Praise for *Narrative Expansions*

'Assembled with intentionality, openness and care, the essays in *Narrative Expansions* present a wide range of perspectives on decolonial library practice and theory. Jess Crilly and Regina Everitt begin with a conversation about how this book came into being, and then offer an important overview of the tensions and significance of what it means to decolonize academic libraries. The authors share their knowledge and experiences in ways that open possibilities for thinking and acting critically and expansively across a range of areas in the field, as well as the colonial epistemological foundations on which librarianship has been built. This is a necessary and engaging volume.'

Melissa Adler, Assistant Professor, Faculty of Information & Media Studies, Western University

'*Narrative Expansions* is the book that any library and information specialist interested in 'decolonising the university/curricula/library' should read. It contextualises the societal, institutional, library and information landscapes, bringing together the different threads and debates around this topic and humanises it with nuanced conversations and presentation of practical examples of enacted change. Decolonisation is a journey in reflection, asking hard questions, having difficult conversations, and action. This book is a first essential step on this urgent journey and expansion of narratives.'

Elizabeth E. Charles, Assistant Director (Digital Services, Systems and Collections), Library Services, Birkbeck, University of London

'This is a rich, harrowing and, above all, generous book that provides a welcome (and long overdue) focal point for decolonial work in libraries. Building upon recent grass-root conference initiatives, the book is not afraid to tackle hard-hitting topics, including the ongoing trauma of libraries' colonial legacies and the dangers of performative allyship, amongst other themes. At the same time, this is a hopeful book, as authors draw from personal narratives and critical theoretical frameworks to outline a powerful vision of what decolonised and anti-racist library work is – and what it could be, when we dare to question the voices, knowledges and pedagogies of our profession.'

Dr Alison Hicks, Assistant Professor and Programme Director for Library and Information Studies, University College London

Narrative
Expansions

Every purchase of a Facet book helps to fund CILIP's advocacy, awareness and accreditation programmes for information professionals.

Narrative Expansions

Interpreting Decolonisation in Academic Libraries

Edited by
Jess Crilly and Regina Everitt

© This compilation: Jess Crilly and Regina Everitt 2022
The chapters: the contributors 2022

Published by Facet Publishing
7 Ridgmount Street, London WC1E 7AE
www.facetpublishing.co.uk

Facet Publishing is wholly owned by CILIP: the Library and Information Association.

The editors and authors of the individual chapters assert their moral right to be identified as such in accordance with the terms of the Copyright, Designs and Patents Act 1988.

Except as otherwise permitted under the Copyright, Designs and Patents Act 1988 this publication may only be reproduced, stored or transmitted in any form or by any means, with the prior permission of the publisher, or, in the case of reprographic reproduction, in accordance with the terms of a licence issued by The Copyright Licensing Agency. Enquiries concerning reproduction outside those terms should be sent to Facet Publishing, 7 Ridgmount Street, London WC1E 7AE.

Every effort has been made to contact the holders of copyright material reproduced in this text, and thanks are due to them for permission to reproduce the material indicated. If there are any queries please contact the publisher.

British Library Cataloguing in Publication Data
A catalogue record for this book is available from the British Library.

ISBN 978-1-78330-497-4 (paperback)
ISBN 978-1-78330-498-1 (hardback)
ISBN 978-1-78330-499-8 (PDF)
ISBN 978-1-78330-521-6 (EPUB)

First published 2022

Text printed on FSC accredited material

Typeset from authors' files in 10/13pt Elegant Garamond and Humanist 521 by Flagholme Publishing Services.
Printed and made in Great Britain by CPI Group (UK) Ltd, Croydon, CR0 4YY.

Contents

Figures and Tables ... ix

Contributors ... xi

Preface ... xvii

Introduction: Decolonise or 'Decolonise'? ... xxi
Jess Crilly and Regina Everitt

Part 1 Contexts and Experiences ... 1

1. **Decolonising the Library: From Personal Experience to Collective Action** ... 3
A conversation with Hillary Gyebi-Ababio

2. **Intelligent Leaders, Intelligent Spaces** ... 13
Regina Everitt

3. **Decolonising Research Methodologies** ... 25
Sara Ewing

4. **Do Black Employees' Rights Matter? The Lived Experience of BAME Staff in UK Academic Libraries** ... 39
Mohammed Ishaq and Asifa Maaria Hussain

5. **Decolonising the Academic Library: Reservations, Fines and Renewals** ... 57
Lurraine Jones and Marcia Wilson

6. **Critical Information Literacy and Structural Oppression: Reflecting on Challenges and Looking Forward** ... 73
Angela Pashia

Part 2 In Practice	89
7 The Contribution of Library and Information Science Education to Decolonising Briony Birdi	91
8 Indigenising Canadian Academic Libraries: Two Librarians' Experiences Rachel Chong and Ashley Edwards	105
9 Liberating the Library: What it Means to Decolonise and Why it is Necessary Marilyn Clarke	127
10 Opening Spaces for Creative and Critical Enquiry Alexandra Duncan, Vivienne Eades-Miller and Adam Ramejkis	139
11 Towards Decolonising the British Library: A Staff-Led Perspective Pardaad Chamsaz on behalf of and in collaboration with the British Library BAME Staff Network Decolonisation Working Group	153
12 Cataloguing, Classification and Critical Librarianship at Cambridge University Cambridge University Decolonising Through Critical Librarianship Group	173
13 Re-membering Kenya: Building Library Infrastructures as Decolonial Practice Syokau Mutonga and Angela Okune	189
14 Challenging its Imperial Origins: Towards Decolonising SOAS Library Ludi Price	213
15 Decolonising Library Collections: Contemporary Issues, Practical Steps and Examples from London School of Economics Kevin Wilson	225
Afterword: Challenging the Narrative of the Storyteller Regina Everitt	251
Index	255

Figures and Tables

Figures

7.1	'A bit racist is still racist' – images of printed materials from 2019 Microaggression campaign	96
7.2	Reading list audit: overall diversity of authors across module reading lists	98
12.1	Basic cartonera record	180
12.2	Basic cartonera record, continuation	180
12.3	Expanded cartonera record	180
12.4	Expanded cartonera record, continuation	181
13.1	The lion's head that can be found – sometimes – in McMillan Library's main branch, Nairobi, Kenya	190
13.2	The entrance to McMillan Library's main branch, Nairobi, Kenya	199

Tables

7.1	Emergent themes from the qualitative staff and student data	99
7.2	Decolonising framework for LIS education	102
15.1	Place of publication, Course Collection	231
15.2	Place of publication, Main Collection	232
15.3	Place of publication, Main Collection Journals	234

Contributors

The editors

Jess Crilly has worked mainly in academic libraries, most recently as Associate Director for Content and Discovery, Library Services, University of the Arts London, up to September 2020. Her interests include critical librarianship; the meaning of and possibilities for the decolonisation of knowledge; and the multiple contexts and uses of archives. Jess was the organiser of the *Towards a Critical (Art) Librarianship* conference in 2018 and has published book chapters (*Inclusion and Intersectionality in Visual Arts Education*, IOP/Trentham, 2019) and articles in *Art Libraries Journal* and other publications.

Regina Everitt is Assistant Chief Operating Officer (Service Excellence) and Director of Library, Archives and Learning Services at the University of East London. She began her professional career as a technical author/trainer working with computer companies that developed software for the manufacturing, pharmaceutical and financial sectors in the USA and UK. After managing a small library at a university in West Africa as a volunteer with the United States Peace Corps, she transitioned into the higher education sector, developing and managing libraries, social learning spaces and other learning resources. She works with sector professional bodies and institutions to address the under-representation of Black, Asian and minoritised ethnic staff members in leadership positions in the LIS profession.

The contributors

Briony Birdi is a Senior Lecturer in Librarianship at the Information School, University of Sheffield, where her research and teaching explore the social, political and educational roles of public and youth libraries, with a particular focus on social justice and diversity. She is the Director of Equality, Diversity and Inclusion for the faculty of Social Sciences, a senior leadership role in the areas of race equality, gender equality, disability equality and well-being. Briony has also served on national and international committees, and has been consulted on public library policy and practice, reading and diversity for regional, national and international academic and professional organisations.

Cambridge University Libraries Decolonising Through Critical Librarianship Group Jennifer Skinner (African Studies Library), Clara Panozzo Zénere and Christopher Greenberg (Latin American and Iberian Collections, Cambridge University Library), Frances Marsh (Polar Library, Scott Polar Research Institute) and Eve Lacey (Newnham

College Library) work together as part of the Decolonising Through Critical Librarianship Group. More information on their case studies, resources and events for librarians in Cambridge and elsewhere can be found online: https://decolonisingthroughcriticallibrarianship.wordpress.com.

Pardaad Chamsaz is a curator at the British Library, responsible for Nordic material and for research projects across the Germanic collections. He is a member of the Library's BAME Staff Network steering committee, representing its Decolonising Working Group, made up of staff from many different departments. The group aims to foster a space for informed, open and safe discussion of ideas related to decolonisation and its implications for the Library and its BAME staff. It focuses on understanding how the colonial history and structures of the institution can manifest in the workplace as racial inequality and discrimination. By understanding those connections, it hopes to re-centre and revalue the experiences of BAME colleagues and of existing and potential communities of BAME researchers and visitors.

Rachel Chong's maternal grandfather is Métis from Manitoba's Red River Settlement, but Rachel was raised on Coast Salish Territory in what is often referred to as Greater Vancouver. She has worked in libraries in a variety of capacities including page, clerk and circulation supervisor. Since completing her Master of Library and Information Studies and First Nations Curriculum Concentration at the University of British Columbia, she has held a number of librarian positions in the public, private and academic sectors. She is currently employed with Kwantlen Polytechnic University as the Indigenous Engagement and Subject Liaison Librarian.

Marilyn Clarke is Director of Library Services at Goldsmiths, University of London, a member of the Goldsmiths Human Resources and Equalities Committee, the Goldsmiths Racial Justice Board, and co-Chair of the Goldsmiths Race Equality Group (BAME staff network). She is a member of the SCONUL Board and was a member of the CILIP BAME Network Steering Group. Marilyn leads the Liberate Our Library Working Group at Goldsmiths and has co-delivered workshops on decolonising research and curricula alongside an academic skills lecturer at the 2018 Advance HE EDI Conference and at Manchester University in 2019. Her work has been published in *UKSG eNews*, *Art Libraries Journal*, and *ALISS Quarterly* and she has spoken at several sector conferences. Marilyn is a social justice activist and has written a chapter in the forthcoming publication, *Critical Library Pedagogy in Practice* (Innovative Libraries Press).

Alexandra Duncan is an Academic Support Librarian at Chelsea College of Arts (University of the Arts London – UAL), supporting Interior and Spatial Design and Product and Furniture Design courses. She has a PgCert in Academic Practice in Art, Design and Communication (UAL) and is a Fellow of the Higher Education Academy.

Alex is interested in how to make art librarianship more critical, and regularly presents and publishes on how to use Wikipedia as a tool for activism within library education. She is a member of the ARLIS/UK & Ireland Council and a regular host of Wikipedia edit-a-thons.

Vivienne Eades-Miller is an Academic Support Librarian for Fashion, Textiles and Materials courses at Central Saint Martins (CSM, University of the Arts London), where she is functional lead on academic support and information skills work. Viv has worked in university libraries for over a decade, and has also set up and run a prison library and has a background in youth work. She manages the zine collection at CSM Library and is interested in empowering students to find their academic voice and self-publish. Her research is focused on creativity and serendipity in library research.

Ashley Edwards has Métis, Dutch and Scottish heritage and is a citizen of Métis Nation British Columbia (MNBC). She was raised in Stó:lō territory, in British Columbia, without connection to her Métis roots. Her parents instilled a sense of pride about her Indigenous heritage as a child, and learning about her Indigeneity has been a journey of personal discovery, without Elders to guide her. She is grateful for the connections being made within the MNBC community. Ashley has a Library Technician diploma (2009) and a BA in Adult Education (2015) from the University of the Fraser Valley, and an MLIS degree from the University of Alberta.

Sara Ewing is a Lecturer in Academic Literacies in the Centre for Academic Language and Literacies at Goldsmiths, University of London, teaching critical reading, writing and research methods across the University. She has a background in community-based organisations, with an emphasis on access to education for marginalised and stigmatised populations. Sara is currently focused on facilitating Decolonising Academic Practices workshops and integrating decolonising theories and praxis with discipline-specific academic skills provision.

Hillary Gyebi-Ababio is the National Union of Students' Vice President for Higher Education 2020–22. Having worked at the University of Bristol Students' Union as the Undergraduate Education Officer, and as the Chair of the Widening Participation Network, she has worked extensively with students in higher education, and has a deep passion for widening participation, anti-racism and decolonisation. The ongoing work she has contributed to looks to the vision of creating an education system that is truly lifelong, liberated and accessible for all.

Asifa Maaria Hussain is an Assistant Professor in Management at Heriot Watt University in Edinburgh. Asifa has previously worked at a number of UK universities and has conducted multidisciplinary research in the field of equality and diversity for almost 20 years. She has undertaken consultancy for the Ministry of Defence, Glasgow City Council and the Equality and Human Rights Commission. Asifa has published widely and is a member of a number of bodies and committees involved in advancing equality and diversity.

Mohammed Ishaq is a Reader in Human Resource Management (HRM) at the University of the West of Scotland, with expertise in the area of equality and diversity. Mohammed has engaged in multidisciplinary research over the past 20 years, spanning the disciplines of sociology, politics and the wider discipline of business and management incorporating HRM. Mohammed has published widely and consulted for the Scottish Government, SCONUL and the Equality and Human Rights Commission. He engages in research of a practical and applied nature with implications for policy makers, societies and organisations and is a member of numerous boards and committees dedicated to advancing equality.

Lurraine Jones is Head of Department for Education and Communities, University of East London, UK. Her research interests are Black Britishness, 'Race', Black feminisms and the policing of Black bodies and communities. Her recent publications are: 'Pain, Anger and Youth Resistance: Police Racial Awareness Training and the Contemplations of a Black Mother', in: Etienne, J. (ed.) (2020) *Communities of Activism: Black Women, Higher Education and the Politics of Representation,* London, UCL/IOE Press; and Wilson, M. and Jones, L. (2020) 'Dear Senior University Leaders: What Will You Say You Did to Address Racism in Higher Education?', *Times Higher Education.*

Syokau Mutonga is an anthropologist – passionate about people in all places across time. She is particularly interested in exploring how intersectional approaches can be utilised to study culture on the African continent so as to reveal the hidden networks, systems and infrastructures that support or undermine collective life and sustainable social change. As the Research and Inventory Manager at Book Bunk Trust, her core responsibilities include ensuring the success and seamless operation of all research-related work. These include leading the overall data aspects of Book Bunk's work and its day-to-day management such as data gathering and presentation, acquisitions, volunteer management/relations, administration and communications.

Angela Okune is an anthropologist of science and technology with over ten years of experience working in and with research and technology communities in Nairobi, Kenya. Angela received her PhD from the Anthropology Department at the University of California, Irvine and serves as an Associate Editor on a collective editorial team for the Open Access journal *Engaging Science, Technology, and Society*. She also serves on the Society for Social Studies of Science (4S) Council and as a Design Team member of the Platform for Experimental Collaborative Ethnography. Angela founded and manages an experimental, open ethnographic data portal called Research Data Share (www.researchdatashare.org).

CONTRIBUTORS xv

Angela Pashia is a Professor and Head of Learning and Research Support at the University of West Georgia. Angela holds a Masters in Anthropology from the University of Virginia and a Masters in Information Studies and Learning Technologies, library science emphasis, from the University of Missouri. Angela also teaches online professional development courses for librarians through the Library Juice Academy. More information, including Angela's full curriculum vitae, is available at angelapashia.com.

Ludi Price is Librarian for China and Inner Asia at SOAS Library, and was previously Far Eastern Cataloguer there for six years. She is also a Visiting Lecturer at City, University of London's library school, #CityLIS. She earned her PhD in Information Science at City, specialising in the information behaviour of media fan communities on the internet. Her current research interests focus on the intersections between fandom, fan studies and library and information science. Other interests include fan information behaviour, fan-tagging and folksonomies, participatory culture, social curation and transcultural fandom. She is also co-chair of SOAS Library's Decolonisation Operational Working Group.

Adam Ramejkis is an Academic Support facilitator and Intercultural Communication trainer at University of the Arts London. He runs student and staff-facing workshops, projects and facilitated discussions on a range of themes centred around culture, communication, criticality, creativity and collaboration. He works in close collaboration with course teams and library services, co-designing and co-delivering workshops which encourage a critical and reflective lens on learning and systems of knowledge. He has an MA in Applied Linguistics (King's College London) and recently gained a Graduate Diploma in Library and Information Management (Ulster University).

Kevin Wilson has worked in academic libraries for over 15 years and has been the Academic Liaison and Collection Development Manager at the London School of Economics and Political Science (LSE) since 2017. He leads both the library's liaison activity with over 20 departments and research centres and the development of the library's collections. Kevin has presented on decolonisation in libraries at several conferences. Prior to joining LSE, Kevin worked at Goldsmiths, University of London and City, University of London in different roles. He can be found on Twitter as @liaisonkevin.

Marcia Wilson works at the Open University as a Professor and the Dean of Equality, Diversity and Inclusion (EDI). She is responsible for implementing and embedding the EDI agenda across the institution. Her work includes equality projects with Universities UK and her research interests focus on racial trauma in sport. She is a multiple award winner and uses her platform to raise awareness about inequalities and generate institutional and sector change.

Preface

The origins of Narrative Expansions

Jess Crilly (JC): *Narrative Expansions* originated with an invitation from Facet Publishing to write something about decolonising libraries and, reflecting on my positionality, I decided not to write something myself but to co-edit a volume, and with someone whom I knew would bring different experiences and perspectives to the work. I had been working with collections and discovery (at University of the Arts London before retiring in September 2020) and concerned for a while to really understand what was meant by decolonisation, and how this was, could or should be interpreted in libraries, so that anything we did was theoretically grounded and we were not jumping on a bandwagon or using a buzzword (Crilly, 2019).

Regina Everitt (RE): When Jess asked me to be part of this project, I accepted without hesitation, though I had reservations about the term 'decolonisation'. As an African American with 400 years of history in the United States – admittedly many of them violent and painful – the term 'decolonisation' did not immediately resonate with me. The issue for me was simply racism to reinforce the notion of White superiority. I grew up learning that *if you are White you are alright, if you are Brown stick around, and if you are Black step back*. So, I wanted the movement to be called what it is and not be dressed up in what I felt was a term to attract popular support – a fad! However, working on this project and learning more about the experiences of those who grew up in Africa and the Caribbean before and after their independence from Europe, 'decolonisation of the mind' certainly resonated. I had read parts of Fanon's *Black Skin, White Masks* during my early undergraduate studies, but did not fully appreciate its impact, as my world was confined to the New York–South Carolina corridor in the north-east of the United States. Although I grew up in a predominantly Black community, colourism and the aspiration towards the media's interpretation of 'Whiteness' (e.g. skin tone, speech, possessions) were pervasive.

Voice

RE: Like the range of authors in this book, Jess and I have differing approaches to writing, which has been a strength for this project. Jess takes a more theoretical approach, which will resonate with those who best consume information from 'academic-style' writing. I take an experiential approach, which on this project foregrounds my 'lived' experience as the 'product' of education through a Eurocentric prism that essentially excluded me. We have intentionally sought to capture both voices so as to challenge accepted epistemology, so there are some individual pieces of writing from us in this Introduction and the Afterword, as well as the two of us writing together.

JC: We really value the different kinds of writing in this book, some of it very grounded in personal experience and reflection, some of it more traditionally academic, and the author's positionality has often determined the approach.

Challenges of writing the book

RE: A key challenge was the uncomfortable and unpopular task of categorising people who do not identify as White. Black, Asian and minority ethnic (BAME), used widely in the UK, has been dismissed as a lazy attempt at 'othering' swathes of people. The Asian categorisation does little to differentiate between people from the Indian subcontinent and East Asia. Traveller communities may identify as minority ethnic, though they may be categorised as White for some statistics. Although 'minority' in the UK context denotes that it is a predominantly White nation, the term also suggests 'political' and 'social' minority – thus marginalising or minoritising those who do not identify as White. The term 'people of color' (POC) or 'Black, Indigenous and people of color' (BIPOC) is used in America, but for me these terms hark back to the days of when Black people were referred to as 'coloured people' – which is now considered derogatory. There is no consensus on the correct term. I find myself shifting between 'Black, Asian and Global Majority', 'Black, Asian and marginalised or minoritised ethnic', again abbreviated as BAME, and 'Black and Brown people', depending on the context. We have left it to the discretion of the authors to determine the appropriate terminology for the context of their chapters.

JC: I have thought too about the appropriateness of the book format for a dynamic topic, but after a series of conferences and writing in the UK in the last few years it seemed a good idea to pull some of it together, as well as integrating what libraries are doing with the bigger picture, especially in the wider discourse of decolonising the university, and from other perspectives than that of the UK. That's why the book has contributions from the student perspective, library and academic literacy workers, anthropologists, researchers, curators and academics, as well as being international in scope. And again, though centred on the academic library, we have taken a broad interpretation of this term and have an important contribution from the British Library – an essential component of the UK library infrastructure – while the chapter by Mutonga and Okune is really cross-sectoral and features a public library case study.

The book presents a snapshot of thought and activity at a particular moment in time. Many of the authors refer to Decolonisation Groups that they are a part of – that work is dynamic and in many ways still emerging, and so will have progressed during the writing of this book.

Our hope for the future

RE: I have had the privilege of speaking with students who are starting careers in the library and information profession about our role in supporting our institutions towards anti-racism and equality, diversity and inclusion. I will now be referring them to this book alongside *Knowledge Justice: Disrupting Library and Information Studies through Critical Race Theory* as essential reading to encourage them to approach their profession through the lens of critical librarianship, questioning the voices, imagery and spaces that tell a single story. As future leaders of these institutions, these students have the power to expand the narratives currently dominating their collections and spaces.

JC: A book like this can only be highly selective and partial, and there are so many other aspects of decolonising work that could be discussed. I hope that this momentum for change continues.

References

Crilly, J. (2019) Decolonising the Library: A Theoretical Exploration, *Spark: UAL Creative Teaching and Learning Journal*, **4** (1), 6–15.

Fanon, F. (1952) *Black Skin, White Masks*, Grove Press.

Leung, S. Y. and Lopez-McKnight, J. R. (2021) *Knowledge Justice: Disrupting Library and Information Studies through Critical Race Theory*, MIT Press.

Introduction: Decolonise or 'Decolonise'?

Jess Crilly and Regina Everitt

Decolonisation is impossible, but we must make her possible.

(Foluke Adebisi)

A contested term

When we were editing this book, and thinking about the title, we discussed at various points whether to use decolonise or 'decolonise', and it's noticeable that the contributing authors to this volume sometimes also use 'decolonise'. So, what is the tension around this term?

Decolonisation as an intention has clarity. The students at the University of Cape Town in 2015 were intent on decolonising: 'For the first time since the anti-apartheid movement, South African students were grabbing international headlines, as they struggled for universal access to an education that did not reproduce the imperial logic their parents' generation fought to dismantle' (Elliott-Cooper, 2018, 290).

The intentions of students and other activists in the UK are also clear, though in the different context of its being a historic European centre of colonialism, as expressed in Keele University's Manifesto for Decolonising the Curriculum:

> Decolonization involves identifying colonial systems, structures and relationships, and working to challenge those systems. It is not 'integration' or simply the token inclusion of the intellectual achievements of non-white cultures. Rather, it involves a paradigm shift from a culture of exclusion and denial to the making of space for other political philosophies and knowledge systems. It's a culture shift to think more widely about why common knowledge is what it is, and in so doing adjusting cultural perceptions and power relations in real and significant ways.
>
> (Keele University, 2018)

So are the tensions around the call to 'decolonise the library/curriculum/university' more about enactment than purpose? In relation to the library, perhaps it is the implication that decolonisation is a definable, finite and measurable process that is problematic; like so many processes that constitute the organisation of libraries, the implication that we can start and one day finish this project. The library is a place that privileges practicality (Hudson, 2017; Nicholson and Seale, 2018), and though there is work to be done, this is not the familiar project process with measurable time scales and impacts that we are so used to implementing, and is about learning and unlearning as well as about activity. Or is it around the accuracy and legitimacy of the term 'decolonisation' as it relates to the work being done under that banner, which should logically be radical and transformative? Or the need to properly contextualise decolonisation, surely one thing in the historic centres of colonialism, another in the settler nation and postcolonial/neocolonial city.

There is a quandary at the heart of the call to decolonise – if the neoliberal university (or national library, or public library) is part of the problem, and systemically racist, is decolonisation a philosophical possibility? And, by association, can libraries decolonise within those structures and constraints, or is coloniality so embedded as to be immutable? Who has the insight, and the wisdom to do this? To quote Audre Lorde, 'The master's tools will never dismantle the master's house. They may allow us temporarily to beat him at his own game but they will never enable us to bring about genuine change' (Lorde, 1984); or, as Adebisi asks, 'How illogical is it that the structure we are attempting to decolonise is the structure we are attempting to use to decolonise?' (Adebisi, 2019).

Despite the rapid uptake of a decolonisation discourse in universities and other institutions, the critiques of this movement are sobering. The influential article by Tuck and Yang (2012) is perhaps one of the more cited references in this book. Tuck and Yang describe decolonising work as a move to settler innocence, and warn of using the term as a metaphor instead of enacting the radical acts that decolonisation should logically entail, including the return of Indigenous land.

> There is a long and bumbled history of non-Indigenous peoples making moves to alleviate the impacts of colonization. The too-easy adoption of decolonizing discourse (making decolonization a metaphor) is just one part of that history and it taps into pre-existing tropes that get in the way of more meaningful potential alliances. We think of the enactment of these tropes as a series of moves to innocence (Malwhinney, 1998), which problematically attempt to reconcile settler guilt and complicity, and rescue settler futurity.
>
> (Tuck and Yang, 2012, 3)

Tuck and Yang are referring to a settler-colonial context, yet colonisation and therefore decolonisation are contextual. As Bhambra states in *Decolonising the University*:

> We think there is value in complicating the substantive claim made by Tuck and Yang (that decolonisation is exclusively about the repatriation of land to indigenous people) in order to extend and deepen their political warning ... colonisation (and hence decolonising) cannot be reduced to a historically specific and geographically particular articulation of the colonial project, namely settler-colonialism in the Americas.
>
> (Bhambra, Gabrial and Nişancıoğlu, 2018, 4)

Regardless of context, the essence of the warning remains, that decolonisation should not be used as a metaphor to stand in for various kinds of social justice.

Other voices critiquing the decolonisation movement (in UK higher education) include Doharty and others (2020), who highlight the ways that staff of colour can be disproportionately burdened with the work, and note that 'the misuse and overuse of the decolonize discourse place the term at (if not beyond) the risk of becoming little more than a superficial buzzword, severed from its radical essence' (Doharty, Madriaga and Joseph-Salisbury, 2020, 3).

Appleton (2019) warns of overclaiming by using the term decolonisation: 'Within the academy, I have seen the sloppy attempt to "decolonize" a syllabus or a programme without any real structural changes.' Appleton proposes a more specific and grounded use of vocabulary, for example, 'Diversify your syllabus and curriculum, Digress from the canon, Decentre knowledge and knowledge production . . .' (Appleton, 2019).

There is also the risk that actions such as diversifying collections and reviewing reading lists can be co-opted into programmes of tokenistic change, to defer the need for more fundamental change.

Decolonising the library

And yet, though these are powerful and important warnings and critiques of how decolonisation is playing out in universities, there *is* clearly decolonising work being done in libraries, and this could be defined as activity that specifically addresses the multiple impacts on the library and knowledge production that result from imperial histories and colonialism. These long-lasting impacts of the colonial persist in 'coloniality', described by Maldonado-Torres: 'Thus coloniality survives colonialism. It is maintained alive in books, in the criteria for academic performance, in cultural patterns, in common sense, in the self-image of peoples, in aspirations of self, and in so many other aspects of our modern experience. In a way, as modern subjects we breathe coloniality all the time and everyday' (Maldonado-Torres, 2007, 243).

The construction of race as a hierarchical system with Whiteness as the pinnacle is a foundational logic of imperialism that justified some people being treated as less than human. 'The Enlightenment was pivotal in the shift into the new age of empire: it provided the universalist, supposedly rational and scientific framework of knowledge that maintained colonial logic. Understanding how the Enlightenment and racism cannot be separated is the first step in truly appreciating that colonial logic still rules the world today' (Andrews, 2021, 2).

Coloniality is evident everywhere in academia, in the persistent Whiteness of institutions, including libraries; in the legacy of Eurocentric collections; in the colonial roots of the academic subjects that form collections in libraries; in the dominance of English language and of academic publishing centred in Europe and the USA; and in many other aspects of scholarly communication. It is evident in the undervaluing and absence of Indigenous forms of knowledge, in accepted notions of research methodologies and forms of knowledge. Coloniality is also evident in the persistence of universalist knowledge systems, classification schemes and cataloguing vocabularies, and these legacies are one of the most pressing challenges for libraries, as in the much-cited case of the Library of Congress Subject Heading 'illegal aliens' (Dartmouth College, 2019; Fox, 2020).

These are the territories where libraries are working to decolonise – through practical interventions, collaboration with academic staff and students, influence with publishers and suppliers and through developing criticality for their own understanding and for engagement with their library users.

The effects of the colonial are still with us, and attempts to disrupt and unsettle them can be described as decolonial – or anti-colonial. Sometimes these impacts of the colonial are absorbed into everyday practices to the point of invisibility, but sometimes there are material reminders, such as the missionary archives held by the SOAS Library, the busts of Sir Joseph Banks and Sir Hans Sloane at the entrance to the British Library and the lion's head in the McMillan Library, Nairobi.

We cannot consider colonisation, 'the darker side of Western modernity' (Mignolo, 2011), in isolation, as it co-exists with patriarchy and capitalism. This is reflected in the way that the authors in this volume have used theoretical frames that are tangential or intersect with decolonisation, particularly critical librarianship, which, as defined by Nicholson and Seale (2018, 2) 'uses a reflexive lens to expose and challenge the ways that libraries and the profession "consciously and unconsciously support systems of oppression", thereby pursuing a socially just, theoretically informed praxis'. Other authors refer to knowledge democracy, critical pedagogy and critical information literacy, progressive librarianship, liberation theory and responses to structural oppressions, particularly anti-racism, and it should be said that libraries have been working in these spaces for decades.

Several authors have referenced critical race theory (CRT), which provides both a theoretical framework and a tool for activism; Leung and Lopez-McKnight (2021) have traced its application within library and information science (LIS) and the many ways that CRT can be used to challenge the foundational principles of the profession.

Contested narratives

Narrative Expansions was written during an extraordinary period of time, over 2020–21, when decolonisation was foregrounded in a struggle over the ownership of national narratives. Following the killing by police of George Floyd on 25 May 2020 in Minneapolis, the subsequent resurgence of Black Lives Matter and widespread protest against police brutality, many institutions in the cultural sector, including universities, responded with statements on anti-racism, frequently referencing the role of the library and its collections, redoubling their commitments to anti-racism and decolonisation. These were sometimes criticised for not reflecting what was actually happening in those institutions. Some iconic British institutions, including Kew Gardens and The National Trust, made public statements reflecting on their organisation's relationship with slavery and imperialism.

The Brutish Museums (Hicks, 2020) was published, with its denunciation of the possession of the looted Benin Bronzes held in many UK and other nations' museums, describing museums such as Pitt Rivers in Oxford as sites of trauma and ongoing violence, and escalating the call for the restitution of looted objects – a call that is slowly being taken up. Some institutions are responding; Aberdeen University Museums and Special Collections have announced that they are returning a Benin Bronze (University of Aberdeen, 2021). The year 2020 was also the year of the toppling of the statue of Bristol slave trader Edward Colston, and a reappraisal and complicating of the role and biography of some revered national figures, particularly Winston Churchill. In summary, this was a time when the national narrative – whom it includes and excludes, whom it celebrates and ignores and how it is taught – was forefronted, and highly contested in what are characterised as culture wars. An example is the recent and controversial report of the UK Commission on Race and Ethnic Disparities that mischaracterises the decolonisation of reading lists as 'banning White authors' (Commission on Race and Ethnic Disparities, 2021, 8).

Conclusion

Though we are critically examining the concept of decolonising the library, and exploring the ways it is being interpreted in different contexts, it is a vital approach to thinking and acting on the colonial legacies that impact libraries and knowledge production. Lessons can be learned from the experiences and ideas of the authors who have contributed to this volume and the theoretical perspectives they bring: if we cannot fully enact the 'de-' of decolonisation, we can continue to work on decolonial or anti-colonial acts.

A key question for libraries is how to reconcile working in this space where decolonisation is impossible but necessary; in the words of Adebisi, 'Decolonisation is impossible, but we must make her possible' (Adebisi, 2019). Perhaps we can use the concept of radical hope, as the Pitt Rivers Museum has done, in order to reimagine museum practice and move forwards against a weight of history and custom. The work of decolonising the library is about understanding how the past has informed the present, but must also be about envisaging a better future, even if how to achieve it isn't always clear.

> Radical Hope is directed toward a future goodness and it anticipates a good for which those who have the hope but as yet lack the appropriate concepts with which to understand it.
> (Jonathan Lear, cited in Pitt Rivers Museum, n.d.)

About the book

The aim of *Narrative Expansions* is to draw together some of the work that has been taking place in libraries as part of the decolonising movement that has swept through higher education in the UK and elsewhere and to ask how decolonisation is being interpreted – and enacted – in academic libraries. *Narrative Expansions* is in two parts: Part 1 describes the contexts that libraries are operating in and the impacts of those contexts through an experiential lens. Part 2 focuses on located practices where the theory and practice of decolonisation intersect and practitioners seek to understand how they can be interpreted and applied. Inevitably these are loose and overlapping categories.

Part 1: Contexts and Experiences

Students have long been instigators for change in higher education, as well as collaborators with libraries. In Chapter 1, Hillary Gyebi-Ababio provides a student's perspective on decolonising the library, outlining key movements in decolonisation of higher education, such as Rhodes Must Fall from its origins in South Africa to campaigns at Oxford University, and Why Is My Curriculum White, calling readers to action by 'grasping the root', in the words of Angela Davis. Gyebi-Ababio explains how the contents of the library are potentially transformative for student identity and belonging, and how students are organising for change through National Union of Students- (NUS) led campaigns. The creation of the NUS Free Black University, and its founding principles of being multiformat and freely accessible to all, is definitely something for libraries to take note of.

The ownership and control of spaces, names and objects has become one of the most high-profile and contested areas of the decolonisation movement, in both public and institutional spaces – centring on statues, paintings and other artefacts and the names of buildings. In Chapter 2, Regina Everitt describes her formative experiences of public and educational spaces and their messages around cultural value and entitlement while growing up in Philadelphia. She explains how this feeling that you belong or don't belong in a space has informed her approach as a leader and manager of spaces in academia, and within the library.

The under-representation of and negative experience of Black, Asian and minoritised ethnic staff in libraries, and in the academy generally, is a recurring theme of the book. Mohammed Ishaq and Asifa Hussain (Chapter 4) draw on their research on the lived experience of these staff members in UK academic libraries, drawing parallels between the findings of a SCONUL-commissioned survey and experience in other areas of the public sector, and recommend actions for change. They conclude that without challenging the organisational culture, structures and processes that perpetuate and sustain racial inequality, decolonisation of the library is unattainable. Lurraine Jones and Marcia Wilson (Chapter 5) are part of an inexcusably paltry number of Black female educators in higher education in the UK. They explore the call to decolonise the library through a personal history of racialisation, learning and working in White institutions. Jones and Wilson use CRT to discuss the prevalence and meaning of Whiteness in the academy and explain the role of white allyship in challenging the misconception of the post-racial society. The library, the authors argue, has a powerful role at the centre of the institution, and must either step up to support decolonisation, or continue to prop up the status quo.

The time of writing the book was dominated by what can be described as Trumpism – a rise in populism in the USA and internationally, characterised by a deliberate attack on the concept of truth, the adoption of conspiracy theories such as QAnon, culminating in the storming of the US Capitol Building on 6 January 2021, and attacks on CRT as a legitimate methodology – alongside a pandemic. In Chapter 6 Angela Pashia reflects on these events and her experience of teaching critical information literacy in this climate, which led her to question the teaching of authoritative sources and alternative media. Pashia provides an important discussion of how the concepts of information literacy can adapt to a more extreme cultural climate of conspiracy and *dis*information. She also explains why, in the US context, though politically aligned with the decolonisation movement, critical information literacy, social justice and structural oppression are foregrounded.

Sara Ewing (Chapter 3) provides a theoretical framework for decolonising research methodologies drawing on the influential work of Linda Tuhiwai Smith and others. Decolonising research methodologies aims to disrupt the colonial epistemology of universal knowledge, representation and legitimacy characterised by the exclusion of different modes of thinking and ways of living. Ewing discusses the power dynamics at play in the classroom, and how a decolonial epistemic shift works to liberate racial, sexual, gender, class, linguistic, religious and epistemic embodied experiences from oppression. She describes work with undergraduate Law students using texts outside the traditional canon to deconstruct moral, ethical and epistemological positions that underpin the study of law.

Part 2: In Practice

Several authors refer in their chapters to a current lack of critical content in UK LIS curricula. In Chapter 7 Briony Birdi considers the contribution of LIS education to the decolonisation movement, noting that calls to decolonise the university have led to reflections about the role of library collections, for example, but have had little, if any, impact on the LIS curriculum. Birdi proposes that decolonisation be embedded in both the theoretical and practice-led elements of the LIS programme. Drawing on her research and teaching, she provides a primer on how to make decolonisation core to the LIS curriculum.

Decolonisation is contextual and relates to specific histories and geographies. Rachel Chong and Ashley Edwards (Chapter 8) write within a settler-colonial context, from their personal experience and roles in Canadian university libraries. They explain the significance of the 2015 Truth and Reconciliation Commission and related legislation, and how universities and their constituent libraries are working to address the recommendations of the Commission. They consider what reconciliation means within this context and how the work of the Commission seeks to acknowledge and redress past wrongs. Syokau Mutonga and Angela Okune (Chapter 13) introduce the concept of progressive librarianship, writing about their work with libraries in Nairobi, Kenya, using the McMillan Library and the work of the Book Bunk Trust as a case study. They pose the question, in the context of decolonisation: what do we remember and what do we forget? And how do we not simply 'forget and move on' but reclaim a radical past? Describing the impact of neo-colonialism (in the form of Structural Adjustment Programs) on the Kenyan infrastructure, Okune and Syokau question the risks and long-term impacts of multinational technology corporations mining, controlling and monetising cultural digital assets.

In Chapter 9, Marilyn Clarke describes why the decolonisation movement is important to academic libraries and how it has informed the Liberate Our Library work at Goldsmiths, University of London, working in collaboration with student campaigns. Clarke outlines the production of Eurocentric epistemologies during colonialism and the epistemicide of non-Western knowledge systems and ways of knowing and being. She argues for moves to a 'knowledge democracy' and the need for an activist stance from library workers.

Alexandra Duncan, Vivienne Eades-Miller and Adam Ramejkis (Chapter 10) draw on critical pedagogy and describe student workshops developed at University of the Arts London, 'Critical Library Research', 'Hack Your Library' and workshops centred on Wikipedia, where learning spaces are framed as places of active critical enquiry and co-production. The workshops centre on critical thinking around library systems of knowledge, and democratisation of information production through empowerment of the student voice.

The British Library has a unique role as the UK's national library, as a library of deposit, serving multiple audiences as an academic and research library, as partner to public libraries and as a cultural institution. As the steward of the nation's knowledge, the British Library is part of every 'decolonisation' conversation, whether it concerns museums and galleries, archives and libraries or education and curricula. The British Library BAME Staff Network Decolonisation Working Group is a staff group committed to understanding how colonial history and structures manifest as racial discrimination in the workplace, and vows to revalue the experiences of minoritised people. In Chapter 11 they describe some recent activities of the Working Group across various areas of the Library – public spaces and exhibitions, the custodianship of physical and digital collections, cataloguing and metadata and discuss the particular challenges of working at scale.

In Chapter 12, Christopher Greenberg, Eve Lacey, Frances Marsh, Clara Panozzo Zénere and Jenni Skinner describe work taking place in Cambridge University Libraries through the Decolonising Through Critical Librarianship Group. Their case studies focus on the African Studies Library and Scott Polar Research Institute, as well as a discussion of how the Library can curate and make discoverable *cartonera* materials (a means of democratising publishing originating in Argentina). They describe how collections and legacy metadata have been critically evaluated and accessibility enhanced through a decolonising lens. In Chapter 14 Ludi Price outlines the history of SOAS

University of London from its roots in providing language instruction for colonial administrators, missionaries and scholars for roles within the British Empire to its present role and reputation as a radical space. Price explains the establishment of the Library Decolonisation Group in this context. The history of the Library means that its special collections, such as missionary archives, have unique research potential for understanding the complexities of the colonial past. Historical donations, some undocumented, raise the question of the provenance of materials, and ideas of repatriation and restitution. With the closure of physical spaces due to the pandemic and reliance on digitised materials, Price asks what stories and voices are lost from collections available in physical form only.

Much of the current work on decolonisation taking place in libraries is centred on collections, on what is selected, acquired and retained, the metadata that describes it and the algorithms within discovery layers. Kevin Wilson (Chapter 15) provides an overview of some contemporary issues in collection management, including the usefulness of collection development policies and how libraries can collaborate with academic staff in the production of reading lists. He uses a case study from the London School of Economics (LSE) to advocate for data-driven collection management. Using analytics from the library management system and reading list software, he describes their rich insights into the composition of collections, bringing into stark relief the bias towards authors of the Global North. Wilson argues that the bias in collections is exacerbated by 'big deals' from publishers that favour publications from the USA and UK, edging out titles from more diverse and small and/or specialist publishers.

Connections and common themes emerge across all the chapters. One example is the experiences of Wilson at LSE, of the Decolonising Through Critical Librarianship Group at Cambridge and of Price at SOAS University of London and how they are addressing colonial legacies in collections and their metadata that reveal the relationship between colonialism and the foundation and focus of academic disciplines such as geography, biology, anthropology, development studies and area studies. Academic library collections form part of an infrastructure that formalised and validated these disciplinary evolutions alongside institutional museums, the establishment of institutions and societies and the infrastructure of journals, academic departments and professorships. Academic libraries are now managing the legacies of Eurocentric collections and outdated metadata, while also advocating these collections as valuable sources for research.

Acknowledgement and thanks

We would like to thank the authors of this book for managing to write during a pandemic while they were grappling with working from home, childcare, anxiety and, for some, sickness and grief. Thank you all for staying the course.

Jess Crilly and Regina Everitt
May 2021

References

Adebisi, F. (2019) Why I Say 'Decolonisation Is Impossible', blog post, https://folukeafrica.com/why-i-say-decolonisation-is-impossible/ (accessed 17 May 2021).

Andrews, K. (2021) *The New Age of Empire: How Racism and Colonialism Still Rule the World*, Allen Lane.

Appleton, N. S. (2019) Do Not 'Decolonise' if You Are Not Decolonizing: Progressive Language and Planning Beyond a Hollow Academic Rebranding, *Critical Ethnic Studies Blog*, University of Minnesota Press, www.criticalethnicstudiesjournal.org/blog/2019/1/21/do-not-decolonize-if-you-are-not-decolonizing-alternate-language-to-navigate-desires-for-progressive-academia-6y5sg (accessed 7 April 2021).

Bhambra, G., Gebrial, D. and Nişancıoğlu, K. (eds) (2018) *Decolonising the University*, Pluto.

Commission on Race and Ethnic Disparities (2021) *The Report*, https://assets.publishing.service.gov.uk/government/uploads/system/uploads/attachment_data/file/974507/20210331_-_CRED_Report_-_FINAL_-_Web_Accessible.pdf (accessed 17 May 2021).

Dartmouth College (2019) Change the Subject – a Documentary about Labels, Libraries, and Activism, https://sites.dartmouth.edu/changethesubject.

Doharty, N., Madriaga, M. and Joseph-Salisbury, R. (2020) The University Went to 'Decolonise' and All They Brought Back was Lousy Diversity Double-Speak! Critical Race Counter-Stories from Faculty of Colour in 'Decolonial' Times, *Educational Philosophy and Theory*, **53** (3), 233–44, https://doi.org/10.1080/00131857.2020.1769601.

Elliott-Cooper, A. (2018) 'Free, Decolonised Education' – a Lesson from the South African Student Struggle. In Arday, J. and Mirza, H. S. (eds), *Dismantling Race in Higher Education: Racism, Whiteness and Decolonising the Academy*, Palgrave Macmillan.

Fox, V. (2020) Report of the SAC Working Group on Alternatives to LCSH 'Illegal Aliens', https://alair.ala.org/bitstream/handle/11213/14582/SAC20-AC_report_SAC-Working-Group-on-Alternatives-to-LCSH-Illegal-aliens.pdf (accessed 2 June 2020).

Hicks, D. (2020) *The Brutish Museums: The Benin Bronzes, Colonial Violence and Cultural Restitution*, Pluto Press.

Hudson, D. J. (2017) The Whiteness of Practicality. In Schlesselman-Tarango, G. (ed.), *Topographies of Whiteness: Mapping Whiteness in Library and Information Studies*, Library Juice Press.

Keele University (2018) Keele Manifesto for Decolonising the Curriculum, www.keele.ac.uk/equalitydiversity/equalityframeworksandactivities/equalityawardsandreports/equalityawards/raceequalitycharter/keeledecolonisingthecurriculumnetwork/#keele-manifesto-for-decolonising-the-curriculum (accessed 14 May 2021).

Leung, S. Y. and Lopez-McKnight, R. (2021) *Knowledge Justice: Disrupting Library and Information Studies through Critical Race Studies,* MIT Press.

Lorde, A. (1984) The Master's Tools Will Never Dismantle the Master's House. In *Sister Outsider: Essays and Speeches*, Crossing Press.

Maldonado-Torres, N. (2007) On the Coloniality of Being: Contributions to the Development of a Concept, *Cultural Studies*, **21** (2–3), 240–70, https://doi.org/10.1080/09502380601162548.

Malwhinney, J. L. (1998) Giving up the Ghost, Disrupting the (Re)production of White Privilege in Anti-Racist Pedagogy and Organizational Change. Masters Thesis, Ontario Institute for Studies in Education of the University of Toronto, https://tspace.library.utoronto.ca/handle/1807/12096 (accessed 21 June 2021).

Mignolo, W. (2011) *The Darker Side of Western Modernity*, Duke University Press.

Nicholson, K. and Seale, M. (2018) *The Politics of Theory and the Practice of Critical Librarianship*, Library Juice Press.

Pitt Rivers Museum (n.d.) Radical Hope, Critical Change, https://prm.web.ox.ac.uk/radical-hope (accessed 19 April 2021).

Tuck, E. and Yang, K. (2012) Decolonisation Is Not a Metaphor, *Decolonisation: Indigeneity, Education & Society*, **1** (1), 1–40.

University of Aberdeen (2021) University to Return Benin Bronze, 21 March, www.abdn.ac.uk/news/14790/ (accessed 19 April 2021).

Part 1
Contexts and Experiences

1
Decolonising the Library: From Personal Experience to Collective Action

A conversation with Hillary Gyebi-Ababio

Editors (Eds): Firstly, what do you understand by decolonisation as a term?
Hillary Gyebi-Ababio (HG): The term 'decolonisation' is now being used very widely – its definition is often disputed and misinterpreted. Fanon's *The Wretched of the Earth* is one of the earliest texts where we see decolonisation defined clearly. Fanon speaks of decolonisation as 'the need to thoroughly challenge the colonial situation' (Fanon, 2004, 2).

In more recent interpretations, decolonisation has been defined as 'a political process and vital internalization of the rejection of colonialist mindsets and "norms"' (Ghillar, 2016).

Mbembe describes decolonisation much more tangibly as being about 'reshaping, turning human beings once again into craftsmen and craftswomen who, in reshaping matters and forms, need not to look at the pre-existing models and need not use them as paradigms' (Mbembe, 2018, 9). The Decolonising LSE Collective refer to 'recognizing, making visible and working to address the legacies that colonialism, empire, racism and patriarchy continue to have and envisioning a world beyond these repressive structures' (Decolonising LSE Collective, n.d.).

Ultimately, as Behari-Leak et al. articulate well, decolonisation is 'a nuanced, layered concept', and we should focus 'more in its detail than its definition' (Behari-Leak et al., 2017). We must ensure that we don't get caught up in lengthy academic discussion over the definition of decolonisation that results in cyclical inaction, and ensure there is focus on how to make this work authentic, wholescale and transformative.

The decolonisation movement is alive and growing – and has been for years and years. So much progress has been made, and a firm foundation has been built for the work that is starting to emerge. Therefore, before speaking about how decolonising the library can come to life, we must pay homage to and, in our work, honour those that have been doing this work before us, especially in times where the work of decolonisation has been criticised, misconstrued and outright rejected. A final point on defining decolonisation: many have tried to misconstrue it to be about the 'erasure of history'. It must be made clear that decolonisation comes to life when there is a real understanding about the justice it seeks to bring to those who have been erased, invisibilised and excluded from the narrative for so long; this comes through rebuilding and reimagining knowledge, the purpose of education, and truly building a world without white supremacy.

Eds: Why is decolonisation so high on the NUS agenda?
HG: Decolonisation is about reimagining education and all aspects of our societies; education is the key that unlocks knowledge, fuels passions and curiosity and defines the truths that allow students to carve out their identity in the world. At the root of the NUS is a deep hunger and determination to rebuild how education is done and remove all the structures that have led to racism, colonialism and imperialism, and in their place, the aim and vision is of a world that is accountable for this violence and works towards restorative justice, by working together towards cultural, psychological and economic freedom. Decolonisation as theory and practice is used to imagine this and create what this change would look like. In our current education system, students are not experiencing that liberation or social justice at the core of their educational experience, and with other members of our education communities, still suffer from the impact of current and historical colonialism that our modern educational system was built on.

Students of all backgrounds need to engage with education in a way that enables them to be architects of their own futures, and partners in its development. The purpose of education should not be to make students consumers or spectators, but, rather, it must be to empower students to share their knowledge, build on it, challenge it, reshape it, critically analyse it, in order to grow as a collective as well as individuals. This is aptly put by the late Martin Luther King Jr, who said: 'Education must enable one to sift and weigh evidence, to discern the true from the false, the real from the unreal, and the facts from the fiction. The function of education, therefore, is to teach one to think intensively and to think critically' (King Jr, 1947, 1).

In King's definition, education is about investigation, a process of learning and unlearning and, crucially, reimagining and recreating. But the purpose goes even further: in order for change to happen not only in the minds of individuals but in the world, social justice must be embedded in education. This is most important in the world today, as we battle health pandemics, and also ongoing social injustices too.

For the generation who have been spearheading the decolonising education movement, this work is about fighting for more than just an 'inclusive' education. It's about fighting for an education that sets a foundation for students and the world they live in – a world they can build that is anti-racist, fully liberated and accessible for all.

Eds: How is decolonisation part of your broader anti-racist work?
HG: Students and grassroots activists, who have ignited the process of decolonisation across their educational institutions over many years, have grounded their anti-racist work in decolonisation – from solidarity with Black South Africans during apartheid through the Rhodes Must Fall campaign, to work on addressing the Black attainment gap, to launching the nationwide campaign Why Is My Curriculum White? That campaign invited academics, staff and students into spaces that confronted the curriculum's Eurocentricity; students have seen decolonisation as not just about the university, but instead about the wider world and, most importantly, about people.

In essence decolonisation calls for us to reassess our notions of humanity, as Fanon does, and reset the very foundations of our assumptions, norms and taught truths. This work for the educational community needs to be about the student – every student, who continues to experience and be wrongly taught about the violence of current and historical colonialism in their education.

Mbembe characterises the heart of this work well in affirming that: 'we are also talking about the creation of those conditions that will allow Black staff and students to say of the university: "This is my home. I am not an outsider here. I do not have to beg or to apologize to be here. I belong here"' (Mbembe, 2018, 4).

The ultimate aim is to liberate and democratise our education systems so that the world becomes free from spaces, institutions and systems that perpetuate colonial violence, and is built for us, by us. The prominence of the Black Lives Matter (BLM) movement following the death of George Floyd in May 2020 has played a massive role in calling out colonialism in education. For many students, particularly Black students, this was a time when they took back the fight for the eradication of the systemic racism that has plagued their lives and hindered their educational experiences.

Eds: Where does the library fit with this work and how have students engaged with decolonising the library?
HG: An example of students working with libraries in this space is the Goldsmiths University and Student Union Liberate Our Library campaign (Goldsmiths, University of London, 2021).

Marilyn Clarke, Goldsmiths Library, states that: 'I as a library worker seek to transgress against the boundaries imposed by racism, classism and heteronormative structures in both knowledge dissemination and organisation, as well as institutional structures' (Clarke, 2019).

Activists and sabbatical officers in and around Goldsmiths Student Union have long been at the forefront of the decolonisation movement. The Goldsmiths Anti-Racist Action group successfully led a 137-day occupation of Deptford Town Hall, where students were able to secure commitments pertaining to an overhaul of the curriculum and wide acknowledgement of the university's colonial ties. In that same vein, the Liberate Our Library campaign came off the back of a wider campaign to 'liberate our degrees' led by the NUS. The importance of the specific work on the library stemmed from the understanding that 'the library as a professional service must play a fundamental role in this work as a conduit for access to learning and teaching resources' (Clarke, 2019). This project is particularly interesting in how it centres students and their vision. At the heart of the democratisation of the library, and education more widely, is the idea that there are no gatekeepers of knowledge or any individual or group that holds a monopoly on owning knowledge.

Students must be central to the work of decolonising the library. The two key components that have blocked the progression of the decolonisation movement are the exclusion and destruction of information for knowledge building, and the lack of safe spaces that enable all, especially those that have been marginalised, to be liberated. The first step to any of this work is to recognise that knowledge is not a commodity and therefore must be regarded as 'a cumulative and shared resource that is available to all' (Keele Decolonising the Curriculum Network, 2020).

Students, staff and institutions must challenge current ways of knowledge accumulation in the building of the decolonised library. Students must build on the work of those who have laid the foundations for decolonisation and honour those whose ancestral knowledge has been destroyed or erased. For liberation to be achieved, academic tradition must be uprooted to allow students to pave a way that leads to transformative change.

Work to decolonise the academic canon and library is very important to students. This is an area of decolonisation that is active and progressing – and for students has been on the agenda long before the advent of the Why Is My Curriculum White? campaign. Dismantling the academic canon and expanding and transforming the library as we know it is a part of the decolonisation process that can produce immediate change and engage people for longer-term change. The library is a place of discovery, of investigation. It is the place where knowledge is produced and held in physical collections and through access to digital resources. For the individual student, it is a place where, consciously or unconsciously, they look to be found, and not only found, but empowered, equipped and validated by and with knowledge. Knowledge is linked with identity; the availability of a full and truly liberated library of knowledge is crucial if education is to meet its true purpose.

Decolonisation is as much a journey as it is a movement and a force for change. For all those starting the journey, the first step must be to learn and unlearn. Access to knowledge – which includes both theoretical information and accounts of experience – draws the individual in to become invested in the work of decolonisation and releases them from the notion of innocent ignorance, leading them to confront current and historical colonial legacies that have afforded power and agency to White supremacy. Students need to become renewed in their power and authority within the institutions they navigate. This work goes beyond updating and adding to reading lists and looks to dismantle and reimagine the library as a space where people are liberated, challenged and are supported in this journey.

For Black students, decolonising the library is a double-edged sword. On the one hand, it allows their stories and histories to be recognised in their truth, with their pain and their joy. They no longer are the subject nor are they victims, but instead they become transformed into the narrator, the liberated and the visionary. On the other hand, they are also exposed to and made alive to the inheritance of pain and violence that has been sustained over generations of current and historical colonialism. For students there is power in being recognised for the narratives, personalities, individuality and diversity of identities they bring to the academy – and even more so in being celebrated for them.

There is also a need to take great care to give Black students and staff the support to be able to go on this first stage of their journey, where they are unlocking and unpicking the lies and mistruths that were placed on them as fact throughout their educational journey. The work of decolonising the library is both about the exchange of knowledge and about the physical spaces in which they can feel safe and supported in the transformation and revelation that brings.

Decolonisation of the library is a great responsibility and requires us to pay homage to and to celebrate those it brings into the light, but it also must be coupled with trauma-informed action to ensure that the potential wounds it opens can be healed. In such a central place as the library, it is important that what is front and centre is the notion of the reimagined humanity that Fanon calls for, and even more so a willingness to liberate our spaces, texts, institutions and student community to really fulfil their full potential. This is essential in understanding the impact that this has for the discovery of self that is central to this work.

Eds: What is the role of allies in decolonising the library?
HG: Students who are allies in this work must be encouraged to be proactive in approaching knowledge critically and be open to the extent that they will be challenged and simultaneously humbled. The library is a place where their eyes must be opened to a world bigger and more complex than they've been exposed to and find themselves removed from the centre of the narrative, to being part of a bigger picture. It is important that this space is one where they can learn independently, without an over-reliance on the victims of colonial violence to teach them. They must learn what it means to have benefited from the colonial legacy and understand the embedded inequalities and injustices that still affect racially marginalised people. It is equally important that in understanding the injustice, allies also understand other cultures and reasons to celebrate them.

Individuals in the student community must learn about cultures, practices and histories that enable those that have been marginalised to be seen as partners in this space and not to be pitied or seen as victims. More importantly, for allies, this work must inspire them to change the way they think and recognise the entitlement they've been brought up to have regarding the ownership of knowledge and spaces.

Eds: What about decolonising teaching and learning practices and spaces?
HG: Decolonisation is about the way students are taught and invited to belong in educational spaces. In order for the work done to have any meaning and true engagement, students – especially Black students – need to be able to feel free to engage with education on their own terms. The current system encourages these students to assimilate for success, or challenge and be shut out. If we were to flip this on its head, whether through doing away with modes of assessment that look only to tick off learning objectives, and instead replacing them with authentic modes of demonstrating engagement and critical thinking, or rethinking what learning environments look like

entirely, we could reconceptualise the university as a place of liberation for all. 'The university curricula will not decolonise itself. It will not happen through the bureaucratised curriculum design reviews. Major curriculum reform cannot be achieved without greater democratisation of the university as an institution, and its relation to wider society' (Keele Decolonising the Curriculum Network, 2020).

We must think radically about the pipeline that enables more Black students to engage with academia, which requires us to look at how we enable their progression. The 'broken pipeline' shows that the progression of Black students in academia is inhibited due to systemic inequalities. Sustainable and real change comes from challenging the system that excludes Black voices, ideas and knowledge from being accepted. Ongoing issues of the BAME degree-awarding gap, where there is clear evidence of gaps in degree awards between Black students, BAME students and White students – who are awarded better degrees than their racialised counterparts.

Eds: Moving from the individual student experience to the NUS role in collective action, what are your current campaigns?
HG: Decolonisation calls for us to move from individualism to collective solidarity and action. The collective is crucial, as it is the place where we recognise that our existences are intertwined with others, and therefore so is our liberation. It is in the collective that we can share knowledge, in order to imagine and build alternatives. The power of community and the collective should never be underestimated when campaigning: decolonisation requires us to abolish the current power structures and repair historical harm by centring those who have been marginalised. It's through collective action that allies meet those directly exposed to colonial violence and understand that decolonisation, although a radical movement for the marginalised, is also about restoring the purpose and function of education and society.

Decolonisation cannot happen in the context of piecemeal reform or as a side project. Its scope requires the involvement of the whole institution to really see impact and change. As Angela Davis states, radical simply means 'grasping at the root' (Davis, 2006). The roots of colonial legacy are too deep to be uprooted by individuals, or even by the marginalised alone. It requires a collective response; decolonisation benefits us all. It gives voice to those who have been 'invisibilised', discredited and shut out of the justice they deserve for years of colonial violence; it opens and expands the world into a truly diverse, liberated and democratised place where there are no longer limits to who and what is classed as 'truth', and an expansion of narratives and perspectives offered to all to explore and engage with.

There are already existing collectives working on decolonisation. The student movement has been at the forefront of this in educational spaces, from work on the curriculum to wider work around mental health support. These are established areas of our work, but the prominence of the BLM movement and campaigns like Rhodes Must Fall have renewed and reinvigorated the decolonisation movement. It is important to highlight these to show the power of collective student campaigning and work that has really moved the decolonisation agenda forwards.

Why Is My Curriculum White? (University College London, 2014): This campaign was started at University College London in 2014, with a focus on exposing the Eurocentricity and White-centred nature of the academy. Supported by successive NUS Black Students' campaigns, this was replicated at many universities across the UK. The campaign was central to the understanding of the roots of colonialism, that the curriculum was shaped by, taught by and constructed by White people for the benefit of White people. The power of this student-led work was that students were able to make spaces that were in themselves decolonial in practice, where students and academics alike were equal counterparts and where student-led sessions and activities brought to light the impact that a Eurocentric curriculum had on their educational experience. In this space the status quo was challenged and, more importantly, institutions started to be confronted with the visceral reality of the continued upholding of colonial legacies and practices. This campaign has led to wider campaigns around decolonising services in universities, like the promotion of culturally competent care, as well as the sprouting up of courses and disciplines centred on Black studies and decolonial practice.

NUS Decolonise Education: The NUS Decolonise Education campaign is focused on building a foundation and community where students and grassroots activists can be connected and equipped to put into action the work of decolonisation; political education and collective power are at the centre of the campaign. Another key component is that Black voices are centred, but in doing this there is an awareness that this is a collective endeavour because 'decolonising education will benefit every one of us' (NUS, 2020), including allies.

There has already been a lot of work done towards decolonising the academic library. The NUS has been building a multimedia library, the Free Black University, an open access e-library (Free Black University, 2020). This initiative seeks to transform the concept of the library and how we handle and distribute knowledge, with a real focus on accessibility and equity, recognising that no one student should have an advantage over another in engaging with this content.

Therefore, the range of media which the library uses is being expanded. Social media, the use of infographics and different forms of learning resources can break down barriers to who can access the knowledge, and has broken stigmas by using approaches to the dissemination of knowledge that have often been rejected from the current academic canon. In the developing library, student voices are amplified through different media – from podcasts to Instagram lives.

Creative expressions of knowledge, alongside reclaimed styles of academic writing, are also ways of making this work much more accessible for all students, staff and academic communities to engage with equitably; expanding membership of the academic community to encourage curation of such forms of knowledge is crucial; students finally will become recognised as authors, project leads, creatives and experts in ways they haven't before. The approach to building this catalogue of knowledge is similar to Goldsmiths' Liberate Our Library in being intersectional and recognising that students are diverse and should have choice and freedom to engage with knowledge in a way that connects with them.

While these campaigns centre on Black students and the marginalised, they recognise the wider impact this work has on the educational experience of all students. The intention is to take people on a journey, meeting them at their starting point, connecting them with others on the journey and guiding them through. While decolonisation has a deep connection to anti-racist work, it also unlocks other spaces of liberation confined by the pillars of colonialism that intersect with capitalism, sexism, homophobia and many more forms of injustice. The meaning of allyship is transformed in this context, with the embedding of a true community that comes from a place of accepting and celebrating difference, as well as celebrating similarities and connections.

As Audre Lorde has said: 'Without community, there is no liberation . . . but community must not mean a shedding of our differences, nor the pathetic pretence that these differences do not exist' (Lorde, 2007).

Eds: What are your thoughts on the decolonisation movement going forwards?
HG: As those who are coming up as the next and new generations, students are well placed to be the force that collectively dismantles, but most importantly rebuilds. At the centre of decolonising the library, the willingness and creativity that come with rebuilding and transforming are energised and sustained by students. It is in the collective spaces that students transform the handling of the knowledge that enables real change and invites all participants to move from their individual experience and learning to collective solidarity and organising. 'If you have come here to help me you are wasting your time, but if you have come because your liberation is bound up with mine, then let us work together' (Aboriginal activists group, Queensland, 1970s, as quoted by Watson, 2004).

Acknowledging the impact of racism, the colonial legacy and systemic oppression, is now unavoidable; ignorance is no longer an excuse and inaction and passive solidarity are no longer acceptable responses. In fact, students now have more power and support to hold their institutions to account. Universities and other educational institutions are in a position to be a real part of change, but it requires the cycle of reproducing and capitalising off colonial violence to be broken. The only way forward is to break the pattern of piecemeal change that has let students and staff down over the years. This requires wholescale and transformative change, all of which is made possible through real investment and commitment to decolonising our libraries, institutions and education system as a whole.

Students are central to seeing a truly decolonised library come to fruition, in a truly liberated and democratised education system. It is work that requires a full and wholescale process that fundamentally centres the voices of Black students – in their full diversity, from every background and identity. It requires a willingness of White staff and institutions to humble themselves, their traditions and their processes in order to make this a fruitful and authentic project.

The work of decolonisation requires the abandonment of traditional practices, replacing them with true decolonial practices and a wider engagement, beyond the educational sphere, with society and the world. This enables students to build and foster a culture and generation that fights injustice and is intentionally anti-racist. This intersects with other key areas of work like sustainability and climate change, gender politics and so many social and global issues that require work that grasps at the root.

References

Behari-Leak, K., Masehela, L., Marhaya, L., Tjabane, M. and Merckel, N. (2017) Decolonising The Curriculum: It's In The Detail, Not Just In The Definition, *The Conversation*, https://theconversation.com/decolonising-the-curriculum-its-in-the-detail-not-just-in-the-definition-73772 (accessed 15 January 2021).

Clarke, M. (2019) Liberate Our Library: Social Justice and the Need for Change, *UKSG eNews*, www.uksg.org/newsletter/uksg-enews-438/liberate-our-library-social-justice-and-need-change (accessed 14 January 2021).

Davis, A. (2006) Decolonising Education, Moe Lectureship in Women's Studies, Gustavus Adolphus College, Minnesota, 2006, www.nus.org.uk/decoloniseeducation (accessed 13 January 2021).

Decolonising LSE Collective, (n.d.) What is Decolonisation? https://decolonisinglse.wordpress.com/about/what-is-decolonisation (accessed 17 September 2021)

Fanon, F. (2004) *The Wretched of the Earth*, Grove Press.

Free Black University (2020) *eLibrary – Free Black University*, www.freeblackuni.com/elibrary (accessed 14 January 2021).

Ghillar, M. A. (2016) What Is 'Decolonisation'? – How Do We Decolonise? Sovereign Union – First Nations Asserting Sovereignty, http://nationalunitygovernment.org/content/what-decolonisation-how-do-we-decononise-1 (accessed 15 January 2021).

Goldsmiths, University of London (2021) Liberate Our Library, www.gold.ac.uk/library/about/liberate-our-library/ (accessed 14 January 2021).

Keele Decolonising the Curriculum Network (2020) Keele's Manifesto For Decolonising The Curriculum, *Journal of Global Faultlines*, **7** (1), 107, DOI: 10.13169/jglobfaul.7.1.0107.

King Jr, M. L. (1947) The Purpose Of Education, *Morehouse College Student Paper*, www.shsu.edu/dept/office-of-the-president/documents/MLK+Speech+2016.pdf (accessed 8 January 2020).

Lorde, A. (2007) The Master's Tools Will Never Dismantle the Master's House. In *Sister Outsider: Essays and Speeches*, Crossing Press.

Mbembe, A. (2018) Decolonising Knowledge and the Question of the Archive. Lecture, Wits Institute for Social and Economic Research, University of the Witwatersrand, Johannesburg.

NUS (2020) Decolonise Education, www.nus.org.uk/campaign-hub/decolonise-education (accessed 19 June 2021).

University College London (2014) *Why Is My Curriculum White?* Video, www.dtmh.ucl.ac.uk/videos/curriculum-white/ (accessed 14 January 2021).

Watson, L. (2004) A Contribution to Change: Cooperation out of Conflict Conference: Celebrating Difference, Embracing Equality, Hobart, Tasmania.

2
Intelligent Leaders, Intelligent Spaces

Regina Everitt

Introduction

As an undergraduate I had an internship at an agency writing recruitment advertisements. The ads ranged from the small 'want' ads for salespeople or programmers to the full-page spreads in newspapers and magazines for directors and executives. I was no Don Draper from *Madmen*. I didn't particularly enjoy the job, but it taught me to know my audience. And I learned that I enjoyed pitching ads for some audiences more than others.

Now, I am the Director of Library, Archives and Learning Services at the University of East London (UEL). The university is located in the Borough of Newham, one of the poorest in London, with an ethnically diverse population that was one of the most adversely impacted by COVID-19. The University has a 70% Black, Asian and minority ethnic (BAME) student population and a staff population of almost 70% White. So, many students do not see themselves in the staff population. Most of the students are the first in their families to attend university. According to UEL internal data, the degree-awarding gap (percentage difference between groups receiving a 1st/2:1 or A/B grade) between BAME and White students was about 13% in 2019/20, down from 21% the previous year. However, the gap between Black and White students was just over 17%, down from roughly 25% the previous year.

The University has undertaken a range of measures to close the degree-awarding gap. It has created an Office of Institutional Equity (OIE), the first of its kind in the UK, to lead on the delivery of an ambitious action plan to achieve the Race Equality Charter (REC). The REC is a framework created by Advance HE to aid institutions in identifying and challenging the barriers that block the progression of BAME students and staff (Advance HE, 2020). The UEL action plan includes staff training on inclusive teaching practices and anti-racism as well as reviews of such institutional policies and procedures as recruitment, performance management and disciplinaries. The OIE also monitors the equality, diversity and inclusion data for trends, sector benchmarking and achievement of targets.

Key to the success of narrowing the degree-awarding gap is staff knowing their audience. We must *see* the whole student – their lived experiences, academic needs, caring responsibilities, work demands – so that we can provide the right level of support to lead to successful outcomes for the students. However, to truly support our students, we must be able to empathise with the challenges that they may face and be aware of and manage our own attitudes towards them. This is called *emotional intelligence*. As a leader, I must support my team in becoming emotionally intelligent and draw on their individual strengths to enable them to effectively support the students; thus, using my *social intelligence*. So, I must be an emotionally and socially intelligent leader to create the culture that enables my team to deliver spaces and services that give our students a sense of belonging and enable them to be academically successful. Ideally, the students will see themselves reflected within the spaces and services that I lead.

Emotional and social intelligence

Psychologist Daniel Goleman defines emotional intelligence as being aware of and managing one's emotions and empathising with others (Big Think, 2012). As a leader, I must be aware of my own strengths, weaknesses and biases and be able to recognise these within my team and organisation. So, if I lack empathy for young parents 'who shouldn't have gotten themselves in that position', I am unlikely to implement support services that accommodate their caring responsibilities. If I am uneasy around young Black men, my interactions with them may be strained, leading to conflict and disciplinary action.

Social intelligence would be my awareness of the feelings of others, reading the signals that they send through their behaviours and interacting accordingly (Goleman, 2007, 84). For example, I may implement interventions to encourage international and home UK students to work collaboratively in a learning space. Or I may facilitate targeted training for staff members who continually have conflict with certain students. Goleman talks about emotions as being how we are wired. So, I would say that social intelligence is our 'internal Bluetooth', allowing individuals to connect and communicate through words and actions. As a leader, I will want to ensure that those connections are constructive.

I help my team to know our audience by understanding how well our students engage with our collections, spaces, imagery and messaging through analysis of usage data, feedback, user experience activities and other qualitative and quantitative methods. I also allocate funding to empower staff to use creative and inclusive resources and practices to support students and develop their skills. Finally, discussions about social and emotional intelligence are embedded in customer-care training.

The best way for leaders to know whether they are emotionally or socially intelligent is to ask those around us, usually through a 360-degree appraisal. A 360-degree appraisal is when peers, stakeholders, customers, line managers and junior and senior staff provide anonymous feedback on a range of behaviours and competencies of a leader. My last appraisal, using the Blended360 tool, showed that I rated in the upper quartile for both emotional and social intelligence, with a slightly higher rating for the former. I won't be self-congratulatory just yet, however. As I have a particular interest in space, I will reflect on how my emotional and social intelligence have influenced how I have developed and used spaces.

Who belongs in what space?

It was a scorching hot day in Washington, DC in July 2019. My friends and I had found a cool, shady patch in Lafayette Square opposite the White House and were just getting stuck into the latest gossip when we were suddenly surrounded by police officers on cycles yelling, 'Get out of the park NOW!' My friends said that this was normal practice when the president was near. (A year later, that same park would be forcibly cleared by security forces during BLM protests about the death of George Floyd so that then President Trump could have a photo opportunity nearby, as described in an article in the *New York Times* on 2 June 2020 (Baker et al., 2020).)

We eventually ended up at the Smithsonian National Portrait Gallery, a free place to beat the heat while visiting the portraits of former President Barack Obama and former First Lady Michelle Obama. Their portraits were stunningly beautiful and regal, within a space filled with predominantly White American historical figures.

However, the portrait that sparked the most animated conversation among me and my friends was that of rapper LL Cool J. It was many years since I had visited the gallery, so it was surreal to see a rapper from my inner-city childhood in the National Portrait Gallery, in the same room as Michelle Obama and Toni Morrison. The LL Cool J portrait had been part of a wider exhibition at the Gallery of portraits of hip-hop icons, according to a Gallery blog (National Portrait Gallery, 2021). A far cry from my childhood memory of a more staid visit to the space!

Artist Kehinde Wiley (who painted Barack Obama's portrait) captured LL Cool J in the same pose as businessman and philanthropist John D. Rockefeller in a portrait by John Singer Sargent, some 100 years ago. Wiley is known for creating portraits of African American men and women in the poses of aristocrats in works by Western and European painters (George, 2020). The portrait was commissioned by the VH1 Hip-Hop honours, for which LL Cool J received recognition. LL Cool J is said to have an interest in art and sits on the Smithsonian National Board (George, 2020).

LL Cool J's portrait stood out for me on that day because I grew up listening to his music, and rap was the music of the streets – a world away from the Smithsonian. Faced with his portrait, I reverted to that inner-city girl from the segregated neighbourhood who grew up to believe that Black people didn't belong in hallowed spaces like art galleries, but only worked there as cleaners or security guards. For that moment I, who have worked on three continents, had to check my feelings of belonging within what I considered to be 'White only' spaces. Like the takeover of the Louvre in 2018 by Beyoncé and Jay-Z, I needed to reclaim my right to be in that or any space, and reaffirmed my vow to help my students to do the same (Chrisafis, 2019).

My experiences of spaces
Growing up in Philly

I was born in Philadelphia, the city where the Declaration of Independence, decolonising the United States from Great Britain, and the Constitution were signed. Located in the north-east of the USA, the city is an hour-and-a-half journey south of New York City on the high-speed train. The Philadelphia of my childhood memory had distinct spaces where everyone knew where they belonged; you ventured into other neighbourhoods and spaces with caution. West Philly, where I was born and grew up, was a predominantly African American community where blue-collar workers had their homes. There was also an aspirational middle class with some teachers, police officers, nurses and social workers. At the turn of the 20th century, renowned baritone, actor and activist Paul Robeson lived just a few blocks from my West Philly home. Many years later, I would occupy another space in Paul Robeson's steps, SOAS University of London. Robeson studied and campaigned for social justice at SOAS and I later ran the library there.

On reflection, the Philly neighbourhoods, spaces of my childhood, which were predominantly working class, were segregated by ethnicity. North Philly had predominantly African American and Latinx communities. South Philly had a large Italian community. In the Southwest and East were Polish and Irish communities. In the Northeast were Jewish communities. I remember being chased from the Elmwood section of Southwest Philly by the local White kids whenever we went to the skating rink there. Centre city was the more affluent and historical area of Philadelphia and home of the Declaration of Independence. West and North Philly were hit hard during the gang war era of the 1970s and the crack era of the 1980s and 1990s and were considered 'no go' areas unless you knew where you were going. It was virtually impossible to get a taxicab to go to West or North Philly at night.

Through my primary and secondary school years, I circulated largely within the confines of my West Philly space. The people in the spaces were just like me. Black. Working class. Family roots in the Southern states like Virginia and the Carolinas, but unclear about the specific location of descendance from Africa. My schools and churches were all within walking distance or a short bus ride or drive away. The local barber's and candy shop were all Black owned. There was a local cinema where we enjoyed scary movies and cop films like *Shaft* and *Dirty Harry*. The barber's, candy shop and cinema had all disappeared by the end of my middle school years; but my local library, the Free Library of Philadelphia, still stands today.

As a teen in West Philly, I escaped from my porch during the summer holidays to go to the library to languish among the stacks of the Black Literature section. I devoured stories from writers from the Harlem Renaissance through the Black Power movement. Langston Hughes. Richard Wright. James Baldwin. Lorraine Hansberry. Angela Davis. It was *The Big Sea* by Langston Hughes that dared me to dream of escaping the gang and drug problems of my inner-city space to travel the world. In that book, Hughes recounts the adventures of his travels as a merchant seaman to Africa and hanging out in the nightclubs of Europe. I wanted that freedom! I was outgrowing my West Philly space.

Belonging at university . . . or not

I was fortunate that the state of Pennsylvania has some outstanding higher education institutions, as I could not afford the cost of studying out of state. In the USA, residents receive significant discounts if they study in their home state. For my undergraduate studies, I attended Temple University, which is located in North Philly with its notable issues with drug-related violence. Temple University has since expanded and regentrified some of its North Philly surroundings, as have the University of Pennsylvania and Drexel University – my postgraduate alma mater – in West Philly. It is not unusual now to see a White person walking just a few blocks from where I grew up, whereas in my youth the only White people in the area were cops and insurance salesmen.

Although Temple University was located in a predominantly Black neighbourhood, its student population was predominantly White. So, all the familiarity, comfort and belonging of being in a neighbourhood of people who were just like me were stripped away the minute I walked into the hallowed walls of the University. The posters showed pictures of the White people that I only saw on television, blonde haired, blue eyed – 'all American' boys and girls. The students in my class were predominantly White. I recall only one or two non-White lecturers. I remember that in my first year a guy whom I attended high school with said that he planned to leave, as he never expected there to be so many White people at the University. I don't think that he had anything against White people per se. He, like me, was thrust into a space that was worlds different from where we were from. The only White adults that we had ever spoken to at length were our schoolteachers. The White kids used to chase us from the skating rink. Keg parties? Toga parties? Nah, we partied differently in West Philly. My friend transferred to one of the historically Black universities in the South. I had to make this work mostly because family finances didn't allow out-of-state options. So, I took a deep breath and dived in.

In her book, *Why Are All the Black Kids Sitting Together in the Cafeteria?*, Beverly Daniel Tatum notes that Black students in predominantly White educational environments think of themselves in terms of race because that is how the rest of the world sees them (Tatum, 1997, 214). In my all Black high school, my school friend and I were the athlete, the cheerleader, the newspaper editor, the head of the honour society. At the predominantly White university, we were the only Black young woman or man on the course. And Black was identifiable by all the nefarious activities that took place outside the university walls: crime, poverty, other. Though Tatum's book was about students in secondary education, I recognised the coping mechanisms of the Black students in these predominantly White spaces (e.g. downplay academic ability to avoid being accused of 'acting White' or amplify use of slang to be 'more Black').

I stayed at the University, and was glad in the end that I did. I graduated with honours and found a multicultural group of lifelong friends. Expectedly, I endured some of the same challenges that Black and Brown students face today: lecturers not calling on me or not valuing my work; being the 'only fly in the sugar bowl' at parties and events; having few Black or Brown role models; and being on the receiving end of back-handed, 'helpful' advice: 'You should get rid of that West Philly accent'. However, during my years at Temple, I proved to myself that I could perform academically just as well as if not better than my White peers, many of whom had attended high schools with more resources than mine. My experience also gave me valuable lessons on how to navigate in the work environment and postgraduate education, where I would be in the minority again. By the time I completed graduate school, I had started to travel and had developed confidence in inhabiting new spaces; spaces that in childhood did not appear to be for people like me.

When Maria Balshaw, Director of the Tate Gallery, was Director of the Whitworth Gallery in Manchester, she led a major renovation of the space, removing the enclosing walls and enabling art to be seen from the outside. During an interview on Radio 4's *Desert Island Discs*, she describes a scene where a child on a scooter rides up to the entrance of the refurbished gallery and, as the doors open proceeds to scoot inside, to the abject horror of his father, who has been chasing behind him (BBC, 2020). Balshaw said that as a gallery staff member welcomed them into the space, she knew that they had done the right thing by making the space more accessible to the local community. I love that story, for I couldn't imagine my early West Philly self walking into a Centre City art gallery and being welcomed. Yet, had I tried, I might have been pleasantly surprised.

I draw on these formative experiences of my emotional and social intelligence about space and belonging as I lead the development of spaces and services to support student learning. As Matthew Syed discusses in *Rebel Ideas*, having a member of a team that has a perspective that is different from the status quo could lead to creative solutions to solve complex problems (Syed, 2020). With the early spaces that I developed and managed, I would like to think that I brought a unique perspective to the homogeneous senior management teams with which I worked in higher education.

My influence and leadership of spaces
Peace Corps service in Africa

In 1961, US President John F. Kennedy signed a declaration to create the Peace Corps, a volunteer agency created to support 'developing' nations and to promote world peace. This was a great opportunity for me to travel, live and work in Africa, so I signed up. I was assigned to teach English as a Second Language in universities and schools in Central and West Africa. The subtext of the teacher training materials were unsubtle messages about how great life was in America. I planned to inject some reality into my teaching and, prior to departure, arranged for book donations about African American history to be sent to my schools and the library I ran. The students were, of course, interested in life in America and how to gain scholarships or sponsorship for study. However, because I was their teacher, they were very interested in contemporary African American life – where we lived, how we dressed, what music we enjoyed, how we spent our leisure time, our slang. I filled my classrooms with images and sounds from African American life as we discussed the Harlem Renaissance, Civil Rights movement and contemporary politics. The students were also interested in the legacy of the transatlantic slave trade. When I called myself a 'Pan Africanist', as I was unsure where on the continent my family originated, they claimed me as their kin. I was most often identified as Malinke, one of the largest ethnic groups in West Africa.

As an English language teacher, I wanted my students to vocalise the language. This sounds obvious, but it was not the approach of my Francophone African colleagues, who taught French. In their classrooms, students sat quietly, conjugating verbs, using different coloured pens to highlight phrases in neat little notebooks, presumably replicating well-mannered French children. Their approach to teaching exemplified what Freire called a 'banking' method, in which the students were expected to regurgitate whatever the teacher deposited in their heads (Freire, 2018). In my classes, we read aloud, sang, did impromptu plays, wrote and performed raps! The Head of Studies was not amused by my noisy lessons, so I kept my classroom door shut to create a safe space for students to express themselves using the English language. The students were engaged and co-created lessons.

UK university libraries and learning spaces

Years later, at the University of the Arts London (UAL), I had the opportunity to develop a social learning space called the Learning Zone, where students were empowered to decide how and where they would study, work collaboratively, reconfigure the space as they wanted, use new technology and eat, drink and use their mobile devices. It was the antithesis of the 'ssh' library environments that I experienced during my undergrad and postgrad studies and worked particularly well for the practical work of art and design students (e.g. sewing, film rendering, sketching). The informal nature of the space fostered students' sense of ownership and belonging in the space. There were few rules about what students couldn't do, and student peer workers to help them to discover what was possible in the space. I tried to limit interventions, allowing students to lead on how the space was used. However, I think we and academic colleagues could have done more to encourage more interactions between home and international students, thus giving all students more of an international experience. For example, Chinese students often sat together, maybe due to language barriers. Like the 'Black kids sitting together in the cafeteria', they self-segregated for whatever reason, possibly to remain within their comfort level with people like themselves. Ideally, their lecturers would have divided students into multicultural teams for collaborative work and they would have used spaces like the Learning Zone to co-create.

From the *tabula rasa* freedom of running the Learning Zone at UAL, I moved on to SOAS University of London, a world-renowned specialist in the study of Asia, Africa and the Middle East. Whereas the SOAS of the past trained civil servants on languages and cultures so that they could manage British colonies, the SOAS of today seeks to lead the fight on anti-racism and social justice. The SOAS team's work on decolonisation is discussed in more detail in Chapter 14. However, access to and use of the spaces in the library changed over the years. Due to its unique collections, the SOAS Library is one of the most popular destinations for reciprocal access schemes with UK and international institutions. Protective of the collections, some front-line staff members during my time there acted as *gatekeepers* as they interrogated users on why they needed to enter the library. I sought to shift that approach to *enabling* users to access the library, as members of the public were welcome to access the collections for reference purposes. I was aware that some long-serving library and academic staff longed for the days when the Reading Room, which later became a computer lab, was a quiet space where international researchers interrogated the collections in their original language under the protective gaze of a library assistant. However, the renovated collaborative study spaces and zoned quiet and silent spaces created a more open and welcoming environment for students and staff.

University of East London (UEL) has two modern libraries: one at the Docklands Campus and one at the Stratford Campus. Both libraries provide zoned spaces for collaborative, quiet and silent study. Both buildings are normally open 24/7 during teaching weeks, with access to PCs, Wi-Fi and self-service machines to enable students to borrow and return items and manage their accounts on demand. Beyond the physical buildings, students have 24/7 access to a range of online resources such as e-books, e-journals, databases and self-paced learning materials with chat support to aid students in navigating the resources.

Like many students, some UEL students have caring and other responsibilities beyond their studies. To support this diverse population of students, the library team implemented a range of targeted services to embed a sense of belonging in the physical and virtual spaces. Baby-changing tables, games and books are available in the libraries for those students who may need to bring children with them to the libraries; students are encouraged to recommend texts for the collection. Library teams have been working with academic staff and students to embed more inclusive teaching practices, with the addition of texts with a range of intellectual thought that speak to the lives of the students. Library staff engage in reading groups where students and academics come together to read and discuss critical race theory. Library staff and students share suggestions for interesting extracurricular reads via a Teams site with author recommendations ranging from Charles Bukowski to Bernadine Evaristo. The library team members enjoy consulting with students through such user-experience tools as graffiti boards or journey mapping, and adapting services and spaces to meet student needs. I support these interests through the allocation of funding for resources or time for staff members to attend events or visit other institutions to share ideas. I also enable them to share their experiences through regular slots at team meetings and host events, where possible. All these actions foster a 'can do' culture that unleashes staff creativity to deliver spaces and services that meet our students' needs.

Designing-in intelligence
On-campus imagery

In her research entitled *Who Is Worthy of these Walls? Postgraduate Students, UK Universities, and Institutional Racism*, Akile Ahmet captures the experiences of BAME postgraduate students in London-based Russell Group institutions through focus groups, in-depth interviews and the use of photography in which participants visualise their experiences. The participants cited a range of experiences that resonated with my time at university decades earlier, such as ill-tempered responses from lecturers when they are engaged in debate (Ahmet, 2020). The feeling of being 'othered' by the imagery of predominantly White leaders and historical figures from the past looming from institution walls was resonant with my childhood memories of visiting spaces like the Smithsonian National Art Gallery.

As a result of the global BLM protests following the killing of George Floyd in America by police, university leaders have been challenged to become emotionally intelligent about the impacts of statue and portrait imagery within their institutions. At UEL, the statue of Sir John Cass, who built his wealth from the slave trade, was removed from the School of Education and Communities amid concerns from students and staff about its negative and painful connotations (UEL, 2020). The School was renamed, dropping Cass from its title. City University of London took a similar approach, removing the name from its Business School (Neate, 2020). Ironically, the Sir John Cass foundation was set up in 1748 to promote the education of young people in London, particularly those from disadvantaged backgrounds, according to the Foundation website.

In solidarity with the Rhodes Must Fall campaign, started at the University of Cape Town in South Africa in 2015, students and staff have demanded the removal of the statue of Cecil B. Rhodes from Oriel College, Oxford University. Rhodes, a businessman during the colonial era in South Africa, presents a symbol of imperialism and racism that is at odds with modern educational values. At the time of this writing, a commission had been set up at Oxford University to determine the future of the statue (Coughlan, 2020).

I think that it is right that educational institutions, particularly, review their spaces and messaging to ensure that they do not alienate the very populations they are meant to educate. As an information professional I do not advocate that history is hidden or rewritten, but it should be contextualised to show societal evolution. As leaders we must be emotionally and socially intelligent enough to continually challenge (or be challenged on) our assumptions and approaches to delivery of spaces and services.

Designing spaces right

In the *Elemental Workplace*, Neil User identifies 12 key elements to create 'fantastic' workplaces for users (User, 2018, 72–144). Among these are:

- **influence:** where a user can create a relationship with the space and reconfigure it to suit them;
- **inclusion:** where the space accommodates the user's needs without need for obvious adjustment.

As discussed above, the ethos around the development of the Learning Zone at UAL was to allow users a choice in how they configured the space, facilitated by lightweight furniture on castors. The space had high and low tech to accommodate practices ranging from knitting to film rendering. The student workers were from a variety of countries, and so spoke different languages, thus mitigating the language barrier to seeking assistance. The imagery used in promotional literature and presentations showed the diversity of the user population.

The light, open and zoned informal-to-formal design are common features in modern academic libraries. Two examples of great practice in my view are Birmingham University Library, opened in 2016, and University of Roehampton Library, opened in 2017. Both award-winning buildings feature a variety of learning spaces providing students with the choice of where and how to study. They both have beautiful outlooks to green spaces that provide a calming respite from intense periods of study. These spaces are a far cry from the university libraries of my past, where the movement of a chair, crackle of a crisp packet or utterance of a single word would bring the ire of some students and staff. In these modern spaces, you don't feel that you need to make yourself unseen and unheard.

Mitigation of the spread of the COVID-19 coronavirus has influenced space accessibility and design considerations. During periods of restriction of public movement (lockdown), academic library buildings were forced to close and teaching moved online, thus disproportionately disadvantaging students living in 'digital poverty' – with no access to IT equipment or Wi-Fi. As restrictions were eased, library spaces were among the first university buildings to open, particularly to make accessible PCs, Wi-Fi and study spaces for students without access at their home residences. In compliance with government guidance, the spaces must: enable students to have 1–2 metres of distance between them (physical distance); be well ventilated to blow away any virus particles; have surfaces that are easily disinfected; and have thoroughfares that can support one-way systems (Department for Higher Education, 2020). Modern library spaces like those at UEL, and presumably Birmingham and Roehampton universities, have generally adapted well to the compliance requirements, thus reinforcing the inclusion element of their design.

Conclusion

London is one of my favourite cities for the arts, shopping and foodie experiences. When I had my son many years ago, I was determined to continue to enjoy the city's many pleasures. So, I popped him in the pram and set off for the Tube. I soon realised how inconveniently few step-free options there were at stations around London and quickly learned which ones to avoid. That experience reinforced my empathy with people who need step-free access to spaces and continues to influence my thinking about the functional aspects of the spaces that I lead.

Not all leaders can walk in the shoes of their service users. A White female library director, for example, cannot truly understand what it feels like to be a Black male undergraduate student. However, she can talk to the student, work with academic teams to create support systems (e.g. resources, spaces, information skills sessions) and learn about effective approaches for supporting the students. Once she and her team have got to truly know their audience, they can reflect on their own attitudes about the students' experiences, and then work together to implement relevant support.

Having grown up in a similar environment to many of my students at UEL, I have the privilege of understanding many of their lived experiences. However, I am decades their senior, with formative experiences that influence how I see the world, how those perceptions manifest in my leadership style and the resultant impact on the work culture in which my team delivers spaces and services. So, if the presence of an inner-city rap icon in a national art gallery gives me pause, then the 'why' really matters.

References

Advance HE (2020) Race Equality Charter, www.advance-he.ac.uk/equality-charters/race-equality-charter (accessed 2 January 2021).

Ahmet, A. (2020) *Who Is Worthy of a Place on These Walls: Postgraduate students, UK Universities, and Institutional Racism*, Royal Geographical Society.

Baker, P., Haberman, M., Rogers, K., Kanno-Youngs, Z. and Benner, K. (2020) How Trump's Idea for a Photo Op Led to Havoc in a Park, *New York Times*, 2 June, updated 17 September, www.nytimes.com/2020/06/02/us/politics/trump-walk-lafayette-square.html (accessed 2 January 2021).

BBC (2020) Desert Island Discs Maria Balshaw: Director of Tate, 9 August www.bbc.co.uk/programmes/m000lnld (accessed 14 May 2021).

Big Think (2012) Daniel Goleman Introduces Emotional Intelligence, www.youtube.com/watch?v=Y7m9eNoB3NU (accessed 2 January 2021).

Chrisafis, A. (2019) Beyoncé and Jay-Z Help Louvre Museum Break Visitor Record in 2018, *The Guardian*, 3 January, www.theguardian.com/world/2019/jan/03/beyonce-jay-z-help-louvre-museum-break-visitor-record (accessed 2 January 2021).

Coughlan, S. (2020) Oxford College's Rhodes Statue Staying Until Next Year, *The Guardian*, 21 July, www.bbc.co.uk/news/education-53487991 (accessed 2 January 2021).

Department for Higher Education (2020) Guidance: Higher Education Coronavirus (COVID-19) Operational Guidance, update 2 March 2020, www.gov.uk/government/publications/higher-education-reopening-buildings-and-campuses/higher-education-reopening-buildings-and-campuses (accessed 6 March 2021).

Freire, P. (2018) *Pedagogy of the Oppressed: 50th Anniversary Edition*, Tantor Media, Inc.

George, A. (2020) How a Maverick Hip-Hop Legend Found Inspiration in a Titan of American Industry, *Smithsonian Magazine*, 24 July, www.smithsonianmag.com/smithsonian-institution/how-maverick-hip-hop-legend-found-inspiration-titan-american-industry-180975399 (accessed 2 January 2021).

Goleman, D. (2007) *Social Intelligence: The New Science of Human Relationships*, Arrow Books.

National Portrait Gallery (2021) Now On View: LL Cool J., https://npg.si.edu/blog/now-on-view-ll-cool-j-kehinde-wiley (accessed 2 January 2021).

Neate, R. (2020) City University Changes Business School Name over Slavery Links, *The Guardian*, 6 July, www.theguardian.com/education/2020/jul/06/city-university-changes-cass-business-school-name-over-slavery-links (accessed 2 January 2021).

Syed, M. (2020) *Rebel Ideas: The Power of Diverse Thinking*, John Murray Press.

Tatum, B. D. (1997) *Why Are All the Black Kids Sitting Together in the Cafeteria?* Basic Books.

UEL (2020) University of East London Moves Forward with Sir John Cass Name Change, 27 August, www.uel.ac.uk/news/2020/08/university-of-east-london-moves-forward-with-sir-john-cass-name-change (accessed 2 January 2021).

User, N. (2018) *The Elemental Workplace*, LID Publishing Limited.

3
Decolonising Research Methodologies

Sara Ewing

Introduction

Research methodology is traditionally understood as the research strategy and rationale that informs approaches to conducting research, including its aim, purpose and methods. It is part of a research paradigm that is based on both ontological (view of the world) and epistemological (relationship with knowledge) orientations. One main ontological orientation is that reality is objective, meaning that objects in the world exist independently of our perception or comprehension, that they can be measured and tested and that it is possible to establish and explain universal principles and facts. A subjective ontological orientation, on the other hand, believes that reality is made up of individual perceptions and interactions, that facts are culturally and historically located, subject to variable behaviours, attitudes, experiences and interpretations, and thus multiple (Bryman, 2016). The tension between these two poles is largely irresolvable, and researchers often choose a position between the two. This position informs what is considered possible to know, and how knowledge is constituted, or an epistemological orientation.

Positivism asserts that genuine knowledge must be confirmed by the senses, gathering facts in a value-free way that provides the basis for generalisable laws and principles. Constructionism, on the other hand, claims that knowledge is a social, cultural and historical artefact, constructed by humans and their interactions with each other. It is not natural or inevitable, just socially agreed (Denzin and Lincoln, 1994). Based on these ontological and epistemological orientations, basic choices are made to pursue quantitative, qualitative or mixed-methods research, which determine the specific methods that are used to gather data and information.

Enlightenment principles such as individuality, rationality, empiricism and universalism were introduced and validated as essential foundations of not just research but also human civilisation, situating them both firmly in the values and contexts of the Western world. Processes of modernity and colonialism thus asserted control over not only politics and the economy but also the categories by which systems of knowledge, social norms, cultural values and social identities could be understood. Colonial epistemologies established hierarchies of superiority and inferiority, naturalising and normalising unequal social and political relationships.

The Western canon, including ways of thinking and educational foundations, divides social reality, including forms of knowledge and their conceptual foundations, into that which is visible and that which is invisible. '[This] division is such that the reality of what is invisible becomes non-existent, and is indeed produced as non-existent. Non-existent means not existing in any relevant or comprehensible way of being. Whatever is produced as non-existent is radically excluded because it lies beyond the realm of what the accepted conception of inclusion considers to be its other' (de Sousa Santos, 2007, 45). This exclusionary dynamic precludes debates that may inform new ways of thinking or insights, and thus has the effect of maintaining and perpetuating the thoughts and practices of the Western canon of knowledge, misrepresenting it as neutral and universal and thereby reproducing the coloniality of knowledge. Ramon Grosfoguel (2007, 212) claims that a decolonial epistemology instead 'requires a broader canon of thought … [that] would have to be the result of the critical dialogue between diverse critical epistemic/ethical/political projects toward a pluriversal' and which seriously considers 'the epistemic perspective/cosmologies/insights of critical thinkers from the Global South thinking from and with subalternized racial/ethnic/sexual spaces and bodies'. Decolonising research methodologies not only deconstructs and critiques Western research paradigms, but also offers a means of constructing knowledges that prioritise these marginalised perspectives and principles.

Decolonisation can be understood in myriad ways, but in higher education it can be defined as 'an expression of the changing geopolitics of knowledge whereby the modern epistemological framework for knowing and understanding the world is no longer interpreted as universal and unbound by geo-historical and biographical contexts' (Baker, 2012, 2). This means that knowledge is plural, subjective and locally situated, requiring an interrogation of who contributes to the production of knowledge, and who and what is considered worthy of being researched. This process is not abstract, but instead indexes identities, relationships and practices in the real world. As such, decolonising research methodologies asserts the agency of people from all backgrounds to theorise and interrogate the presumptions of academic research. According to Linda Tuhiwai Smith (2012, ix), the primary concern is 'not so much with the actual technique of selecting a method but much more with the context in which research questions are designed, and with the implications of research for its participants and their communities. It is also concerned with the institution of research, its claims, its values and practices and its relationships to power.' Rather than simply disseminating research methods and the knowledge they produce, the institution of research must be questioned and reinterpreted in context as a means of recovering the memories silenced by the legacy of colonial research practices (Meneses, 2011, 124). This includes the 'historical epistemicide' (Darder, Mayo and Paraskeve, 2016, 1) that currently constitutes legitimate disciplinary concepts and theories.

Academic literacies and academic research

Proponents of a traditional conception of literacy, sometimes known as the autonomous model, see literacy as composed of 'a set of portable, decontextualized information processing skills which individuals apply' (Reder and Davila, 2005, 172) that are unrelated to social and cultural context. This theory of literacy asserts that reading and writing alter an individual's cognitive and organisational ability such that he is able to think abstractly and reason logically (e.g. Goody, 1986; Ong, 1982). An alternative argument to this perspective is that literacy is more complex than just a neutral set of skills and is instead a context-specific and socially constructed practice, where reading and writing are rooted in 'conceptions of knowledge, identity and being' (Street, 2003, 78). Accordingly, the definition of literacy is contested and dependent on a particular worldview, hence ideological, and so its emphasis is less on the acquisition of skills, and more, rather, on the implications and effects of literacy use embedded in social practice. This perspective entails recognising that, instead of a single decontextualised literacy, there are multiple literacies whose practice, applicability and efficacy are dependent on when and where they are practised. Because the organisation of these practices takes place within a given society in a particular time, it is necessary to investigate how this hierarchy develops and how their relative values are assigned. Whether legislated and codified, or informally and socially determined, each society or subgroup of society has an established and commonly understood system for deciding which literacy practices are practised where and when, and what meanings are associated with those practices.

As a discipline, academic literacies emphasise English fluency as a tool for addressing 'specific academic and other institutional purposes' (Seidlhofer 2004, 223), which at university level typically involves independent research and writing. 'Literacies' is used in the plural because academic practices consist of multiple possible social relations and disciplinary expectations (Leung and Street, 2012, 9), and thus cannot be considered independently of institutional context, academic disciplines and social practices. This represents a significant challenge to the idealised and universalised ethnocentrism of the autonomous model of literacy, characterising it instead in terms of the worldviews and practices of Western academics (Brandt and Clinton, 2002, 339). Gee sees these as discourses that are socially constructed, ideological products of history (1996, 142–5) and which necessarily involve participants in relations of power. In this sense, then, academic literacies are attained as a means of becoming proficient within this power dynamic. At Goldsmiths, University of London, proficiency is constituted by not only the English language, but also the intellectual command of the critical and postmodern theories that underpin disciplinary analysis and compose valid academic discourses. In this context, discourses are not simply ideas, discussions or language, but are 'ways of displaying (through words, actions, values and beliefs) *membership* in a particular social group or social network' (Gee, 1996, 142–3), which in higher education is rooted in particular ways of conceptualising knowledge, identity and being (Street, 2003, 78). Academic discourses are embedded in particular social identities and roles within broader cultural and socio-economic contexts (e.g. Bourdieu, 1991; Gee, 1996) that precede and accompany entry into higher education.

Constructed of language and knowledge, academic writing can be seen as a discourse, which is the use of language as a social activity and is a means of representing, signifying and interacting with the world that is inextricably tied to social structure and the distribution of power (Fairclough, 1992, 63–4). The only way to succeed academically is by performing 'the social practices associated with the written word' (Barton, 2007, 37). Brandt and Clinton would see this origination and reception of written assessment as a relationship between 'sponsor' and 'sponsored', where the sponsor creates the assignment and monitors the terms of access and success, while the sponsored accepts and addresses it, with some incentive for compliance with conventions (Brandt and Clinton, 2002, 349). The incentive could be a good mark, which demonstrates an ability to practically apply disciplinary knowledge. Practical knowledge is inextricably tied to ideology, which is inserted into practices and manifested through actions (Althusser, 1971, 114). Accordingly, this definition of literacy emphasises common activities as well as shared language use, and highlights 'the everyday processes whereby people ... are made into subjects' (Ong, 1996, 737). The construction of knowledge in relation to 'ways of being' is a multifaceted exchange between disciplinary conventions and an intricate network of subjective experiences and expectations on the part of both the students and the lecturer. Engaging with institutionally promoted knowledge and practices creates an identity with which the student can conform and engage by 'doing' (Wenger, 1998, 193). This can be seen as a process of acculturation through which students must develop new modes of conduct and new sets of knowledge and literacy practices.

Resistance research and writing

Power is traditionally characterised in terms of either getting someone to do something they would not otherwise do (e.g. Dahl, 1958) or preventing someone from doing something they would otherwise do (e.g. Bachrach and Baratz, 1962). These positive and negative conceptualisations are elaborated by the acknowledgement that power can also shape social and institutional norms and expectations, influencing individual decisions and behaviours (Hay, 1997, 51). Agar (1985, 164) describes an institution as 'a socially legitimated expertise together with those persons authorized to implement it', a notion of presupposed knowledge similar to Fowler's (2005) definition of dominant discourses as unstated and unquestioned propositions that permeate social life. In fact, it has been argued that categories and their discursive counterparts, or specific conceptual assumptions and judgements, form the basis of institutional motivation and action (Makitalo and Saljo, 2002, 59). As a result, there is an interactional framework through which the respective roles of the institution and the individual are negotiated. The actual nature of the power of institutions has been debated at length, with some theorists seeing them as dominant entities imposing their will on unwilling parties (Althusser, 1971), and others seeing their power as derived from the complicity of the subordinate party (Foucault, 1972). However, in either case the interactionally enacted power can be seen as the result of a complex historical process of social reinforcement, variously identified as 'genealogy' (Foucault, 1977), 'genre' (Bakhtin, 1986) or 'iteration' (Butler, 1997) which impacts on the role of individual agency in the context of institutional norms and discourses. As such, literacy operates as a function of epistemological colonisation.

This perspective asserts that these power relations are composed of implicit and unquestioned discourses which serve to reinforce cultural, political and academic hierarchies. Within this context, research and writing can also be seen in terms of its potential for the expression of ideas and perspectives that may challenge the status quo (Barton, 2007, 70). It can be inferred that this entails creativity and activism, a perspective central to critical literacy, which promotes engaging critically with language as it is related to ideology and power relations. What can be interpreted as complicity in completing formal assessments can also be seen as a means for the writer to pursue and achieve their own goals, so it could be identified as a form of resistance. Because writers do have agency, they are presumably able to mediate both imposed literacy practices and ideology, imbuing them with their own intentions, resisting their hegemonic imperatives, and recrafting them to fulfil the needs at hand (Brandt and Clinton, 2002, 46). The incorporation of critical thought and analysis into education through their own research practices is '[t]he process in which [people], not as recipients but as knowing subjects, achieve a deepening awareness both of the socio-cultural reality that shapes their lives and of their capacity to transform that reality' (Freire, 1985, 93). It is with this potential in mind that I move to the work of embedding decolonising practices into academic literacies provision.

Decolonising academic practices

The underlying orientation to knowledge and the associated decolonial critiques are relevant to any discipline, as it is Western research itself which constructs and maintains the core conceptual and contextual assumptions that determine what is relevant and what is not. There is a foundation of presumed legitimacy that crosses all disciplines and, as such, there are common concerns and approaches to learning for anyone who enters the classroom. Such an epistemological orientation positions some students in terms of deficit, in which they are perceived to lack the necessary knowledge to participate in the class, a 'discourse [which] works to reproduce colonial binaries and maintain social hierarchies – us and them, the educated and uneducated, agents and beneficiaries, the prepared and the under-prepared, the advantaged and the disadvantaged, white and black' (Luckett and Shay, 2017, 8). This constructs a stigmatised expectation that is experienced and embodied by individual students in the classroom, and feeds into the interactions between students and teachers. As such, there are important pedagogical implications for the development of activities which integrate not only formal conventions of academic research but also individualised contexts and purposes.

Regardless of discipline, genre and rhetorical purpose, academic study and assessment requires a critical, analytical engagement with academic language, in both reading and writing. This involves a reciprocal relationship between the epistemological orientations of postmodern theory and its use as an analytical framework for discipline-specific academic research and writing, which can be seen as a 'community of practice' (Lave and Wenger, 1991). Learning to apply language in a relevant academic context can be seen as a process of conscious reflection in response to teaching that is able to break language down into its analytic parts. This includes highlighting and articulating the ways in which commonly used abstract concepts can be interpreted and understood in a wide variety of concrete ways. Frameworks of interpretations and assumptions of shared meaning 'organize and regulate social practices, influence our conduct and consequently have real, practical effects' (Hall, 2013). Indeed, for literacy to function as liberating rather than restrictive, it must be able to critique the language of these frameworks and assumptions, including words, attitudes and values, and use this as a foundation for both analysis and criticism (Gee, 1996, 156). Situating learning in this way, within authentic contexts of subject-specific material, remediates the gap between mastering content and its accurate expression within disciplinary conventions, both of which are required in order to succeed in higher education. This pedagogical emphasis is necessary to meet the needs of students that do not have experience with these specific uses of language, but it also enables students to utilise embedded academic practices as resources for engaging with and pursuing their own creative and intellectual goals.

Identity and agency

Communication is a process of representing ourselves to others, thus 'who we are to each other ... is accomplished, disputed, ascribed, resisted, managed and negotiated in discourse' (Benwell and Stokoe, 2006, 4). But the starting point of expression is our own understanding of ourselves, and who we are to ourselves, which makes identity construction an interaction between how we negotiate our self-understanding, how other people interpret those representations, and how we are perceived and represented by others. The discourses and ideologies that are raised implicitly or explicitly throughout an interaction can therefore provide the basis for categorisation, representation and negotiation. As such, they provide a point of orientation, as well as an opportunity to identify with or establish distance from other people on that basis. In many cases, students express that they do not in fact even see themselves in these categories and classifications, particularly in the way that they have been interpreted and used as justification for particular choices, approaches or policies (Akel, 2019). In this way, the categories and hierarchies of an academic discourse can perpetuate the subordination of individuals and groups while validating its own prestige and power (Gee, 1996, 155), a continuity of colonial systems of classification. Redressing this imbalance requires 'rewriting and *rerighting*' (Smith, 2012), or permitting the inclusion of typically excluded or invalidated ideas, experiences, values, relationships and identities.

An individual is described as having agency when he is considered to be free to construct his own identity; in contrast, he is seen to be bound within the structure of existing discourses if he does not exhibit that freedom (Benwell and Stokoe, 2006, 10). However, performed identity is based on individual circumstances and how they are negotiated within specific discursive contexts, so it is not possible to fully align with one extreme or the other, despite the temptation. Indeed, such negotiations can be complicated by how institutional power influences how and to what extent agency is realised, as where we are can situate a very personal manifestation of power struggle and exclusion (Benwell and Stokoe, 2006, 13). Agency is an active process that reinforces the interactional relationship between discourse and institutional power, as both are motivated by and react to each other. Liberal higher education is predicated on an encouragement and acceptance of diversity, or 'just difference and democratic dialogue' (Held, 2010, 77). However, what constitutes 'just difference' is debatable, and a failure to engage with this unfixed meaning obfuscates the mechanisms of power that underpin teacher–student relationships and likewise constitute the norms associated with these interactions. An emphasis on diversity presumes the prioritisation of tolerance in theoretical discussions in the classroom, which is based on the assumption that the lecturer/tutor is impartial and can thus assess the distinction between legitimacy as 'rightness' or 'correctness' (Held, 2010, 89–90). These are normative assumptions that naturalise cultural hierarchies without conscious reflection, and risk misrepresenting education as neutral, particularly with regard to the dominance of the English language. This can be seen as a 'recolonization of social relations' (Balibar, 2004, 41) which reinforces endemic assumptions about what constitutes knowledge 'within the bounds of established conventions, naturalizing its exclusions, and pre-empting the possibility of its radicalization' (Butler, 1997, 49).

Reflexive pedagogy

A socio-cultural linguistic awareness of the relationship between research, pedagogy and cultural hierarchies enables the consideration of student diversity in terms of the rich potential range of perspectives and insights, not in terms of cultural and linguistic deficit. This pedagogical perspective depends on ongoing reflexivity in the classroom that critically analyses how meaning is negotiated, by both lecturer/tutor and students, as it is equally important to understand what those interpretations of meaning are doing with us as it is to understand what we are doing with those interpretations of meaning. Such determinations are intimately related to endemic power relations in higher education. The tension between interpretations of legitimacy and meaning maintains the conflicts that underpin the pursuit of an inclusive educational system. In this sense, decolonisation is articulated in terms of 'epistemic disobedience' (Mignolo, 2011), or a delinking from the dominant narrative of Western modernity, which is constructed under pretensions of universality. Decolonising research operates in the context of the domination of Western modernity and its associated epistemologies. It is based on efforts to denaturalise the universalising narrative that Western modernity is a project in pursuit of the global common good, a history which produced a 'cognitive imperialism' (Battiste and Henderson, 2009) that presumes the superiority of Eurocentric researching and theorising. Removing this authority over content and interpretation confronts the assumption that some students are prepared or unprepared; it opposes the typically embedded notion of conformity to or deviation from the epistemological norms associated with colonial governance strategies (Luckett and Shay, 2017, 4). Recentring the meaning-making processes in this way allows multiple and diverse voices to be heard and validated, perspectives which are often silenced.

Critical pedagogy promotes an intentional democratisation of the classroom, in the interest of creating an inclusive and participatory space (Freire, 1985) that does not privilege one set of experiences or ways of theorising over another. Despite this insistence on democratisation, 'the histories, memories, knowledges and experiences of [marginalized] groups escape from the space of this democratization. In this sense, the "silences" that other memories have been subjected to and their absence from imperial academic circuits strongly indicates the presence of alternative discourses that question insistently the centrality of a single, universal history' (Meneses, 2011, 126). To confront this tacit silencing, classes can be centred on the generation and discussion of participants' ideas, assumptions, experiences and values. Such diverse opinions and perspectives on multiple topics constitute experiential knowledge, which can challenge hegemonic Eurocentric theorising and meaning-making and thus make explicit possible alternatives.

Collaboration and integration

This has begun to be implemented in an embedded way by integrating decolonising approaches into guest lectures on the 21st Century Legal Skills core module for the new Department of Law at Goldsmiths, University of London. These classes aim to develop critical reading and writing skills within the subject of law at Goldsmiths. They are based on ideas and assessment types from other core modules, and also involve discussing attitudes, assumptions, motivations and values related to their theoretical and practical contexts. This involves considering the deconstruction of commonly accepted conceptual categories and classifications, including the ways in which individual identities, experiences and meaning-making have influenced the perception of validity and relevance. From this frame of reference, the body-politics (Anzaldua, 2012), or an embodied experience, is invoked in the classroom, a space marked by the physical presence of and interactions between students.

Rather than focusing on traditional legal texts, the class instead uses decolonising texts to deconstruct moral, ethical and epistemological positions that underpin the study of law. For example, the critical reading class considers the notion of international law and human rights as a continuity of colonial domination (Anghie, 2016). Integrating these perspectives into the critical writing class consolidates the importance of linking personally meaningful contexts and experiences to disciplinary conventions and decolonising theories in order to develop an informed and original argument. This approach reflects the innovative nature of the programme and facilitates critical research and writing practices which normalise decolonial thinking at the very start of the degree programme. In this way, the classes are able to incorporate and reflect on a wide range of academic and non-academic experiences that enable students to 'actively engage in a conceptualization from whence they can actively negotiate and/or reject the particular understandings, historical interpretations, and theorizations' (Tejada, 2008, 29) of the class. In turn, this helps them to link concepts and theories to their practical approaches to research and writing, highlighting the significance of deconstructing and reconstructing conceptual foundations, as well as the implications for academic research and the production of written assessment. Making decisions and forming judgements about what evidence is legitimate and relevant is a key aspect of this process.

The understanding and application of research and writing in a particular social, institutional and disciplinary context is a form of academic literacy. This is often conflated with information literacy, which is commonly seen to emphasise identifying and locating relevant information and resources, although it is not limited to that (MacMillan and Mackenzie, 2012). Disciplinary expertise is conceptual, theoretical and contextual. Links and crossovers in expertise make collaborations particularly effective. Wilkes, Godwin and Gurney (2015, 171) call the Venn diagram between academic skills lecturers, subject librarians and discipline-specific lecturers a 'super skill set'. As part of an evolving practice, academic literacies lecturers have collaborated with disciplinary lecturers to ensure that provision aimed at helping students meet the expectations of their written assessments is contextualised within the concepts, theories, contexts and genres of their discipline. They also work with subject librarians to link these foundations with the search strategies and resources that are necessary to independently research and substantiate their academic arguments. Academic literacies lecturers have increasingly collaborated with subject librarians to promote inclusive citation as a central feature of decolonising academic literacies.

Sessions focusing on inclusive citation examine what is included on reading lists: what is considered essential reading, what is additional optional reading and what is excluded entirely. It looks at the order in which these assigned readings are presented, as what are perceived to be the most important foundations of the topic tend to be presented first, and everything else builds on those foundations. This reveals both the theoretical and practical priorities and hierarchies that are implicitly validated and legitimised in that discipline or subject and perpetuates the hierarchies of inclusion and exclusion, superiority and inferiority, visibility and invisibility, centre and periphery that sustain the institution of higher education (hooks, 1994). An experience shared by students and academics alike (Gabriel and Tate, 2017) is that '[w]hen I read texts … I frequently have to orientate myself to a text world in which the centre of academic knowledge is either in Britain, the United States or Western Europe; in which words such as "we", "us", "our", "I" actually exclude me' (Smith, 2012, 37). Inclusive citation offers counter-narratives based on locally constructed and validated meanings, a more inclusive representation that confronts the supposed truth-telling power of research that is based almost entirely in the Global North.

Conclusion

Decolonising research methodologies disrupts the colonial epistemology that aimed to universalise knowledge, representation and legitimacy, and which constructed an epistemic regime characterised by the exclusion of different modes of thinking and ways of living. There remains a historical and methodological consistency in the invisible administrative authority that colonialism continues to exert over knowledge, its processes, goals and outcomes, and the explanations, predictions and policies it incurs (Quijano, 2000). Consequently, decolonising research methodologies cannot simply challenge or refine research but requires instead a broad and purposeful strategy for transforming the structures that underpin the institution of research, and the ways in which it relies uncritically on traditional ways of organising, conducting and disseminating the knowledge produced by research (Smith, 2005). Decolonising research therefore considers on what basis the interests of marginalised groups can be elevated and prioritised over the interests of institutions intent on preserving their own power. Decolonising research requires the interrogation and critique of the modes of thinking and inherited imaginaries of academia, as well as the popular discourses of legitimacy it informs.

By examining the participants and interactions that colonial processes have defined, constructed and perpetuated, decolonising research methodologies considers who is involved, how these processes have been maintained, why they continue to be legitimised and in what ways they can be deconstructed and reconstructed in the interests of a more inclusive, just and equitable society. It explores how epistemic resources can be redistributed in a way that counters colonial hierarchies and their consequences of degradation. A decolonial epistemic shift endeavours to liberate racial, sexual, gender, class, linguistic, religious and epistemic embodied experiences from oppression. It aims to change not just the ways in which these categories are conceptualised but also the structures of power in which knowledge about them is produced, naturalised and enacted (Mignolo and Tlostanova, 2016). Part of this process means acknowledging and interrogating how notions of racial and ethnic inferiority are built into the basic assumptions of research practices (Smith, 2005).

Decolonising research methodologies motivates a necessary intervention into these assumptions and practices, undoing the epistemological hierarchies that prioritise Western worldviews. It reconsiders the foundations of and approaches to academic research, as well as their implications for the production of written assessment, knowledge and identity.

Analysing the discursive interactions that comprise and maintain the institution makes possible a 'critical positioning of revolutionary approaches to research [that] is crucial to the successful emergence of new paradigms' (Barrett, 2018, 1). Working within the genres and conventions of particular disciplines, incorporating strategies for decolonising research may enable the emergence of new approaches to constructing and validating research. In direct contrast to the pretence of a singular and neutral epistemology embedded in a Eurocentric research paradigm (Mignolo and Tlostanova, 2016, 133), ideas, principles and ethics originating in the Global South can become equally legitimate sources of knowledge rather than simply the object of research. This is also a means by which we can challenge the long-standing biases which limit how we understand knowledge, learning, society and the world around us. Destabilising the organisation of systems is of central importance in this process, including the structure of curricula, the expectations of classroom interactions and the historical and ideological orientations that have benefited and sustain academic institutions. The oppression of marginalised peoples can never be politically neutral, and thus decolonising research must take an explicitly activist stance.

References

Agar, M. (1985) Institutional Discourse, *Text*, **5** (3), 147–68.
Akel, S. (2019) *Insider-Outsider: The Role of Race in Shaping the Experiences of Black and Minority Ethnic Students*, Goldsmiths.
Althusser, L. (1971) Ideology and Ideological State Apparatuses. In *Lenin and Philosophy and Other Essays*, New Left Books.
Anghie, A. (2016) Imperialism and International Legal Theory. In Orford, A. and Hoffman, F. (eds), *The Oxford Handbook of the Theory of International Law*, Oxford University Press.
Anzaldua, G. (2012) *Borderlands/La Frontera: The New Mestiza, Second Edition*, Aunt Lute Books.
Bachrach, P. and Baratz, M. S. (1962) Two Faces of Power, *The American Political Science Review*, **56** (4), 947–52.
Baker, M. (2012) Decolonial Education: Meanings, Contexts and Possibilities. In *Interpreting, Researching and Transforming Colonial/Imperial Legacies in Education*, American Educational Studies Association, Annual Conference Seattle, www.academia.edu/3266939/Decolonial_Education_Meanings_Contexts_and_Possiblities (accessed 22 November 2019).
Bakhtin, M. (1986) *Speech Genres and Other Late Essays*, Texas University Press.
Balibar, E. (2004) *We, the People of Europe: Reflections on Transnational Citizenship*, Princeton University Press.
Barrett, E. (2018) New Frontiers of Research: Indigenous Knowledge Systems and Artistic Practice. In Kumar, M. and Pattanayak, S. (eds), *Positioning Research: Shifting Paradigms, Interdisciplinarity and Indigineity*, SAGE, 181–95.
Barton, D. (2007) *Literacy: An Introduction to the Ecology of Written Language*, Blackwell Publishing.
Battiste, M. and Henderson, J. Y. (2009) Naturalizing Indigenous Knowledge in Eurocentric Education, *Indian Journal of Native Education*, **32** (1), 5–18.
Benwell, B. and Stokoe, E. (2006) *Discourse and Identity*, Edinburgh University Press.

Blommaert, J., Heller, M. and Slembrouk, S. (2001) *Reflections from Overseas Guests*, www.ling-ethnog.org.uk/publications.html (accessed 24 July 2012).
Bourdieu, P. (1991) *Language and Symbolic Power*, Polity Press.
Brandt, D. and Clinton, K. (2002) Limits of the Local: Expanding Perspectives on Literacy as a Social Practice, *Journal of Literacy Research*, **34** (3), 337–56.
Bryman, A. (2016) *Social Research Methods*, Oxford University Press.
Butler, J. (1997) *Excitable Speech: A Politics of the Performative*, Routledge.
Dahl, R. A. (1958) A Critique of the Ruling Elite Model, *American Political Science Review*, **52** (2), 463–9, www.jstor.org/stable/1952327 (accessed 19 November 2012).
Darder, A., Mayo, P. and Paraskeve, J. (eds) (2016) *International Critical Pedagogy Reader*, Routledge.
de Sousa Santos, B. (2007) *Another Knowledge is Possible*, Verso.
Denzin, N. K. and Lincoln, Y. S. (eds) (1994) *Handbook of Qualitative Research*, SAGE Publications, Inc.
Fairclough, N. (1992) *Discourse and Social Change*, Polity Press.
Foucault, M. (1972) *The Archaeology of Knowledge*, Tavistock Press.
Foucault, M. (1977) *Language, Counter-memory, Practice: Selected Essays and Interviews*, edited by D. F. Bouchard, translated by D. F. Bouchard and S. Simon, Cornell University Press.
Fowler, R. (2005) *Language in the News: Discourse and Ideology in the Press*, Routledge.
Freire, P. (1985) *The Politics of Education: Culture, Power and Liberation*, Bergin and Garvey.
Gabriel, D. and Tate, S. A. (eds) (2017) *Inside the Ivory Tower: Narratives of Women of Colour Surviving and Thriving in British Academia*, Trentham.
Gee, J. P. (1996) *Social Linguistics and Literacies: Ideology in Discourses*, RoutledgeFalmer.
Goody, J. (1986) *The Logic of Writing and the Organization of Society*, Cambridge University Press.
Grosfoguel, R. (2007) The Epistemic Decolonial Turn, *Cultural Studies*, **21** (2–3), 211–23.
Hall, S. (2013) The Work of Representation. In Hall, S., Evans, J. and Nixon, S. (eds), *Representation, 2nd edn*, SAGE Publications.
Hay, C. (1997) Divided by a Common Language: Political Theory and the Concept of Power, *Politics*, **17** (1), 45–52.
Held, D. (2010) *Cosmopolitanism: Ideals and Realities*, Polity Press.
hooks, b. (1994) *Teaching to Transgress: Education as the Practice of Freedom*, Routledge.
Lave, J. and Wenger, E. (1991) *Situated Learning: Legitimate Peripheral Participation*, Cambridge University Press.
Leung, C. and Street, B. V. (eds) (2012) *English: A Changing Medium for Education*, Multilingual Matters.
Luckett, K. and Shay, S. (2017) Reframing the Curriculum: A Transformative Approach, *Critical Studies in Education*,

www.tandfonline.com/doi/full/10.1080/17508487.2017.1356341 (accessed 11 November 2019).

MacMillan, M. and Mackenzie, A. (2012) Strategies for Integrating Information Literacy and Academic Literacy: Helping Undergraduate Students Make the Most of Scholarly Articles. In *Proceedings of the IATUL Conferences*, Paper 16, http://docs.lib.purdue.edu/iatul/2012/papers/16 (accessed 24 February 2021).

Makitalo, A. and Saljo, R. (2002) Talk in Institutional Context and Institutional Context in Talk: Categories as Situated Practices, *Text*, **22** (1), 57–82.

Meneses, M. P. (2011) Images outside the Mirror: Mozambique and Portugal in World History. In Darder, A., Mayo, P. and Paraskeve, J. (eds), *International Critical Pedagogy Reader*, Routledge.

Mignolo, W. (2011) Geopolitics of Sensing and Knowing: On (De)coloniality, Border Thinking and Epistemic Disobedience, *Postcolonial Studies*, **14** (3), 273–83.

Mignolo, W. and Tlostanova, M. (2016) Theorizing from the Borders. In Darder, A., Mayo, P. and Paraskeve, J. (eds), *International Critical Pedagogy Reader*, Routledge.

Ong, A. (1996) Cultural Citizenship as Subject-Making: Immigrants Negotiate Racial and Cultural Boundaries in the United States, *Current Anthropology*, **27** (5), 737–62, www.jstor.org/stable/2744412?seq=1#metadata_info_tab_contents (accessed 16 April 2012).

Ong, W. (1982) *Orality and Literacy: The Technologizing of the Word*, Methuen.

Quijano, A. (2000) Coloniality of Power, Eurocentrism and Latin America, *Nepantla*, **1**, 533–80, www.decolonialtranslation.com/english/quijano-coloniality-of-power.pdf (accessed 12 October 2019).

Reder, S. and Davila, E. (2005) Context and Literacy Practices, *Annual Review of Applied Linguistics*, **25**, 170–97.

Seidlhofer, B. (2004) Research Perspectives on Teaching English as a Lingua Franca, *Annual Review of Applied Linguistics*, **24**, 209–39.

Smith, L. T. (2005) On Tricky Ground: Researching the Native in an Age of Uncertainty. In Denzin, N. K. and Lincoln, Y. S. (eds), *Handbook of Qualitative Research,* 85–107, SAGE Publications, Inc.

Smith, L. T. (2012) *Decolonising Methodologies: Research and Indigenous Peoples*, Zed Books.

Street, B. (2003) What's 'New' in New Literacy Studies? *Current Issues in Comparative Education*, **5** (2), 77–91.

Tejada, C. (2008) Dancing with the Dilemmas of a Decolonising Pedagogy, *Radical History Review*, **102**, 27–31, https://read.dukeupress.edu/radical-history-review/article-abstract/2008/102/27/22125/Dancing-with-the-Dilemmas-of-a-Decolonising?redirectedFrom=PDF (accessed 13 September 2019).

Wenger, E. (1998) *Communities of Practice: Learning, Meaning, and Identity*, Cambridge University Press.

Wilkes, J., Godwin, J. and Gurney, L. J. (2015) Developing Information Literacy and Academic Writing Skills Through the Collaborative Design of an Assessment Task for First Year Engineering Students, *Australian Academic and Research Libraries*, **46** (3), 164–75, http://doi.org/10.1080/00048623.2015.1062260 (accessed 24 February 2021).

4
Do Black Employees' Rights Matter? The Lived Experience of BAME Staff in UK Academic Libraries

Mohammed Ishaq and Asifa Maaria Hussain

Introduction

The theme of this book is timely, given the emergence of the Black Lives Matter (BLM) movement in the USA. Although originating in America, the movement has struck a chord with Black Asian and Minority Ethnic (BAME) communities in other Anglophone countries such as the UK. While the BLM movement was initially a response to police brutality and racial violence against Black people, it has helped to generate a wider debate about the need to advance racial diversity and fight racial inequalities faced by BAME people. More pertinently, in the context of this book, the movement has placed the experience of BAME employees under greater scrutiny and initiated difficult but necessary conversations in organisations and workplaces about what employers are doing or should be doing to advance the rights of BAME workers.

This chapter's particular contribution is to focus on the academic library sector, which has been under-researched in relation to race equality. The authors argue that if successful decolonisation of libraries is to be achieved, then it is important to understand and reflect on the 'lived' experience of BAME staff currently working in academic and research libraries across the UK. The research reported in this chapter represents part of a wider project established to investigate aspects of developing the workforce and fostering diversity across the library sector (Ishaq and Hussain, 2019). It is hoped that the outcomes from the research will allow the leadership and management of academic libraries to take stock of where they are in relation to their race equality agenda and where they need to be to ensure that they demonstrate their commitment to the effective decolonising of libraries.

Summarising BAME employees' work experience in UK organisations: evidence from the literature

Literature documenting the work experience of BAME staff in the academic and non-academic library sectors is virtually non-existent. The closest is research conducted in the USA which centred on the issue of racial microaggression in academic libraries (Alabi, 2015) and on the existence of racism and a culture of Whiteness in US academic libraries

(Brook, Ellenwood and Lazzaro, 2015). In the context of the UK, there is a small-scale qualitative study exploring the low representation of BAME staff in the library and information science (LIS) profession in London (Williams and Nicholas, 2009). However, there is a body of knowledge on the contemporary workplace experience of BAME employees in various sectors of the UK economy. Overall, these experiences reveal common issues and challenges encountered by Black workers. These are presented in this section of the chapter, drawing on examples from a range of professions within the public sector as reported in academic literature and documentary sources.

Workplace racism and discrimination

Racism and racial discrimination in the form of physical and verbal abuse have been experienced by BAME staff in the workplace. In the National Health Service (NHS), BAME staff have reported instances of bullying and discrimination from White colleagues as well as from service users (Chand, 2018). A similar picture emerges in the Metropolitan Police, where BAME officers have complained of a toxic culture of bullying and harassment in the workplace (Warren, 2020). It appears that the use of inappropriate language, including racial microaggression and stereotypical views, pervade some of the UK's biggest public sector organisations. What has been more concerning is that such behaviours have not been adequately addressed, with organisational approaches to tackling racial discrimination lacking effectiveness and willpower.

BAME employees undervalued and on lower pay

Evidence suggests that while there has been a narrowing of pay differentials between ethnic groups in recent years, marked differences still exist for some ethnic minority groups (EHRC, 2017). The Equality and Human Rights Commission's study revealed that BAME workers earned less than their White counterparts. This was especially the experience among men of BAME origin. The low pay among BAME employees was attributed to a combination of factors such as discrimination and social disadvantage, including horizontal segregation – the over-representation of BAME people in specific low-paid sectors and occupations. This included jobs that are insecure, involving zero-hours contracts. The consequences on BAME communities of this type of structural racism have been profound and, according to the Living Wage Foundation (2020), have affected the physical and mental health of BAME individuals.

Occupational segregation

The vertical segregation of BAME workers, with little opportunity for promotion and representation in leadership roles, and horizontal segregation – over-representation in specific occupational sectors where pay is typically low and opportunities for career progression and promotion opportunities are limited – are a hallmark of the UK labour market (Kirton and Greene, 2016). Horizontal segregation on the lines of ethnicity and race in the UK reveals that many people from ethnic minority backgrounds are concentrated in lower-status occupations in the hotel, restaurant and distribution industries (McIntrye, Mohdin and Thomas, 2020). Interestingly, during the current economic crisis generated by COVID-19, these are the very sectors that have been among the hardest hit with redundancies.

Vertical segregation on ethnic lines is a feature of the leadership and management in a number of key public sector employers in the UK, including the NHS (Randhawa, 2018), universities (ECU, 2017; Khan, 2017) and local government (The Global Recruiter, 2018). Studies show that systemic barriers within organisations mean that BAME employees become stuck at lower levels of the organisational ladder. The work of Miller (2019) has revealed a significant lack of racial diversity at the top of big UK organisations as a consequence of racial inequalities in career progression.

Linked to vertical segregation or 'the glass ceiling', another prominent theme emerging from the extant literature is the lack of opportunities for BAME employees to carve out a clear pathway to progressing their careers, including being overlooked for promotion, with many feeling that their career progression has failed to meet their expectations (Miller, 2019). Research has revealed that ethnic minorities are less likely to get top jobs in the UK public sector than they are in some of the biggest private sector companies (Ramesh, 2014). A further connection to the theme of career progression is lack of access to resources, including lack of access to training opportunities. A study by the Chartered Institute of Personnel and Development (CIPD, 2017) revealed a perception among BAME workers that they were not given adequate opportunities to access training to help them to conduct their jobs effectively and to further their careers.

Lack of workplace diversity

Many organisations in the UK public sector fail to have workforces that reflect the communities they serve. Despite the three-pillar framework advanced by Dickens (1999) emphasising the legal, social justice and business cases for advancing equality and diversity in organisations, the reality is different. Studies show that some of the most powerful UK public sector employers do not have ethnically representative workforces. These include the armed forces, the police and judiciary, who research by Duncan, Dodd and Madsen (2018) noted were 'decades away from becoming as ethnically diverse as the population they serve'. A small-scale study of the library sector focusing on London revealed that even the UK's biggest and most ethnically diverse city has been grappling with the issue of low representation of BAME staff in the LIS sector (Williams and Nicholas, 2009).

The literature referenced in this section highlights that discrimination and disadvantage are characteristics of the UK labour market encountered by BAME people. BAME employees experience lack of opportunities and poorer outcomes in their workplace in relation to a number of variables such as career progression, promotion, training, salary and treatment from White co-workers.

Methodology
Research design and approach

The research reported in this chapter was essentially qualitative in nature, involving a focus group and a series of interviews with BAME staff working in academic and research libraries across the UK that are members of SCONUL, the Society of College, National and University Libraries (Ishaq and Hussain, 2019). The recruitment of participants for the study was aided by a questionnaire conducted to gather some demographic data on BAME employees working in the academic library sector. The questionnaire gave respondents the opportunity to indicate their interest in taking part in the qualitative stage of the research. This allowed the authors to generate a sample of BAME staff interested in participating in the focus group and in the series of interviews. The focus group represented stage one of the qualitative research and was aimed at extracting the views of BAME staff in relation to key themes agreed among the research team. Emerging themes from the analysis of the focus group subsequently helped to inform the construction of an interview schedule that served as the basis for a series of one-to-one interviews with BAME staff, representing stage two of the qualitative research.

Research participants

Ethical approval was obtained from the authors' institutions for all stages of the data-collection process. The ethical approval process took full cognisance of issues such as confidentiality, anonymity, data protection and consent. All participants who indicated their willingness to participate in the research were asked to sign a consent form. In total, nine participants took part in the focus group, which was hosted by a university and moderated by the authors, while the in-depth interviews were conducted via phone from the premises of the authors. In total, 16 interviewees participated in the interview stage.

Findings

In this section some of the key findings from the focus group and in-depth interviews are presented to shed light on the 'lived' experience of BAME staff. Details of the wider study conducted, from which the findings have been extracted, can be found in the full report (Ishaq and Hussain, 2019). To comply with the ethical requirements of the research and maintain the anonymity of individuals, those participants to whom quotes have been attributed have been assigned either a letter or a numeral to differentiate between them. The findings reveal a plethora of issues faced by library staff from a BAME background.

Self-identity: awareness of ethnicity and impact on workplace experience

Those BAME staff whose ethnicity was particularly marked were more conscious of this, and it appeared to have an impact on how they felt they were treated in the workplace.

The lack of diversity among library staff perpetuated the feeling of belonging to an ethnic minority group. This further created a sense of being monitored and singled out. These perceptions are highlighted in the following comments:

'It's just sometimes you feel that you don't have the face that fits.'

(Interviewee J)

'As a BAME member of staff, I tend to keep myself to myself … because I don't trust them, fundamentally. So, they may have views of the fact that I keep myself to myself.'

(Interviewee H)

'I don't know if we are more closely monitored but I definitely feel that I have to get recognition. I feel that I have had to work harder than my White colleagues.'

(Interviewee K)

'When I talk with a couple of my colleagues, and one of them who's been giving me really superb off-the-record mentoring, like really has helped me … I've really benefited from that kind of advice …, every time she and I would have a meet by our desks or around the library … when one of the heads of service would go past they would make eyes like this [makes staring gesture]. Like, "oh the brown people are talking. I wonder what they're plotting", and that kind of reverberated attitude … It made me feel watched. It made me feel like someone's observing you, someone's expecting me to plot something horrific.'

(Focus group participant 7)

'I think it kind of puts a lot of pressure on you if there's very few ethnic minorities represented in the staff … I'm a perfectionist but I feel that I have to try that bit harder because I feel that not only am I representing myself as a member of staff and doing things to the best of my ability, I'm also in some way representing how White people are gonna see every [reference to participant's nationality] person from hereon in because they might not see another [reference to participant's nationality] person for a very long time. So, you do feel that extra, you know, pressure of representing not just your profession but your race as well.'

(Focus group participant 4)

Existence and manifestation of racism in the workplace

The research also explored whether BAME staff had experienced racism in their job. The findings reveal that while racism was not rampant it did exist and manifested itself through the use of inappropriate language and ignorance about cultural issues in the workplace, including what would be classed as racial microaggression.

'I have had instances with colleagues who keep getting my name wrong and I don't think my first name is that difficult. Maybe it is some sort of unconscious bias. I have people make comments about the fact that you know, I'm vegetarian and it's because I'm a Hindu. … I had a colleague who on multiple occasions said "is it okay if I talk about meat in front you?" And then I've had a supervisor in a previous job that during Ramadan she just turned around and said "why aren't you fasting?" And made an assumption that I was Muslim. And then I had to say I'm not, then she said "oh well what are you then?" And it was just the phrasing of it, just quite confrontational and abrupt.'

(Interviewee K)

'People making comments about Travellers and thinking it is okay to do it and because everyone knows Travellers are not good people because what you see on TV is the negative side of it. I have experienced this at school and here at the university.'

(Interviewee I)

'For some reason we seem to get each other's e-mails. There is another colleague called ****. Or people call us each other's names. They are totally different names aren't they and we don't look alike and we don't work closely at all, so why does this keep happening?'

(Interviewee J)

'Well it tends to be comments. So, for example, a while ago it was the supervisor. Another colleague had made a comment. I think it was something like he was arguing with another colleague about religion or about belief in God. I was sat at a different desk but he walked over and said "what about Islam what kind of religion is that'?" And I said "sorry what was that?" He said "oh nothing".'

(Interviewee M)

'You have a sense of the fact that somebody is not treating you or treating someone else in a way that they ought to or that they're not giving people perhaps the opportunity that they ought to give them. But it's often at times difficult to pin that that is exactly what is happening and to prove it. And this isn't uncommon for, for any type of institution, this is true, libraries are no different. So ... I, I think that we do, I think we have issues at the point of co-workers that I have some lovely people that I work with. Really, you know, great people that I work with and who are particularly supportive. Probably the best that I've had is right now. But I have some that I know are just seeking to put a dagger in.'

(Focus group participant 2)

What was concerning based on the views of research participants was the fact that libraries were not viewed as having systems and procedures to deal effectively with complaints of racism raised by staff. A fundamental problem was the belief among some participants that there was a lack of appetite and willpower among management and HR departments to address the issue:

'Like we've just introduced a sexual harassment, you know, online reporting system but there's not one for racism.'

(Interviewee C)

'What I think is the ineffectiveness of the personnel department. There is a lack of willingness to be sued or to take it anywhere. So anything potentially negative happens, personnel will do everything in their power, as far as I'm concerned, to mitigate the circumstance. So you will lose because they will not support you.'

(Focus group respondent 3)

'I think sometimes they're afraid to do some things because students pay X amount of money for an academic library. You know, they don't wanna take it further, you know …'

(Focus group participant 6)

There was a feeling that BAME employees lacked voice and adequate representation in the employment relationship and there was lack of trust in trade unions, who were viewed as unhelpful when BAME employees raise concerns:

'The unions are useless … I wouldn't join a union … Unions were formed to keep Black people out of work anyway. I've never had a positive or constructive engagement with a union. I don't see what the unions do in a way to make my experience as a BAME person any better within the organisation and I'd be loath to give them my money …'

(Interviewee H)

Disproportionate impact of training and development opportunities on BAME staff

While training and development opportunities were viewed as generally adequate, BAME staff were negatively impacted, as such opportunities were less for those at the lower end of the job spectrum, such as library assistants, and it is at the lower end where BAME staff are over-represented. Lack of funding was seen as a further threat, and it was feared that lack of training and development opportunities would hinder attempts to get more BAME staff into management and leadership, thereby failing to break the glass ceiling.

'If you have got a lack of BAME people in management you are basically saying to them you can't have those equal opportunities of training. You know you are creating a barrier that should not exist and you should instead offer it to them much more to give them that thing.'

(Interviewee C)

'I think that's interesting (the lack of training opportunities), because when I was working as a library assistant there were very few opportunities beyond the mandatory training for me, whereas as a librarian, they're a bit more sort of open to suggestions and allowed me to go to any events or training that I've asked for … If you are sort of higher level the training opportunities are potentially greater.'

(Interviewee K)

Occupational structure and limited opportunities for promotion

The nature of the job structure in academic libraries is such that opportunities for promotion are limited. However, as noted in relation to training and development, the impact on BAME staff is considerably more detrimental as they are already under-represented at higher levels and the lack of promotion opportunities hinders the possibility of addressing the lack of racial diversity at senior level:

> 'I think the promotion opportunities are limited. Unless, I think, my director dies, there is very limited experience for promotion within the library services.'
>
> (Interviewee H)

> 'I would say that they [promotion opportunities] are pretty limited. That's my personal experience as well as a kind of general sentiment that I hear quite a lot from people.'
>
> (Interviewee O)

> 'I think the highest grade that you'll see a person of colour would be librarian grade. You wouldn't see anything higher up than that. I mean in terms of like promotion.'
>
> (Focus group participant 7)

A further obstacle faced by BAME library staff was the perception that line managers did not actively encourage BAME employees to pursue the limited promotion opportunities that arose:

> [M]y experience has been I will go around that [my line manager] because I don't feel as though somebody's actually looking for me, to take me up. So, I have to find a path, another path. We are always looking to find other ways to, to move around the system to get up, because actually even if you are performing well, it's very hard to get somebody to acknowledge it.'
>
> (Focus group participant 2)

> 'I've asked my line manager about it. You know, what are the opportunities for progression, and I wouldn't say she was overly enthusiastic.'
>
> (Interviewee D)

Ethnic diversity of the library workforce

There was a strong sentiment that greater racial diversity of the library workforce was required from both a business case perspective and a social justice standpoint. Concerns centring on the overall lack of diversity among the workforce of libraries, as well as the failure of the workforce to reflect its user base were noted by participants:

> 'I do enjoy it, but because I am such a minority there is a subconscious feeling that you are not part of the whole big library team. You feel that there is some sort of subconscious racism there.'
>
> (Interviewee J)

> 'It's essential especially for my current workplace. I would probably say 80 to 90% of students are from an ethnic minority background … the workforce does not reflect the student demographic.'
>
> (Interviewee E)

> 'There is a whiteness in libraries that certainly where, the university I'm working at is not reflected in our, in our student cohort.'
>
> (Focus group participant 3)

> 'I think an ethnically diverse workforce is really important. You are able to experience different things from a diverse workforce. A diverse workforce is more successful. They are more innovative and more creative. I am the only BAME person among around 90 library staff.'
>
> (Interviewee H)

Disquiet about the lack of ethnic diversity among the workforce of academic libraries extended to the upper layers of the job hierarchy, with perceptions that senior roles in the library profession were dominated by White individuals. There was a feeling that institutional barriers hinder the progression of BAME staff. BAME staff were perceived as experiencing a glass ceiling.

> 'It's incredibly important. You know, as I mentioned before. There are no people of colour in our senior leadership team … there is a concentration of Black staff members in the lower grades. People that use the library … we don't reflect that. We live in London and we don't reflect the London communities.'
>
> (Interviewee O)

> 'The top layers definitely [lack diversity] because they are only White managers in the library and there have been where I've worked. And we've never had somebody who isn't White in a management position. So, I think the same is replicated you know in like CILIP [the Chartered Institute of Library and Information Professionals] and other organisations.'
>
> (Interviewee C)

Suggestions on how academic libraries can advance equality and diversity

Participants offered a basket of recommendations as to how academic libraries can advance equality and diversity, ranging from increasing the diversity of staff, making it a strategic priority, to educating the essentially 'White' leadership about equality and diversity issues:

> 'Increasing the number of staff, the diverse workforce you have and it needs to be prioritised as a key strategic area. It is not seen as a priority and it keeps getting mentioned and then forgotten about and nothing is being done about it really.'
>
> (Interviewee J)

'I think it would be first of all to educate themselves 'cause I think almost exclusively they (the management and leadership) will all be White would be my guess.'

(Interviewee C)

'Awareness is fundamental, I mean there are some people who are probably not even aware what these things [equality and diversity] mean.'

(Interviewee N)

Discussion

This section of the chapter considers the research findings holistically with a focus on how they should be interpreted and the extent to which some concepts and theories provide context and explanation for the experiences reported by BAME staff. The interpretation of the findings will also help in constructing recommendations to address the issues that have emerged.

This research has demonstrated that the issues faced by BAME library staff are not endemic to the academic library sector. The behaviours, attitudes and practices experienced by BAME staff in academic libraries are typical of many workplaces in the UK as highlighted in the review of literature. The 'lived' experiences of BAME library staff reported in this chapter therefore resonate with those in numerous other sectors and professions within the UK (see CIPD, 2017; Chand, 2018; Rollock, 2019). Lack of racial diversity among the workforce, failure of leadership and management to reflect racial diversity, lack of opportunities for training and career progression for BAME staff, the existence and persistence of racism and discrimination including verbal bullying, harassment and microaggression are some of the key findings in this research. The findings provide further validity to the concepts of vertical and horizontal segregation, which explain the lack of diversity in the leadership of organisations and the over-representation of minority groups in specific occupations and roles (Kirton and Greene, 2016). The findings also suggest the existence of a 'canteen culture' where inappropriate behaviours, attitudes and prejudice against diverse and minority groups are demonstrated by employees. The term 'canteen culture' was used in the late 1980s to refer to the organisational culture present in police forces that was characterised as discriminatory, initially in relation to women but later also towards ethnic minorities (Bennetto, 1998). The term is now applied to any organisation or profession where discriminatory views and attitudes are shared by employees.

There are a number of theories and frameworks which provide some foundation and explanation for the origins and causes of racial inequalities experienced by BAME people both in society and in employment. These theories are rooted in multiple disciplines such as sociology, cultural psychology, socio-economics, politics, history, legal studies, management and philosophy. Although a detailed explanation and debate on the causes and origins of racial inequalities is not the main purpose of this chapter, it is nevertheless useful to note the experience of BAME library staff as being rooted in theories and racial discourse.

Proponents of critical race theory (CRT) would argue that the existence of racial inequalities is not unexpected, given that race is a socially constructed concept that is used by White people to advance their economic and political interests at the expense of non-White people (Delgado and Stefancic, 1998). Inspired by, among others, Dr Martin Luther King Jr and Malcolm X, CRT focuses on the attempts of White people to continue their historical advantages over non-White people. Because supporters of CRT argue that the socially constructed view of race means that 'Whiteness' is seen as the norm and White is seen as being dominant, this would then aid our understanding of the discrimination and inequalities experienced by BAME staff reported in this research.

Further concepts that may aid our understanding of racist and discriminatory behaviour both in society and in the workplace include the theory of social constructionism, which stresses the way in which individuals and society make sense of the world around them and how differing perceptions lead to differing views of people and hence their treatment (Berger and Luckmann, 1967). The following extract from the work of Salter, Adams and Perez (2018) captures how the principles of CRT and social constructionism support our understanding of resultant racism and racial inequalities:

> racism is also systemic, existing in the advantages and disadvantages imprinted in cultural artifacts, ideological discourse and institutional realities that work together with individual biases … historically derived ideas and cultural patterns that maintain present-day racial inequalities … through our preferences and selections, we maintain racialized contexts in everyday action … we inhabit cultural worlds that in turn promote racialized ways of seeing, being in and acting in the world.
>
> (Salter, Adams and Perez, 2018, 150)

Neoclassical and labour market segmentation theories provide a socio-economic explanation for the existence of occupational segregation – both vertical and horizontal (Watts and Rich, 1993; Beardwell and Thompson, 2014). Acker's concept of the 'inequality regime', defined as 'loosely interrelated practices, processes, actions and meanings that result in and maintain class, gender, and racial inequalities within particular organizations' (Acker, 2006, 43), makes a significant contribution in aiding our understanding of the unequal treatment and experience of BAME employees in organisational settings, including those in academic libraries reported in this research. Acker's work conceptualises how inequality regimes perpetuate inequalities in organisational settings.

Recommendations

The main contribution of this research is practical rather than theoretical, therefore it is only logical to make recommendations for the academic library sector to consider based on the main research outcomes that could help to improve BAME staff experience in the workplace.

Some BAME staff are made to feel self-conscious about their identity. This creates a sense that they are being monitored. The lack of ethnic diversity among the workforce accentuates those feelings. Academic libraries need to take steps to create a positive climate for diversity in the work environment. This can be facilitated by instigating measures to recruit more racially diverse staff and reassuring BAME staff that there is a zero-tolerance approach to racism and prejudice.

Addressing workplace racism

In this research, racism, primarily verbal, appears to be a concern for some BAME staff. In particular, racial microaggression seems to be a feature of the workplace experience. The leadership of academic libraries and the wider institutions within which they operate must ensure that as well as taking a zero-tolerance approach to unacceptable behaviour there is a robust race-awareness training programme in place. Such training should particularly target unconscious or implicit bias. This would help to address racial microaggression – including inappropriate and derogatory language – and cultural ignorance and to challenge stereotypical views that some BAME staff have experienced. Training should be conducted in an environment that allows participants to engage in constructive dialogue and reflective conversations, providing an opportunity for difficult but necessary debate and discussion that challenges inappropriate and unacceptable co-worker behaviour.

At present there is a lack of trust among BAME staff about the effectiveness of processes and procedures designed to deal with complaints of workplace racism. There is a need therefore to reassess current systems to ensure that they are effective. The human resources function in particular can lead on implementing a more effective system of reporting racial discrimination that instils confidence and trust among those experiencing workplace racism. This is especially critical, given the perception among BAME staff that there is a lack of adequate mechanisms for employee voice that cater for the unique challenges experienced by BAME employees.

Academic libraries acting in unison with the wider institutions within which they are embedded should sign up to the Race at Work Charter, which is evidence based and would demonstrate both that equality and diversity is valued and that there is commitment to practising and implementing equality of opportunity in the workplace (BITC, 2020). Academic libraries should target approaches that help to dismantle the structures that are perpetuating racism and discrimination. Many organisations across both the UK public and private sectors are already signatories to the Charter (BITC, 2020), including a number of higher education institutions. In addition to the Race at Work Charter, academic libraries should also consider the Race Equality Charter, which is more specific to the higher education sector and which is aimed at improving the representation, progression and success of ethnic minority staff and students within higher education (Advance HE, 2020).

Outreach work and community engagement

Academic libraries should do more outreach work in line with other public sector institutions such as the uniformed services to promote the library profession to the BAME community as a career option. This endeavour should also take the opportunity to showcase current BAME staff in the academic library sector as role models. The BAME staff who participated in this research stressed that such an approach would send a positive message to members of the BAME community considering a career in academic libraries. Police forces across England have stepped up outreach work in recent years to deal with the lack of ethnic diversity in their workforce (see Bury et al., 2018).

The role of leadership

The leadership of libraries need to lead from the top and champion equality and diversity. They should demonstrate that they view equality and diversity as a strategic priority rather than a peripheral endeavour. This would prevent the marginalisation of the equality and diversity agenda and allow adequate financial resources to be set aside to protect the agenda from current and future financial pressures. The powerful role of leadership in advancing the cause of equality and diversity in organisations cannot be overstated. A case in point is the role of leadership in changing the fortunes of the armed forces in Anglophone countries including the UK and Canada, where senior leaders have championed the cause of diversity and have not been afraid to tackle the White male-dominated culture that led to accusations of racism, sexism and homophobia for decades (Hussain and Ishaq, 2016). One way of ensuring universal buy-in from all organisational stakeholders is to elevate the business case for diversity and the merits associated with it (Dickens, 1999). Managers and leaders are responsible for navigating resistance from White colleagues to any approaches for advancing the equality and diversity agenda. This would ensure that the agenda can be successfully implemented.

Concerns about lack of career progression and promotion opportunities were highlighted by several BAME staff who took part in this research. There was also a view that internal recruitment practices need to be reviewed to allow BAME staff to take advantage of promotion opportunities that arose. This suggests the need for managers to take action, including ensuring that they identify BAME staff with managerial potential and encourage line managers to engage in conversations with those staff during performance appraisals. This would allow BAME staff to have a trajectory towards career progression. Furthermore, consideration should be given to a coaching and/or mentoring programme to develop BAME staff, especially at the lower levels, to prepare them for managerial or other senior roles, thus creating a talent pipeline. Academic libraries should contemplate approaches similar to those adopted by other big public sector organisations such as the BBC, who have developed a number of trainee and leadership programmes to improve diversity among the Corporation (BBC, 2018). Similar approaches have been noted in the civil service (Ethnic Dimension, 2015).

Ethnic monitoring

While higher education institutions do monitor the ethnicity of their employees, there is no ethnic monitoring across the academic library sector and SCONUL does not collect data on the ethnic make-up of the academic library workforce (Ishaq and Hussain, 2019). This has to be addressed because, without monitoring, it is difficult to track the career development and progression of BAME staff. Moreover, ethnic monitoring data can provide a further evidence base and help in assessing the impact of policies and practices and identify gaps.

The authors feel that the aforementioned recommendations represent reasonable and realistic approaches in the light of the research findings. They would help to build trust and confidence among BAME staff and generate collateral benefits such as greater employee engagement, loyalty and identity with the organisation. While measures to improve BAME staff experience and tackle workplace racial inequalities should not rule out the need to take into account the unique circumstances prevailing within individual sectors and organisations, there is merit in having a co-ordinated approach across the public sector, given the homogeneity of experience and issues faced by BAME employees in other organisations.

Although it is worth considering the lessons that can be learned from the response of those sectors and organisations that face similar issues, there is less evidence available at present on the success or otherwise of policy approaches adopted by academic libraries. If academic libraries implement successful programmes of recommendations, they can become effective agents of change and therefore make the successful transition – using Kirton and Greene's adaptation of Healey's typology of equality of opportunity organisations (Kirton and Greene, 2016, 214) – from being classed merely as 'compliant' organisations to 'comprehensive proactive' organisations when it comes to equality and diversity. Neither the liberal nor the radical approach to equality has been wholly successful. However their successor – diversity management – despite having its critics, incorporates an important characteristic that, if realised in practice, can make the difference, which is the need for transformation of organisational cultures (Kirton and Greene, 2016, 130).

Conclusion

The reported findings shed light on the real-life experience of BAME staff engaged in the execution of their duties in academic and research libraries and previously reported in the research commissioned by SCONUL (Ishaq and Hussain, 2019). They reveal that academic and research libraries have some way to go in addressing institutional, structural and systemic bias against BAME staff, which manifests itself in a variety of ways. The main theme of this book centres on the decolonisation of libraries. This chapter argues that the effective decolonisation of libraries will remain a myth until BAME staff employed in academic libraries experience fair treatment, have equal opportunities for career progression and promotion and are viewed as a valuable human resource. Reflecting on the negative perceptions expressed by BAME staff about their workplace and starting the process of addressing these perceptions must be an integral part of the decolonising of libraries agenda.

While decolonisation remains a controversial and contested term, even in librarianship, there is no doubt that its intentions are credible (EARLL, 2020). It can play a role in seeking to address the disadvantage and discrimination faced by BAME employees by critically reflecting on and influencing and shaping organisational culture, values and attitudes that reflect a modern and diverse society, where there is zero tolerance for inequality, discrimination and prejudice.

Despite the existence of racism and unequal opportunities, the majority of BAME staff in this research did not reveal an inclination to exit the profession and there is little evidence of large-scale flight from the profession. Rather, BAME staff expressed resilience and a desire to fight for their rights in a profession that they appear to cherish. If academic libraries are willing to implement strategies to address the challenges faced by BAME staff, then they would go some way towards rewarding that loyalty. Challenging organisational culture, structures and processes that perpetuate and sustain racial inequality would be a good starting point in moving the decolonisation or similar agenda forward and being able to answer in the affirmative: do Black employees' rights matter?

References

Acker, J. (2006) Inequality Regimes: Gender, Class and Race in Organisations, *Gender and Society*, **20** (4), 441–64.

Advance HE (2020) Race Equality Charter, www.advance-he.ac.uk/equality-charters/race-equality-charter (accessed 17 February 2021).

Alabi, J. (2015) Racial Microaggressions in Academic Libraries: Results of a Survey of Minority and Non-minority Librarians, *The Journal of Academic Librarianship*, **41** (1), 47–53.

BBC (2018) BBC Publishes Landmark Report on BAME Career Progression and Culture, www.bbc.co.uk/mediacentre/latestnews/2018/bame-career-progression-and-culture-report (accessed 3 December 2020).

Beardwell, J. and Thompson, A. (2014) *Human Resource Management: a Contemporary Approach*, Pearson Education Limited.

Bennetto, J. (1998) Canteen Culture: The Language of Bigotry, www.independent.co.uk/news/canteen-culture-the-language-of-bigotry-1175592.html (accessed 17 February 2021).

Berger, P. L. and Luckmann, T. (1967) *The Social Construction of Reality: A Treatise in the Sociology of Knowledge*, Anchor Books.

BITC (Business in the Community) (2020) Race at Work Charter, www.bitc.org.uk/race-at-work-charter-signatories (accessed 5 December 2020).

Brook, F., Ellenwood, D. and Lazzaro, A. (2015) In Pursuit of Anti-racist Social Justice: Denaturalising Whiteness in the Academic Library, *Library Trends*, **64** (2), 246–84.

Bury, J., Pullerits, M., Edwards, S., Davies, C. and DeMarco, J. (2018) *Enhancing Diversity in Policing*, NatCen Social Research.

Chand, K. (2018) The NHS Relies on its BME Staff – So Why Do They Still Face Discrimination? *The Guardian*, www/theguardian.com/society/2018/Jul/09/nhs-bme-staff-discrimination (accessed 9 October 2020).

CIPD (2017) *Addressing the Barriers to BAME Employee Career Progression to the Top*, Chartered Institute of Personnel and Development.

Delgado, R. and Stefancic, J. (1998) Critical Race Theory: Past, Present and Future, *Current Legal Problems*, **51** (1), 467–91.

Dickens, L. (1999) Beyond the Business Case: A Three Pronged Approach to Equality Action, *Human Resource Management Journal*, **9** (1), 9–19.

Duncan, P., Dodd, V. and Madsen, K. S. (2018) Police, Military and Courts Lagging Decades Behind on Ethnic Diversity, www.theguardian.com/uk-news/2018/dec/05/police-military-and-courts-lagging-decades-behind-on-ethnic-diversity (accessed 25 November 2020).

EARLL (2020) How Effective Are Academic Libraries' Attempts at Dismantling Racism? www.earll.co.uk/post/how-effective-are-academic-libraries-attempts-at-dismantling-racism (accessed 2 December 2020).

ECU (2017) Equality in Higher Education: Staff Statistical Report 2017, www.ecu.ac.uk/publications/equality-in-higher-education-statistical-report-2017 (accessed 8 December 2020).

Equality and Human Rights Commission (2017) The Ethnicity Pay Gap, www.equalityhumanrights.com/en/publication-download/research-report-108-ethnicity-pay-gap (accessed 9 December 2020).

Ethnic Dimension (2015) *Identifying and Removing Barriers to Talented BAME Staff Progression in the Civil Service*, Civil Service, www.gov.uk/government/publications/identifying-and-removing-barriers-to-talented-bame-staff-progression-in-the-civil-service.

Hussain, A. and Ishaq, M. (2016) Equality and Diversity in the British Armed Forces: Progress, Challenges and Prospects, *Defence and Security Analysis*, **32** (1), 36–50.

Ishaq, M. and Hussain, A. (2019) *BAME Staff Experiences of Academic and Research Libraries*, SCONUL.

Khan, C. (2017) Do Universities Have a Problem with Promoting Their BAME Staff?, *The Guardian*, 16 November, www.theguardian.com/higher-education-network/2017/nov/16/do-universities-have-a-problem-with-promoting-their-bame-staff (accessed 29 November 2020).

Kirton, G. and Greene, A.-M. (2016) *The Dynamics of Managing Diversity: A Critical Approach*, 4th edn, Routledge.

Living Wage Foundation (2020) Low Pay Disproportionately Affects Black, Asian and Minority Ethnic (BAME) Workers, www.livingwage.org.uk/news/news-low-pay-disproportionately affects BAME workers (accessed 25 November 2020).

McIntrye, N., Mohdin, A. and Thomas, T. (2020) BAME Workers Disproportionately Hit by UK Covid-19 Downturn, Data Shows, *The Guardian*, 4 August, www.theguardian.com/society/2020/aug/04/bame-workers-disproportionately-hit-uk-economic-downturn-data-shows-coronavirus (accessed 21 October 2020).

Miller, J. (2019) Tackling Racial Inequalities in Career Progression in UK Organisations. In Nachmias, S. and Craven, V. (eds), *Inequality and Organisational Practice* (vol. 1), Palgrave Macmillan.

Ramesh, R. (2014) Public Sector Lacks Diversity Despite Obligation to Promote Equality, *The Guardian*, 11 September, www.theguardian.com/society/2014/sep/11/public-sector-uk-lacks-diversity-study-trevor-phillips (accessed 9 November 2020).

Randhawa, M. (2018) Closing the Gap on BME Representation in NHS Leadership: Not Rocket Science, www.kingsfund.org.uk/blog/2018/03/bme-representation-nhs-leadership (accessed 9 November 2020).

Rollock, N. (2019) Staying Power: the Career Experiences and Strategies of UK Black Female Professors, www.ucu.org.uk/media/10075/staying-power/pdf/ucu_rollock_february_2019.pdf (accessed 15 November 2020).

Salter, P., Adams, G. and Perez, M. (2018) Racism in the Structure of Everyday Worlds: A Cultural-Psychological Perspective, *Current Directions in Psychological Science*, **27** (3), 150–5.

The Global Recruiter (2018) Report Shows Lack of Diversity in Local Government Leaders, www.theglobalrecruiter.com/report-shows-lack-of-diversity-in-local-government-leaders (accessed 9 December 2020).

Warren, R. (2020) Former Officer Claims Racism Forced Her Out of Met Police, *The Guardian*, 24 June, www.theguardian.com/uk-news/2020/jun/24/bame-ex-officer-claims-racism-forced-her-out-met-police (accessed 9 December 2020).

Watts, M. and Rich. J. (1993) Occupational Sex Segregation in Britain 1979–1989: The Persistence of Sexual Stereotyping, *Cambridge Journal of Economics*, **17**, 159–77.

Williams, P. and Nicholas, D. (2009) Exploring the Low Representation of Black and Minority Ethnic Staff in the Library and Information Science Profession: A Case Study of London, CIBER Research, Department of Information Studies, University College London.

5
Decolonising the Academic Library: Reservations, Fines and Renewals

Lurraine Jones and Marcia Wilson

Advisory: this chapter contains an offensive term to identify a historical book title.

> In a 1930s child psychology study in the USA, White children were tested on their perceptions of 'race' by being shown a picture of a library. After glancing at it they had to answer a number of questions, among them: 'what was the Negro doing?' In fact, there were no Black people in the picture at all, but the answers all ran in a similar vein: 'He is busy scrubbing the floor', 'He is dusting the bookcases'. As Pieterse points out, no child said 'he is reading a book' (Pieterse, 1992, 11).

Introduction

Our concern in this chapter is to develop our thinking through our personal history of racialisation, learning and working in White educational spaces in order to explore the call to decolonise academic libraries. Toni Morrison posits that higher education is an 'unabashedly theological and consciously value-ridden and value-seeking moral project' (cited in Law, Phillips and Turney, 2004, 7). Much of Western archival methodology is embedded in colonialism and imperialism with a cultural bias towards Eurocentricity, Christian values and the Enlightenment, and therefore libraries are not inherently neutral spaces. We argue that libraries, as collectors and producers of White heteropatriarchal knowledge, are culpable in legitimising and reproducing colonialist and racist ideologies. As Nina de Jesus (2014) suggests,

> realizing the emancipatory potential of the library as institution would require breaking and disrupting the system of intellectual property and other aspects of capitalism, especially the publishing industry. It would require disrupting the empire's mechanisms for creating 'knowledge' by being more than a repository for imperial knowledge products. It would require supporting Indigenous resistance to the settler state and working towards dismantling anti-Blackness.
>
> (de Jesus, 2014)

As Black educators in a post-1992 London institution (University of East London, UEL) we are committed to the decoloniality of education and the dismantling of institutional Whiteness. In the same way that there have been calls to decolonise the university curriculum, the university library must be considered along the same lines. It is not appropriate to attempt to decolonise one part of an institution but leave all others steeped in Whiteness.

Here is Peter. Here is Jane. I like Peter. I like Jane.

Lurraine Jones: A child of Irish and Montserratian immigrant parents, I was born in Hackney, East London and, along with all the other local catchment working-class British and immigrant kids, went to London Fields Primary School. There, we learned to read and write from the Ladybird Key Word Reading scheme, which was the British school reading scheme in the 1960s and 1970s (Wikipedia, 2021). The Ladybird books were first published in 1964, with 1950s nostalgic, gendered illustrations reflecting the life of a nuclear White, middle-class, heterosexual family which was alien to our own family experiences. My mum took my sister and me to the local library on Saturdays, where my main memories are reading Miffy, Dr Seuss and Enid Blyton's middle-class books of the Famous Five and Malory Towers, although I must admit I never read Agatha Christie's popular tale of *Ten Little Niggers*. As I grew up, the library was always a special place for me – I have always 'loved a book'. It was a place of quiet contemplation, meeting my friend Jackie to talk about school, and then our first jobs and boyfriends, 'ssssshhhing' and reading about White histories for school (Tudors and Stuarts and Shakespeare) and White romance for love (Mills and Boon). Regina Everitt, the Black Director of Library, Archives and Learning Services (one of few in the UK) where I work at the UEL wrote in a piece about the need for greater diversity in higher education (HE) libraries that 'in my teens, during long, hot summers in Philly, I sought refuge in the black literature section of my local library, devouring stories from writers from the Harlem Renaissance through to the Black Power movement' (Everitt, 2020). How envious I was on reading that!

I came to HE late as a divorced mother of four. Like so many other student mothers who have said the same to me over the years, I wanted to study to 'make something of myself' and 'be an example to my kids'. Growing up as a mixed-heritage Black person in the UK, I have always had an emotional response to 'race', due to my experiences of racism and colourism. I did Psychosocial Studies and learned European male psychoanalytic and social theories. I did not question learning about these theories as I struggled with them; Eurocentricity was the norm.

However, it was when I came to the theories of 'race' in my second year of study that I began to learn and understand that education, indeed every Western and colonial institution, is based on a racial epistemological framework created, built and shaped by Whiteness. It was revelatory to me and has changed me in every way since. I reflected that my secondary school sports teams – headed up, of course, by White sports teachers – were predominantly Black: rounders, netball, track and field. However, so few of these girls were taking subject exams, the lower Certificate of Secondary Education (CSE) never mind the higher Ordinary Level (O Levels). Although we girls knew that this was 'how it was', I now understood *why* many of the Black girls at my secondary school did not take exams at 16. They were in the General Class, as the selection and separation into sets was based on supposed 'natural' intelligence.

At university I was enlightened by Grenadian Bernard Coard's book *How the West Indian Child is made Educationally Sub-Normal in the British School System* (Coard, 1971). Writing in *The Guardian* in 2004, Coard said:

> the issues raised in the book, however, applied to the plight of black children throughout the British school system, and not just to those sent to ESN [educationally sub-normal] schools. Racist policies, racist curricula, problems of low self-esteem and low teacher expectations, and so on, infected the entire school system. This had devastating consequences for the overall performance of black children throughout Britain.
>
> (Coard, 2004)

Coard made the further critical point about the contemporary educational crisis for many Black children that:

> What is particularly important to note is that the children of the 1960's and 1970's whom the British education system failed are the parents and grandparents of today's children – large numbers of whom are being suspended and 'excluded' from schools, or placed in 'special units' or streams . . . The lesson to be learned for today's problems in the school system is that they were 'hatched' decades ago, in the previous two generations.
>
> (Coard, 2004)

It was as an adult in my second year of undergraduate study that I *understood* that my schooling and library experiences had been spaces of Whiteness – White teachers, White authors, White theories, White histories and White librarians. I never saw 'me' anywhere positively in education, in books, in top jobs, in romance, hair, models, fashion – anywhere. I *knew* I was as clever as some of my White peers who were put forward for the 11-Plus – the grammar school admissions test. In the words of Rocky Balboa, 'I cudda been a contender'. The revelation was as devastating to me as it was enlightening.

Marcia Wilson: My early experiences are slightly different to Lurraine's, but many are the same. I was born in East London to Jamaican parents, and my very early memories are of reading book after book, mostly Ladybird books. My mother used to take me and my brother to the local library on a Saturday morning and I was excited to choose a handful of books that would be mine for a week or so until it was time to return them and select more. I do not recall seeing or reading any book that had images of characters who looked like me. I grew up in a working-class home and, although money was tight, we always had encyclopaedias, dictionaries and grammar/punctuation books: reading and writing (the Queen's English) was regarded as important in my home. Being a teenager opened a whole new, exciting world for me in relation to books. I always had a Saturday and/or Sunday job and willingly spent my money on cheap (but fashionable!)

clothes from market stalls and on books. However, the books I read during my teenage years were very different from the ones I read when I was younger. I discovered books written by Black authors and I was a regular visitor to WH Smith and Waterstones, where they had a section entitled 'Black Writing' and I made a beeline for it. Later, I discovered Black-owned bookshops that sold a huge range of the much-loved authors that I was reading such as Terry Macmillan, Bebe Moore Campbell, Toni Morrison (yes, I struggled and re-read each page multiple times, but it was worth it), Richard Wright and the list goes on. The feeling of being in those shops was new and exhilarating and I felt a sense of community as I was with like-minded people who shared my passion for literature. I was feeling nourished after reading the books in a way that I never felt when studying my A Level English Literature. It was a thirst that could not be quenched as I discovered my Blackness through literature and movies.

Here is Amahl. Here is Imani. I like Amahl. I like Imani.

Marcia Wilson: For some, Whiteness can be normalised without even questioning it. I recall as a child watching films that featured majority White actors such as Shirley Temple, Fred Astaire and Ginger Rogers, *Lassie*, *Black Beauty*, etc. The only time I saw Black people in films was when they were being subservient to White people. Seeing Black people on TV was such a rarity that I used to shout out to my parents when I saw someone so that they could come into the living room and see for themselves. However, when *Babylon* (1980) and *Burning an Illusion* (1981) were released, and then Spike Lee's work was a regular feature at the box office, I was hooked on films that had majority Black actors. I knew that the curriculum in school was White, but I never questioned it. It was the norm, and I catered for what was missing in my own time and with my own money.

As I studied for my A Levels, I knew the classics that were regarded as essential (Shakespeare, Chaucer, etc.), but I was also developing a deep love for literature that included characters who looked like me and that centralised Black people. It was almost like existing in two different spheres – learning what was deemed important knowledge in the school curriculum but also learning and embracing a different world of Black literature. Whiteness reigned supreme in the education system and, therefore, in our school and local library. As a child, I looked at the library as the gateway to the opportunity to broaden my mind, learn about different cultures and go on imaginary journeys that transported me to places beyond the East End of London. It did all of that, but the destinations were always White spaces.

There have been many debates concerning the nature of the relationship between the power structure and education, and some have documented persistent inequalities in Black children's education (Eggleston et al., 1986; Gillborn and Mirza, 2000; Wright, Weekes and McLaughlin, 2000; Wright, 2010; Wright, 2012). As a mother, I vowed that my children would not have the same schooling experience as me in terms of 'seeing' themselves or being presumed intellectually inferior. As an educator specialising in 'race',

I committed to anti-racist and decolonial practice, and I have to say that every Black academic I have met thus far, regardless of their subject discipline, is engaged in the same, not least because they are only too well aware they are one of the very few who have 'made it'. Indeed, as Ahmed draws attention to in her discussion of diversity practitioners, 'the institution can be experienced *as* resistance' (Ahmed, 2012, 26). The somatic norm underlying the normality of Whiteness in academic libraries is brought to the fore in this chapter by discussing our own experiences, first of learning in the British school system and then of working and studying in the White dominated sector of HE, where our presence enables us to highlight the synchronic relationship between racialised bodies and elite spaces in the body politic (Puwar, 2004).

We the people
Critical race theory

Having discussed the normality of Whiteness in education and our places as learners and academics within it, we now turn to critical race theory (CRT) to explore this topic further. An important theme related to CRT is the development of experiential knowledge as a method to document experiences with racism in order to apply our own perspective to the situation. This point is crucial in informing and tackling racism. Arguably, one of the best illustrations of this is by Chinua Achebe who said that 'Until the lion has its own historians, the history of the hunt will always glorify the hunter'. Documenting experiences about Whiteness in the education system is a critical story to tell, especially for White allies to know that Black people's experiences are very different from theirs (Anderson, 2015).

Originally developed in the USA in the 1970s in the fields of law and radical feminism by Black activists and scholars such as Derrick Bell, Alan Freeman, Richard Delgado and Kimberlé Crenshaw, CRT questions the fundamental principles on which a supposedly democratic USA was founded when 'race' was central to its foundations. CRT asserts that 'race' and therefore racism is central, permanent and an ordinary part of our society where Whiteness is 'the norm' and the dominant force of power in social roles and relationships in society. CRT offers an invaluable insight and tool to examine how 'race', although normalised in society, is a social construct, is hierarchical in its nature with societal resources distributed inequitably, which Bonilla-Silva (2015) asserts is 'a racialised social system'. Many Black academics through their lived experiences of racialisation and racism engage with CRT as a theoretical and methodological framework to expose that institutions are underpinned and dominated by White supremacy. Joseph-Salisbury describes CRT as 'a political, economic and cultural system in which whites overwhelmingly control power and material resources, conscious and unconscious ideas of white superiority and entitlement are widespread, and relations of white dominance and non-white subordination are daily re-enacted across a broad array of institutions and social settings' (Joseph-Salisbury, 2019). Invoking CRT, Cecile Wright's research into young Black students' aspirations and performance concurs with Rollock et al.'s (2011) study of Black middle-class parents who used their own privileged positions in education through their access to economic, social and cultural capital to support their children's educational aspirations and attainment (Wright, 2013). Wright posits, however, that class or the inequalities of access to cultural and economic capital are not a determinant of aspiration for the next generation and that Black families have long persisted in their endeavours to improve their livelihoods via the education system. However, despite the unequal outcomes between White and Black students in tertiary schooling, Black students are disproportionately more likely to go on to HE (Wright, 2013). Recent statistics evidence, however, that universities are failing Black students in comparison to their White peers in degree award outcomes. As we have argued elsewhere, White students are 13.2% more likely to be awarded a good degree (1st or 2:1). Higher Education Statistics Agency data indicates similar outcomes for Black students with regard to retention on their degree programme, progression from one level of study to the next and graduate employability rates (Wilson and Jones, 2020).

Institutional racism

Ahmed asks, 'if diversity is a way of viewing or even picturing an institution, then it might allow only *some* things to come in to view' (Ahmed, 2012, 14, emphasis added). What is not in the view of senior leaders in educational institutions is the existence of structural and systemic racism, which fails to recognise the power and influence that, in this case, the academic library has. We have argued elsewhere it is time for leaders to perform a deep dive into examining the deficits of their institutions rather than of their students, and to be held accountable for the policies, practices and culture that may affect Black students' progression, retention and award outcomes (Wilson and Jones, 2020).

As argued earlier regarding tertiary schooling and Coard's thesis, intellect becomes associated only with Whiteness, the Whiteness of academic thought becomes natural and logical, rather than racial (Joseph-Salisbury, 2019). Academic debates and enquiries as to why educational inequalities continue to persist in tertiary schooling for Black students in comparison to their White peers have in more recent years also entered the HE spectrum as, of course, the children of today become the undergraduate students of tomorrow. Global movements such as #Rhodesmustfall, #whyismycurriculumwhite? and Why Isn't My Professor Black? demand that knowledge, artefacts, canons and praxis from the Global South are given equal importance to those of the Global North in HE institutions. Building on these movements, there is more recently a strong and urgent Decolonise The Curriculum agenda impacting upon HE. Elizabeth Charles (Assistant Director of Library Services, Birkbeck, University of London) posits:

> In critically re-examining what is included in the curriculum – the voice, narratives and different sources of knowledge – education could be transformative of both the individual (staff and/or student) and the impact this might have on the subject discipline and society. It will not

be an easy transition, but it is long overdue and must be addressed, as well as the lack of other representation and senior representation in the staff of [higher education institutions], scholarly communication and the library and information sectors.

(Charles, 2019)

A decolonial lens certainly focuses attention on the Whiteness of HE institutions. As Joseph-Salisbury argues, it is the illusion that universities are racial meritocracies that acts to reaffirm the dominance of Whiteness; that dominance is understood merely as the proverbial cream rising to the top (Joseph-Salisbury, 2019). However, Doharty, Madriaga and Joseph-Salisbury argue that, 'despite the paradox of working under (what purports to be) a 'decolonial' agenda, widespread calls to decolonise our universities have further embedded rather than dismantled Whiteness, thus continuing to characterise the careers, wellbeing, and daily lives of faculty of colour' (Doharty, Madriaga and Joseph-Salisbury, 2021). We can both speak of our HE experiences of having 'to do the work' in either taking on the burden or moving the decoloniality agenda forward because we feel we 'owe' poorly served Black students and we are 'experts'. Or, more insidiously, of being *expected* by White colleagues to take on the burden of 'race issues' for the institution or even when a Black student has personal issues. We have both had many conversations with Black colleagues over the years about the extra pastoral work, done willingly or otherwise to try to help students or institutional agendas, in addition to normal workloads. Thus, one's career can be structured and limited by 'race' even if this is not a research or career interest, and the emotional labour involved in the personal and institutional agendas can impact on Black academics' well-being. As Rollock argues, 'navigating this inequitable terrain for BME staff can become mentally exhausting and taxing, subsequently impacting on aspects of professional performance within an uncompromising inequitable landscape' (Rollock, 2016).

In his discussion of academia and racism Les Back suggests that two 'antagonistic forces' are at play in HE, the first being 'a deep resistance in the academy to reckon with what might be called the sheer weight of whiteness' (Back, 2004, 1) and the second being multiculturalism (i.e. an increasing international and cosmopolitan student body) and White resistance and resentment to this force. Back posits that through mission statements universities claim to embrace widening participation and diversity without acknowledging the fallacies of impartiality and neutrality of institutions based on Eurocentric knowledge and values (Back, 2004). Let's think about the academic library in this context, the lifeblood that runs through the veins of a university and intellectual life which must adjust to the resources, information needs and interests of an increasingly diverse student body. In a 2015 survey by the Chartered Institute of Library and Information Professionals (CILIP) and the Archives and Records Association (ARA) of library and information professionals in the UK, 97% of respondents identified as White, out of a workforce of about 86,000 (Everitt, 2020). That means that White staff, most of whom, as Vaughan suggests, 'control the language of categorization and control access to the information categorized within the system' (Vaughan, 2018), can be said to be culpable in legitimising and reproducing racism unless they are committed anti-racists. Derrida asserts that 'there is no political power without control of the archive' (Derrida, 1996, 4), which begs the question we ask: 'are all members of CILIP and the ARA *active* anti-racists?' Without library and archive staff having anti-racism training and understanding institutional Whiteness, the project of decolonising education is a non-starter.

Colour-blind racism

Many White liberals (which most academic staff are), perhaps not wanting to appear racist or feeling ill equipped to address the subject, have operated on a 'colour blind' basis, treating students with respect and good intentions but not according to student needs. CRT challenges dominant claims of colour-blindness and equal opportunity which are particularly prevalent and standpoints in the UK. Well-intentioned White people would probably be devastated to be labelled racist (Burke, 2018). However, many people have not found the tools to effectively discuss racism or have an appreciation of what it actually is, and this is evident in how different people explain and understand racism. In general, White people and Black people view racism differently. Some White people view racism as an attitudinal behaviour, meaning that a person does not like someone who is Black or Brown and treats that person unfavourably; whereas many Black people view racism as a systemic problem that impacts on every area of society and institutions.

Colour-blind racism is built on the premise that equal opportunity exists, and inequality can be explained by individual or cultural differences (Burke, 2018). Bonilla-Silva (2010) proposed four frames to understand how colour-blindness operates in different spheres. First, abstract liberalism relates to the ideas associated with political liberalism, such as equal opportunity. The premise of this notion is that preferential treatment of certain groups is inappropriate, and individuals should attain positions without the assistance of initiatives such as positive action. There is no acknowledgement that society is not a level playing field and Black people are severely under-represented in positions of power in all the major UK institutions.

Naturalisation is the second frame presented by Bonilla-Silva. This is based on the premise that inequalities in society are natural because people tend to gravitate towards those whom they feel most comfortable with and identify with. The third frame is cultural racism and is based on stereotypes of specific groups such as believing that the Black degree-awarding gap is the result of deficits in Black people (e.g. laziness and lacking in academic skills). The fourth and final frame, minimisation of racism, suggests that our society is mostly post-racial and that racism is no longer the problem that it was many years ago. A prime example of this is when people point to success stories, such as successful and wealthy sportspeople and singers, as clear evidence that racism is no longer a problem in UK society because, with hard work, these individuals were able to rise to the top of their chosen professions. Once again, this argument ignores where power resides in UK institutions.

White allyship

The concept of White allyship has gained prominence in the discussion of dismantling racism. However, the conversation has not been without its misgivings, misunderstandings and tensions. One of the issues that has arisen relates to the role of White people as 'saviours' of Black and Brown people. In other words, Black people are portrayed as victims or are positioned from a deficit perspective where they need looking after or are in charitable need (Endres and Gould, 2009). This paternalistic perspective was highlighted when a flurry of White celebrities (e.g. Madonna, Angelina Jolie, Stephen Spielberg, Tom Cruise and Nicole Kidman) adopted Black babies, which led to the infants being known as the latest Hollywood trend (Fisher, 2009).

Spanierman and Smith (2017) provide a useful starting point for understanding what constitutes allyship. Probably one of the most important aspects is that being an ally involves continual work. It is important that White allies have a nuanced understanding of racism and White privilege and are engaged in an ongoing process of reflecting on their own positionality with respect to racism. Allies develop ways to use their privilege to promote racial equity and dismantle racist structures. It is important to note that the dismantling of these structures is key. Unfortunately, when allies see their role as one of mainly supporting Black and Brown people, this lends itself more to the paternalistic aspect and reinforces White privilege and supremacy (Endres and Gould, 2009).

True allies must seek ways to develop partnerships with other allies and people of colour and invariably, throughout the process, encounter challenges and resistance from other people who believe that society is post-racial. Following the murder of George Floyd in 2020, there was an increase in White people wanting to know what role they could play in understanding and dismantling institutional racism. This was evidenced by the increase in anti-racist books by authors such as Reni Eddo-Lodge and Kendi X Ibrahim. Unfortunately, what has become apparent is that some 'allies' expect credit for the work they do and this can at times be seen via social media posts. This broadcasting of their role as an ally and inability to accept criticism from others, especially Black and Brown people, indicates that 'allyship' is not authentic and can clearly be questionable (Spanierman and Smith, 2017).

In addition to White allies being aware of institutional racism and White privilege, it can be argued that effective allies are aware of their racial identity. Although there are different models identifying the stages of racial identity (Hardiman, 1982; Ponterotto, 1988), Helms (1995) is arguably the most comprehensive. She identifies six stages of development, described as (1) contact, where there is a denial of racism or individuals argue that they operate on a colour-blind basis; (2) disintegration, where there is tension and conflict in choosing between one's ethnic group and greater humanity goals; (3) reintegration, where one resolves the tension by taking a racially superior stance. Individuals may justify this by aligning their thinking with stereotypes that exist about people from other ethnic groups; (4) pseudo-independence, where limited contact is made with people from other ethnic groups but those people are seen as acceptable and possibly like minded; (5) immersion/emersion, where there is an increased understanding of White privilege and institutional racism but feelings of guilt may still be prevalent; and (6) where someone fully accepts their racial positioning, adopts an anti-racist perspective and values diversity. It can be argued that when allies are at the final stage of embracing their White identity, they are in a position to be more effective in dismantling institutional racism, and feelings of guilt about Whiteness do not hamper the ability to do the work needed to progress towards equality.

As we drew attention to earlier, university libraries are not neutral spaces (Ferretti, 2018). They are gateways to knowledge and can provide avenues to enhance understanding about social justice issues. This was demonstrated by a decolonisation project at the UEL led by librarian Ian Clark. Starting in 2017, UEL worked towards submission for Advance HE's Race Equality Charter Mark. Clark's contribution was significant in that he organised a 'Decolonisation' exhibition at the entrance of the university library. Relevant informative journal articles were on display for library users to see and take away on entering the building. In parallel, Clark worked with colleagues to undertake an audit of the key reading lists for the modules (units) across the university. Without exception, over 90% of the key authors in the reading list were White males. Importantly, this information was shared with colleagues, along with the importance of diversifying the reading list and suggestions for ways to do this. Clark's work is a prime example of effective allyship in that their work actively focused on dismantling the Whiteness of the library. Clark argues that the library has a significant role in building 'connections and solidarity'. He argues that it is vital for White colleagues to understand the role of the library in decolonisation, which isn't about traditional library work and is not about upholding or maintaining the status quo (Clark, 2019).

In May 2019 Marcia Wilson delivered a keynote address at the M25 Library Consortium conference. The presentation was about racism in HE and the audience was overwhelmingly White. There were fewer than ten non-White people in attendance, including the presenter, and, on reflection, some of the content discussed probably made uncomfortable listening. Marcia reflects:

> It was the first time that I have delivered a keynote and I did not have many delegates wanting to discuss the issues raised after the session. I still think about that session and wonder how the librarians are committing to change in their institutions. It is my hope that out of the uncomfortableness came something to spark change. Why must it always take an event or incident that is traumatic and catastrophic for White people to recognise that inequalities exist in society and therefore in our institutions? It is deeply troubling that it was only after George Floyd was murdered in May 2020 at the hands of a White police officer that outrage was sparked across the globe. It was that traumatic event that was a catalyst for people to explore how to be an ally and ask questions about how they can use their privilege to generate change.

This is effectively illustrated by a graphical depiction of the lack of Black representation at the senior levels of more than 1,000 senior posts in UK organisations in the Colour of Power Index (Tulsiani, 2017). Just 17 positions out of 1,099 of the most senior roles within the UK's most powerful institutions are held by Black people. This lack of representation impacts on the power to engage in decision-making processes within organisations. Thus, it becomes normalised to see a majority of White people in senior roles in every major institution in the UK. Furthermore, their status in often perceived as attained through meritocracy (Littler, 2017).

Conclusion

In this chapter we have been thinking through our personal histories of racialisation, learning and working in White educational spaces to explore the contemporary call to decolonise libraries. Although we concur that there has been a positive change in British educational curricula from early childhood through to non-tertiary in terms of the inclusion of minoritised writers and educational role models since our own experiences, we argue that not much has changed in tertiary education.

Some of the inertia around Decolonising the Curriculum is arguably because most librarians are white and 'not racist', and whilst personally committed to liberating the curriculum are professionally unwilling to take risks with increasingly tighter budgets and continue to collect and reproduce established White heteropatriarchal knowledge. This is what Trepagnier calls 'silent racism', a non-racist rather than anti-racist attitude and practice (Trepagnier, 2016) that can become entangled with starker interpersonal or institutional racism, such as the obvious lack of Black of students at Red Brick universities. DiTomaso's argument is useful to draw on here, where she posits that 'racial inequality is reproduced primarily by the advantage or favouritism whites provide to other whites more so than from the discrimination and racism of whites toward non-whites' (DiTomaso, 2015). While DiTomaso's position has merit in terms of highlighting often White liberalist silent racism, we draw on the strident principles of CRT to argue that libraries are not neutral places in Britain but, rather, are spaces of White epistemic totality (Mignolo and Walsh, 2018, 197).

In an incredible paradox of publishing, on 31 March 2021, the 50th anniversary and the internet launch of lauded Bernard Coard's updated book *How the West Indian Child is made Educationally Sub-Normal in the British School System*, the UK government's Commission on Race and Ethnic Disparities (CRED) report (the Sewell Report) was published. In the report's section on education, the Commissioners (several of whom were Black and global majority) stated:

> Education is the single most emphatic success story of the British ethnic minority experience. Over the last half century, new arrivals to Britain have seized on the opportunities afforded by the state school system and access to university. The story for some ethnic groups has been one

of remarkable social mobility, outperforming the national average and enabling them to attain success at the highest levels within a generation. Put simply we no longer see a Britain where the system is deliberately rigged against ethnic minorities. The impediments and disparities do exist, they are varied, and ironically very few of them are directly to do with racism. Too often 'racism' is the catch-all explanation and can be simply implicitly accepted rather than explicitly examined. The evidence shows that geography, family influence, socio-economic background, culture and religion have more significant impact on life chances than the existence of racism.
(Commission on Race and Ethnic Disparities, 2021)

Much applauded among Conservatives, one justification for the report's findings was that the people holding four senior positions in the government, the Chancellor of the Exchequer, the Business Secretary, the Home Secretary and the Attorney General, are from ethnic minority backgrounds. The CRED report was denigrated by Black and White academics, activists, institutions and intellectuals alike for presenting ideals from what seemed to many to be a parallel universe. As White Emeritus Professor Max Farrar pointed out, '[the report] … chaired by Dr Tony Sewell, published on 31st March 2021, shows that poverty of analysis is not confined to white people', which is a searing truth. Furthermore, in his critique of the CRED report's denial of institutional racism while evidencing of the lack of Black Caribbean educational progression, Farrar stated that 'somehow it didn't occur to Sewell and his people that the Windrush generation of Caribbean migrants put enormous emphasis on their children's education in the 1950s, 60s and 70s' (Farrar, 2021). In placing the lack of educational progression on individuals (and it is undeniable there are Black families and individuals who have no interest in or do not value education), the CRED's report is akin to the Ladybird books of 1950s nostalgia reflecting the idealised life of a nuclear White, middle-class, heterosexual family which is still alien to most Black family experiences in Britain.

University libraries are an essential part of the educational experience. The benefits they offer the university community are immense. Good libraries can play a pivotal role in strengthening research and developing researchers (Rasul and Singh, 2011; Research Information Network, 2011) as well as in supporting learning and teaching activities (Hickman, 2017). The library could be regarded as the heart of the campus because this is the space that can be accessed by all, regardless of whether that is physically or within the digital realm. It stands to reason, given the importance of libraries, that they could also be the most appropriate and fitting site that is central within institutions for resisting Whiteness and engaging in renewed calls to bring about change across the sector. Librarians have the power to decide whether they will contribute to decolonisation work or maintain the status quo. This decision is an important one because it also impacts on what kind of message is being sent to students about what constitutes knowledge and who the producers of knowledge are. The library, in all its power, will either work towards dismantling racist structures or reinforce them.

References

Ahmed, S. (2012) *On Being Included: Racism and Diversity in Institutional Life*, Duke University Press.

Anderson, E. (2015) The White Space, *Sociology of Race and Ethnicity*, **1** (1), 10–21.

Back, L. (2004) Ivory Towers? The Academy and Racism. In Law, I., Phillips, D. and Turney, L. (eds), *Institutional Racism in Higher Education*, Trentham Books.

Bonilla-Silva, E. (2010) *Racism without Racists: Colour-Blind Racism and Racial Inequality in Contemporary America*, Rowman and Littlefield.

Bonilla-Silva, E. (2015) More than Prejudice: Restatement, Reflections, and New Directions in Critical Race Theory, *Sociology of Race and Ethnicity*, **1** (1), 73–87.

Burke, M. (2018) *Colorblind Racism*, Polity.

Charles, E. (2019) Decolonizing the Curriculum, *Insights*, **32** (1), 24, http://doi.org/10.1629/uksg.475 (accessed 10 May 2021).

Clark, I. (2019) The Role of the Library in Decolonising, *Medium*, http://orcid.org/0000-0002-0205-1915 (accessed 20 November 2020).

Coard, B. (1971) *How the West Indian Child is Made Educationally Sub-Normal in the British School System*, New Beacon Books.

Coard, B. (2004) Why I Wrote the ESN Book, *The Guardian*, 5 February, www.theguardian.com/education/2005/feb/05/schools.uk (accessed 30 December 2020).

Commission on Race and Ethnic Disparities (2021) *The Report of the Commission on Race and Ethnic Disparities,* www.gov.uk/government/organisations/commission-on-race-and-ethnic-disparities (accessed 20 April 2021).

de Jesus, N. (2014) Locating the Library in Institutional Oppression, *In The Library With the Lead Pipe*, www.inthelibrarywiththeleadpipe.org/2014/locatingthe-library-in-institutional-oppression (accessed 27 January 2021).

Derrida, J. (1996) *Archive Fever: A Freudian Impression*, University of Chicago Press.

DiTomaso, N. (2015) Racism and Discrimination versus Advantage and Favoritism: Bias for versus Bias against, *Research in Organizational Behavior*, **35**, 57–77, 10.1016/j.riob.2015.10.001.

Doharty, N., Madriaga, M. and Joseph-Salisbury, R. (2021) The University Went to 'Decolonise' and All They Brought Back was Lousy Diversity Double-Speak! Critical Race Counter-Stories from Faculty of Colour in 'Decolonial' Times, *Education Philosophy and Theory*, **52** (3), 233–44, www.tandfonline.com/doi/full/10.1080/00131857.2020.1769601?src=recsys.

Eggleston, J., Dunn, D., Anjali, M. and Wright, C. (1986) *Education for Some*, Trentham Books.

Endres, D. and Gould, M. (2009) I am also in the Position to Use my Whiteness to Help Them Out: The Communication of Whiteness in Service Learning, *Western Journal of Communication*, **73**, 418–36.

Everitt, R. (2020) Why We Need More BAME Representation in Academic Libraries, *THE*, www.timeshighereducation.com/career/why-we-need-more-bame-representation-academic-libraries (accessed 20 January 2021).

Farrar, M. (2021) Why the Sewell Commission on Race and Ethnic Diversity got it so Wrong, www.maxfarrar.org.uk/wp-content/uploads/2021/04/Why-Sewells-2021-Commission-Report-is-so-wrong.pdf (accessed 15 April 2021).

Ferretti, J. A. (2018) Neutrality Is Hostility: The impact of (False) Neutrality in Academic Librarianship, *Medium*, https://medium.com/@CityThatReads/neutrality-is-hostility-the-impact-of-false-neutrality-in-academic-librarianship-c0755879fb09.

Fisher, L. (2009) Black Babies: Hollywood's Latest Accessory? *ABC News*, 31 March, https://abcnews.go.com/Entertainment/story?id=7218470&page=1 (accessed 2 June 2021).

Gillborn, D. and Mirza, H. S. (2000) *Educational Inequality: Mapping Race, Class and Gender*, Ofsted.

Hardiman, R. (1982) White Identity Development: A Process Oriented Model for Describing the Racial Consciousness of White Americans, unpublished PhD dissertation, University of Massachusetts, https://doi.org/10.1017/CBO9781107415324.004.

Helms, J. E. (1995) An Update of Helm's White and People of Color Racial Identity Models. In *Handbook of Multicultural Counseling*, SAGE Publications, Inc.

Hickman, B. (2017) University Libraries Need to Start Putting the Student First, *The Guardian*, 3 August, https://www.theguardian.com/higher-education-network/2017/aug/03/university-libraries-need-to-start-putting-the-student-first (accessed 19 June 2021).

Joseph-Salisbury, R. (2019) Institutionalised Whiteness, Racial Microaggressions and Black Bodies out of Place in Higher Education, *Whiteness and Education*, 4, 1–17. 10.1080/23793406.2019.1620629.

Law, I., Phillips, D. and Turney, T. (2004) *Institutional Racism in Higher Education*, Trentham Books.

Littler, J. (2017) Meritocracy: The Great Delusion that Ingrains Inequality, *The Guardian*, 20 March, https://www.theguardian.com/commentisfree/2017/mar/20/meritocracy-inequality-theresa-may-donald-trump (accessed 19 June 2021).

Mignolo, W. D. and Walsh, C. (2018) *On Decoloniality: Concepts, Analysis Praxis*, Duke University Press.

Pieterse, J. N. (1992) *White on Black: Images of Africa and Blacks in Western Popular Culture*, Yale University Press.

Ponterotto, J. G. (1988) Racial Consciousness Development among White Counsellor Trainees: A Stage Model, *Journal of Multicultural Counselling and Development*, **16**, 146–56.

Puwar, N. (2004) *Space Invaders: Race, Gender and Bodies Out of Place*, Berg.

Rasul, A. and Singh, D. (2011) The Role of Academic Libraries in Facilitating Postgraduate Students' Research, *Malaysian Journal of Library and Information Science*, **15** (3), 75–84.

Research Information Network and Research Libraries UK (2011) *The Value of Libraries for Research and Researchers*, www.rin.ac.uk/value-of-libraries.

Rollock, N. (2016) How Much does your University do for Racial Equality?, *The Guardian*, 19 January, www.theguardian.com/higher-education-network/2016/jan/19/how-much-does-your-university-do-for-racial-equality (accessed 20 April 2021).

Rollock, N., Gillborn, D., Vincent, C. and Ball, S. (2011) The Public Identities of the Black Middle Classes: Managing Race in Public Spaces, *Sociology*, **45** (6), 1078–93.

Spanierman, L. B. and Smith, L. (2017) Roles and Responsibilities of White Allies: Implications for Research, Teaching, and Practice, *The Counselling Psychologist*, **45** (5), 606–17.

Trepagnier, B. (2016) *Silent Racism: How Well-Meaning White People Perpetuate the Racial Divide*, 2nd edn, Routledge.

Tulsiani, R. (2017) The Colour of Power Index, Green Park, https://thecolourofpower.com (accessed 20 January 2021).

Vaughan, C. (2018) The Language of Cataloguing: Deconstructing and Decolonizing Systems of Organizations in Libraries, *Dalhousie Journal of Interdisciplinary Management*, **14**, https://doi.org/10.5931/djim.v14i0.7853.

Wikipedia (2021) The Key Words Reading Scheme, 29 March (updated), https://en.wikipedia.org/wiki/Key_Words_Reading_Scheme (accessed 10 May 2021).

Wilson, M. and Jones, L. (2020) Dear Senior University Leaders: What Will You Say You Did to Address Racism in Higher Education? *THE*, www.timeshighereducation.com/blog/dear-senior-university-leaders-what-will-you-say-you-did-address-racism-higher-education (accessed 10 January 2021).

Wright, C. (2010) Othering Difference: Framing Identities and Representation in Black Children's Schooling in the British Context, *Irish Educational Studies*, **29** (3), 289–304.

Wright, C. (2012) Black Students, Schooling in the UK. In Freeman, K. (ed.), *Education in the Black Diaspora*, Routledge.

Wright. C. (2013) Understanding Black Academic Attainment, *Education Inquiry*, **4** (1), 87–102, DOI: 10.3402/edui.v4i1.22063.

Wright, C., Weekes, D. and McLaughlin, A. (2000) *Race, Gender and Class in Exclusion from School*, RoutledgeFalmer.

6
Critical Information Literacy and Structural Oppression: Reflecting on Challenges and Looking Forward

Angela Pashia

Introduction

It has been a challenging time to be concerned about teaching information literacy in the USA. For a while, it felt like librarianship was shifting towards becoming a more justice-focused field. There was a shift towards critical information literacy (CIL), an approach incorporating critical pedagogy and/or critical theory into one's teaching. The Black Lives Matter movement brought the topic of racism into the national discourse. A growing number of librarians were writing articles using critical race theory (CRT) and other theoretical perspectives that used a critical lens to examine structural racism in libraries and librarianship. In addition, librarians were beginning to engage with decolonisation, including explicitly discussing the need for CIL to decolonise the assumptions inherent in most discussions of information literacy (e.g. Langille, 2018).

As those positive shifts were becoming more mainstream within librarianship, a pandemic of anti-intellectualism was spreading through the population. Large portions of the population were taking conspiracy theories as seriously as, or sometimes more seriously than, verifiable facts. The election of Donald Trump as the 45th President of the United States felt like a turning point. These conspiracy theories felt more influential than ever before, because the President of the United States regularly contributed to spreading them.

And then the COVID-19 pandemic struck. Conspiracy theories and anti-scientific perspectives continued running rampant, spurred on by the US President. Simple preventive measures, like wearing a mask in public, were politicised, while millions of people repeated the disinformation (Box 6.1 on the next page) claims that this was no worse than the flu. Meanwhile, colleges and universities across the country shifted to fully online education. Some libraries stayed open, while others went fully remote along with the rest of the institutions they operate within. Even at those colleges and universities that returned to in-person classes and reopened libraries early, COVID-19 safety measures influenced the on-campus experience.

In this chapter, I reflect on where we have been, the challenges we faced and some directions that I see as opportunities for working towards more justice in libraries and librarianship going forward.

> **Box 6.1: Disinformation or misinformation?**
> I use the term disinformation, rather than misinformation, when discussing factually incorrect information disseminated by political figures. Misinformation refers to information that is factually incorrect, regardless of intent. Disinformation includes intent – so it is the intentional dissemination of misinformation, such as government propaganda campaigns. In this case, I chose this term because Donald Trump admitted in an interview with Bob Woodward in early February 2020 that he knew the novel coronavirus was a significant threat and intentionally downplayed the severity (Costa and Rucker, 2020; Gregorian, 2020).

Background and context

Librarianship, like any profession in the USA, has a long history of structural oppressions. This is not an indictment of librarianship itself, but a symptom of having been shaped by people who exist in a country that practised White supremacist legal apartheid until the 1960s. As late as the early 1960s, many states had established laws, known as Jim Crow laws, which explicitly required segregation in many public spaces, including libraries. These laws are popularly associated with the American South, largely in states that fought on the side of the Confederacy in the American Civil War, but Wikipedia lists Jim Crow laws found in 38 American states, ranging far beyond the South (Wikipedia, 2009). This was a national problem that was only more visible in the South because, prior to the Great Migration, in which large numbers of Black Americans moved to Northern and Western cities to work in manufacturing, from the mid-1910s to around 1970, the majority of Black people in the USA lived in the South.

The Civil Rights Act of 1964 struck down Jim Crow laws. Still, many communities across the country had racial covenants written into the deeds of homes, explicitly prohibiting owners from selling or renting to anyone deemed not White (Rothstein, 2017). Even in areas without explicit racial covenants, residential segregation was accomplished through Federal Housing Authority (FHA) policies tied to underwriting mortgage loans. The FHA mapped out cities and categorised neighbourhoods in terms of risk of default, with the racial composition of the residents factored into those determinations. These policies resulted in segregated schools and public services, even in areas without explicit laws demanding segregation. The Fair Housing Act of 1968 outlawed discrimination on the basis of race, religion, national origin or sex. However, racism is adaptable and laws are only effective when enforced. Legally invalidating racial covenants did not immediately end their impact. Policies for underwriting mortgages no longer explicitly refer to the racial composition of neighbourhoods, but the language of risk, coupled with the outcomes of centuries of systemic oppression in terms of income and wealth, has enabled mortgage companies to continue to disproportionately deny mortgages, or promote predatory mortgages that increase the cost to the lender, for minoritised groups (Zonta, 2019; Olick, 2020; Glantz and Martinez, 2018).

Libraries and structural oppression

This means that modern libraries in the USA were established in a culture that accepted racial apartheid, enforced by explicit law in some regions, enforced by contract law in other regions and enforced in less direct ways by federal and state funding policies. Many of the foundations of public library practices, structures and organisational schema can be traced to the dominant ideologies of that time (Honma, 2005). Academic libraries exist within colleges and universities, many of which were segregated until the middle of the 20th century. In this context, a separate system of Historically Black Colleges and Universities (HBCUs) developed, but even those libraries were subjected to the dominant White supremacist ideology as a condition of being selected to receive grant funding (Walker, 2017).

Many Americans prefer to view these laws and practices as ancient history that is somehow not relevant today. However, my dad was born in 1953. He has shared with me some of his childhood memories of growing up in an explicitly segregated St Louis, Missouri. Racial segregation shaped the childhood of every American who was born before about 1960 – which includes many of our prominent national politicians. However, we have yet to have any official Truth and Reconciliation process. As a culture, for a long time, we turned to either 'colour-blindness', in which we pretend not to see a person's race, or celebratory multiculturalism, in which we focus on representation and celebrate superficial differences, both of which provide cover to avoid discussing the deep and enduring harms that have been done and the structures that continue to shape our institutions (Hudson, 2017a).

Institutions can retain structures long after dominant cultural attitudes have changed. One recent example of this is the lengthy process of attempting to update a Library of Congress subject heading. The term currently used for materials related to undocumented immigrants is 'illegal aliens'. After a long process and support from the American Library Association (ALA), the Library of Congress agreed to replace the term with two different subject headings: 'noncitizens' and 'unauthorized immigration'. Before this could be enacted, however, Congress stepped in to require the Library of Congress to continue using the offensive term (Baron et al., 2019). In January 2021, the ALA passed a resolution referencing more recent legislation and President Biden's proposal to remove the term 'alien' from US immigration laws, which again calls on the Library of Congress to change this subject heading (ALA, 2021). Institutional resistance to change can be even more stubborn when the practice in question is more easily cloaked in the myth of neutrality.

A growing body of research has examined the myriad ways in which libraries have been shaped by and continue to uphold structural oppression (Strand, 2019). Many of these studies draw on either CRT or Whiteness Studies. CRT is an approach that examines the structures that uphold racist (and other oppressive) outcomes, regardless of the intent of any actors involved. Whiteness Studies also takes a structural approach, but explicitly addresses the construction of Whiteness as a category that provides access to privileges, in order to counter the ways in which Whiteness has often gone unnamed and treated as the default state. However, a study published in 2018 examined the assigned readings for required courses in the top 20 ALA-accredited Library and Information Science programmes and found that 'the vast majority of the examined required foundational courses provided students with little to no exposure to CRT or critical theory' (Gibson, Hughes-Hassell and Threats, 2018, 64). The authors of this study analysed and categorised each article using a broad definition of CRT that included all articles that used a critical framework to analyse race, regardless of the stated theoretical foundation (Gibson, Hughes-Hassell and Threats, 2018, 59).

Social structures function to uphold 'common sense' assumptions about what is normal and good. An ideology is a set of ideas, assumptions and beliefs. Though we can generally identify a dominant ideology in a given society, ideologies on their own can shift and compete. Structures are built in accordance with the dominant ideology – this can be intentional when ideologies come into conflict, but is often a result of people making decisions about policies, practices, building design and so on without having questioned why they believe that is the best way to proceed. These structures then reinforce that ideological perspective, regardless of any actor's intent. Without a societal Truth and Reconciliation process that examines the ways in which a White supremacist ideology shaped the structures that Americans have grown up viewing as the norm, and without explicit systematic professional education on the ways a White supremacist ideology shaped many of the structures libraries operate within, many librarians continue to uphold problematic structures. Even those who support equity and inclusion may act in ways that uphold racist structures if they have not had the opportunity and support to learn about those underlying structures.

Critical information literacy

Turning specifically to the literature on information literacy, there has been a shift towards a critical approach, but less explicit discussion of race, CRT or Whiteness Studies. This is unsurprising in the context of a culture that has largely attempted to avoid discussing racism as a structural issue, rather than as a personal attitude. Additionally, most librarians who teach information literacy primarily teach guest lectures in courses taught by faculty in other academic disciplines, which brings an additional layer of power dynamics to the classroom.

The Association for College and Research Libraries (ACRL) Framework for Information Literacy for Higher Education defines information literacy as 'the set of integrated abilities encompassing the reflective discovery of information, the understanding of how information is produced and valued, and the use of information in creating new knowledge and participating ethically in communities of learning' (ACRL, 2015). The Framework outlines six threshold concepts with related 'knowledge practices' and dispositions. This document includes elements that are consistent with a critical approach. For example, the 'Authority Is Constructed and Contextual' frame raises issues of how different communities of practice may have different ways of determining who counts as an authoritative voice and includes recognition of 'the value of diverse ideas and worldviews' as one of the related dispositions (ACRL, 2015). However, this document fails to explicitly address race or racism, even in contexts where its omission is conspicuous (Rapchak, 2019).

CIL encompasses work that applies some form of critical theoretical approach and/or critical pedagogy to teaching information literacy, but is not on its own a single theoretical foundation. CIL calls on librarians to address the ways in which 'the existing information system mirrors the larger social and political order, which is characterized by a radically asymmetrical distribution of power, and is shot through, systematically and structurally, by racism, sexism, homophobia, militarism, and class oppression' (Beilin, 2015). This includes a range of approaches, including work grounded in CRT, as well as work that focuses primarily on sexism, class oppression, or capitalism (monetisation of data, for example), without necessarily addressing race or racism explicitly.

Early in my career as an instruction librarian, I began incorporating elements of critical pedagogy into my teaching. My first attempts at this maintained the pretence of 'neutrality' with regard to structural oppressions. The messages I had received about best practices in librarianship and teaching through the course of my education had emphasised the need for the teacher/librarian to be 'neutral', and I never received formal preparation to do otherwise. The critical element at the time was in the way I designed lessons and assessments, focusing on active learning instead of the 'banking model' of education (Freire, 1993), in which students are empty vessels who receive knowledge from expert teachers. I also included some critique of the capitalist structure of academic publishing, but framed within discussions of the public domain, open access and Creative Commons licensing of content.

Then, in August 2014, Ferguson, Missouri erupted into massive protests. I followed these events more closely than I had during previous responses to police brutality because it was close to home for me – I grew up in north St Louis County, not far from where the protests were happening. I followed activists on Twitter and followed the links they shared to articles that led me towards a new research focus.

In spring 2015 I began incorporating discussions of structural racism into a 2-credit-hour credit-bearing information literacy course, Information Literacy and Research. This course was not required, but was one of the electives students could choose to fill a general education requirement. Most students take the course during their first or second year of university, though it is not uncommon to have a couple of upper-level students in a course section. I have published elsewhere (Pashia, 2017) about teaching lessons on three major topics related to structural racism and information literacy. Early in the semester, I included a lesson in which I showed a 20-minute video titled *Why Is My Curriculum White?* (UCLTV, 2014), and then spent the rest of the 50-minute class period facilitating a class discussion of the video in relation to their educational experiences. I also described lessons addressing bias in algorithms, including the ways Google results reinforce biases (Noble, 2018). The third topic I outlined in 2017 was alternative media, relating to the ACRL Frame 'Authority is Constructed and Contextual'. Structures of exclusion have been built into traditional publishing, privileging certain voices over others, and so learning to identify credible alternative sources can provide access to a wider range of perspectives. In addition to these topics, I included lessons on ideology, hegemony and critical thinking, attempting to develop students' abilities to identify connections between 'common sense' assumptions and particular ideological perspectives.

These are heavy topics for students in their first or second year of higher education. No matter how hard we try as teachers, there are always students who enthusiastically engage with course content, and others who engage only enough to earn the grade they want to get. This is an entirely rational choice, particularly for students who are balancing a full load of classes and work and family obligations. This pattern is exacerbated in this course by academic advisors who have advised students to take this course as 'an easy A' – which sets them up to expect to be able to succeed with minimal effort or critical thinking.

For a while, I felt like my efforts to get students to question their assumptions and interrogate the ideological perspectives that shaped their core assumption might not always bloom as fully as I had hoped in a single semester, but at least I was planting seeds Maybe some students didn't fully 'get it' in my class, but I could hope that next semester, or next year, they'd learn something that would put those lessons in a new light and spark the critical approach I had hoped to get them to understand.

Trumpism

In November 2016, shortly after Trump was elected to fill the role of President of the United States, journalist and anthropologist Sarah Kendzior asked Americans to write down who they are, what they value and 'Write a list of things you would never do. Because it is possible that in the next year, you will do them. Write a list of things you would never believe. Because it is possible that in the next year, you will either believe them or be forced to say you believe them' (Kendzior, 2016).

Kendzior earned a PhD in anthropology before becoming a journalist. Having completed doctoral research focused on the rise of an authoritarian leader in Uzbekistan, she has a unique perspective that led to some frighteningly accurate predictions about the flagrant attacks on journalists, expertise and basic facts that we experienced during Trump's time in office.

In reality, the rise of disinformation had begun long before Trump took office. A survey about current national and international events by Fairleigh Dickinson University's PublicMind in 2012 reported that, 'all else being equal, someone who watched only Fox News' performed 'significantly worse than if they had reported watching no media at all' (PublicMind, 2012). Citing significant concerns about the design and interpretation of the

PublicMind survey, further research sought to examine this relationship in more detail. This study found

> no differences in knowledge concerning how the US political system works (what I call process-related knowledge) but do find a significant, negative relationship between visiting foxnews.com and facts about society writ large (what I call society-oriented knowledge). These effects persist even when controlling for party, ideology, and conservative-group affinity and in the preponderance of matching procedures employed to reduce concerns of self-selection.
>
> (Licari, 2020, 792)

Increasing use of social media seemed to contribute to spreading conspiracy theories more widely, though it is possible social media just made them more visible. During the Obama administration I learned the term 'birtherism' – the conspiracy theory that President Obama had actually been born outside of the United States, and therefore was ineligible to hold the office of President. In 2011, Donald Trump participated in openly spreading this conspiracy theory (Smith and Tau, 2011), with the result that he 'rose sharply in the primary polls, but never formally ran' (Serwer, 2020).

Despite these trends, in the summer of 2016 I could never have guessed that these conspiracy theorists would ever be taken seriously or that one would be elected to the highest government office in the USA. In 2016, Americans watched Pizzagate unfold, culminating in a man attacking a pizza parlour with an AR-15-style assault rifle. This conspiracy theory claimed that several high-ranking members of the Democratic Party were conspiring with the owners of certain restaurants in a human trafficking and paedophilia ring (Wikipedia, 2016). This sounds outrageous – of course the people spreading this theory are just unhinged and not to be taken seriously, right? Like many American librarians at the time, I lamented that so many people needed better information literacy skills, but otherwise had no idea how bad things would get.

And then Donald Trump won the election and took office in January 2017. In the same year that the White House Press Secretary, Sean Spicer, presented easily falsifiable information to the media as though it were true, and Counsellor to the President Kellyanne Conway defended those lies as 'alternative facts', a new conspiracy theory, QAnon, began spreading like a plague. Started in October 2017, QAnon seems to have been inspired by the Pizzagate conspiracy. It has morphed to include a wide range of claims, all centring on the idea that Donald Trump was (and perhaps still is) working against a powerful group of Satan-worshipping paedophiles that control the government and media (Wikipedia, 2018). Proponents of this conspiracy theory contributed significantly to the armed insurrection at the US Capitol Building on 6 January 2021.

Against this backdrop, I started to question the effects of my teaching, particularly in terms of the lessons on alternative media. Did my lessons encouraging students to consider alternative perspectives make it easier for any of them, particularly those who were less engaged in class, to accept the QAnon claims?

Writing in 2017, I noted that lessons on alternative media can get into some murky areas. Citing attention to 'fake news', I emphasised the need to include discussions of power dynamics and structural -isms, like racism and sexism, when encouraging students to critically evaluate the value of an alternative media source. But the events that happened since then have seriously shaken my confidence in teaching those lessons. When I planted seeds of ideas that I hoped would bloom into a critical consciousness, or at least a critical information literacy, did the seeds that didn't bloom wind up festering into fuel for conspiracy theories?

Examining structural oppression as a component of information literacy remains imperative. But the experience of living through the Trump administration has shaken my confidence and beaten down my morale.

Coronavirus

From an information literacy perspective, 2020 was a fascinating and surreal year. The contradictory messages put out by people who would traditionally be considered authoritative sources fuelled massive public distrust in experts, even before factoring in the way that many members of the Republican Party politicised the virus and protective measures.

Early in the pandemic, people began stockpiling N95 masks, which led to shortages. Before we had solid scientific evidence about how this particular virus spread, doctors took to social media platforms to describe the complicated fitting procedures doctors must go through, in order to explain that the masks wouldn't really protect you if you didn't have the perfect fit. I must admit that I remember watching and retweeting one such video; it was medical advice from a doctor, so why wouldn't I listen to this expert? Early on, even the Surgeon General advised the public not to worry about wearing masks (Tufekci, 2020a). Then, more evidence started coming out that the virus spread by droplets and airborne transmission. Zeynep Tufekci published several articles (SILS UNC, 2020 lists some of these) and tweeted several threads compiling evidence from around the world that wearing masks was correlated with lower rates of transmission and arguing for more attention to ventilation (Tufekci, 2020b). Yet authoritative sources like the US Centers for Disease Control and Prevention (CDC) and the World Health Organization (WHO) seemed slow to respond to the growing body of evidence that the novel strain of coronavirus was airborne, transmitted by aerosol particles that could spread much further than the droplets that much official advice was focused on.

Some of the shifting messaging can be explained as shifting understanding of a new scenario. We protect ourselves as well as we can, using limited information, and then, once we have gathered more information, we shift our tactics to fit the new information. However, in a climate of rampant conspiracy theories, 'alternative facts' and claims of 'fake news', some people seemed to take changing advice as evidence that 'they', the experts, didn't really know what they were talking about. On top of that, politicians and right-wing groups actively politicised the response to COVID-19. The simple act of (not) wearing a mask became a political statement, regardless of what advice doctors, epidemiologists, the CDC or the WHO presented. Viewing this situation through traditional models of information literacy that construct authority as tied to official positions, the anti-mask crowds were simply choosing between authoritative sources, and decided to believe the President of the United States rather than medical experts, who, Trump claimed, were artificially inflating the numbers of deaths attributed to COVID-19 (D'Ambrosio, 2020).

Meanwhile, colleges and universities had to drastically change their operations, including the way classes were taught. At my university we received notice on 12 March 2020 that instruction would be suspended for two weeks, 16 March through 29 March. During that two-week period, it was decided that all courses would be moved online for the duration of the semester. We began offering some courses in person, with distancing and masks required, in the fall 2020 semester. Faculty who were not already teaching online were often unprepared to teach online, and were scrambling to adapt. Faculty who were required to teach in person, beginning in fall 2020, were expected to offer 'dual modality' – making the content available online, in case a student must quarantine for 14 days, while also teaching in person. This effectively doubled their workloads. During this time at my university, requests for library instruction were much lower than usual. While faculty struggle to teach full loads of courses while coping with living through a historic pandemic – which by 28 April 2021 had killed over 574,000 people in the USA alone (Johns Hopkins, 2021) – it is even more difficult than usual to identify what information literacy concepts students are learning in their courses from their professors while they are receiving fewer library instruction sessions.

Where do we go from here?

At the time of writing this chapter, vaccines are slowly becoming more widely available in the USA. Donald Trump is no longer President of the United States. The 46th President, Joe Biden, seems to have made an effort to emphasise facts and science – a stark contrast to the 'fake news' claims of his predecessor. QAnon is still out there, but less visible, since major social media outlets took action against those spreading associated claims – including Twitter banning Donald Trump. It feels like a return to some form of 'normal' is on the horizon.

We have a great deal of work to get back to. First, I continue to encourage librarians to educate themselves on structural oppression. This must be the foundation for all subsequent work in critical librarianship and CIL. In the USA, structural racism is an ongoing pandemic that continues to materially affect the lives of a significant portion of the population.

Living in Atlanta, Georgia, issues of structural racism seem more pressing than issues related to colonisation, but that is the result of an ethnic cleansing campaign in the 1800s (Wikipedia, 2001) that forced the Indigenous populations in this region either to move to reservations hundreds of miles to the west or to assimilate. The national mythos of the United States of America emphasises our role as a former colony that won independence, while minimising our ongoing role as a coloniser. In keeping with this, the education system has worked to relegate the Indigenous populations of the US to history. A report from the Reclaiming Native Truth (RNT) project examined persistent narratives about Native Americans in the USA. Participants in focus groups 'often express disappointment or anger that what they were taught' in school about Native Americans 'was so sparse or misleading' (RNT, 2018, 13). Relatedly, 'a study of schools in 2011–2012 found that nearly 87% of state history standards failed to cover Native American history in a post-1900 context and that 27 states did not specifically name any individual Native Americans in their standards at all' (RNT, 2018, 31). These erasures in the curriculum, a lack of representation in media and the historic removal of Native Americans to distant reservations have made Indigenous issues out of sight, and therefore out of mind, for many in the US. Participants in the focus groups who do not live near Indian Country 'admit that they do not think about Native American issues and largely believe the population is declining' (RNT, 2018, 8). The invisibility of Indigenous issues, combined with ongoing high-profile instances of anti-Black and anti-Asian racism, has made it difficult to sustain focus on decolonisation efforts, though the colonising worldview and structural racism are fundamentally intertwined.

Decolonisation is becoming more widely discussed in the USA. However, it still doesn't appear in the recent programmes from long-established information literacy conferences, such as Georgia International Conference on Information Literacy (no mention of decolon* in the programme from 2020 or 2021), Library Instruction West (no mention in the programme from 2020) and LOEX (Library Orientation Exchange) (a self-supporting, non-profit educational clearing house for library instruction and information literacy information; no mention in the programme from 2020 or 2021). That's another area in which we librarians will need to educate ourselves. I have done a considerable amount of work learning about structural racism and CRT, but am just learning about the decolonisation movement and where that overlaps with and differs from the structures that uphold anti-Black racism in the USA.

In many ways, librarianship focuses heavily on practicality. As a group, we tend to want practical solutions to problems, instead of detailed theoretical examinations of the deep roots of those problems. David Hudson directly connects this emphasis on practicality to hegemonic Whiteness, arguing that by privileging practicality we limit theoretical and critical examinations of the structures underlying our assumptions, thereby allowing problematic narratives to continue unchallenged (Hudson, 2017b). While engaging with theory does not necessarily lead to anti-racist outcomes, the library field needs to create more space and place a higher value on engagement with critical theory in order to effectively challenge the status quo.

Librarians have been discussing issues related to diversity and multiculturalism for decades. Despite a wide range of initiatives and training programmes, we still have a long way to go towards dismantling structural racism in libraries. This tells me that we need to shift our strategy from checklists of practical suggestions for making the library more inclusive to a deep professional engagement with CRT and other critical research.

Since 2018, I have co-taught a course through an online platform for continuing professional education for librarians, examining institutional racism in libraries. It is a four-week course, designed as a seminar with discussions of journal articles each week. For some participants, it is the first opportunity they have had to engage with critical scholarship on structural racism in a library context. This is not surprising in light of the research discussed above, which found little or no engagement with critical theory or CRT in foundational courses in LIS degree programmes in the USA (Gibson, Hughes-Hassell and Threats, 2018). We need to provide more opportunities for library workers to engage with this critical literature, whether through professional development coursework, journal article discussion groups supported by library administrators or some other framework. Of course, shifting the curriculum in LIS degree programmes would also be valuable.

In the realm of critical information literacy, there are many ways to incorporate discussions of structural oppression and decolonisation into our professional work. Earlier, I discussed some of the ways I have taught lessons directly addressing these topics in a general education course. Partnering with faculty to co-teach more advanced courses can provide opportunities to challenge the Whiteness of academic discourse in ways that are not practical in other settings. For example, a graduate-level course focusing on marginalised knowledge, including Indigenous knowledge, traditional ecological knowledge, working-class knowledge and feminist knowledge, enables a deep examination of what gets left out of much of the scholarly discourse, along with extensive attention to strategies for evaluating the credibility of these sources (Larson and Vaughan, 2019).

Addressing structural oppression through information literacy instruction does not need to be limited to the content of our lessons, though. How we talk about information literacy within the field and with faculty, as well as how we assess information literacy programmes, can affect what lessons are prioritised. Folk (2019) recommends reframing information literacy as a form of cultural capital, which can be taught as a tool to help close the opportunity gap for marginalised students. While this runs the risk of invoking the Lady Bountiful archetype (Schlesselman-Tarango, 2016), a well-designed assessment plan, along with critical engagement with CRT scholarship among those delivering instruction, can incentivise teaching practices that break down structural barriers for students.

We can also do work with faculty to influence what materials they use. While I remain less confident about discussing the value of credible alternative media sources with undergraduate students, it is imperative that faculty include more diverse voices in course materials. In addition to working to diversify the library collection, promoting the development and use of Open Educational Resources (OERs) provides an opportunity to bring credible alternative perspectives into the curriculum through assigned materials. I am currently co-editing a book on using OERs to promote social justice (Ivory and Pashia, forthcoming), and have been impressed with the range of work being done around the world to develop OERs that give voice to scholarship that has traditionally been excluded from the canon in various fields.

I can't end this reflection without noting that, despite citing Hudson's critique of the emphasis on practicality within librarianship, I find myself outlining a set of practical areas for future action. Knowing that our habits are shaped by Whiteness does not automatically change those habits. But also, I will reiterate that there is no simple solution, and the success of any actions I propose depends on having done the work to study history and critical theory.

References

ALA (American Library Association) (2021) Resolution on Replacing the Library of Congress Subject Heading 'Illegal Aliens' with 'Undocumented Immigrants', www.ala.org/aboutala/sites/ala.org.aboutala/files/content/ALA%20CD%2044%20Resolution%20on%20replacing%20the%20Library%20of%20Congress%20Subject%20Heading%20Illegal%20aliens%20with%20Undocumented%20immigrants_0.pdf.

ACRL (Association for College and Research Libraries) (2015) Framework for Information Literacy for Higher Education, www.ala.org/acrl/standards/ilframework (accessed 28 April 2021).

Baron, J., Broadley, S., Cornejo Cásares, Ó., Padilla Castellanos, M., Castro, J. and Schultz, D. (2019) *Change the Subject*, documentary film, Trustees of Dartmouth College.

Beilin, I. (2015) Beyond the Threshold: Conformity, Resistance, and the ACRL Information Literacy Framework for Higher Education, *In the Library with the Lead Pipe*, www.inthelibrarywiththeleadpipe.org/2015/beyond-the-threshold-conformity-resistance-and-the-aclr-information-literacy-framework-for-higher-education/ (accessed 28 April 2021).

Costa, R. and Rucker, P. (2020) Woodward Book: Trump Says He Knew Coronavirus Was 'Deadly' and Worse than the Flu While Intentionally Misleading Americans, *Washington Post*, September 9, www.washingtonpost.com/politics/bob-woodward-rage-book-trump/2020/09/09/0368fe3c-efd2-11ea-b4bc-3a2098fc73d4_story.html (accessed 30 April 2021).

D'Ambrosio, A. (2020) Physicians Push Back on Trump's Claim of Inflated COVID Deaths, *Medpage Today*, 27 October, www.medpagetoday.com/infectiousdisease/covid19/89351 (accessed 28 April 2021).

Folk, A. (2019) Reframing Information Literacy as Academic Cultural Capital: A Critical and Equity-Based Foundation for Practice, Assessment, and Scholarship, *College & Research Libraries*, **80** (5), 658–73, https://doi.org/10.5860/crl.80.5.658.

Freire, P. (1993) *Pedagogy of the Oppressed*, Penguin.

Gibson, A., Hughes-Hassell, S. and Threats, M. (2018) Critical Race Theory in the LIS Curriculum. In Percell, J., Sarin, L. C., Jaeger, P. T. and Bertot, J. C. (eds),

Re-Envisioning the MLS: Perspectives on the Future of Library and Information Science Education (Advances in Librarianship, 44B), Emerald Publishing Limited.

Glantz, A. and Martinez, E. (2018) For People of Color, Banks are Shutting the Door to Homeownership, *Reveal News*, 15 February, https://revealnews.org/article/for-people-of-color-banks-are-shutting-the-door-to-homeownership (accessed 28 April 2021).

Gregorian, D. (2020) Trump Told Bob Woodward he Knew in February that COVID-19 was 'Deadly Stuff' but Wanted to 'Play it Down', *NBC News*, 9 September, www.nbcnews.com/politics/donald-trump/trump-told-bob-woodward-he-knew-february-covid-19-was-n1239658 (accessed 28 April 2021).

Honma, T. (2005) Trippin' Over the Color Line: The Invisibility of Race in Library and Information Studies, *InterActions: UCLA Journal of Education and Information Studies*, **1** (2), 1–26, http://escholarship.org/uc/item/4nj0w1mp.

Hudson, D. J. (2017a) On 'Diversity' as Anti-Racism in Library and Information Studies: A Critique, *Journal of Critical Library and Information Studies*, **1**, 1–36.

Hudson, D. J. (2017b) The Whiteness of Practicality. In Schlesselman-Tarango, G. (ed.), *Topographies of Whiteness: Mapping Whiteness in Library and Information Science*, Library Juice Press, http://hdl.handle.net/10214/11619.

Ivory, C. J. and Pashia, A. (forthcoming) *Using Open Educational Resources to Promote Social Justice*, ACRL Press.

Johns Hopkins (2021) COVID-19 Dashboard by the Center for Systems Science and Engineering (CSSE) at Johns Hopkins University, last modified 28 April, https://coronavirus.jhu.edu/map.html (accessed 28 April 2021).

Kendzior, S. (2016) We're Heading into Dark Times. This is how to be your Own Light in the Age of Trump, *The Correspondent*, 18 November, https://thecorrespondent.com/5696/were-heading-into-dark-times-this-is-how-to-be-your-own-light-in-the-age-of-trump/1611114266432-e23ea1a6 (accessed 28 April 2021).

Langille, D. (2018) Decolonizing Academic Libraries: Critical Information Literacy and Truth and Reconciliation, *Canadian Association of Professional Academic Librarians Conference, Regina, SK, May 29*, presentation slides, https://capalibrarians.org/wp/wp-content/uploads/2018/07/1B_Donna-Langille_slides.pdf.

Larson, C. M. and Vaughan, M. (2019) Opening to the Margins: Information Literacy and Marginalized Knowledge. In Pashia, A. and Critten, J. (eds), *Critical Approaches to Credit-Bearing Information Literacy Courses*, ACRL Press.

Licari, P. R. (2020) Sharp as a Fox: Are Foxnews.Com Visitors Less Politically Knowledgeable?, *American Politics Research*, **48** (6), 792–806, https://doi.org/10.1177/1532673X20915222.

Noble, S. U. (2018) *Algorithms of Oppression: How Search Engines Reinforce Racism*, New York University Press.

Olick, D. (2020) A Troubling Tale of a Black Man Trying to Refinance his Mortgage, *CNBC*, 19 August, www.cnbc.com/2020/08/19/lenders-deny-mortgages-for-blacks-at-a-rate-80percent-higher-than-whites.html (accessed 28 April 2021).

Pashia, A. (2017) Examining Structural Oppression as a Component of Information Literacy: A Call for Librarians to Support #BlackLivesMatter Through Our Teaching, *Journal of Information Literacy*, **11** (2), 86–104, https://doi.org/10.11645/11.2.2245 .

PublicMind (2012) What You Know Depends on What You Watch: Current Events Knowledge Across Popular News Sources, 3 May, press release, http://publicmind.fdu.edu/2012/confirmed/final.pdf.

Rapchak, M. (2019) That which cannot be Named: The Absence of Race in the Framework for Information Literacy for Higher Education, *Journal of Radical Librarianship*, **5**, 173–96, https://journal.radicallibrarianship.org/index.php/journal/article/view/33.

RNT (Reclaiming Native Truth) (2018) *Research Findings: Compilation of All Research*, www.firstnations.org/wp-content/uploads/2018/12/FullFindingsReport-screen.pdf.

Rothstein, R. (2017) *The Color of Law: A Forgotten History of How Our Government Segregated America*, Liveright Publishing Corporation.

Schlesselman-Tarango, G. (2016) The Legacy of Lady Bountiful: White Women in the Library, *Library Trends*, **64** (4), 667–86, https://scholarworks.lib.csusb.edu/library-publications/34.

Serwer, A. (2020) Birtherism of a Nation, *The Atlantic*, 14 May www.theatlantic.com/ideas/archive/2020/05/birtherism-and-trump/610978/ (accessed 28 April 2021).

SILS UNC (2020) Zeynep Tufekci Advocates Mask Wearing in Open Letter to US Governors and Op-Eds in USA Today and The Atlantic, *School of Information and Library Science, University of North Carolina*, 18 May, https://sils.unc.edu/news/2020/tufecki-masks (accessed 28 April 2021).

Smith, B. and Tau, B. (2011) Birtherism: Where It All Began, *Politico*, 22 April, www.politico.com/story/2011/04/birtherism-where-it-all-began-053563 (accessed 28 April 2021).

Strand, K. J. (2019) Disrupting Whiteness in Libraries and Librarianship: A Reading List (last modified March 2021), www.library.wisc.edu/gwslibrarian/bibliographies/disrupting-whiteness-in-libraries/ (accessed 28 April 2021).

Tufekci, Z. (2020a) Why Telling People they don't Need Masks Backfired, *New York Times*, 17 March, www.nytimes.com/2020/03/17/opinion/coronavirus-face-masks.html (accessed 28 April 2021).

Tufekci, Z. (2020b) We Need to Talk About Ventilation, *The Atlantic*, 30 July, www.theatlantic.com/health/archive/2020/07/why-arent-we-talking-more-about-airborne-transmission/614737/ (accessed 28 April 2021).

UCLTV (2014) *Why Is My Curriculum White?* [video], https://youtu.be/Dscx4h2l-Pk (accessed 28 April 2021).

Walker, S. (2017) A Revisionist History of Andrew Carnegie's Library Grants to Black Colleges. In Schlesselman-Tarango, G. (ed.), *Topographies of Whiteness: Mapping Whiteness in Library and Information Science*, Library Juice Press, https://kb.gcsu.edu/lib/3.

Wikipedia (2001) Indian Removal (last modified 27 April 2021), https://en.wikipedia.org/wiki/Indian_removal (accessed 28 April 2021).

Wikipedia (2009) List of Jim Crow Law Examples by State (last modified 27 April 2021), https://en.wikipedia.org/wiki/List_of_Jim_Crow_law_examples_by_state (accessed 28 April 2021).

Wikipedia (2016) Pizzagate Conspiracy Theory (last modified 15 April 2021), https://en.wikipedia.org/wiki/Pizzagate_conspiracy_theory (accessed 28 April 2021).

Wikipedia (2018) QAnon (last modified 28 April 2021), https://en.wikipedia.org/wiki/QAnon (accessed 28 April 2021).

Zonta, M. (2019) Racial Disparities in Home Appreciation, *Center for American Progress*, 15 July, www.americanprogress.org/issues/economy/reports/2019/07/15/469838/racial-disparities-home-appreciation (accessed 28 April 2021).

Part 2
In Practice

7
The Contribution of Library and Information Science Education to Decolonising

Briony Birdi

Introduction

This chapter considers the contribution of library and information science (LIS) education to the 'decolonising' of our university curricula, and how students on LIS degree programmes can be supported to explore the concept of decolonising as students both in a higher education environment and in the workplace as LIS professionals.

There has been a growing agenda – shaped by both protest movements and intellectual debate – to 'decolonise the university', to draw attention to the colonial history of the campus and how higher education remains in the shadow of that colonialism. This process has included much reflection on what it might mean to 'decolonise' both the university (Bhambra, Gebrial and Nişancıoğlu, 2018) and its library collections (Dali and Caidi, 2021). However, our understanding of where LIS education fits into this discussion is arguably less advanced. This seems a little surprising, as LIS education is the academic discipline which bridges the gap between higher education and the LIS professions. This chapter is informed both by the author's experience as an LIS academic and by her involvement in a 2020 study, 'Decolonising the Curriculum in the Faculty of Social Sciences' by Williams et al., as part of her role as Co-Director of Equality, Diversity and Inclusion for the Faculty of Social Sciences at the University of Sheffield.

LIS as delivered in higher education tends to be situated within a broader social sciences school or faculty, and the reach of colonialism across the social sciences is widely acknowledged in the literature. As Williams et al. (2020) state, 'The division of labour among the disciplines of the social sciences, for example, follows the distinction between the "modern" world of colonisers (Sociology, Political Science, Economics) and the "traditional" formerly colonised world (Development Studies, Anthropology).' Although they observe that 'much has been done to blur these geographical boundaries, which made sense in the age of empires', Williams et al. argue that we are nonetheless still working with 'these dichotomies (First World/Third World, Global North/Global South, Developed/Developing, etc.) in how we understand the disciplinary division of labour within the Social Sciences today' (Williams et al., 2020, 7).

The education of LIS students is therefore inevitably affected by colonialism on several fronts, whether in the higher education environment in which it is studied, in the academic libraries which provide the resources supporting the learning process or in the libraries and information services in which the students work now and in the future. This chapter therefore focuses on the intersection between the academic discipline and the profession, using three simple steps we can take in order to engage LIS students with the concept of decolonising and how it relates to education and libraries. It will explore how students on LIS degree programmes can work through their ideas about the nature of universities and libraries as inclusive or exclusive spaces, being given time to think first about their own place in the classroom and the LIS profession, and then to think about what a decolonised curriculum and working environment could look like.

It does need to be acknowledged, however, that LIS academics may face an uphill struggle in first convincing colleagues that the space needs to be found for this type of material in the curriculum. For those who are already convinced of the centrality of social justice to a public-serving profession, this can be mystifying, as Dali and Caidi observe:

> If every librarian or information professional inevitably finds themselves working in a diverse environment, why are courses on diversity not part of the LIS core curriculum? Every LIS program realizes the vitality and ubiquity of technology and offers core technology courses, despite the fact that not every LIS graduate will end up in a highly technology-saturated environment. At the same time, practically every LIS graduate will work in a diverse setting with diverse community members, regardless of the type of library or information technology (IT) setting. Yet, courses on diversity are not built into the core.
>
> (Dali and Caidi, 2021, 14–15)

Indeed, after two decades of LIS teaching and research, the author of this chapter agrees with Dali and Caidi that our discipline may have somewhat lost its focus on the human, in favour of systems. The desire to 'decolonise' is gaining momentum in higher education, but we have some way to go before any aspect of 'diversity' occupies a core position in all LIS curricula. This brief chapter aims to help to redress this, providing simple steps which can either be worked through in sequence, as presented, or used as a source of stimulus for discussion with LIS students. The first considers the wider higher education environment, the second its academic programmes and the third its libraries and the LIS profession.

Step 1: starting the conversation: the colonial legacy and Whiteness of our university campuses

The university context

The first step enables us to find the space we need to talk through the context in which our universities and libraries are based, and to think about how others might experience the same space quite differently. The conversation can begin by considering our universities and what we know about them. At this stage the focus has not shifted to the LIS discipline, but remains on the broader, university context and student experience. Three factors can be used as a starting point:

1 that the colonial past continues to affect today's university campus;
2 that BAME (Black, Asian and Minority Ethnic) students regularly experience microaggression (and aggression) on our campuses;
3 that there is a 'degree-awarding gap' between BAME and White students in higher education.

The term on which this publication is centred is 'decolonising', but in order to begin to *de*colonise a teaching space, or a module, or an entire curriculum, it is first important to understand what has been *colonised* in the first place. An excellent introduction to a classroom discussion from a UK BAME perspective is provided by Melz Owusu, formerly the Education Officer at the University of Leeds and now a decolonial theorist and activist. In a widely viewed 2017 TEDx talk, Owusu gives the following reminder of the British Empire's continued influence on the UK education system and its students:

> Colonialism wasn't just the physical brutality and theft of land and resource, it was also the intellectual colonialisms of the minds of the colonial subjects ... the sun has not set on the British Empire, and one of the places where that is most pronounced is within our education system.
>
> [A colonised curriculum has emerged from] the coupling of lower expectations for students of colour with an unrepresentative curriculum, which had its base in the pain of colonialism.
>
> (Owusu, 2017)

The 'Whiteness' of campuses

Central to this colonial legacy are the continued Whiteness of our university campuses and the fact that, despite increasing BAME student populations (the proportion of students in UK universities identifying as BAME has increased steadily, rising from 14.9% in 2003/4 to 23.9% in 2017/18 – Advance HE, 2019), degree programmes tend to deliver White-led and White-inspired curricula. A starting point for discussion is to ask what does this mean, and how does this Whiteness manifest itself? Looking to recent research for examples, the Whiteness of the university campus itself is described by BAME student focus group participants in a 2017 study of BAME student attainment at the University of Sheffield in the following terms:

> 'It's quite difficult because there is not a lot of black students on my course or in Sheffield at all, so it's very hard to kind of fit in.' (*Focus group female, undergraduate*)
> 'When you are the only one it's like, did they let me in because they needed to have one?' (*Focus group female, PhD student*)
>
> (Awan et al., 2017, 14).

This Whiteness is visible not only in a university's student body but in its staff and the teaching materials they deliver. The following is taken from a description of the BAME student's university experience from a second University of Sheffield study in 2020:

> They are very unlikely to be taught by a member of staff who is not white, which means that they lack role models ... They are unlikely to encounter major theorists or scholars who are not white, or to see literature on their reading lists that [is] written by someone who is not white. Within their disciplines ... race and racism are either not taught at all, or side-lined into a specialised module rather than made central to a range of social issues and contexts.
>
> (Williams et al., 2020, 6)

Critically, we now know that these omissions – however apparently unintentional – can combine and contribute to institutional racism, defined in the Stephen Lawrence Inquiry report as 'The collective failure of an organisation to provide an appropriate and professional service to people of colour, culture or ethnic origin' (Macpherson, 1999, para. 6.34). This failure, Macpherson argues, can be 'seen or detected in processes, attitudes and behaviour which amount to discrimination through unwitting prejudice, ignorance, thoughtlessness and racist stereotyping which disadvantage minority ethnic people' (Macpherson, 1999, para. 6.34).

White privilege and the degree-awarding gap

In our discussion of Whiteness, it is easy to think only of the negative impact of the existing system on the BAME student; but equally important to the learning process is an exploration of the 'advantage', or privilege, which can be experienced at the other end of the scale for the White student and staff member. The next step in this conversation is therefore to provide space to think about and discuss White privilege, and White power. The ground-breaking writing of US academic Peggy McIntosh is helpful in explaining this frequent omission in the learning process:

> As a white person, I realised I had been taught about racism as something that puts others at a disadvantage, but had been taught not to see one of its corollary aspects, white privilege, which puts me at an advantage. I was taught to see racism only in individual acts of meanness, not in invisible systems conferring dominance on my group.
>
> (McIntosh, 1989, 10)

For a more recent illustration of this dominance, in 2014 University College London released a short video, *Why Is My Curriculum White?*, which gave valuable student perspectives on the Whiteness of their university experiences, from all faculties across the university. Particularly striking in the students' accounts is the dominant contribution of, and recognition for, the White, largely male perspective: 'What I see a lot in academic environments is the hero-worshipping of a small but significant minority of privileged people throughout history who have had access easily to the academic environment, as opposed to those who have been making history by living!' (UCL, 2014). McIntosh's widely used definition of White privilege is as 'an invisible package of unearned assets', which she set outs as a list of 26 items or 'conditions' which 'attach somewhat more to skin-colour privilege than to class, religion, ethnic status, or geographic location'. This list can be used – in full or in part – as the basis for a reflection of our own privilege, or otherwise. It is important that this process does not require reporting a 'score', but is used to reflect privately and learn from the experience. The following examples are given as an illustration.

> 'When I am told about our national heritage or about "civilization", I am shown that people of my color made it what it is.'
> 'I can be sure that my children will be given curricular materials that testify to the existence of their race.'
> 'I am never asked to speak for all the people of my racial group.'
>
> (McIntosh, 1989, 11)

Secondly, any BAME student will inevitably have experienced some degree of racism during their educational experience, ranging from unambiguously racist words or actions to a more subtle, but still hurtful and harmful, form of behaviour. As per the previous discussion of White privilege, given the sensitivity of the topic, the LIS students considering this point in the classroom are not required to share their own experience or observations of racist behaviour, but examples as stimuli for discussion and reflection can be found and shared relatively easily from within the literature (Awan et al., 2017; Morales, 2014). As a further example, a 2019 campaign, 'A Bit Racist Is Still Racist', from the University of Sheffield's BME Committee, aimed to highlight the harm caused by microaggressive comments and behaviour. Committee members talked to BAME students during a one-week period in 2019, collating their comments for dissemination both online and in spaces throughout the campus, as illustrated in Figure 7.1 on the next page.

Thirdly, it has become increasingly evident that another notable difference between the student experience of BAME and White students relates to their final degree classification. Commonly termed the 'attainment gap' or the 'award gap' (the author's preferred term which arguably shifts the 'blame' for a lower degree classification from the student to the awarding institution), this refers to the difference between the proportion of White British students receiving the highest degree classifications (First or 2:1) and the proportion of UK-domiciled BAME students who are awarded the same degrees. LIS students may already be familiar with the term, but in understanding the wider institution in which an academic library is based it can be illuminating to review the data together. Taking the most recent available example, in 2019 Advance HE reported a 'BAME degree attainment gap of 13.2 percentage points' (Advance HE, 2019, 110). If this homogenised group 'BAME students' is broken down further, it is clear that Black students are most negatively affected by the attainment gap, with Black African

Figure 7.1 *'A Bit Racist Is Still Racist'* – images of printed materials from 2019 Microaggression campaign, the University of Sheffield's BME Committee

students facing a gap that is more than five times the lowest differential recorded, which is for Chinese students, as shown in decreasing order (and using the Advance HE category labels) in the following list:

- Other Black – 24.6 percentage points
- Black African – 23.9 percentage points
- Black Caribbean – 21.7 percentage points
- Asian Indian – 5.2 percentage points
- Chinese – 4.3 percentage points
- Mixed race – 3.7 percentage points. (Advance HE, 2019, 110)

Where available, it can also be a useful exercise to compare a student's own institutional data to the national data, and to encourage them to continue this practice in future work so that they have a greater understanding of the student experience and how this may differ dramatically between groups.

Step 2: understanding the continued impact of colonialism and Whiteness on our curricula

Our discussion of decolonising can now move from the broader higher education context to the content of the degree programmes themselves. The introduction to this chapter referred to the continued 'reach of colonialism' within the social sciences in which LIS is generally located, a point reflected in US LIS academics Dali and Caidi's reference to the 'hegemonic legacy of a colonial (or imperialist) information science mandate with origins in Anglo/Euro-centric roots' (Dali and Caidi, 2021, 110). Their brief account of 'Biased trends in historical and contemporary LIS education' (Dali and Caidi, 2021, 110–11) provides an excellent text for students to critique and consider in the light of their own experiences and observations both as LIS students and new professionals. Furthermore, their wider development as LIS professionals will benefit from additional disciplinary and geographical perspectives. For example, in a study from the University of Cape Town, Sebidi and Morreira argue that 'the social sciences in South Africa are strongly influenced by European studies and epistemologies … such that curricula emphasise particular ontological positions, and expect students to reproduce these positions in their work' (Sebidi and Morreira, 2018, 37).

Using a second example, in 2019–20 a group of four BAME student researchers at the University of Sheffield worked with a team of academic staff to conduct an investigation of decolonising work in its Social Sciences faculty. Focusing on four of the 13 academic departments in the faculty (Education, Management School, Politics, Sociological Studies), the project had two phases. Phase One was a quantitative audit of selected core module reading lists in the four departments, looking at the extent to which people of colour are presented to students as the producers of knowledge. The research team felt that predominantly White-led reading lists were 'central to the institutionalised message that people of colour are not knowledge producers' (Williams et al., 2020, 10). Phase Two was informed by the first phase, and involved collecting qualitative data from staff and students regarding their perceptions of decolonising beyond reading lists. Topics covered included student experiences of the curriculum, classroom practices, flexibility of assessment and institution-level decolonisation and staff understanding of the decolonising agenda and how it related to or informed their academic work. A brief summary of key findings from each phase follows.

1. *Reading list audit*. White male authors dominated reading lists across the four disciplinary areas. As Figure 7.2 on the following page illustrates, each audit highlighted the poor representation of authors from a BAME background, particularly female authors. Very similar recent findings have been reported by researchers from other UK universities (Schucan Bird and Pitman, 2019; Stockdale and Sweeney, 2019).
2. *Student and staff perceptions*. Three main themes were identified in the qualitative data from both students and staff. These provide a brief but helpful checklist of issues

to consider when supporting a decolonising process, and illustrative comments from each are shown in Table 7.1 opposite.

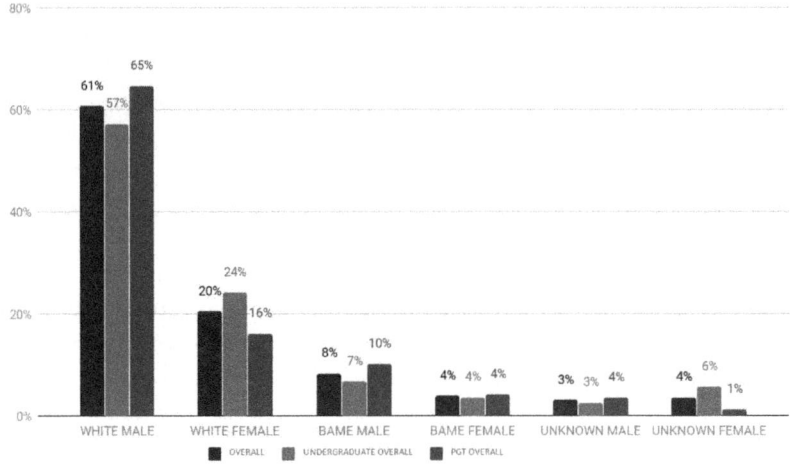

Figure 7.2 *Reading list audit: overall diversity of authors across module reading lists* (adapted from Williams et al., 2020)

Even a brief discussion of this type of report – however small scale – will help LIS students to understand the need for academic libraries to support module leaders to use more varied knowledge banks and to provide their students with a more diverse range of perspectives. It also illustrates that taking action to decolonise a degree must go beyond a review of reading lists, beyond a simple encouragement by library staff to include more texts by BAME authors, in order to understand both the learning and teaching experience in the modules they are required to support.

Step 3: the colonial imprint on academic libraries, and the White LIS profession

The third and final part of the decolonising conversation takes us from the university context in which the LIS student is based and moves into the LIS profession they are joining, its workforce and the services it provides.

Given the colonial legacy of our university campuses, it is first important to remember that this will have inevitably affected the contemporary services and collections of the academic libraries which support them. A brief but balanced perspective is given by Farnel et al. (2021), who observe, 'Postsecondary institutions and the libraries within them are deeply rooted in the imperial enterprise', asking the vital question whether any efforts made by academic libraries to decolonise or indigenise could ever be truly effective when

Table 7.1 *Emergent themes from the qualitative staff and student data* (Williams et al., 2020)

Emergent issues	Student and staff perspectives, with illustrative comment
Staff and student knowledge and understanding of decolonising	Students felt that they would all benefit from developing their cultural awareness and mutual respect for those from other backgrounds.
	'If students learn outside perspectives in-class then they will be able to move through their day-to-days with a greater respect for those around them.'
	For staff, there was a clear sense of feeling daunted by the prospect of decolonising their curricula, and of not knowing where to start.
	'We've got to unravel a huge amount of the institution to properly decolonise …'
The dominance of Eurocentrism and Whiteness in the curriculum	Students noted that even where non-white or non-European examples were provided, they would be related back to the White/European perspectives as the normative culture.
	'The normalisation or the assumption is that we must compare everything with White. Like, the White European culture is the norm.'
	Staff commented that taking time to do EDI- (equality, diversity and inclusion) related work such as decolonising – in teaching or as a subject of research – was not highly valued in academic terms, either within academic publishing or even in terms of promotion to the next academic level.
	'The pressure is to homogenise and to go the other way from decolonisation … very leading academics thinking of this kind of planetary scale.'
	'And then you have all the other work that many in the department do but it's just not viewed as … global and big-hitting … race, identity, gender, culture are seen as add-ons, still …'
Perceived barriers to decolonising	Students repeatedly asked to be given space and time to think and talk about anti-racism, anti-colonialism, decolonising, and felt that this wasn't generally provided in class.
	'I can't think of an instance when we have been explicitly encouraged to approach something from an anti-colonial or anti-racist perspective.'
	Staff were concerned that the decolonising discussions within academia were starting to question their purpose as academics, and even rendered invalid the work they had done to this point. This concern arguably relates to the notion of 'White fragility', which describes the defensiveness White people can reveal when their ideas about race and racism are challenged in some way.
	'it's not just the idea that what you teach is wrong or … even harmful, or even violent, but that your entire career, your entire education and basically everything you stand for as an academic, is potentially invalid and illegitimate.'

they are 'unfolding within a system that continues to be part of the colonial project' (Farnel et al., 2021, 168–9). In order to consider this question, Farnel et al. draw from the museums and archives sectors, using firstly Romero's argument that 'Being a part of a history does not necessarily lock you into any one particular future' (Romero, 2019, para. 2), and secondly Christen and Anderson's statement of 'commitment' and 'obligation' for their archival work at the University of Alberta to 'undo, redo, and build again structures that embody meaningful and mutual obligations to see, hear, and enact different ways of knowing, being, and relating' (Christen and Anderson, 2019, 107). After reading the brief section from Farnel et al. (2021, 168–9), students can then reflect on their own position on this question.

Statements from both research and practice can next be used to prompt initial discussion about the LIS workforce, for example the following quotes illustrate some of the perceptions frequently voiced about gender, ethnicity, class, stereotypes and leadership within the LIS professions:

> Librarianship has long been a profession dominated by women, specifically white women.
> (Cooke, 2017, 3)

> Libraries are organised and structured mainly by middle class professionals who have absorbed the norms of their profession and class.
> (Campbell, 2005, 271)

> '[Asked whether the homogenous LIS workforce had implications for the delivery of socially inclusive services] I'm inclined to say yes it should, but I'm not so sure in practice, as long as the white middle-aged women are open minded and good at their job.'
> (Public library manager, quoted in Birdi, Wilson and Mansoor, 2012, 122)

Having considered these initial perceptions, we can see if they are reflected in the data. A recommended source is the 2015 workforce mapping study commissioned by the Chartered Institute of Library and Information Professionals and the Archives and Records Association (ARA) and conducted by a team from the Centre for Social Informatics at Edinburgh Napier University. Based on a data set of 10,628 survey responses from library and information staff in the UK, this large-scale and statistically significant 2015 study (Hall et al., 2015) estimated the size of the UK LIS workforce at that point as 86,376. It is a valuable exercise to review the key findings of this study in confirming the gender-based perceptions described above (78.1% of the LIS workforce are female, compared to 50.1% of the UK workforce as a whole). The findings also indicate that, in terms of leadership roles, male employees are more likely to occupy senior management roles than their female peers, with 10.2% of male employees in senior leadership, compared to 5.9% of female employees.

Arguably more significantly, the study provides evidence of the predominant Whiteness of the LIS profession in 2015, as 96.7% of survey respondents identified as 'White', which was 9.2% more than those in UK *Labour Force Survey* data from the same year.

Within the academic and research libraries sector specifically, a second piece of research by Ishaq and Hussain (2019) reported that BAME staff felt that this lack of diversity 'was not being acknowledged, nor taken seriously, by the senior management of academic and research libraries' (Ishaq and Hussain, 2019, 6). The whole of this report makes valuable reading, but the key findings in the Executive Summary (Ishaq and

Hussain, 2019, 5–8) provide an excellent basis for class discussion, using for example the following prompts: *Were any of the findings surprising to you? Which were you expecting to see? Make recommendations to academic library managers to address three of the issues identified.*

After considering the experiences of BAME academic library staff, the discussion can then move to those of the students who use them. They inevitably represent multiple diversities, yet Cooke (2017) argues that these are not always reflected or considered in the design or delivery of library services, despite the legal obligation (under the 2010 Equality Act in the UK) to provide a service without discrimination: '[Pluralistic and intersectional] community members are often still considered the "other" and not served in the manner in which they deserve, with staff and resources that look like them and represent their experiences and information needs' (Cooke, 2017, 5).

Students can consider the different ways in which Cooke's description could apply to an academic library service's staff and resources, based on their own observations and experience. Do they think that Cooke's accusation is fair, that some library users are not 'served in the manner in which they deserve'?

In terms of the library resources themselves, students can explore what form a 'diverse' collection could take: one which reflects the needs and interests of its user communities instead of providing a 'prepared slate of services and resources deemed suitable for them' (Cooke, 2017, 1), and one which draws from an appropriately wide range of sources. To support the discussion, they could read Thethi's stark reminder (in Chilcott, 2019) of the potential limitation of providing only the 'prepared slate' of resources, given that a collection 'could be defined as diverse because it spans different countries but have each item in the collection written in the same language by an English, cis-gendered, straight, middle class, white man' (Chilcott, 2019).

After working through these issues, students will have a deeper understanding of the potential impact of a continued lack of diversity on the effective delivery of the service all library users 'deserve': a fair and equitable environment; a collection of resources representing a wide range of geographical and cultural perspectives; and a diverse workforce with the empathy and cultural awareness to deliver them.

Conclusion: taking steps towards a decolonised curriculum and profession

The previous sections have presented a structured conversation about decolonising, considering in turn the colonial imprint of our universities (Step 1), their degree programmes (Step 2) and their libraries (Step 3). In combination, they form a simple framework for the inclusion of decolonising as both a theoretical and practice-led element of an LIS education programme, as summarised in Table 7.2 on the next page.

The inclusion of such a framework in LIS education will not in itself 'decolonise' either our universities or the programmes they teach. Far from it: decolonisation is a

Table 7.2 *Decolonising framework for LIS Education*

	Theme	Key points for LIS student discussion	Suggested resources to use as a starting point (for full details see References)
Step 1	The colonial legacy and Whiteness of our university campuses	Understanding 'colonialism' and its continued impact on the university campus: • the Whiteness of Higher Education. Considering the BAME student experience: • microaggression and racism; • the attainment ('award') gap between BAME and White students.	• An introduction to decolonising, origins and definitions: Bhambra, Gebrial and Nişancıoğlu, 2018 (e.g. Chapters 1–2) • A clear definition of institutional racism: the Macpherson Report (Macpherson, 1999) • An overview of national (UK) student data: Advance HE (2019) • A reflection on the UK BAME student experience: TEDx talk *Decolonising the Curriculum*, Owusu (2017) • Microaggressions in higher education: Morales, E. (2014) • White privilege and White power: classic seminal text McIntosh (1989)
Step 2	The continued impact of colonialism and Whiteness on our curricula	The reach of colonialism and Eurocentric epistemologies to the social sciences, including Library and LIS. Reviewing today's social sciences curricula: • the reading list audit; • student and staff perceptions of decolonising: knowledge and understanding, Eurocentrism, perceived barriers.	• *Why Is My Curriculum White?* (UCL, 2014), video • Biased trends in historical and contemporary LIS education: Dali and Caidi (2021, 110–11) • An example of European/colonial influence on non-European degree programmes: Sebidi and Morreira (2018) • An example of a small-scale university study of decolonising practice and attitudes: Williams et al. (2020)
Step 3	The colonial imprint on academic libraries; the White LIS profession	Understanding the impact of colonialism and dominant Whiteness on academic libraries: • their services, their workforce, their user community. Considering 'diversity' in relation to library staffing, services and resources.	• The academic library context: Decolonizing and indigenizing in a colonial setting': Dali and Caidi (2021, 168–9) • Understanding the LIS workforce: Cooke (2017, 1–10). • Statistical data on the UK LIS workforce: CILIP/ARA Workforce Mapping report (Hall et al., 2015) • BAME academic library staff experience report: Ishaq and Hussain (2019) • The complex nature of 'diversity' in the provision of services and resources: Jasspreet Thethi's blog post (Chilcott, 2019)

complex and multifaceted concept which will require many years of work to achieve. However, the intention is that this work will support the LIS student and researcher in their academic engagement with the topic, and in their continued development as effective and empathic professionals in their field.

References

Advance HE (2019) *Equality in Higher Education: Students Statistical Report 2019*, www.advance-he.ac.uk/knowledge-hub/equality-higher-education-statistical-report-2019 (accessed 18 January 2021).

Awan, N., Williams, A. R., Crockford, J., Huntley, S., Hyatt, D., McClelland, N., Miller, M., Padmore, J., Philpott, S., Atom, A. and Claasen, C. M. (2017) *'You Have to Put on Your White Self to Progress': BME Attainment and Progression Task and Finish Group Report*, May, University of Sheffield.

Bhambra, G. K., Gebrial, D. and Nişancıoğlu, K. (eds) (2018) *Decolonising the University*, Pluto Press.

Birdi, B., Wilson, K. and Mansoor, S. (2012) 'What We Should Strive for is Britishness': an Attitudinal Investigation of Ethnic Diversity and the Public Library, *Journal of Librarianship and Information Science*, **44** (2), 118–28.

Campbell, B. (2005) 'In' versus 'With' the Community: Using a Community Approach to Public Library Services, *Feliciter*, **51**, 271–3.

Chilcott, A. (2019) Archives and Diversity are Cancelled. We Need Archival Intersectionality – Jasspreet Thethi, *Off the Record*, October 25, https://aranewprofessionals.wordpress.com/2019/10/25/archives-and-diversity-are-cancelled-we-need-archival-intersectionality-jasspreet-thethi/ (accessed 18 January 2021).

Christen, K. and Anderson, J. (2019) Toward Slow Archives, *Archival Science*, **19** (2), 87–116.

CILIP and ARA (2015) *A Study of the UK Information Workforce*, https://archive.cilip.org.uk/research/workforce-mapping (accessed 24 January 2019).

Cooke, N. (2017) *Information Services to Diverse Populations: Developing Culturally Competent Library Professionals*, Libraries Unlimited.

Dali, K. and Caidi, N. (2021) *Humanizing LIS Education and Practice: Diversity by Design*, Routledge.

Farnel, S., Carr-Wiggin, A., Lar-Son, K. and DeLong, K. (2021) Academic Library Initiatives 'For the Public Good': Diversity by Design or Retrofitting? In Dali, K. and Caidi, N. (eds), *Humanizing LIS Education and Practice*, Routledge.

Ishaq, M. and Hussain, A. M. (2019) BAME Staff Experiences of Academic and Research Libraries, SCONUL, www.sconul.ac.uk/page/bame-staff-experiences-of-academic-and-research-libraries (accessed 18 January 2021).

Macpherson, W. (1999) *The Stephen Lawrence Enquiry: Report of an Inquiry*, The Stationery Office, https://assets.publishing.service.gov.uk/government/uploads/system/uploads/attachment_data/file/277111/4262.pdf (accessed 18 January 2021).

McIntosh, P. (1989) White Privilege: Unpacking the Invisible Knapsack, *Peace and Freedom*, July/August, Women's International League for Peace and Freedom. In P. McIntosh, Extending the Knapsack: Using the White Privilege Analysis to Examine

Conferred Advantage and Disadvantage, *Women & Therapy*, **38** (3–4), 232–45, DOI: 10.1080/02703149.2015.1059195.

Morales, E. (2014) Intersectional Impact: Black Students and Race, Gender and Class Microaggressions in Higher Education, *Race, Gender & Class*, **21** (3–4), 48–66.

Owusu, M. (2017) *Decolonising the Curriculum*, YouTube video, 10:59 mins, TEDx talk, University of Leeds, 14 April, https://youtu.be/zeKHOTDwZxU (accessed 18 January 2021).

Romero, A. (2019) Museum Resolution: Build Social Relations over Property Relations, Walker Art Center, 8 January, https://walkerart.org/magazine/soundboard-museum-resolutions-anthony-romero (accessed 18 January 2021).

Schucan Bird, K. and Pitman, L. (2019) How Diverse Is Your Reading List? Exploring Issues of Representation and Decolonisation in the UK, *Higher Education*, **79**, 903–20.

Sebidi, K. and Morreira, S. (2018) Accessing Powerful Knowledge: A Comparative Study of Two First Year Sociology Courses in a South African University, *Critical Studies in Teaching & Learning*, **5** (2), 33–49, DOI: 10.14426/cristal.v5i2.87.

Stockdale, K. J. and Sweeney, R. (2019) Exploring the Criminology Curriculum, *Papers from the British Criminology Conference*, **19**, 84–105.

UCL (2014) *Why Is My Curriculum White?*, YouTube video, 20:09, University College London, 9 December, https://youtu.be/Dscx4h2l-Pk.

Williams, T., Mayblin, L., Birdi, B., Carnegie, E., Fields, D., Gadhia, M., Igali, F., Kiyumbu, W., Ladipo, D., Mills, C., Pinney, M. and Stampnitzky, L. (2020) *Decolonising the Curriculum in the Faculty of Social Sciences*, University of Sheffield.

8
Indigenising Canadian Academic Libraries: Two Librarians' Experiences

Rachel Chong and Ashley Edwards

Introduction

Since 2015, institutions across the land we now call Canada have been increasingly engaged in reconciliation efforts as laid out in Canada's Truth and Reconciliation Commission's Calls to Action. While only three of the 94 Calls to Action are directed at libraries, the overarching theme of educational change resonates within all library sectors. Academic libraries are uniquely positioned both to engage in their own decolonising and Indigenising initiatives and to support those of their parent institutions. Caution should be taken, though, since often people and institutions seem to want to move quickly to reconciliation, as if it were a destination and not a journey. As Rhiannon Bennett [Musqueam] said during a panel discussion at Kwantlen Polytechnic University on 25 November 2020, you need to learn the truth before you can work on reconciliation.

This chapter presents some of that truth by providing a brief background on the colonisation of the country known today as Canada and how that colonisation was carried out through education. Part of this is learning what we mean by Indigenous, and who the three Indigenous Peoples in Canada are. We also share our learning on what reconciliation means, and how legal documents set up a framework to support our work. Complementing this, we unpack decolonising and Indigenising in relation to each other. This leads to a section on education, imparting why Indigenisation initiatives are important both within post-secondary institutions and in the libraries that serve them. We conclude our chapter by sharing our stories as Indigenous academic librarians contributing towards Indigenising our institutions.

Before we begin

Following the government definition and current practice (Joseph [Gwawaenuk], 2018; Justice [Cherokee Nation], 2018; Vowel [Métis], 2016; Younging [Opaskwayak Cree], 2018), the term Indigenous will be used when discussing First Nations, Métis and Inuit. Older and outdated terms may be used in context when discussing practices or as used by an author. Additionally, where possible, the name of an author's community or Nation has been included the first time we cite them. We are responsible for any omissions or mistakes and apologise in advance for them. We have used Gregory Younging's 2018 work *Elements of Indigenous Style* (EIS) to compose this chapter; where there are discrepancies in publication styles, we have followed EIS.

We also should acknowledge that we are two Métis librarians displaced from our home territory, born and raised on the West Coast of British Columbia. This impacts on how we engage with our Indigeneity and, in turn, on our work as Indigenous librarians. The land we now refer to as Canada is home to over 600 sovereign First Nations (Gadacz and Gallant, 2019) and more than 50 Inuit communities (Gray [Tsimshian Nation], 2011, 40), while the Métis homelands are located on what are now seven provinces and territories (Métis Nation Canada, n.d.) (Box 8.1). There is a rich cultural diversity across the country, and we would be remiss not to acknowledge that our voices are only two among many.

> **Box 8.1: The Indigenous Peoples of Canada**
> **First Nations** 'refers to that group of people officially known as Indians under the *Indian Act*, and does not include Inuit or Métis peoples' (Vowel, 2016, 11). First Nations have unique recognised rights in addition to their rights as Canadian citizens. These Nations are distinct and unique.
>
> **Inuit** (plural) or **Inuk** (singular) refers to the Indigenous Peoples who live in the Arctic regions (Joseph, 2018, 112; Younging, 2018, 66–7).
>
> **Métis** are self-identified and distinct from other Indigenous Peoples. They share historic Métis Nation Ancestry and must be accepted by the Métis Nation (Métis Nation Canada, n.d.).
>
> Indigenous Peoples in Canada are united by experiences of colonial trauma; they are also united by their resilience, their commitment to each other and the relationships they value and share with all their relations.

Locating the self: building relationship

Within an Indigenous paradigm, connections are foundational. When looking at connection in relation to storytelling, such as we are doing now, 'connection is made not only through a storyteller's relationship to the topic of their tale, but also through a storyteller's ability to develop a relationship with their audience. Though this can be done through a multitude of methods, an important part of beginning any relationship is getting to know a little bit about one another' (Penak, 2018, 259).

Following the Indigenous Protocol and research practice of numerous Indigenous scholars including Opaskwayak Cree scholar Shawn Wilson (2008, 97–125) and Nisga'a scholar Amy Parent (2018, 65), we will start by locating or situating ourselves. This is an act of humility, acknowledging those people who have guided and shaped us, as well as the land that is a part of us. In doing this we recognise that our experience and perception can never be complete, but we are grateful to all our relations. In the tradition of our host Nations, we raise our hands in thanks.

Ashley Edwards

Taanshi ķiyawaaw, Ashley Edwards *moñ noñ*. Chilliwack, British Columbia *oschi niya, maaķa* Burnaby, British Columbia *ni-wiiķin. En Michif*, Dutch, *pi* Scottish *niya*. This is a greeting in southern Michif, which is spoken by some Métis communities. I said: hello everyone. My name is Ashley Edwards. I'm from Chilliwack, but live in Burnaby now. I'm Métis, Dutch, and Scottish. Chilliwack is located in the heart of Stó:lō territory, and Burnaby is located on the homelands of the Tsleil-Waututh, Stó:lō, Qayqayt, Stz'uminus, xʷməθkʷəy̓əm (Musqueam), and Kwikwetlem First Nations.

My interest in Indigenous librarianship and Indigenising education is a mix of personal and professional. As mentioned, I grew up in Chilliwack, which is Stó:lō territory, yet it was not until I began work at the Stó:lō Research and Resource Management Centre (SRRMC) as a library technician that I learned anything about the Indigenous history of that area. My time with the SRRMC opened my eyes to the inequity of library practices in relation to Indigenous Peoples and topics, particularly around subject headings and classification. It also encouraged me to ask questions about my own Indigenous heritage. I had grown up knowing my dad was Indigenous and Dutch, but I did not know from what community until 2016, when I learned that his mother's family is Métis, from the Red River settlement area of Manitoba. My mother's family is Scottish, having settled in Nova Scotia and Ontario.

My time at the SRRMC taught me to view the world around me differently; to see how stories and information can be held not only in books, but in the mountains, trees and animals all around us. As a librarian, I think about how to bring this land-based storytelling to our traditionally text-based profession and collection. I have been with the Simon Fraser University (SFU) Library since 2013, starting as a library assistant in the Learning and Instructional Services Division. After graduating with my Master of Library and Information Studies (MLIS) from University of Alberta in June 2020, I began my position as the Indigenous Curriculum Resource Centre (ICRC) Librarian.

I want to extend a heartfelt *maarsi* (thank you) to the editors for providing this opportunity to share on this important topic. For me as a recent graduate it is incredibly humbling. There are many people who are supporting and guiding me on this journey of reconciliation and identity. An equal (and often the same people!) number of people supported and encouraged my education interests and career ambitions. I am grateful that Rachel is here with me, sharing her experiences and wisdom. We have had many wonderful conversations leading up to this, and I look forward to more over the years. My Mom, Kimberly, and sister Jennifer are towers of strength and inspiration. And last but never least, my husband Bob. Without him, I would not be who I am today. *Kishchiitaymitin* (I adore you).

Rachel Chong

Taanishi, Rachel Chong *dishiniķaawshon*. Delta, British Columbia *niwiķen*. I am grateful to the Gabriel Dumont Institute Heritage Michif To Go app for teaching me to introduce myself in the language of my ancestors – Michif. To translate: hello, my name is Rachel Chong. I reside in Delta, British Columbia, on the traditional unceded territories of the Kwantlen, sq̓əc̓iy̓aʔɬ təməxʷ (Katzie), Stó:lō, Stz'iminus, Á, LE̱NENEȻ ŁTE (W̱SÁNEĆ), and sc̓əwaθenaʔɬ təməxʷ (Tsawwassen) First Nation. I am of mixed European and Métis ancestry and married into a Chinese-migrant family. My maternal grandfather, Maurice Bousquet, is Métis from St Boniface, Red River settlement in what we now call Manitoba and it is through his legacy that I claim my Métis Nation citizenship. My grandfather prematurely passed to the spirit world shortly after I was born and I deeply feel his loss as I meander my way culturally.

Growing up as an urban Métis, I was disconnected from my culture, language and land. I am grateful to my mother, Michele Bousquet, who raised my siblings and me. As a single parent, she instilled in us the importance of education. While working on my undergraduate degree at SFU, I was employed as page, clerk and later circulation supervisor at my local public library. Thanks to my employer's encouragement, I had the opportunity to study for my MLIS at the University of British Columbia and learn more about my history through the First Nations Curriculum Concentration. I am forever grateful to many Indigenous scholars, colleagues, family and friends who have helped me navigate my understanding of Indigeneity, Canadian history, my place in the world and how I might contribute.

When Ashley approached me to co-author this piece, I considered this work with caution, smudge (an Indigenous spirituality practice) and prayer. I am mindful that words have the ability both to wound and to heal. Printed texts are not the traditional way of our people, as thoughts, like people, grow and evolve. What is said today has a different context tomorrow. With this in mind, I continue the Protocol to smudge and pray to my ancestors for guidance as I write and edit this piece in the hopes that these words resonate, that their healing intent is not lost.

What is in a word?

Words can have multiple meanings, and their context changes over time. In his book, *How to Be an Antiracist*, Ibrahim X. Kendi (2019) discusses the importance of defining what concepts and terms mean before engaging with them. Following his advice, before we can begin sharing what a decolonised or Indigenised academic library could look like we need to examine what some of these words and phrases mean. In the following sections we will provide some definitions and explanations of Indigenous terms, followed by a brief discussion on some vocabulary around reconciliation.

More than a name

Many people are apprehensive about how to refer to Indigenous Peoples, not wanting to cause offence or not knowing how best to refer to a specific group of people (Vowel, 2016,

7–13; Younging, 2018, 50). It's important to take cues from the Nation or community you are engaging with; this could mean checking the Nation or community's website to see how they identify, or asking community members. For example, when writing our introductions and positionality statements both of us confirmed Nation and community names using a combination of Native-Land.ca (an ontology created by the Indigenous Matters Committee of the Canadian Federated Library Association) and confirmed names using the Nation or community's website. There is always the possibility of making mistakes, and being open to feedback or corrections is important (Vowel, 2016, 7–13).

Métis scholar Chelsea Vowel notes that 'there is no across-the-board agreement on a term' (Vowel, 2016, 8) because terms and names evolve over time (Vowel, 2016, 7–13; Younging, 2018, 50–73). For example, in Canada the terms Indian, Aboriginal and Indigenous have all been used to identify someone who is First Nations (these terms will be expanded on below). This is why following the practice of checking and being receptive to correction is important. Today, the term Indian is considered inappropriate; however, some Nations (such as the Musqueam Indian Band) have decided to continue using it.

Aboriginal vs Indigenous

When referring to Indigenous groups in Canada, you need to understand some history and terminology. The blog for Indigenous Corporate Training, a company founded by Bob Joseph [Gwawaenuk Nation] has a post titled 'Indigenous or Aboriginal, which is correct?' and teaches us that for hundreds of years the original inhabitants in Canada were termed Indians – a mistake made by Christopher Columbus, who thought he had reached India (Indigenous Corporate Training, 2016). It was not until 1982 that 'Aboriginal' replaced 'Indian' as the appropriate term for Indigenous Peoples in Canada, when Aboriginal rights were included in the Constitution (Vowel, 2016, 10; Younging, 2018, 62). In 2016 the federal government adopted Indigenous as the preferred term for all government communications (Joseph, 2018, 12), and this term is gaining recognition in organisations and literature (Younging, 2018, 64–5).

Indigenous is used collectively to refer to First Nations, Métis and Inuit Peoples in Canada (Joseph, 2018, 111; Younging, 2018, 64–5), and is not intended to 'imply homogeneity of culture or of linguistic representations' (SFU Aboriginal Reconciliation Council, 2017, v). It is important to recognise and acknowledge 'that Indigenous peoples are diverse, multicultural, and multinational' (SFU Aboriginal Reconciliation Council, 2017, v). When possible, refer to the specific Nation by their name (Younging, 2018, 69–72).

A note on Canada

Canada is a relatively new concept. Officially, confederation took place in 1867, but some provinces, such as Newfoundland, did not confederate until 1949 (Waite, 2019). Canada is a young country with a complex past.

Before confederation, this land was home to hundreds of sovereign Nations that created treaties with foreign nations, mainly England (Waite, 2019). As history progressed, Canada shifted from seeing the original inhabitants as sovereign Nations, and in 1876, through the Indian Act, made these sovereign Nations wards of the state of Canada (Joseph, 2018, 8; Burton and Point [Stó:lō], 2006, 39–42).

Reconcile, decolonise, indigenise

Before we share our experiences within our institutions, we need to examine a few more terms. In Canada, the term 'reconciliation' gained traction in the media and in scholarly and popular literature following the 2015 final report and Calls to Action released by the Truth and Reconciliation Commission (TRC). Many of the Calls to Action are related to education, and call on professions to be 'properly educated and trained about the history and impacts of residential schools' (TRC, 2015a, 1). As a result, many Canadian academic institutions created reconciliation committees, as found in an environmental scan conducted by Ashley Edwards (2020a). These committees produced initiatives concerning Indigenising and/or decolonising. A first step in this work is understanding how these terms intersect and connect.

Reconciliation focuses on relationships, and definitions include reconciling one belief with another (Korff, 2020). So, this term has a twofold meaning in this work. The relationship between Indigenous Peoples and Canada requires work to arrive at a mutually trusting and respectful relationship. Like all relationships, this is going to take communication, commitment and renewal. Relationship reparation can only happen with 'awareness of the past, acknowledgement of the harm that has been inflicted, atonement for the causes, and action to change behaviour' (TRC, 2015b, 3). To enact transformative change this should be done at a personal level as well as an institutional and systemic level. For many, it will include unlearning myths about Canada and learning about Canada's genocidal history. People need to connect history with the realities Canada faces today, a nation that provides settlers with privilege derived from the wealth of the land and Indigenous Peoples without that privilege.

In their reconciliation efforts many people and institutions are engaged in decolonising and/or Indigenising practices. Often these terms are used interchangeably or together; however, they mean and imply different things. In their 2012 article, authors Tuck [Unangax̂] and Yang discuss how 'decolonisation' refers to giving the land back, to decolonise the physical space known today as Canada. They remind us that 'it is not a metaphor for other things we want to do to improve our societies and schools' (Tuck and Yang, 2012, 1). True decolonisation is not possible, since Canada is a settler-colonial country, meaning 'settlers come with the intention of making a new home on the land, a homemaking that insists on settler sovereignty over all things in their new domain' (Tuck and Yang, 2012, 5). True decolonisation can happen only if/when land is repatriated, otherwise it's symbolic (Tuck and Yang, 2012, 7). What institutions can participate in and enact are practices of Indigenisation.

When looked up in the dictionary, 'Indigenise' has a simple meaning, to make something Indigenous (Merriam-Webster). It's a simple word that in practice has complex and nuanced impacts. The actions of Indigenising create deep and transformative change, as it 'indicates incorporating Indigenous knowledge and ways of knowing into the core practice of the institution' (SFU Aboriginal Reconciliation Council, 2017, v). Authors Adam Gaudry [Métis] and Danielle Lorenz (2018) posit that Indigenisation is a spectrum, with three categories: Indigenous inclusion, reconciliation Indigenisation and decolonial Indigenisation (Gaudry and Lorenz, 2018, 218). Each of these categories has the ability to build off the others, yet often universities practise only Indigenous inclusion. Gaudry and Lorenz make the point that this isn't a criticism of the work Indigenous inclusion does; however, it should not be the only work an institution undertakes. Both reconciliation and decolonial Indigenisation would result in foundational changes to the academy, from governance to curriculum and teaching. In this way, an Indigenised academy could be the start of changes within society as students were exposed to different knowledges and ways of understanding the world.

With these understandings and background, we will now look at key legal documents that guide much of the current reconciliation and Indigenisation work within Canadian institutions.

Truth before reconciliation
Legal documents

There are a number of documents that have accelerated the development of Indigenous efforts throughout Canadian academic institutions. Within Canada the Truth and Reconciliation *Final Report* (TRC 2015b) and *Calls to Action* (2015a) are, arguably, the most pivotal, as of 2015. The TRC acknowledges Canada's abhorrent role in the formation and deployment of Residential Schools, in which children were forcibly removed from their families and communities (some as young as two), displaced under the guise of boarding school education, forced into what were essentially work camps modelled after the British Workhouses (Cooper-Bolam, 2019, 144–54), where the children were molested and abused (Gray, 2011, 61). The Residential School system became the template for racial atrocities throughout the world: Deputy Superintendent General of Indian Affairs Duncan Campbell Scott referred to the department and Residential Schools as part of the 'final solution of our Indian Problem' in 1910 (Joseph, 2018, 60), a turn of phrase more commonly associated with Nazi Germany and the Holocaust. Residential Schools did not fully close their doors until 1996 (Gray, 2011, 61).

Because the TRC identifies 'education' as a historic means of genocide, it strongly calls on education institutes to rectify and reconcile. Some key points include providing 'the necessary funding to post-secondary institutions to educate teachers on integrating Indigenous knowledge and teaching methods into the classroom' (TRC, 2015a, 10ii), as well as '[b]uilding student capacity for intercultural understanding, empathy, and mutual respect' (TRC, 2015a, 63iii). The TRC relies heavily on the United Nations (2007) Declaration on the Rights of Indigenous Peoples (UNDRIP) and often makes reference to this document (TRC, 2015b); so, while TRC's final report and Calls to Action may be the most pivotal documents within Canada, UNDRIP was absolutely necessary for laying the foundation.

Adopted in 2007, UNDRIP supports the Indigenous right to land and culture. Officially, Canada objected to UNDRIP until 2016; in 2019 Prime Minister Justin Trudeau announced his government's interest in implementing UNDRIP at the federal level. While there has been consultation with various Nations, Jorge Barrera (2019) reported in CBC News on 4 December 2019 that UNDRIP had yet to be passed federally. Without proper implementation and legal protection, UNDRIP cannot support Indigenous land, water and resource activism. How this impacts on information sharing and Indigenous ways of knowing is that the land can be viewed as a library. Indigenous '[l]iterature and stories can be found in more places than the Western standard ink and paper, extending to the "wampum belts, winter counts, birchbark scrolls, hieroglyphs, petroglyphs and pictographs"' (Edwards, 2006, 5; Edwards, 2019, 3). Assaults on the land often seek to eradicate Indigenous stories, histories, culture and Peoples.

Another key Canadian document is the 2019 *Murdered and Missing Indigenous Women and Girls* (MMIWG) report, which outlines the excessive rate of murders of Indigenous women and girls and the lack of recourse to justice within Canada. The MMIWG report explicitly states '[w]e call upon all … post-secondary institutions and education authorities to educate and provide awareness to the public about missing and murdered Indigenous women, girls, and 2SLGBTQQIA [Two Spirit, lesbian, gay, bisexual, transgender, queer, questioning, intersex, asexual] people, and about the issues and root causes of violence they experience' (MMIWG, 11.1). Many of these root causes have linked the rape and murder of Indigenous women and girls to the plunder and death of the land, and there have been numerous studies that link resource-extraction 'man-camps' to increased violence experienced by Indigenous women and girls (Dorries and Harjo, 2020, 214; Knott [Dane-Zaa, Nehiyaw, Métis], 2018, 150–7).

Sadly, government failure to engage in a meaningful response to the TRC *Calls to Action* and MMIWG is not an isolated event. Canada has failed to begin reconciliation, on numerous occasions. The Royal Commission on Aboriginal People (RCAP) consulted 96 communities over five years and released a final report in 1996 (Gray, 2011, 88–9). Canada's inaction led to 'the United Nations urging Canada to live up to their already limited commitments in *Gathering Strength*' (Minister of Indian Affairs and Northern Development, 1997) formal response (Gray, 2011, 88–9). RCAP's failure is compounded by broken treaties and lack of meaningful action with the TRC and MMIWG. It is no wonder that there are strained relations between Indigenous Peoples in Canada and the Government of Canada.

Education

Before sharing what our two institutions are doing to Indigenise their libraries, it's important to understand why this work is necessary. Education of Indigenous Peoples in Canada has a horrific history, with a sole purpose of assimilation. Residential Schools operated to 'kill the Indian in the child' and the Indian Act forced people to choose between post-secondary education and retaining their cultural identity (Joseph, 2018, 53). Today, the Western-European dominance of the curriculum and discipline-specific canons continue this assimilation, providing few opportunities for Indigenous students to 'see' themselves in their courses (Archibald, 2008, 14–15; Battiste, 2013, 23–33; Cote-Meek, 2014, 10; Gaudry and Lorenz, 2018, 221). Battiste (2013) refers to this as cognitive imperialism, which is the 'white-washing [of] the mind as a result of forced assimilation, English education, Eurocentric humanities and sciences, and living in a Eurocentric context complete with media, books, laws, values' (Battiste, 2013, 26).

Within this current state of education, educators need to be aware that by simply adding Indigenous readings – a form of Indigenisation described by Gaudry and Lorenz (2018, 218) as Indigenous inclusion – there is a risk of retraumatising students (Cote-Meek, 2014, 9). While it is important for both Indigenous and non-Indigenous students to learn about topics such as Residential Schools and the Sixties Scoop (a government shift where Indigenous children were forcibly removed from their homes and placed into foster care and/or adopted into non-Indigenous families in the 1960s, but which still continues today), it needs to be done with care. Students may have close family members who are survivors of either system, or be survivors themselves (Cote-Meek, 2014, 9). Many Indigenous communities are dealing with the intergenerational trauma of Canada's continued colonial and assimilationist policies (Cote-Meek, 2014, 10). Additionally, education should incorporate more than these negative aspects of Indigenous history. They should not be overlooked, but they are not representative of the culturally rich and diverse communities who have lived here since time immemorial. Integration of Indigenous knowledge and information needs to be done respectfully, and not as a token gesture towards reconciliation. To do this work in a good way, educators will themselves need to learn about Indigenous pedagogies and Indigenous scholars in their subject areas.

Libraries

Libraries are also sites of education and must come to terms with their own colonial history. As information professionals, we must ask how our profession inadvertently harmed Indigenous Peoples; followed up by, how can we do better? There has been a plethora of papers on the need to decolonise and Indigenise subject headings and classification schemes (e.g. Dudley, 2017; Vaughan, 2018), building inclusive collections (*Collection Management*, **42** (3–4), 2017) and diversifying programming (for examples see Roy and Frydman, 2017). It's important that libraries engage in transformative change and not stay in the Indigenous inclusion stage as identified by Gaudry and Lorenz (2018, 218). Our own education also needs to change (see Edwards, 2019) if we are going to make the transformative changes that are so needed.

While the TRC had few Calls to Action aimed at libraries specifically, the overarching call for educational changes includes libraries in all sectors. As extensions of post-secondary institutions, academic libraries are well placed to assist with reconciliation efforts within their institutions, providing assistance for faculty, staff and students (see Edwards, 2020b). In the final section of this chapter, we share some initiatives we have been involved with.

Our stories of indigenising libraries

Using a storywork methodology framework, we will next highlight some of our initiatives. Jo-ann Archibald [Stó:lō] reminds us that '[s]haring [stories] can take the form of a story of personal life experience' (Archibald, 2008, 2). For Indigenous Peoples, storytelling is an active experience for both the teller and the listener. Nicole Penak [Maliseet and Mi'kmaq First Nations] notes: 'Indigenous storytelling, which is predominantly based on oral delivery and aural reception, requires an active audience, listener, or reader. With this understanding, your contribution to this story is of great importance. I want to invite you to consider your role in this tale as participatory, actively engaging with the other beings, stories, and experiences shared in this chapter' (Penak, 2018, 259).

It is our hope that you will see this as a participatory invitation. Too often the discourse of decolonisation and Indigenisation gets trapped in the perils of settler guilt or fear (Lowman and Barker, 2015, 90–5). Jo-ann Archibald emphasises that storytelling 'is done with a compassionate mind and love for others' (Archibald, 2008, 2); as such, we ask that you also practise self-compassion and self-love. We recognise and acknowledge that colonisation inflicts wounds on everyone, and we are mindful of this as we write.

The beauty and joy of storytelling is that it allows the listener to take meaning as they are ready. Stories 'touch us where we are, today, here, in our bodies and our hearts, to challenge us to think, to examine our emotional reactions, and to reflect on a story's connectedness to our own lives and spirit and extend that connectedness to the rest of creation' (Penak, 2018, 259). The stories we share today are 'not prescriptive in nature, with an index to follow applicable solutions to life's challenges' (Penak, 2018, 262). We humbly present our stories in the hopes that some elements will resonate with you – our readers – in helping to see 'the upside down, the opposite, and the other balances of things around us' (Graveline, 1998, 11, quoted in Penak, 2018, 262).

Simon Fraser University

When I (Ashley) started my role as Indigenous Curriculum Resource Centre Librarian in 2020, I started by conducting an environmental scan of academic libraries and their reconciliatory action. It was clear that universities across the nation were seeking ways to address the TRC's *Calls to Action*. Often, institutions created a committee or council to look at ways reconciliation efforts could be enacted, and centres with variations on the name of Teaching and Learning provided lists of resources to support these efforts.

Simon Fraser University was no different, with the Aboriginal Reconciliation Council (ARC) forming in 2016. Over fall 2016 and spring 2017, ARC consulted with Indigenous communities both on campus and off to gather information used to develop reconciliation goals (SFU Aboriginal Reconciliation Council, 2017, 11). In the fall of 2017 the ARC released its report, *Walk This Path with Us*, which provided a brief history of Indigenous education in Canada, and 34 Calls to Action. SFU Library responded to this report by forming its own Decolonizing the Library Task Group (which became a Working Group), and I was asked to join. Like many people starting decolonising and Indigenising work, we all came to this work with different levels of understanding and education on Indigenous topics, so, initially, the work was focused on self-education and reflection. This time also allowed us to create a strong sense of community within the group, something I believe is necessary when people are in a process of unlearning (i.e. Canada's mythology as a multicultural country) and learning (i.e. the genocidal history of the colonisation of Canada). In practice this work may not have an immediate tangible outcome. The Decolonizing the Library Working Group spent between six and nine months working on self-education before beginning any outreach. After this initial process, an action plan was drafted, and we held kitchen table conversations (Box 8.2) with Indigenous faculty, students and on-campus groups such as the Indigenous Student Centre (ISC). The action plan was focused on staff education, Indigenising library practices (e.g. cataloguing practices, and Indigenising library spaces).

> **Box 8.2: Kitchen table conversations**
> Kitchen table conversations are informal group gatherings, sometimes called circles, often at someone's house. People come together, with something to eat and drink, to discuss an issue, share information, or teach. For more information on this methodology see Kovach (2009) or O'Connor (2020).

Building a relationship with the ISC and listening to what the students identify as needs requires time. For example, the ISC closes each afternoon at 4:30 and the students expressed the problem of not having anywhere to go as a group and continue working together. The Library offered one of its bookable group study spaces and (in pre-COVID times) set one aside for the students to use. The ISC provided some art to make it feel more like a continuation of ISC space, and students often gathered there in the late afternoons and evenings. Additionally, the ISC used the Library's Media and Maker Commons to host a drum-making workshop for Indigenous students. This relationship between the Library and the ISC remains strong, even during the 2020 work-from-home situation. Library staff have provided workshops and drop-in sessions and assisted with a book club, all virtually.

For library staff, initiatives have been around education and the sharing of fiction titles and podcasts that Working Group members enjoy on the staff blog. A separate group has formed, the Decolonising the Library Interest Group (DIG), to help facilitate that work. Each semester a reading circle is held, with books picked by staff; so far we have read *Bad Endings* by Carleigh Baker, *Braiding Sweetgrass* by Robin Wall Kimmerer and one summer focused on how to Indigenise library instruction. In 2019 a colleague and I presented a workshop at the Canadian Association of Professional Academic Librarians (CAPAL) conference held in Vancouver, where we shared a brief outline of education's – and by extension academic libraries' – colonial roots. We talked about the Indian Act, its assimilation tactics and why it is important to understand this when talking about reconciliation both in libraries and in post-secondary institutions. At the request of SFU Library management and training co-ordinators we have facilitated the workshop several times for library staff. In the fall of 2020 the members of DIG created a workshop on how to write a personal land acknowledgement, after examining personal positionality (see www.lib.sfu.ca/help/academic-integrity/indigenous-initiatives/icrc/land-acknowledgement-workshop). This workshop was well received and will be offered again in the future.

In addition to seeking ways to Indigenise library space and provide education for staff, the Library has undertaken a response to ARC's Calls to Action 12 and 21, which call for the Indigenisation of curriculum and the creation of an Indigenous Curriculum Resource Centre. It is this Centre that I have been hired to develop, and it will focus primarily on providing faculty and instructors with the resources to Indigenise their pedagogy and curriculum. During the consultations done by ARC members, it was found that while many faculty are keen to engage in this work, and recognise its importance, they don't know where or how to start. The collection is made up of titles to support this work, which will complement the titles in the general collection. What this means is that while there wouldn't be books in the ICRC on linguistic theory, for example, but there would be books on language revitalisation or Indigenous language programmes.

One exciting aspect of the collection is how it is going to be catalogued. Rather than using the Library of Congress Classification system that many academic libraries use, I am creating a locally modified version of the Brian Deer Classification System. The Deer system was created in the 1970s by Mohawk librarian Brian Deer while he was working at the National Indian Brotherhood (now known as the Assembly of First Nations) (Cherry and Mukunda, 2015, 552). He wanted a system that better represented Indigenous worldviews and relationships, neither of which is well represented in the Library of Congress or the Dewey Decimal System (Cherry and Mukunda, 2015, 549–50; Bosum and Dunne, 2017, 284). The system was also designed to be flexible, allowing for modifications to suit the collection rather than forcing the collection to fit into a system (Cherry and Mukunda, 2015, 553; Bosum and Dunne, 2017, 284, 286); this is why the system is referred to as a locally modified version. In British Columbia, the two most well-known versions of the Deer system are from the Xwi7xwa branch of the University of British Columbia Library and the Union of BC Indian Chiefs library. For the ICRC version I have relied heavily on both, plus conversations with staff at Xwi7xwa. While a full discussion about the Deer system is out of scope for this chapter, some highlights of its importance and value as an Indigenous classification system include: organising communities geographically rather than alphabetically, moving Indigenous knowledge and topics out of the History of North America section, and in general treating Indigenous topics and knowledge with more respect.

As 2020 draws to a close, I am looking forward to what opportunities and initiatives the Library and the ICRC have in the planning stages for next year. I have been working with SFU's Centre for Educational Excellence to develop resources, and scheduling informal gatherings for faculty across disciplines to share their experiences – with the hope of breaking down some discipline-specific silos so often found on campuses. Some colleagues and I are working together to examine ways of supporting faculty in decolonial and anti-racist assignment design and evaluation practices. It is an exciting time to be working in academic libraries as an Indigenous librarian, and I am full of optimism for the impacts this work will have for future generations.

Kwantlen Polytechnic University (KPU)

Upon viewing the job posting for Indigenous Engagement and Subject Liaison Librarian at KPU in 2019, I (Rachel) applied with trepidation. I was acutely aware that while I was a card-carrying Métis person, I did not want to misrepresent my experience as being immersed in culture. My learning of Indigeneity was a result of personal interest and efforts, not passed onto me via Protocol and respected community Elders. Despite my shortcomings, I was delighted when KPU Library contacted me as the successful candidate for the newly created Indigenous Librarian position. I have always been attracted to new projects, and the blank slate (of sorts) that this new position provided was the perfect place to start.

It takes a while to become acclimated to a new work environment. I was most grateful for a warm welcome to KPU's Indigenous Advisory Committee and to the established Gathering Place managed by KPU's Indigenous Services for Students, where I had the privilege of connecting with Indigenous staff, faculty and the Elder in Residence Lekeyten. Through my time at the Gathering Place I learned much, including the need for some form of Indigenous Information Literacy – at the request of both faculty and Indigenous Peoples on campus.

As I was deliberating how best to deliver Indigenous Information Literacy in a way that honoured Indigenous learning strategies, COVID-19 descended. This provided a unique opportunity to deliver video content that more closely mirrored face-to-face oral instruction. Before this, the resources for developing video content were slim and fractured, but with the move to online learning suddenly an abundance of financial and technical support transformed this method of instruction.

Working from my template for live instruction, I began with a short video, which I thought might be ten minutes in length, for instructors to integrate into their classes at

KPU. After consulting with a number of people both within KPU Library and in the broader Indigenous Librarian network, it became apparent that there was an appetite for this content beyond my own institution. The short video evolved into a video series exceeding 40 minutes in length and covering topics from source evaluation, Elder and Knowledge Keeper citation, to Tri-Council Policy Statement: Ethical Conduct for Research (TCPS2) (Kwantlen Polytechnic University, 2020). I would not consider myself an expert on any of these topics, but I did research to the best of my ability to select credible sources that support this work. It is my hope that this series will serve both the KPU community and the broader academic community in terms of expanding student and faculty knowledge on Indigenous information best practices.

While working on the Indigenous Information Literacy instruction, other, simultaneous activities were in the works, including an 'Indigenous Authors' local subject term addition to our catalogue to amplify Indigenous voices. Authors are researched manually and Indigenous authors are individually noted to facilitate diverse voices within student and faculty research.

I was also heavily involved in the development of the KPU Library's Strategic Plan, with one of the six pillars being 'Indigenising Library Practices and Inspiring Reciprocal Reconciliatory Relationships' (Kwantlen Polytechnic University Library, 2020, 8). The Library's Strategic Plan includes pieces on respectful use of Traditional Knowledge, Elder sources and citation. It also includes educating employees both for their own personal interest and in pedagogical content integration for students. One of the personal education pieces the Library contributes to is the Indigenous Book Club, which is a collaboration with KPU's Indigenous Services for Students. We select Indigenous-authored titles and often have the author make a visit. Titles vary to emphasise the diversity of Indigenous Peoples, and include *Life Stages of Native Women* by Cree/Métis educator Kim Anderson and *Potlatch as Pedagogy* by Sara Florence Davidson and Robert Davidson of Haida and Tlingit ancestry.

It has been so incredibly rewarding to come to academic libraries at a time when momentum is growing for Indigenous voices. Having supportive management greatly facilitates this work. Thanks to documents and organisations like UNDRIP, TRC, MMIWG, and RCAP, there is growing awareness and interest in this information both within academia and beyond. I am optimistic that the future our children will inherit will be one that is more accepting, inclusive and respectful of Indigenous voices, experiences and place in the world.

Conclusion

Post-secondary institutions are making some efforts to Indigenise. Still, much work needs to be done to make the university an inviting and welcoming space for Indigenous Peoples to want to participate in. This includes library space. In this chapter we have offered a glimpse into our own experiences in embracing and learning about our

Indigeneity. We have shared with you some initiatives and programmes that we are each involved with in our respective academic libraries, as well as a brief overview of what Indigenising means.

This work cannot happen without learning more of the truth behind Canadian interactions with Indigenous Peoples. If we understand reconciliation to be a relationship, then both Indigenous and non-Indigenous people need to participate in this learning process. Indigenising libraries and academic institutions requires an open mind and heart. Only then will we be engaged in reconciliation work.

In the tradition of our host Nations, we raise our hands in thanks for your active listening, witnessing and participation. Hay cep q̓ə/hay čxʷ q̓ə ('thank you', in Downriver Halkomelem) and ch'íthométsel ('I thank you', in Upriver Halq'eméylem).

Reflections

As we come to the end of our stories, we want to take some time to reflect on our experiences and challenges. While writing this chapter, we had many conversations which can be thought of as learning and/or research circles (Kovach, 2009, 123–4, 152–3; Wilson, 2008, 32, 70). The following section is arranged thematically, and loosely transcribed from our own kitchen table talks where, through informal conversation, 'knowledge is shared and relationships are strengthened' (O'Connor, 2020, 93).

Experiences within educational institutions

Rachel Chong (RC): There was a noticeable lack of visible Indigenous students and faculty in school – both Kindergarten to Grade 12 (K–12) and in post-secondary – and little to no Indigenous content or voices within the curriculum. What was there was often negative. When you look at the statistics and see that few Indigenous students are continuing to post-secondary, you can see why! Relationships between students and instructors are so important.

The typically 300 people in a lecture hall or the 'sage on the stage approach' doesn't work for an Indigenous worldview. It's one thing to talk about Indigenising the MLIS (Masters in Library and Information Science) or undergrad degrees, another to actually do this work.

Ashley Edwards (AE): I also had little to no Indigenous content in my K–12, but it seems so normal, I didn't question the lack in my undergrad studies until well after I graduated. I suppose that's how assimilist education works? It perpetuates the erasure of history, culture, knowledge. So I didn't have any connections to Indigenous communities or people, nor did I know how to seek them out. The one time I tried in high school, I was told by the Aboriginal Support Worker or whatever the job title was that my heritage didn't count because I was not status 'Indian'. Because of that, I never sought out Indigenous support at my university. Reflecting back, it was a huge rejection and act of lateral violence.

Library education

RC: Even working towards making the MLIS more attractive to Indigenous students, there are barriers in terms of undergrad completion and getting interested people into the programmes. Barriers particularly with time and money.

AE: Yes!! And geography. Remote communities don't have the same opportunity, even for online education, because many don't have the infrastructure. Have you read Deborah Lee's [Cree-Métis] 2017 article, 'Indigenous Librarians: Knowledge Keepers in the 21st Century'? She talked with Indigenous library workers, and the barriers of location and money were mentioned, but also having to move from your community to attend academic programmes.

RC: We see the same problems with many post-secondary programmes; hopefully this is changing. Lack of Indigenous curriculum, faculty, funding and peer support.

AE: As you know, I recently graduated. There were few Indigenous voices in the assigned readings; the only one that comes to mind was a chapter on Indigenous research methodologies from Māori scholar Linda Tuhiwai Smith's (1999) book. It was a great chapter, but there should have been more, and from Indigenous Peoples in Canada. There are so many amazing Indigenous scholars we could have read – many we've used writing this chapter!

RC: What about your lib tech school?

AE: There was nothing. Even in all the required courses on classification and cataloguing, we only looked at the mainstream systems, Dewey, Library of Congress and Sears. Reflecting back, this just perpetuates all the issues we talk about now with language used (such as 'Indians of North America') and representation. If you don't see yourself in the work, especially in a respectful way, why would you apply to the programme?

RC: Why would you want to work in an environment like that!

AE: Exactly. I think libraries need to acknowledge their colonial roots, like academic institutions. From there, make changes to better represent and reflect society as a whole rather than colonial society. To be more inclusive.

Indigenous representation

AE: Let's talk about inclusion within educational institutions. There's been a lot of papers and book chapters that examine the lack of Indigenous faculty within Canadian institutions (for example, *The Equity Myth*, by Henry et al., 2017). So, the only way to become a faculty member is through a graduate degree, and for that you need an undergrad degree. That's a lot of education, formal education, that presents barriers to Indigenous people, like we talked about a minute ago.

The other aspect to keep in mind is that until 1952 the Indian Act forced enfranchisement, which was when a person became a Canadian citizen and was removed from their community. So they could no longer live on reserve, lost their status, lost community and family support.

RC: That's a lot to give up just for a colonial education. Communities had their own education systems, and ways of educating themselves.

You aren't going to get Indigenous deans if the barriers are preventing Indigenous PhDs. If the leadership isn't Indigenous, you aren't able to address those deep systemic issues.

Indigenisation

RC: Systemic issues can't be addressed without people doing some hard, internal work first. That can take a lot of time.

AE: Time, and openness. We probably both grew up hearing how 'superior' Canada is compared to the USA in terms of racism, and how we're multicultural. Except when you start learning about Indigenous history and colonialism, you really see that that idea of Canada is a myth. That can be really hard for some people to understand, and accept.

RC: So much was missing from public school education, and that is changing but it's a slow process. For many adults it's going to be self-directed learning, and it's hard to know where to start.

AE: Even for ourselves! Not growing up in community, everything that I'm learning is coming from my seeking it out both through Indigenous popular media (books, podcasts, films) and more scholarly work that is also informing my work as a librarian.

RC: Supportive management really fosters this learning. Ashley, I know Jenna has been really supportive of your work, and Todd with mine, whether learning from academic text or otherwise. A lot of learning happens in community and sharing space with other Indigenous Peoples. Ashley, I know you've mentioned attending Pow Wows. Going to Métis Nation meetings and National Indigenous Peoples' Day events. But even participating in online communities popping up on Facebook, Instagram, these are really powerful tools for Indigenous Peoples to connect. It's really remarkable to see Indigenous Peoples reclaim cultural traditions, empower themselves politically and growing community. These are all things that were taken from us via colonialism.

AE: Engaging with community is so important – it's how we met! But people need to come to events prepared to learn. Sometimes that might mean doing some learning through reading or watching a film or listening to a podcast beforehand. Not expecting the Indigenous people at an event to teach you everything.

RC: Or anything! Colonial learning styles are so different from Indigenous learning styles. You might not pick up on the learning that's available at an event. It isn't a question-and-answer situation; deep learning happens when you internalise what you're hearing or seeing or reading. You need to work through it yourself, experience it yourself. You don't get that internalised knowledge from a quick response.

AE: Because both Indigenous learning and relationships take time, supportive management is really important. The whole team really needs to be on board to support systemic change, and supportive management has the greatest impact on actualising these changes. I think we've both been really fortunate to have support from Jenna, Gwen (SFU Library's Dean) and Todd, respectively; it isn't always the case. One place I think that could be improved is having more continuing, full-time positions for this work. Too often positions related to Indigenising (or equality, diversity and inclusion) are short-term contracts, which can make it tough or impossible to enact meaningful change and build lasting relationships with other departments and Indigenous communities.

[Short pause, both of us deep in thought.]

AE: Which brings us back to Indigenising academic institutions, including libraries. Library staff need to have the support, particularly time and funding, to participate in professional development around Indigenous librarianship. Which, to me, includes Indigenising our libraries.

References

Archibald, J. (2008) *Indigenous Storywork: Educating the Heart, Mind, Body, and Spirit*, University of British Columbia Press.

Barrera, J. (2019) Trudeau Government Moving Forward on UNDRIP Legislation, says Minister, *CBC News*, 4 December, www.cbc.ca/news/indigenous/trudeau-undrip-bill-1.5383755 (accessed 1 March 2021).

Battiste, M. (2013) *Decolonizing Education: Nourishing the Learning Spirit*, Purich.

Bosum, A. and Dunne, A. (2017) Implementing the Brian Deer Classification Scheme for Aanischaaukamikw Cree Cultural Institute, *Collection Management*, 42 (3–4), 280–93, DOI: 10.1080/01462679.2017.1340858.

Burton, W. and Point, G. (2006) Histories of Aboriginal Adult Education in Canada. In Fenwick, T., Nesbit, T. and Spencer, B. (eds), *Contexts of Adult Education: Canadian Perspectives*, Thompson Educational Publishing Inc.

Cherry, A. and Mukunda, K. (2015) A Case Study in Indigenous Classification: Revisiting and Reviving the Brian Deer Scheme, *Cataloging & Classification Quarterly*, 53 (5–6), 548–67, DOI: 10.1080/01639374.2015.1008717.

Cooper-Bolam, T. (2019) Workhouses and Residential Schools: From Institutional Models to Museums. In Pyne, S. and Fraser Taylor, D. R. (eds), *Cybercartography in a Reconciliation Community: Engaging Intersecting Perspectives*, Elsevier, www.elsevier.com/books/cybercartography-in-a-reconciliation-community/pyne/978-0-12-815343-7.

Cote-Meek, S. (2014) *Colonized Classrooms: Racism, Trauma and Resistance in Post-Secondary Education*, Fernwood Publishing.

Dorries, H. and Harjo, L. (2020) Beyond Safety: Refusing Colonial Violence through Indigenous Feminist Planning, *Journal of Planning Education and Research*, **40** (2), 210–19, DOI: 10.1177/0739456x19894382.

Dudley, M. Q. (2017) A Library Matter of Genocide: The Library of Congress and the Historiography of the Native American Holocaust, *The International Indigenous Policy Journal*, **8** (2), DOI: 10.18584/iipj.2017.8.2.9.

Edwards, B. F. R. (2006) *Paper Talk: A History of Libraries, Print Culture, and Aboriginal Peoples in Canada before 1960*, Scarecrow Press.

Edwards, A. (2019) Unsettling the Future by Uncovering the Past: Decolonising Academic Libraries and Librarianship, *Partnership: The Canadian Journal of Library and Information Practice and Research*, **14** (1), https://doi.org/10.21083/partnership.v14i1.5161.

Edwards, A. (2020a) External Environmental Scan (unpublished manuscript, 7 August).

Edwards, A. (2020b) When Knowledge Goes Underground: Cultural Information Poverty, and Canada's Indian Act, *Pathfinder: A Canadian Journal for Information Science Students and Early Career Professionals*, **1** (2), 19–35, https://doi.org/10.29173/pathfinder14.

Gadacz, R. and Gallant, D. (2019) First Nations. In *The Canadian Encyclopedia*. Article published 7 February 2006; last modified 6 August 2019, https://thecanadianencyclopedia.ca/en/article/first-nations (accessed 1 March 2021).

Gaudry, A. and Lorenz, D. (2018) Indigenization as Inclusion, Reconciliation, and Decolonization: Navigating the Different Visions for Indigenizing the Canadian Academy, *AlterNative: An International Journal of Indigenous Peoples*, **14** (3), 218–27, https://doi.org/10.1177/1177180118785382.

Gray, L. (2011) *First Nations 101: Tons of Stuff You Need to Know About First Nations People*, Adaawx Publishing.

Henry, F., James, C. E., Kobayashi, A., Li, P., Ramos, H. and Smith, M. S. (2017) *The Equity Myth: Racialization and Indigeneity at Canadian Universities*, University of British Columbia Press.

Indigenous Corporate Training (2016) Indigenous or Aboriginal: Which Is Correct? (blog), 5 January, www.ictinc.ca/blog/indigenous-or-aboriginal-which-is-correct (accessed 1 March 2021).

Joseph, B. (2018) *21 Things You May Not Know About the Indian Act: Helping Canadians Make Reconciliation with Indigenous Peoples a Reality*, Indigenous Relations Press.

Justice, D. H. (2018) *Why Indigenous Literature Matters*, Wilfrid Laurier University Press.

Kendi, I. X. (2019) *How to Be an Antiracist*, Penguin Random House.

Knott, H. (2018) Violence and Extraction: Stories from the Oil Fields. In Campbell, M., Anderson, K. and Belcourt, C. (eds), *Keetsahnak/Our Missing and Murdered Indigenous Sisters*, University of Alberta Press.

Korff, J. (2020) What You Need to Know About Reconciliation, *Creative Spirits*, www.creativespirits.info/aboriginalculture/people/what-you-need-to-know-about-reconciliation#:~:text=In%20its%20broadest%20sense%20%27reconciliation,again%20after%20they%20have%20argued.&text=Reconciliation%20has%20elements%20of%20truth,healing%2C%20reparation%2C%20and%20love (accessed 1 March 2021).

Kovach, M. (2009) *Indigenous Methodologies: Characteristics, Conversations, and Contexts*, University of Toronto Press.

Kwantlen Polytechnic University (2020) *Indigenous Information Literacy*, https://libguides.kpu.ca/indigenous/indigenousinformationliteracy (accessed 1 March 2021).

Kwantlen Polytechnic University Library (2020) *KPU Library Strategic Plan*, www.kpu.ca/sites/default/files/Library/KPU%20Library%20Strategic%20Plan%20draft_Final_0.pdf (accessed 1 March 2021).

Lee, D. (2017) Discussion Section: Indigenous Librarians: Knowledge Keepers in the 21st Century, *Canadian Journal of Native Studies*, 37 (1), 175–99.

Lowman, E. B. and Barker, A. J. (2015) *Settler: Identity and Colonialism in 21st Century Canada*, Fernwood Press.

Merriam-Webster, s.v. Indigenize, www.merriam-webster.com/dictionary/Indigenise (accessed 1 March 2021).

Métis Nation Canada (n.d.) Citizenship, www2.Metisnation.ca/about/citizenship.

Minister of Indian Affairs and Northern Development (1997) *Gathering Strength: Canada's Aboriginal Action Plan*, https://www.ahf.ca/downloads/gathering-strength.pdf (accessed 23 June 2021).

National Enquiry into Missing and Murdered Indigenous Women and Girls. (MMIWG) (2019) *Reclaiming Power and Place*, https://www.mmiwg-ffada.ca/final-report (accessed 23 June 2021).

O'Connor, C. J. (2020) Colonial and Indigenous Language Policies at McGill University: Beliefs, Mechanisms, and Practices, MA thesis, McGill University.

Parent, A. (2018) Research Tales with Txeemsim (Raven, the Trickster). In McGregor, D., Restoule, J. and Johnston, R. (eds), *Indigenous Research: Theories, Practices, and Relationships*, Canadian Scholars.

Penak, N. (2018) A Story Pathway: Restoring Wholeness in the Research Process. In McGregor, D., Restoule, J. and Johnston, R. (eds), *Indigenous Research: Theories, Practices, and Relationships*, Canadian Scholars.

Roy, L. and Frydman, A. (2017) *Library Services to Indigenous Populations: Case Studies*, www.ifla.org/publications/library-services-to-indigenous-populations—case-studies (accessed 1 March 2021).

SFU (Simon Fraser University) Aboriginal Reconciliation Council (2017) *Walk This Path with Us*, www.sfu.ca/aboriginalpeoples/sfu-reconciliation.html (accessed 1 March 2021).

Smith, L. T. (1999) *Decolonizing Methodologies: Research and Indigenous Peoples*, Zed Books.

TRC (Truth and Reconciliation Commission) (2015a) *Calls to Action*, http://nctr.ca/reports.php (accessed 1 March 2021).

TRC (2015b) *Canada's Residential Schools: Reconciliation: The Final Report of the Truth and Reconciliation Commission of Canada Volume 6,* http://nctr.ca/reports.php (accessed 1 March 2021).

Tuck, E. and Yang, K. W. (2012) Decolonization Is Not a Metaphor, *Decolonization: Indigeneity, Education & Society*, **1** (1), 1–40.

United Nations (2007) *United Nations Declaration on the Rights of Indigenous Peoples*, www.un.org/development/desa/indigenouspeoples/wp-content/uploads/sites/19/2018/11/UNDRIP_E_web.pdf (accessed 1 March 2021).

Vaughan, C. (2018) The Language of Cataloguing: Deconstructing and Decolonizing Systems of Organization in Libraries, *Dalhousie Journal of Interdisciplinary Management*, **14**, 1–15, https://doi.org/10.5931/djim.v14i0.7853.

Vowel, C. (2016) *Indigenous Writes: A Guide to First Nations, Métis and Inuit Issues in Canada*, Highwater Press.

Waite, P. B. (2019) Confederation. In *The Canadian Encyclopedia*. Article first published 22 September 2013, modified October 2019, www.thecanadianencyclopedia.ca/en/article/confederation (accessed 1 March 2021).

Wilson, S. (2008) *Research is Ceremony: Indigenous Research Methods*, Fernwood Publishing.

Younging, G. (2018) *Elements of Indigenous Style: A Guide for Writing By and About Indigenous Peoples*, Brush Education.

9
Liberating the Library: What it Means to Decolonise and Why it is Necessary

Marilyn Clarke

Introduction

> I celebrate teaching that enables transgressions – a movement against and beyond boundaries. It is that movement which makes education the practice of freedom.
>
> (hooks, 1994, 12)

This chapter will discuss the commitment to anti-racist practice by library workers who seek to engage with social movements – predominantly led and created by university students and progressive academics – calling for social justice in educational spaces, in particular, in the westernised university, which has many sites around the world due to the ongoing influence of empire and colonialism. It will look at how our praxis as library workers is steeped in racism and coloniality, hence the use of the term 'decolonisation' and/or 'decoloniality'. It will also focus on the work of the Liberate Our Library initiative at my current institution, Goldsmiths, University of London, which posits itself in the arena of critical librarianship, which draws from critical theory, critical information literacy and critical race theory (CRT), which asks library workers to 'consider the historical, cultural, social, economic, political and other forces that affect information' (Gregory and Higgins, 2013, 7). hooks writes of the classroom as a space to experience freedom, and eventually empowerment, through rethinking teaching practices that lead to systemic changes around race and representation. So too can library workers 'transgress' by rethinking professional practices that disempower and silence certain voices and experiences, and instead work with educators and users to empower the voices kept silent for far too long.

Using such terminologies can often depend on the racial and cultural identity of the author, their geographical location, their class, their socio-economic status and their experience of the education system in which they were taught. I am a Black, British, working-class woman of mixed heritage (German/Hungarian–Jamaican) born and raised in London and educated in the comprehensive, state school system – a system that to this day does not teach Black British history to school children. A UK-based social enterprise called The Black Curriculum (2019), with its roots in student-led activism, has taken up the mantle to go into schools and teach Black British history, due to the 'lack of Black British history in the UK Curriculum'. A Black British school child is more likely to leave school with more knowledge of Black African American history (particularly the civil rights period) than of their own Black British history. The academic year 2020–21 saw the launch of the MA in Black British History at Goldsmiths, University of London. 'You'll not only learn about Black British histories, which have been marginalised from our public understandings of British history and are too often invisible in education and in the media, you'll also join in the work of researching and sharing the histories of Black people in Britain' (Goldsmiths, University of London, 2020b).

To me, the experience of growing up intersectional in the UK, with both its history and its present steeped in the British Empire and colonialism, requires a dismantling of the systems that exist as a result of Britain's invasive, more often violent, presence at one time across almost three-fifths of the world. I cannot divorce my intersectional identities and experiences from the terminologies used to describe what I see as essentially liberation work, leading towards social justice and demonstrable change. I seek to liberate and decolonise myself and my thinking as well as the spaces – both physical and virtual – in which I work and practice. In turn, I seek to use practices that work towards liberating the library, in all its manifestations, as discussed in this chapter.

Before we can talk about decolonising the library, we have to talk about building a movement of people to lead and do the necessary work, without whom nothing will change. The inspirational Executive Director of the American Library Association, Tracie D. Hall, commented in *Information Professional* (2020) on the necessary role of library workers as 'activists': 'to be a librarian in the 21st century is to recognise that we must attend to the social issues that make for the differences in information access and equity. I think that we have to imagine ourselves as activists.' I wholeheartedly agree; without the people as activists, the work will not happen. Change rarely comes from those at the top or in positions of power. Change comes from grassroots organisers, often from those who are themselves marginalised and under-represented in well-established systems of power.

It is all too easy to catch the *zeitgeist* and adapt our language without fully understanding what one is actually committing to. Society at its performative best, can profess to be 'multicultural', 'post-racial' and still be racist. Employers can commit to 'equal opportunities', 'diversity', 'inclusion' and still be racist. This has been all too evident in 2020 following the racist murder of George Floyd in Minneapolis, Minnesota. Statements and commitments to change and finally address racism in all its forms were released in what is viewed as a turning point in our history on the road to eradicate racism. Similarly, universities can cry 'No to racism!' yet fail to recognise their own deeply entrenched systemic racism. The academic library exists within the environment of the university structure and is therefore by default systemically racist. Today, one must be cognisant of social injustice and social inequity in order to participate in social justice.

Knowledge democracy

If we are to talk of decolonising collections, we must first understand where we exist and reside in the world and through which lens the knowledge within our collections has come. Boaventura de Sousa Santos (Professor of Sociology at the University of Coimbra, Portugal and Distinguished Legal Scholar at the University of Wisconsin–Madison) declares, 'there will be no global social justice until there is global cognitive justice' (de Sousa Santos, 2014, vii). De Sousa Santos is a world-leading intellectual who is part of a movement of Global South scholars who challenge the dominance of Western and Global North ideologies at the expense of all other world knowledge. In other words, it is Eurocentrism that dominates because of the legacy of empire, colonialism and the transatlantic slave trade. Similarly, Cupples and Grosfoguel speak of the 'westernized' university where 'the production, acquisition and dissemination of knowledge are embedded in Eurocentric epistemologies that are posited as objective, disembodied and universal and in which non-Eurocentric knowledges such as black and indigenous knowledges are largely ignored, marginalized or dismissed' (Cupples and Grosfoguel, 2019, 2).

If we are in the UK, then that knowledge is Eurocentric, and it essentially relies on a Eurocentric canon. Mbembe (2015, 10) posits that 'the emerging consensus is that our institutions must undergo a process of decolonization both of knowledge and of the university as an institution'. As a result of being an adjunct of the academy, libraries are also part of the Eurocentric academic model, and therefore engaged in 'epistemic coloniality'. If one looks at the production of academic knowledge, it is evident that the USA dominates academic publishing. It is because of imperialism and colonialism that the Western canon dominates the curricula of the vast majority of universities across the world. However, the call for 'knowledge democracy' and 'decoloniality' grows louder by the day particularly from Latin American scholars pushing for the representation of different voices in a move away from the predominance of Western knowledge and culture. In a blog piece from 2013, Rajesh Tandon posits that 'different voices represent different forms and expressions of knowledge – different modes and articulations of knowledge from diverse experiences, locations and perspectives. This is the essence of "knowledge democracy" – a movement that respects multiple modes, forms, sources and idioms of knowledge production, representation and dissemination' (Tandon, 2013).

These scholars envision a knowledge that embraces multiple forms, from texts to drama and from story to ceremony. Grosfoguel (2013) writes of the 'four Genocides/Epistemicides of the Long 16th Century', which explain how the colonisation of knowledge happened from its Islamic centre to its European centre. The four epistemicides are: the displacement of Muslims and Jews from Europe; the invasion of the Indigenous Peoples of the Americas; the transatlantic slave trade; and the murder of Indo-European women deemed to be witches because of their knowledge practices. Grosfoguel highlights the burning of libraries as the physical manifestation of conquest:

> In addition to the genocide of people, the conquest of Al-Andalus was accompanied by epistemicide. For example, the burning of libraries was a fundamental method used in the conquest of Al-Andalus. The library of Cordoba, that had around 500,000 books at a time when the largest library of Christian Europe did not have more than 1000 books, was burned in the 13th century. Many other libraries had the same destiny during the conquest of Al-Andalus until the final burning of more than 250,000 books of the Granada library by Cardinal Cisneros in the early 16th century. These methods were extrapolated to the Americas. Thus, the same happened with the indigenous 'códices' which was the written practice used by Amerindians to archive knowledge. Thousands of 'códices' were also burned destroying indigenous knowledges in the Americas. Genocide and epistemicide went together in the process of conquest in both the Americas and Al-Andalus.
>
> (Grosfoguel, 2013, 79–80)

As librarians, it is important that as the gatekeepers of knowledges that exist within collections we recognise and acknowledge 'this violence, that detached and disaffiliated colonized people from their rich pre-invasion worlds and is still shielded in Western museums, archives and libraries …' (Azoulay, 2019, 77). Alongside the movement to tear down statues that glorify the Empire, so too there are many movements towards repatriating violently plundered objects which adorn the walls, display cases and floors of the Western world's museums, galleries and archives. In her seminal publication, *Decolonising Methodologies: Research and Indigenous Peoples*, Linda Tuhiwai Smith (2012, 10) states that 'I wrote [it] primarily to disrupt relationships between a colonizing institution of knowledge and colonized peoples whose own knowledge was subjugated, between academic theories and academic values, between institutions and communities …'. Through the decolonisation of research methods, Smith reclaims control over Indigenous knowledge and knowledge gathering, thus rewriting and re-legitimising what was thwarted, disregarded and destroyed through the processes of colonisation.

Student activism and the birth of Liberate Our Library

The Rhodes Must Fall protest movement which began at the University of Cape Town (UCT), South Africa in March 2015 set off a swathe of student protest across the world, calling for racial justice and to expose the open institutional racism of university life in South Africa and Britain, as well as to decolonise education. This movement also inspired student counterparts in the UK, with the creation of the Rhodes Must Fall Oxford campaign, calling for the removal of the Rhodes statue at Oriel College. As noted in an article in *The Guardian* by Amit Chauduri (2016), the UCT movement declared itself as 'a collective movement of students and staff members mobilising for direct action against the reality of institutional racism at the University of Cape Town. The chief focus of this movement is to create avenues for REAL transformation that students and staff alike have been calling for.'

The UCT campaign led to the removal of a statue of Cecil Rhodes, a white supremacist. Rhodes was the founder of the southern African colony of (South) Rhodesia, modern-day Zimbabwe, which was named after him in 1895, served as prime minister of the Cape Colony in the early 1890s and has been linked to apartheid-style policies that disenfranchised most Africans.

In 2016, at a time when UK student social movements were beginning to campaign around anti-racism, the Library learned of a Goldsmiths Student Union-led (SU) initiative to diversify the book collection by placing bookmarks in books with suggested titles for purchase. The hope was that these bookmarks would find their way back to the library team for future acquisition. Although very few of the bookmarks did in fact reach the library team, the idea did not die. Instead, library staff met with the SU to scope how to collaboratively grow the idea and make it a significant and impactful success. This campaign inspired the Library's first steps towards its decolonisation work, and ultimately led to the creation of the Liberate Our Library initiative, led by the Liberate Our Library Working Group. The working group, established in autumn 2018, consists of a range of colleagues from several teams and is primarily made up of staff who volunteered to join the group. The group also benefited from the membership of some SU members, namely, the Education Officer, the Welfare and Liberation Officer and the Liberation Coordinator, who give their unique insight and perspective from the voice of the student body.

For geographical context, Goldsmiths is located in the South East London inner-city area of New Cross. It is a single-site campus and a constituent college of the University of London, specialising in arts, design, humanities, social sciences, business and computing. Its student population – from undergraduates to post-doctoral researchers – is circa 10,000. The international student cohort represents over 100 different countries, and 44% are from Black, Asian, mixed or minority ethnic (BAME) backgrounds, including UK residents.

In spring 2019 a group of Goldsmiths students under the name of Goldsmiths Anti-Racist Action (GARA) held a four-month-long occupation of a university building, Deptford Town Hall, calling for an end to systemic and institutional racism. The building itself was and still is contentious, due to the presence of four statues in the niches of its exterior depicting four naval figures:

- **Sir Francis Drake** (c. 1540–96), a pioneer of the slave trade who made at least three royally sponsored trips to West Africa to kidnap Africans and sell them. Elizabeth I awarded Drake a knighthood in 1581, which he received on board the *Golden Hind* in Deptford;
- **Robert Blake** (1598–1657), an admiral who served under Oliver Cromwell throughout the English Civil War. He fought the Dutch to secure the trade triangle between the Caribbean, West Africa and England. Cromwell was responsible for

trafficking the first waves of enslaved people to and from the Caribbean, installing the plantation system in Jamaica and the massacres in Drogheda, Ireland (1649);
- **Horatio Nelson** (1758–1805), a naval flag officer whose leadership is credited with a number of decisive British victories, particularly during the Napoleonic Wars (1803–15). Nelson spent a large part of his career in the Caribbean and developed an affinity with the slave owners there, using his influence to argue against the abolitionist movement in Britain;
- **The fourth statue**, understood to be a 'representative' figure rather than a specific person, from the period when the building was constructed, shows a modern admiral, with sextant and binoculars (Goldsmiths, University of London, n.d.).

Due to its location close to Deptford's Royal Naval Dockyards, the connection to the transatlantic slave trade remains to this day, and was publicly acknowledged only because of the GARA occupation.

The focus of the Library's decolonisation work was also in answer to the Goldsmiths Learning, Teaching, and Assessment Strategy's (LTAS) first objective, to 'liberate our degrees' (Goldsmiths, University of London, 2017). This objective was put forward by the SU to the Pro Warden for Education and is central to the Library's social justice commitments. The Library created a dedicated web page to promote the work of the initiative, explaining the rationale and motivations behind it. The intention is conveyed from the opening lines:

> As part of the Library's strategy, we will engage with the aims of LTAS commitment to 'Liberate our degrees'.
>
> - We will work to diversify our collections, to de-centre Whiteness, to challenge non-inclusive structures in knowledge management and their impact on library collections, users, and services.
> - We will take an intersectional approach to our liberation work to encompass the many parts of a person's identity.
>
> We are doing this work to decolonise and diversify our collections as part of an effort to ensure the library collections speak to all voices, particularly those that are traditionally underrepresented in curricula and on reading lists. We want to work in a collaborative way with our users in identifying the subject areas that do not address their experiences and identities, and where the canon excludes them.
>
> (Goldsmiths, University of London, 2020a)

Liberatemydegree book collection

The fledgling bookmark project eventually led to the group's first piece of work: to identify the excluded voices and lived experiences, and to highlight Global South scholars missing from curriculum reading lists. The aim is to capture book suggestions from students and staff to address what they see as gaps in the collection, addressing the lack of diversity and inclusion of under-represented or marginalised voices and histories. Suggestions can be made via a dedicated e-mail address on the Liberate Our Library web page, which goes directly to the acquisitions team for purchase. These titles then go on to form part of the liberatemydegree collection. The MARC records for the books have a 500 'liberatemydegree' note field, making them all searchable as a full collection in the discovery layer. A member of the library staff and artist, Lizzie Cannon, designed a bookplate which is used for all the print titles, making them easily identifiable as a part of the collection. The bookplate depicts a group of fists raised in protest with the wording 'This book was purchased on request as part of Liberate Our Degrees'. The suggestions are logged in a spreadsheet with the academic department of the requester as well as any comment they may have shared about the suggestion. To date, staff and/or students from almost all academic departments have contributed to the growth of the collection (Box 9.1). Most pleasingly, some of the books have gone on to be included on reading lists.

> **Box 9.1: The Liberatemydegree collection**
> The following are some of the titles that have been suggested for the Liberatemydegree collection.
> Grisel Acosta (ed.) (2019) *Latina Outsiders Remaking Latina Identity*, Routledge.
> Gerald R. Alfred (2009) *Wasase: Indigenous Pathways of Action and Freedom*, University of Toronto Press.
> Stephanie Athey (2004) *Sharpened Edge: Women of Color, Resistance, and Writing*, Praeger.
> Max Belkin and Cleonie White (eds) (2020) *Intersectionality and Relational Psychoanalysis: New Perspectives on Race, Gender, and Sexuality*, Routledge.
> Phylis Johnson and Michael Keith (2001) *Queer Airwaves: The Story of Gay and Lesbian Broadcasting*, M. E. Sharpe.
> Sabrina Mahfouz (ed.) (2017) *The Things I Would Tell You: British Muslim Women Write*, Saqi Books.
> D. S. Marriott (2008) *Hoodoo Voodoo*, Shearsman Books.
> Nandini Sundar (2001) *Subalterns and Sovereigns: An Anthropological History of Bastar, 1854–2006*, Oxford University Press India.

Information literacy through a decolonised lens

A further and extremely important strand to the decolonisation work is led by the Academic Support Team through information literacy and academic skills workshops. A series of what came to be called 'Resistance Researching' workshops began in 2019, 'designed to help students think more critically about how we find and why we use information from a social justice perspective'. In the 'Critical Approaches to Information Gathering' workshop, the objectives are to:

- empower participants to understand why all the books they need aren't shelved in one place, to critically assess bias in library systems, and to proactively seek multiple perspectives in information gathering, by:
- examining the socio-historical construction of library classification systems in order to understand how bias is built into them;
- identifying a range of library search tools and techniques to effectively find resources.

In the 'Open Access for Resistance Researching' workshop, the objectives are to:

> Explore how alternative publishing practices and platforms such as Open Access [OA] and social media can extend academic engagement and promote open and inclusive scholarship. This workshop shows how an ethos of OA can contribute to 'decolonisation', gain an understanding of how mainstream academic publishing privileges certain voices, and critically evaluate academic social platforms such as ResearchGate, Academia.Edu and Mendeley.
>
> (Goldsmiths, University of London, 2020a)

In February 2021, as part of the UK's LGBT+ History Month celebrations, the Library organised a 'Resistance Researching: LGBT+ History Month' workshop to highlight LGBT+ library resources. The aims of the workshop were to equip attendees with the skills to:

- look critically at the language we use in libraries to organise and categorise LGBT+ resources;
- identify a range of library search tools and techniques to effectively find resources;
- know more about our specialist LGBT+ resources.

Internal and external collaboration

Decolonisation and liberation work cannot happen solely within the library space of the university if it is to have meaningful impact and inspire change leading to social justice. As the people who acquire, organise and disseminate knowledge, library workers must also work collaboratively both internally and externally with colleagues and partners. At Goldsmiths, it was recognised that in order to push for institutional change, academic departments had to be part of the conversation. It is they who are also knowledge gatekeepers. What was their role in meeting the strategic goal of liberating degrees? Members of the Liberate Our Library group set a goal to meet all academic heads of department or heads of learning and teaching committees in order to both share the Library's decolonisation work and find out what they were doing to liberate degrees. For the Library, the purpose was not only to gather that knowledge, but also to seek to work collaboratively with departments by sharing what suggestions were being made as part of the collection diversification work, to show those teaching the disciplines what students deemed to be missing in their curriculum based on their own multiple identities and lived experiences. Without this knowledge, how would they know, unless they themselves were asking the same sets of questions of themselves and their students? These meetings proved to be fruitful all round. They showed a mixed picture, with some departments already engaged in decolonising work through diversifying reading lists and pedagogical approaches, to those at the very beginning stages looking to the Library for support with alternative suggestions for reading lists. As a result of some of these departmental meetings, decolonisation/liberation groups were established, with representation from subject librarians being seen as key to the work.

The importance of what the library was doing in this area was also recognised by the university's senior leadership team, who viewed the liberation initiative as an exemplar of institutional good practice. In October 2019 a university-wide UK Black History Month event called 'Decolonising Goldsmiths: mission impossible?' led by Dr Nicola Rollock, a leading Black female professor, launched an internal report on institutional racism – 'Insider-Outsider' by Sofia Akel. The event was introduced by the Warden (Vice Chancellor), and a member of the Liberate Our Library group gave a presentation on the work the Library was engaged in towards social justice.

Externally, the decolonisation work that Goldsmiths Library was doing began to get noticed in the library and higher education sector, leading to invitations to speak at conferences and on panels and to write articles and book chapters. It was clear that a major force for change addressing social justice was beginning to take place across UK higher education institutions and their libraries. This was clearly evidenced when, in January 2020, Goldsmiths – along with library colleagues from Birkbeck, University of London and the University of East London – co-organised a free conference called 'Decolonising the Curriculum: The Library's Role' (Goldsmiths, University of London, 2020c). It attracted 82 people from across the UK. Presentations and lightning talks ranged from liberating reading lists to decolonising through critical librarianship, to inviting marginalised voices into libraries and tackling the attainment gap. It was most evident that libraries were beginning to really question their roles, their practices and their profession, as well as recognising how large a role they have to play towards the advancement of the social justice agenda.

Diversification of the workforce and activism

In 2018 the UK Chartered Institute of Library and Information Professionals (CILIP) and the Archives and Records Association (UK and Ireland) (ARA) published a report containing the results of a survey of staff in the UK information sectors, where 96.7% identified as White (CILIP, 2018). The picture in the USA is not much different. In 2020, figures from the American Federation of Labor and Congress of Industrial Organizations Department for Professional Employees (DPE) showed that 6.8% of the 300,000 librarians in the workforce today identify as Black, 8.6% as Latino, 4.6% as Asian

American or Pacific Islander and less than 1% as Native American (DPE, 2020). In 2016 Carla Hayden – under President Barack Obama – became the 14th Librarian of Congress, overseeing the vast collection of the Library of Congress, the world's largest library. Hayden is the first woman and the first African American to hold the position – the first Librarian of Congress who is not a White man. Her appointment came surrounded by accusations of being unqualified, of succumbing to political correctness, of being a diversity pick; some even questioned her credentials. In January 2020, Tracie D. Hall was named as the ALA's (American Library Association) first female African American executive director. She has put tackling racism at the forefront of her work as leader. 'It is clear that the work of dismantling racism is overdue in our society and in library and information services. Racism, bigotry, and bias threaten the reach and impact of our field and the full promise and potential of an equitably informed public. It cannot abide' (ALA, 2020).

Hall stipulates the importance of building and nurturing library workforces that look like the communities they serve. This is all too keenly observed in the UK, where many students, particularly from non-White backgrounds, report on the negative impact from a pedagogical point of view of not seeing themselves reflected in the staff who teach them, as well as the front-facing student support teams. Hall emphasises the importance of equality, diversity and inclusion (EDI) training to ensure staff commitment in this area: 'We have to diversify the ranks of the library and information workforce. But we also have to make sure that the current corps of library workers are retrained to see the work we do through an equity lens. I cannot overstate how important that is. Today equity, diversity and inclusion are core to the work we do' (Hall, 2020).

To change this picture requires us to be more intentional in our efforts. It is not enough to engage in EDI initiatives at a theoretical level. It is the practical application that informs implementation. The requirement of the profession is for reflective practice. The fundamental questions we must ask ourselves are what is it we need to do now, why do we need to do it and how?

Conclusion

In summary, if libraries are to decolonise, liberate and diversify their collections, workforces and practices within the higher education context, then the work must begin at the source or the heart of why the university exists and what it purports to do. If it is to disseminate knowledge, then that knowledge must be examined through a critical lens, which means acknowledging the roots of how that knowledge has come about, how it is taught, how it is experienced and how it is represented through the learning resources that exist in the library. The aim must be to democratise knowledge and shift away from the westernised dominance and perspective, to look to the majority world by unpacking epistemology and asking what is knowledge, and paying attention to how Indigenous knowledges have been marginalised. This work must be a collaborative learning process for all involved. It must be embraced by the institution if it is to have any meaningful, change-making and lasting impact.

References

ALA (American Library Association) (2020) ALA Executive Director Tracie D. Hall says Dismantling Racism in Library and Information Services is Overdue, press release, 26 June, www.ala.org/news/press-releases/2020/06/ala-executive-director-tracie-d-hall-says-dismantling-racism-library-and (accessed November 2020).

Azoulay, A. A. (2019) *Potential History: Unlearning Imperialism*, Verso.

Black Curriculum (2019) https://theblackcurriculum.com (accessed October 2020).

Chauduri, A. (2016) The Real Meaning of Rhodes Must Fall, *The Guardian*, 16 March, www.theguardian.com/uk-news/2016/mar/16/the-real-meaning-of-rhodes-must-fall (accessed October 2020).

CILIP (2018) CILIP and ARA Release Full Report on 2015 UK Information Sector Workforce Survey, www.cilip.org.uk/page/Workforcesurvey (accessed November 2020).

Cupples, J. and Grosfoguel, R. (eds) (2019) *Unsettling Eurocentrism in the Westernized University*, Routledge.

de Sousa Santos, B. (2014) *Epistemologies of the South: Justice against Epistemicide*, Paradigm Publishers.

DPE (American Federation of Labor and Congress of Industrial Organizations Department for Professional Employees) (2020) Library Professionals: Facts and Figures, 2020 Fact Sheet, www.dpeaflcio.org/factsheets/library-professionals-facts-and-figures (accessed January 2021).

Goldsmiths, University of London (2017) Learning, Teaching, and Assessment Strategy, www.gold.ac.uk/learning (accessed November 2020).

Goldsmiths, University of London (2020a) Liberate Our Library, www.gold.ac.uk/library/about/liberate-our-library (accessed November 2020).

Goldsmiths, University of London (2020b) MA Black British History, www.gold.ac.uk/pg/ma-black-british-history (accessed November 2020).

Goldsmiths, University of London (2020c) *Decolonising the Curriculum: The Library's Role Conference*, https://decolonisethelibrary.wordpress.com (accessed November 2020).

Goldsmiths, University of London (n.d.) Deptford Town Hall External Statues, www.gold.ac.uk/about/history/dth-statues (accessed November 2020).

Gregory, L. and Higgins, S. (2013) *Information Literacy and Social Justice: Radical Professional Praxis*, Library Juice Press.

Grosfoguel, R. (2013) The Structure of Knowledge in Westernized Universities: Epistemic Racism/Sexism and the Four Genocides/Epistemicides of the Long 16th Century, *Human Architecture*, **11** (1), 73–90, http://scholarworks.umb.edu/humanarchitecture/vol11/iss1/8 (accessed October 2020).

Hall, T. D. (2020) Professional Associations Have Work to Do, www.cilip.org.uk/news/527177/Professional-associations-have-work-to-do.htm (accessed April 2021).

hooks, b. (1994) *Teaching to Transgress*, Routledge.

Mbembe, A. (2015) Decolonizing Knowledge and the Question of the Archive, https://wiser.wits.ac.za/system/files/Achille%20Mbembe%20-%20Decolonizing%20Knowledge%20and%20the%20Question%20of%20the%20Archive.pdf (accessed November 2020).

Smith, L. T. (2012) *Decolonizing Methodologies: Research and Indigenous Peoples*, Zed Books.

Tandon, R. (2013) *Global Democracy Requires Knowledge Democracy* (blog), http://unescochair-cbrsr.org/index.php/2013/09/15/globaldemocracy-requires-knowledge-democracy (accessed October 2020).

10
Opening Spaces for Creative and Critical Enquiry

Alexandra Duncan, Vivienne Eades-Miller and Adam Ramejkis

Preamble

A lot of thought has gone into how to write this book chapter – partly in terms of content, but primarily in relation to the awareness that, as three collaborating authors, we are all different in terms of how we approach what we do. We acknowledge that, while our aims and motivations in doing what we do connect and are similar, one of the greatest strengths (and, at least potentially, challenges) lies in the different perspectives and knowledges we bring to planning, developing and delivering workshops. This in itself is not a challenge, our co-operation developing organically and synergistically to take full advantage of what we each bring to the work we do. The challenge presents itself when considering how to share our practice(s) with others in the form of a co-written book chapter! There is a tendency for co-written texts to be presented as a singular, unified voice. When discussing how to write this chapter we realised this was not how we wanted to proceed. Instead, we recognised the need to write in a way that mirrored how we work together: disparate voices and perspectives that complement each other.

To some extent, we want our text to illustrate the overarching objective of decolonising – that of questioning the validity of a universally relevant and approved theory or system, by recognising and truly valuing different voices. We are all too aware of the 'conventions' of academic writing, but equally, if not more, aware that this is exactly the kind of thing we are challenging when we talk about the need to decolonise. Decolonisation is not only about diversifying library collections, reading lists and course curricula (although this is absolutely necessary), and it's also not only about highlighting how limited and limiting canons of knowledge are (again, this is much needed). It's about recognising and decrying how the very fabric of our system of education, and of society as a whole, not only values one way above others but also presents this as *the way*, with other ways disregarded or ignored – excluded.

The way we approach our practices, and the workshops detailed below, is shaped by this belief in inclusivity and the need to engage with different knowledges. They come from a place of curiosity and interest, a belief in social justice as a key tenet of our roles and in response to conversations with peers and students. Centred on a willingness to be open, to discuss and explore themes without a measurable outcome in mind, the focus is on challenging and asking questions of education, systems of power and society as a whole. In this sense, all the workshops are inherently hopeful, advocating the need to expose the inherent bias and *curatedness* of systems of knowledge, and calling for a fully inclusive celebration of diverse ways of thinking, knowing, learning, doing, being, becoming and living together.

It seems therefore not only appropriate but crucial that how we write about our work echoes this very focus on valuing difference. At the same time, we recognise the need to situate our writing within its specific and specified context. We had initially explored more radical approaches to this text, but agreed to compromise in order for this account of our practices to potentially trigger more and wider discussions and actions.

In context

In higher education there is currently a concerted drive towards decolonisation, a process which can work only by 'recognising and reorienting where power is drawn from' and adopting approaches which encourage 'exchanging rather than transferring knowledge' (Gus and Gurmider, in Felix, 2019). By viewing learning environments as spaces of exchange, the focus shifts from one of *transaction* to *interaction*, from a *product-driven approach* which provides answers, to a *process of active critical enquiry* which posits questions. These in turn lead to further critical explorations of structures and systems.

These explorations can be achieved through the adoption of an experiential learning approach (Dewey, 2008; Kolb, 1984) – utilising pre-existing knowledges as a means of exploring instinctual connections with each participants' internalised logic, which can help to develop learners' confidence in their own ways of engaging with the world (or worlds). A key tenet here is that learning is active and independently navigated, triggered by the interests, personal views and perspectives of those present, and shaped on-the-go in response to the themes and directions arising from shared critical explorations within the learning space. Through opening up these spaces to explore, and advocating for self-directed critical enquiry, opportunities are provided for participants to learn with, and within, their own learning.

A strong resonance can be seen here with critical pedagogy (Freire, 1970; hooks, 1994) – an approach which proposes that 'learners can only truly learn to think critically if they are also able to challenge the problems within power and knowledge structures in their educational environment as well as the wider world' (Smith, 2013, 19). Within a critical pedagogy, learning environments provide space and support for participants to be/become active agents in their own (and others') learning (Freire, 1998). In this sense, teaching (and learning) is a political act (Giroux, 1997), one which challenges dominant systems of knowledge and calls for a critical enquiry into issues of social justice and fairness. This is emphasised by Freire when he stresses the importance of *'conscientizagao'*: critical consciousness (Freire, 1970, 35). In his writings about the role of education in liberation from oppressions, there is a focus on equipping and empowering learners. Freire asserts the importance of what he terms *praxis* in education: 'reflection and action upon the world in order to transform it' (Freire, 1970, 51). For Freire, critical reflection must be directly linked to a call to action in some form, as realisation and reflection without action only make oppression more oppressive (Freire, 1970, 51).

Academic libraries, and librarians, are recognised as having a key role to play in the drive to decolonise. Questions must be raised about which resources and knowledges are included and, more importantly, which are *not included*. Reframing this through a critical pedagogy lens, we can say that particular perspectives and knowledges have been – at least to some extent – consciously *excluded*. This decision is often rationalised by the argument that they are not part of the *legitimised knowledge* which is preserved and presented in the established canon.

The understanding of neutrality as positioned in opposition to the idea of curated spaces is an important theme within librarianship. Librarians know to critique this; they know the impact of homogeneous spaces on library users because they are culpable in creating them. Libraries are born of colonial legacies; this is seen in the organisation and structure of their spaces. Drabinski (2019) wrote that in their quest for order librarians have overlaid their own technologies of power onto knowledge construction. In an attempt to introduce order to the world, librarians have naturally impacted upon it, curating it and, consequently, changing it. As Adler (2017) suggests, the systems or order which librarians wield could themselves be viewed as primary historical documents, which contribute to constructed notions of national history and identity. In libraries, one can unmake and remake meaning through the organisation of knowledge. Thereby, in recognising the curated nature of these spaces, and their custodians as the gatekeepers, one also acknowledges the idea of legitimatised knowledge.

This is also present in the idea of open access platforms, where, in deciding what constitutes a good or authoritative source, notability of a subject or neutrality itself, there is consensus. But that consensus is too often reached by a homogeneous group of people – a predominantly White, male editorship – and qualified through a Western lens. This leaves little or no space for other types of knowledge, languages or thought, including Indigenous knowledges – which cannot then fit into these supposedly neutral and open spaces (Gallert and Van der Velden, 2015).

In order to redress this imbalance, then, academic libraries need to adopt a process of 'decanonisation' (Mambrol, 2016), encouraging active participation through a combination of (a) adding new and hitherto under-represented voices and perspectives to their collections and (b) adopting an activist stance towards becoming true 'advocates of diversity, equality and inclusion' (Poole, 2019) through creating opportunities and spaces for students to recognise and critically engage with the current colonised/canonised state of play and the injustices enacted by the systems in place. The focus here is not one of delegitimising canonised knowledge, but of advocating for the legitimisation of a whole range of knowledges. This call for an all-inclusive celebration of voices echoes Morrison's insistence for curriculum design to be 'marked by richness, diversity, discordant voices, fecundity, multiple rationalities, and theories ... touched by humanity and practicality in a hundred thousand contexts' (Morrison, 2004, 487). The overarching aim here is to 'catch the untidy but authentic lived experiences of ... every hue, draw on emergent disciplines outside education, and touch major issues in everyday life' (Morrison, 2004, 487) – as this will allow for multitudinous opportunities to exchange and engage with knowledges, and learn about ourselves and others in a variety of ways.

Given the potential (inevitable?) discordance of the voices we aim to engage with, there is a need for us all to adopt 'intellectual humility' (Paul, 1992) and recognise that the way we see the world is merely one of many ways – that what seems to be *the way* for us, in given contexts, is not and cannot be the way in all contexts and for all people. A link can be made here with Ron Barnett's assertion that, in order to *think*, *learn* and *be* in the radically unknowable and indescribable supercomplexity (and superdiversity) of the world we live in, we need to develop Mode 3 knowledge: 'a knowing in and with uncertainty ... a knowledge which is itself a complex of personal, tacit, experiential and propositional knowledges' (Barnett, 2004, 251).

Within the context of decolonising the academic library, not-knowing and openness-to-possibility are important tools in operating against oppressive systems of control. Akomolafe asserts that we need to 'see activism as a politics of encountering the unsaid' so as not to be hindered, by the violence of existing systems, from experiencing the newness 'that lingers on the edges of awareness' (Akomolafe, 2017, 249). When we think about the impact of colonialism on libraries and publishing as systematic oppression and exclusion of knowledges and thought, we need to question both the modes in which information skills sessions operate *and* the content or collections they use or promote.

By encouraging an approach that embraces uncertainty, openness, serendipity and randomness, we allow for potentially infinitesimal spaces of enquiry to open, and for connections and insights to arise which are of intrinsic value to the learners in the space (by learners, we mean this in a Freirean sense, with no distinction made between teachers and students). This not only runs counter to more traditional colonial models of education, which view randomness and unpredictability as unproductive and unquantifiable; it also threatens the authority of the said models – the simple reframing of *the way* as *a way* potentially leading to a repositioning of perception(s) as a result of not only new learning, but also unlearning of previously unquestioned ways of thinking.

In practice

We will now discuss what this can look like in practice, with reference to three workshops we have (co-)designed and (co-)facilitated at University of the Arts London (UAL), and (co-)presented at conferences. While decolonisation was not necessarily the explicitly stated focus of these workshops, some of the commonalities that highlight these as decolonising sessions are critical thinking around (library) systems of knowledge, and democratisation of information production through a praxis and an empowerment of the student voice(s). Representation of voices, perspectives and information is a key thread that runs through all three sessions.

By critically questioning the authority of dominant knowledges legitimised by library and information – and other – systems, and facilitating the consideration of knowledges which are effectively *illegitimised*, the sessions address lack of representation and ally themselves with under-represented, if not unheard, voices. The sessions critique ideas of libraries as neutral spaces and highlight the nature of curated collections and information systems. Drabinski outlined five principles of critical librarianship, the fifth acknowledging that 'critical librarianship knows that the world could be different' (Drabinski, 2019, 53). This principle underpins the design and delivery of the workshops discussed here, our practices in general and the inherent hope which fuels the drive to decolonise.

In this sense, it may be more useful to think of the workshops we facilitate as forums, defined by Bruner as spaces and opportunities which advocate for the adoption of 'an *active* role as participants rather than as performing spectators who play out their canonical [and canonised] roles according to rule when the appropriate cues occur' (Bruner, 1986, 123).

What follows is a walk-through reflection on three different, yet intrinsically connected, workshops – each written in the voice and style that fits our respective approaches.

Creative Library Research
Adam Ramejkis

Creative Library Research (CLR) workshops aim to encourage critical engagement with libraries as systems of knowledge. When developing the sessions, we started with the following keywords/themes: *criticality*, *creativity*, *systems of knowledge*, *bias*, *neutrality* and *curatedness*. The idea was to open an exploratory space through engaging with diverse knowledges and making connections between seemingly disparate ways of thinking. This aimed at encouraging learners to recognise and value a wider range of perspectives and approaches to knowledge – beyond their own individual contexts and, crucially, beyond the *legitimised knowledge* of subject canon(s). To emphasise this, and to highlight the curatedness and bias of all library collections, CLR workshops are held in non-UAL libraries – partly to encourage students to see and think beyond an Art/Design perspective, but also to explore the complementarity of differing systems of knowledge(s).

CLR developed from a workshop I ran for students from across UAL, centred on discussing and challenging definitions of *critical thinking*. To encourage a less-institutionalised engagement the sessions took place in a non-UAL library space (Conway Hall Humanist Library), chosen because of the stated mission of Conway Hall Ethical Society and its library (and collection) to be/remain 'a haven for the radicals, political and social reformers and freethinkers who dared to dream of a better world' (Conway

Hall, n.d.). The hope was that participants would be inspired by the ethos of the space – feeling more comfortable engaging in critical and radical discussions, and freer in challenging the *legitimised* notions and definitions of thinking, knowledge and learning. In one of these workshops, a discussion ensued about how we could explore and connect with the 'millions of pages of knowledge and thinking' within the library collection – engage '*with* the library, not just *in* the library' (student feedback). Recognising this as an opportunity for potential collaboration with library services, I arranged a series of workshops with academic support librarians across UAL (including Alex and Viv, and May Warren – former academic support librarian at Central St Martins). This resulted in further discussions, culminating in the co-design of CLR workshops, which have been held in a range of non-UAL libraries. CLR – both the workshop and its approach – has been presented at library conferences (Art Libraries Society (ARLIS) 2018, ARLIS 2019, Decolonising the Curriculum – The Library's Role, 2020), and has also informed course-based projects encouraging critical engagement with libraries and systems of knowledge (D'Clark, 2019; Ramejkis, 2019; Knight and Ramejkis, 2020).

The workshops start with a presentation and discussion of a selection of short texts around thinking and learning; these having been carefully chosen to match the context and focus (and, by extension, the bias) of the hosting library. For example, for a workshop in the Institute of International Visual Arts (INIVA) library, we included a short extract from Assata Shakur's autobiography (about the innate inequality of Western education) and one from Patricia Hill Collins (about the need to develop critical consciousness). After reading and sharing initial thoughts, we discussed the texts in relation to INIVA's focus on championing knowledges and practices from around the world as a way of challenging White, Western-centric systems and approaches (Iniva.org, n.d.). The purpose of this discussion is to encourage an openness to what we understand by the term *critical thinking*, and an awareness of how this differs across contexts, through engaging with a deliberately diverse range of thinkers and text types. Other examples used to date are: John Dewey, bell hooks, Umberto Eco, Jiddu Krishnamurti, Marcel Proust, Akala, Immanuel Kant, Peter Kropotkin and Charlene Tan. Through exploring a range of perspectives and discussing possible points of accord and disconnect between them, learners are encouraged not only to challenge canonised views but also to recognise their own individual ways of thinking as simply one of many possible perspectives. The aim here is to foster intellectual humility (Paul, 1992), as a pre-requisite to developing a 'willingness to endure [the] condition of mental unrest' (Dewey, 1997, 13) that uncertainty brings. The message here is to recognise uncertainty as an *open and creative* space for learning about ourselves, others and the world(s) we share.

After a brief introduction to the space, learners are given a short period of time to explore the unfamiliar library collection and to find a book (or books) which they feel connects to their creative practice and/or current research focus. This is a deliberately vague prompt, with no specific criteria given, the aim being to open up new angles on the familiar, to highlight the benefits of widening perspectives through exploring and connecting with new knowledges. Participants being unfamiliar with the layout or contents of the library, there is an added sense of adventure to this search, with the potential for a more creative interpretation of their own areas of interest/research. Once all participants have found their connections, everyone returns to the group and these books are swapped (e.g. passed to the person on the right) so that everybody now has a new book. Learners are then challenged to find a connection between this new, randomly assigned book and their practice/research. In a similar but more pronounced way to the previous activity, this advocates an openness to serendipity, with learners encouraged to recognise the value of even the most tenuous/indirect links. The connections found/made with the self-selected and other-selected books are then shared with the group, followed by a discussion around recurring themes. Through asking for these connections to be articulated in words, the aim is to trigger a metacognitive focus, as students need to critically engage with their own thinking to create links that are credible and make sense to them. Through doing this, learners can develop confidence in, and a feeling of comfort with, the spaces of uncertainty and confusion that come with living in a supercomplex and superdiverse world.

The session closes with a discussion on the *bias* and *curatedness* of libraries, as well as within systems of knowledge and society at large. This leads to shared reflections on the value of critiquing *canonised knowledge*, and opening ourselves to new and different ways of thinking, knowing, learning, doing, being, becoming and living together. The hope is that learners will take this approach into their further studies and creative endeavours, not only by questioning dominant systems of knowledge but by reflecting on how this can lead to 'action upon the world in order to transform it' (Freire, 1970, 51).

Wikipedia
Alexandra Duncan

The Wikipedia workshops are both an acknowledgement of and a response to the multitude of ways the internet has failed. What was conceived as a tool for democracy has resulted in a space estranged from notions of knowledge equity, in which the norm is under-representation based on gender, race and geographic location; a hegemonic model in which knowledge has become another means by which to have power and control.

This project began with a conversation with a colleague, Cassy Sachar, about Wikipedia Art+Feminism edit-a-thons, a sense they were the sort of thing librarians ought to be doing. The statistics on the Art+Feminism organisation website (Art+Feminism, 2021) told us that representation was where certain open access resources were failing.

We cannot avoid looking to open access tools like Wikipedia with the hope that they can redress wider issues with the democracy of information. It is one of the most significant websites in the world – the fifth most visited (Routley, 2019), and the largest and most popular general reference work on the internet (Wikipedia, 2021). 'Imagine a world in which every single person on the planet is given free access to the sum of all human knowledge,' Jimmy Wales, founder of Wikipedia tells us (Roblimo, 2004). A closer look at collective participation tells us that 80% of the global content of Wikipedia is written by White men from Europe and North America, a demographic that makes up just 20% of the world's population (Whose Knowledge, 2018).

So, in 2018 we began hosting UAL/ARLIS Wikipedia edit-a-thons. While this was initially in response to the under-representation of women on Wikipedia (in both the content and the make-up of the editorship), in acknowledging the need for a more intersectional approach they later became focused on women of colour. Using source material from the UAL libraries, in particular the collections at Chelsea College of Arts, attendees are given examples of rudimentary or non-existent articles on under-represented artists, and sources containing information they can easily populate the articles with. One invaluable example of such a work is *Recordings: A Select Bibliography of Contemporary African, Afro-Caribbean and Asian British Art* (Keen and Ward, 1996), published by INIVA in collaboration with Chelsea College of Art and Design. The publication has an index that documents the African-Caribbean, Asian and African Art in Britain Archive, up until 1996.

The editing process is closely aligned with the information literacy learning outcomes in place at UAL. The necessity of edits being backed up by *appropriate* secondary sources forces any editor to not only find sources but read and evaluate them to understand the mechanics of both writing and referencing. This is not new – there are plenty of examples of Wikipedia being successfully embedded in higher education curricula for these exact reasons. However, from questioning edit-a-thon participants, it seemed that the most valuable reason for participating was activism, the awareness that they have a valid voice, with as much right as anyone to participate in the scholarly conversation, and that in doing so they can change the world. As one participant put it: 'finding your own voice in the conversation is empowering' (Duncan and Sachar, 2018). This is a concept at the heart of information literacy, but being able to give it a tangible outcome is significant.

This recognition of the potential of Wikipedia's being a tool with which to explore what representation means in society, and the impact of colonial legacies on the information landscape, led Adam and me to facilitate our own Wikipedia workshop in December 2019. Presented as an activist event, its aim was to consider the politics and culture of Wikipedia, and the possibilities for activism it offered, posing the questions 'Does its open-source nature mean it is unreliable or does it conform to a different, more collaborative, system of checks and controls?' and, 'Can it be used for research as well as a tool for change'?

We began with a discussion and mind-map creation – asking participants to consider Wikipedia's positives and negatives. Participants acknowledged the lack of diversity and open editing as a double-edged sword, and critiqued the West acting as the knowledge gatekeeper. They already understood how and why open source products sometimes fail, and wanted to address this with practical activism. The rest of the workshop was spent doing live editing of Wikipedia articles, using *Recordings* as our key source material. As had become common at edit-a-thons, the takeaway was understanding that there are not enough secondary sources on under-represented subjects, and the awareness that, at the very least, Wikipedia is a useful tool to highlight this. Wikipedia, like Western publishing, prefers *traditional* methods of knowledge production and documentation, relying on published secondary sources to ratify knowledge. There is limited space for Indigenous knowledge corroborated by, for example, oral histories and established systems of verbal peer review, which ensures that its content remains skewed towards Western sources, subjects and perspectives (Duncan, 2020, 156).

At UAL there is institutional interest in Wikipedia as a tool for decolonisation. In early 2020 I met with senior academic colleagues at London College of Communication (LCC) interested in exploring Wikipedia within education. Two Wikimedians also attended, and we shared our varied experiences of engaging with Wikipedia educationally. The possibility of the decolonial lens resulted in Lucy Panesar, LCC Progression and Attainment Project Manager, and the LCC Changemakers – students with a partnership role in developing pedagogy and the curriculum via a decolonial and liberating lens – taking on the running of the project. So far this has produced a three-part edit-a-thon in summer 2020, on decolonisation, and has now led to the creation of the Decolonising Wikipedia Network – a network of LCC staff and students run by Lucy and the Changemakers in collaboration with Richard Neville from Wikimedia, with input from myself.

Wikipedia workshops offer a concrete way to fulfil institutional outcomes. Using dashboards to track the number of edits, and thus the possibility of making an immediate and positive change in the space of an hour, or a day, fits into the wider institutional framework. But the true and most interesting criticality is under the radar. This happens in the accompanying discussions on questioning legitimacy: what makes an authoritative source, or a notable subject? What is neutrality? Their worth is found in this combination of criticality and praxis.

The workshops are reflexive – openly acknowledging that we are not sure how or what is the *best way* to decolonise, and this idea of reflexivity feels very apt when examining Wikipedia as a product or tool. It is familiar to us as librarians, akin to our quest for *neutrality*, and the compromise we make in continuing to engage with structures of knowledge categorisation that are structures of oppression. It is making the best of it. This speaks to the inherent tension of libraries being colonial spaces that we have created. In the workshops the process begins with understanding Wikipedia as an open access tool, inherently democratic. But we constantly reassess it, to move to understanding it as part of the problem. Finally, we understand it as something in between – a mirror that reflects and displays publishing and society's shortcomings. And a way to make change.

Hack Your Library
Vivienne Eades-Miller

Hack Your Library is a workshop exploring the politics of library knowledge systems, labelling and publishing. The session facilitates critical reflection on these systems, their bias, curation and information not adequately represented. We provide students with tools to analyse the historic and inadequate nature of the subject classification and structures they navigate with library research.

After looking at zines as independent publications and discussing them in the context of library collections, we critically examine knowledge systems and discuss broader ideas of labelling and neutrality. In an active session, we then ask students to make a generative critique using their own knowledge and perspective to imagine and recreate knowledge structures and labels in zine form.

My colleague Vanessa Govinden and I designed the session structure after reflections with colleagues around offensive or inadequate subject headings, classification categories and positionings. After co-facilitating Creative Library Research sessions with Adam and Alex, I wanted again to focus with students on exploring library knowledge structures, this time with a social justice lens. Influenced by student artworks reflecting on their experience as students of colour at UAL, we wanted to support critical engagement with the complexity of issues like naming, categorising, highlighting and othering in libraries and broader contexts.

We begin sessions by asking questions about the value of zines to academic collections, looking at a range of zines and then asking how they are different to the rest of the library collections and what they offer that other formats don't. Like Wikipedia, zines (which usually aren't classified) show up the inadequacies of commercial and academic knowledge production, and also colonial ideas of static classification. They help to highlight inadequacy, bias and inaccuracies of categories and labels from limited singular perspectives.

Zines provide a divergence in content, tone, language and authorship from mainstream collections. Personal and contemporary content contrasts starkly with academic sources and knowledge categories. Zines (and later the use of queer theory) provide a context which highlights ideals of universal, correct and static naming and organisation of knowledge as bizarre concepts.

The sessions then facilitate discussion of representation of knowledge (mis and lack of) in Dewey Decimal Classification (DDC), using examples relating to aspects of identity including race, nationality, gender and religion.

As facilitators, we choose examples of positioning or decisions we are forced to make as librarians that we find personally offensive, inadequate or exclusionary. We explain why, and how we think these could impact on the library user navigating information. We use examples to which we feel a connection, because talking about aspects of identity and representation in an information skills forum is relatively new to us, and having considered bell hooks' affirmation that it is our responsibility to share too. 'When education is the practice of freedom, students are not the only ones who are asked to share, to confess. […] empowerment cannot happen if we refuse to be vulnerable while encouraging students to take risks' (hooks, 1994, 21). This also helps to create space for critical discussion and validate multiple opinions and perspectives, rather than projecting a static politics of correctness onto the session.

Ideas of neutrality, naming and positioning knowledge are then explored in the context of the politics of correction: using two queer library theory quotes to frame thinking about possible solutions for placement of specific books. This theory 'resists the idea that stable identities like lesbian or gay exist outside of time. Rather, these identities exist only temporarily in social and political contexts that both produce and require them' (Drabinski, 2013, 101). We ask students to question if 'there can be no "correct" categorical or linguistic structures, only those that discursively emerge and circulate in a particular context' (Drabinski, 2013, 102).

This provides a generative critical framework to discuss student opinions on complex issues. Students share differing opinions on issues such as foregrounding resources by less-represented voices (with categories such as Black female artists, for instance) and othering (because while highlighting and making content accessible, without changes to other categories you are also reinforcing the white male as *default* or *norm*).

Rather than a dynamic of conflicting or opposing opinions, this has thus far produced questioning of and reflection on opinion. Questioning the *correct* way to correct systems of knowledge allows students to consider different approaches, and the complexity (and possibilities) of decolonisation as an idea in this context, in some small way, bringing an element of self-reflexivity to approaching decolonisation. The system doesn't offer enough choices to make a *correct choice* within it; the system needs reconceiving, but framing critically allows us to approach solutions thoughtfully with students.

Hack Your Library sessions encourage generative critique of the curatedness of libraries and classification categories through praxis (Freire, 1970, 32–65). This takes the form of students reimagining and remaking subject categories, labels and structures. At the end of a session students make zine pages around a subject of interest in DDC and create, or recreate, knowledge categories which they feel are important but ignored or framed incorrectly in the structure. As facilitators we endorse the importance of the students' personal and individual perspective in this activity. The experiential learning mode of the sessions utilises students' prior knowledge and their own logic and aims to build confidence in that. Using zines in the sessions helps to validate personal experience and narrative in this context.

We hope that this activity, channelling criticality into praxis, empowers students as to their own academic voice and perspective. Hopefully, the sessions question classification in a way which also expands consideration of the ways students *can* immediately explore their own ideas in libraries, in order to work past limitations of inherently colonial and White classification structures.

Hack Your Library pitches knowledge and labels as contextual and fluid and has students remaking categories from a multiplicity of perceptions, rather than singularly disconnecting static topics in a colonial logic. Supporting ideas of emergent knowledges, these sessions attempt to facilitate the imagining of new spaces of knowledge and academic libraries.

In conclusion

All of the workshops provide a space to question, to challenge the default. It is in this sense that they decolonise. These sessions grew in part out of an openness and eagerness to explore information skills and critical enquiry outside of dominant modes and structures, in terms of collections and resources explored, ideas of what librarians 'teach' and how, and definitions of learning and criticality.

There is often a perceived need in the field of information skills (and in higher education) to revert to a model or a framework. This has the benefit of supporting staff, but can also deny openness and creativity outside of the social and academic structures within which the library or institution operates. It can be difficult for library staff to get time and support to explore information skills work outside of the expected lens and structures of transactional library skills. Explorative work or a focus on critical thinking or questioning may not be seen as immediately productive. Some of the sessions discussed in this chapter don't generally fit with the modes of information skills, or academic support, that we are often used to facilitating in academic libraries: not having easily measurable outcomes or delivering a clear product of mechanical skills, but seeking deeper, and perhaps immeasurable, learning (or unlearning.)

Deeper learning is less strategic, difficult to measure and often impossible to measure in the short term. It is not necessarily directed at a single skill or outcome but relates more to ideas of lived experience and the connectivity of holistic learning. Facilitators running these sessions, and the institutions they work within may need to look to different values and 'surrender [the] need for immediate affirmation of successful teaching' (hooks, 1994, 42).

Key to creating space for learning in these sessions is embracing multiplicities of knowing. There is acknowledgement and practice within the sessions of different knowledges and systems of knowledge co-existing in a beneficial way. Wikipedia edit-a-thons and use of zines engage with the advantages of different sources. Creative Library Research aims to open up responsive and self-generated possibilities of what critical thinking can mean. Hack Your Library emphasises the importance of self-publishing in the knowledge sphere and encourages students to reimagine systems of knowledge.

An important aspect of the sessions is their hopefulness, which supports the imagining of new spaces in libraries and knowledge sectors. All the sessions have an active element of creation, making or practising in response to critiques of libraries, publishing and higher education, encouraging and supporting students to add to multiplicities of knowing as a generative critique, hopefully achieving or working towards some form of praxis (Freire, 1970, 32–65). Channelling criticality into creative making tasks in the workshops, we hope, empowers the student voice(s) through action, whether in the academic sphere or more broadly.

References

Adler, M. (2017) *Cruising the Library: Perversities in the Organization of Knowledge*, Fordham University Press.
Akomolafe, B. (2017) *These Wilds Beyond Our Fences*, North Atlantic Books.
Art+Feminism (2021) About Art+Feminism, https://artandfeminism.org/about (accessed 19 March 2021).
Barnett, R. (2004) Learning for an Unknown Future, *Higher Education Research and Development*, **23** (3).
Bruner, J. (1986) *Actual Minds, Possible Worlds*, Harvard University Press.
Conway Hall (n.d.) *Conway Hall Library – About the Collection*, https://conwayhall.org.uk/library/about-the-collection (accessed 19 March 2021).
D'Clark, R. S. (2019) Whose History? *Shades of Noir*, www.shadesofnoir.org.uk/whose-history (accessed 19 March 2021).
Dewey, J. (1997 [1910]) *How We Think*, Dover Publications.
Dewey, J. (2008 [1938]) *Experience and Education*, Free Press.
Drabinski, E. (2013) Queering the Catalog: Queer Theory and the Politics of Correction, *Library Quarterly: Information, Community, Policy*, **83** (2), 94–111.
Drabinski, E. (2019) What is Critical about Critical Librarianship? *Art Libraries Journal*, **44** (2), 49–57.
Duncan, A. (2020) Towards an Activist Research: Is Wikipedia the Problem or the Solution? *Art Libraries Journal*, **45** (4), 155–61.
Duncan, A. and Sachar, C. (2018) ARLISmatters 03:#FightThePower (podcast), 18 March, https://soundcloud.com/user-819912910/episode-03-fightthepower (accessed 19 March 2021).
Felix, M. (2019) To Decolonise the Curriculum, We Have to Decolonise Ourselves, https://wonkhe.com/blogs/to-decolonise-the-curriculum-we-have-to-decolonise-ourselves (accessed 19 March 2021).
Freire, P. (1970) *Pedagogy of the Oppressed*, Penguin.
Freire, P. (1998) *Teachers as Cultural Workers: Letters to Those who Dare to Teach the Edge, Critical Studies in Educational Theory*, Westview Press.
Gallert, P. and Van der Velden, M. (2015) The Sum of All Human Knowledge? Wikipedia and Indigenous knowledge. In Bidwell, N. and Winschiers-Theophilus, K. (eds), *At the Intersection of Indigenous and Traditional Knowledge and Technology Design*, Informing Science Press.
Giroux, H. (1997) *Pedagogy and the Politics of Hope: Theory, Culture, and Schooling. A Critical Reader*, Westview Press.

hooks, b. (1994) *Teaching to Transgress: Education as the Practice of Freedom,* Routledge.

Iniva.org (n.d.) *Institute of International Visual Arts,* https://iniva.org/about/institute-of-international-visual-arts (accessed 19 March 2021).

Keen, M. and Ward, E. (1996) *Recordings: A Select Bibliography of Contemporary African, Afro-Caribbean and Asian British Art,* Institute of International Visual Arts and Chelsea College of Art and Design, www.arts.ac.uk/__data/assets/pdf_file/0036/199467/Recordings-A-Select-Bibliography-of-Contemporary-African,-Afro-Caribbean-and-Asian-British-Art2.pdf (accessed 14 April 2021).

Knight, L. and Ramejkis, A. (2020) In Response, *The Ethical Record,* **125** (2), 12–16, https://conwayhall.org.uk/wp-content/uploads/2020/03/EthicalRecord-Apr-May-Jun-20-ONLINE.pdf (accessed 19 March 2021).

Kolb, D. (1984) *Experiential Learning, Experience as the Source of Learning and Development,* Prentice Hall.

Mambrol, N. (2016) *Decanonisation,* Literary Theory and Criticism, https://literariness.org/2016/03/22/decanonisation (accessed 19 March 2021).

Morrison, K. R. B. (2004) The Poverty of Curriculum Theory: A Critique of Wraga and Hlebowitsh, *Journal of Curriculum Studies,* **36** (4), 487–94.

Paul, R. W. (1992) *Critical Thinking: What Every Person Needs to Survive in a Rapidly Changing World,* Foundation for Critical Thinking.

Poole, N. (2019) *Diversity within the Profession* – speech to CILIP West Midlands Members Day (8 February 2019), https://cilip.org.uk/general/custom.asp?page=DiversitywithintheProfession (accessed 19 March 2021).

Ramejkis, A. (2019) Fighting Inequality, Interrupting the Canon, Questioning the Status Quo, *The Ethical Record,* **124** (Special Edition), 19–21, https://conwayhall.org.uk/wp-content/uploads/2019/09/EthicalRecord-VictorianBlogging-FINAL.pdf (accessed 19 March 2021).

Roblimo (Robin Miller) (2004) Wikipedia Founder Jimmy Wales Responds, *Slashdot,* 28 July, https://slashdot.org/story/04/07/28/1351230/wikipedia-founder-jimmy-wales-responds.

Routley, N. (2019) Ranking the Top 100 Websites in the World, *Visual Capitalist,* 7 August, www.visualcapitalist.com/ranking-the-top-100-websites-in-the-world (accessed 19 March 2021).

Smith, L. (2013) Towards a Model of Critical Information Literacy Instruction for the Development of Political Agency, *Journal of Information Literacy,* **7** (2), 15–32.

Whose Knowledge (2018) De-colonizing the Internet, https://whoseknowledge.org/decolonizing-the-internet-conference (accessed 19 March 2021).

Wikipedia (2021) Size of Wikipedia, https://en.wikipedia.org/wiki/Wikipedia:Size_of_Wikipedia (accessed 19 March 2021).

11
Towards Decolonising the British Library: A Staff-Led Perspective

Pardaad Chamsaz on behalf of and in collaboration with the British Library BAME Staff Network Decolonisation Working Group

Introduction

In September 2020 the British Library added captions beneath the previously undescribed busts of four major figures proudly displayed at the main entrance of the Library's St Pancras building in London. We begin this chapter by reproducing two of those captions in their entirety, as they capture the essence of efforts by many within the Library to show how the institution's colonial entanglements resonate in the experience of staff and visitors every day.

> Sir Joseph Banks (1743–1820)
> Joseph Banks was a prominent botanist, who served as President of the Royal Society, and advised on the development of the Royal Botanic Gardens at Kew. He was a key figure in the British Empire's expansion in, and exploitation of, the Pacific. Banks self-funded his journey to join James Cook's first voyage to the Pacific in 1768. As well as collecting thousands of plant and animal specimens from across the globe, Banks and his party described and documented 'other' peoples they encountered.
>
> In a series of violent clashes during Cook's voyage around Aotearoa (New Zealand), Banks was involved in the murder of at least one Māori warrior and was also party to the kidnapping of three Māori youths in which four other Māori were shot and killed. A decade after returning to England, Banks advocated for the establishment of a British prison colony in 'New South Wales', and later of the British colonial settlement of Australia, which has resulted in the ongoing displacement and oppression of the continent's indigenous peoples. After his death, Banks' collections were left to the British Museum, later passing in part to the British Library.
>
> *Joseph Banks was a key player in the opening up of the Pacific and Australia for exploitation and enforced colonisation. Less publicised is his direct involvement in the murder of several Māori during his voyage with Cook on the* Endeavour. *My Ngati Kahungunu ancestors were among those killed – a trauma we still feel heavily today. For the indigenous peoples of the Pacific, Banks is a symbol for violence and oppression under the guise of exploration and science.*
> Scott Ratima Nolan, Conservation Support Assistant, British Library

Sir Hans Sloane (1660–1753)
Hans Sloane was born in Ulster, in the north of Ireland, and trained as a physician. An avid collector from an early age, he acquired over 200,000 plant and animal specimens, 71,000 objects, and over 50,000 books, manuscripts, prints and drawings. These later became the foundation collection of the British Museum.

Sloane travelled to Jamaica in 1687 as physician to the island's British colonial Governor and worked as a doctor on slave plantations. Using the expertise of enslaved West Africans and English planters, he collected hundreds of plant and animal specimens. When he returned to London, Sloane married Elizabeth Langley Rose, an heiress to sugar plantations in Jamaica. He was a shareholder in the Royal African and South Sea Companies, both of which profited from the slave trade. His medical income, his investments, and the profits from the forced labour on his wife's plantations enabled Sloane to build such a large collection.

It is too often said that the transatlantic slave trade is long behind us. An untold number of our ancestors' lives were completely ruined by men like Hans Sloane. Every one of their waking moments filled with violent abuse, torture, unpaid manual labour, rape and treatment as if less than human. That pain and trauma is still with us as we fight to make a world that is truly anti-racist. We cannot allow the glorification of enslavers and their legacies to continue through succeeding generations. We must remember these men for who they truly were, for their crimes as well as their accomplishments.

Reuben Massiah, Learning Facilitator, British Library
Chantelle Richardson, Chevening British Library Fellow 2019–2020/Librarian, National Library of Jamaica

The reinterpretation of the busts of Joseph Banks and Hans Sloane is the most emphatic manifestation to date of the Library's July 2020 commitment to becoming 'an actively anti-racist organisation' (BL, 2020a). Three distinct aspects of the reinterpretation mark a step change and an official engagement in the perpetual task of decolonising, namely:

- the open and public acknowledgement of institutionalised connections to empire and slavery, and the centrality of their associated violence and subjugation in the very foundations of the collections and the institution;
- the shift in perspective from institution to individual, centring the lived experience of coloniality in national cultural institutions;
- the participatory process, which brought together curators responsible for the artworks and interpretation, senior managers and, crucially, representatives from the BAME Staff Network, to develop caption texts that would make a material impact on the staff, researchers and communities the Library serves.

This chapter will first contextualise the recent history of 'decolonising' at the British Library, reflecting on the appropriateness of the term itself, before exploring ongoing work in a broad spectrum of areas from acquisitions to exhibitions, from public spaces to metadata. It will touch on the ongoing internal Anti-Racism Project, which has encouraged many colleagues to contribute towards the Library's gradual anti-racist transformation.

Contexts
The British Library

The British Library is a unique institution. As the national library it holds historical written material dating back to the founding collections of the British Museum. It is also one of six legal deposit libraries charged with collecting the UK's published output, both print and digital. It makes those vast collections 'accessible to everyone, for research, inspiration and enjoyment' (BL, 2015) in its reading rooms, its multiple catalogues, its ever-increasing digital offerings, its expanding research programme and in events and exhibitions on-site and online. An academic research library *and* cultural institution, responsible to the nation, the British Library is part of every 'decolonisation' conversation, whether that concerns museums and galleries, archives and libraries or education and curricula.

It carries a dual history, as both a relatively recent institution – with the British Library Act 1972 creating a national centre for reference, bibliographic and information services, uniting science, technological, business and arts and humanities research, and with the doors to its main building opening in the late 1990s – *and* a historic collection of items spanning worlds and millennia, rooted in the British Museum Library founded in 1753. Furthermore, over its near 50-year institutional history, the Library has integrated the National Central Library, the Patent Office Library, the National Lending Library for Science and Technology (Boston Spa, Yorkshire), the National Sound Archive and the India Office Collection (on loan from the Foreign Office). Since 2013 it has massively expanded its digital collecting through the UK Web Archive, in partnership with the other five legal deposit libraries. The Library's online and in-person learning offer has also grown with the continued expansion of national activities via the Living Knowledge Network, a partnership between the Library and over 20 public libraries in cities and towns. It also plans to develop a cultural space in Leeds to complement exhibition spaces at the Library's London site. This immense scope means that the Library reaches into numerous facets of public life, and it influences how a broad range of national and international audiences, including future generations, engage with and understand national historic narratives and cultural memory.

A colonial past

Considering the millions of born-digital and contemporary printed items in the Library's collections, it might be argued that disproportionate attention has been paid to its historic collections in depictions of the Library, especially by those focusing on colonial connections. Yet it is precisely the historic collections that have been favoured in the 'treasures' on display in permanent and temporary exhibitions, or on collections pages online. This is not to suggest that modern and contemporary material is absent from these spaces, nor that the Library's approach to contemporary material is beyond contention; rather, it is important to situate the historic collections at the core of the Library's identity and enmeshed in the spaces of its St Pancras site, emphatically highlighted by the prominent King's Library Tower of early printed books at the heart of the building. This is replicated in the Library's collections structure, with staffing resources weighted towards areas responsible for these collections.

Until very recently, the colonial acquisition histories of many items, or the implication of major collectors and donors in violent and coercive acts, were left unspoken. Worse, many of these same figures – as with Banks and Sloane, or with the presence of East India Company portraits and insignia in the Asian and African Reading Room and elsewhere – were displayed with little or the most benign description, effectively venerating these figures and Empire itself. In *Libraries within the Library: The Origins of the British Library's Printed Collections*, Sloane, for example, is described as a 'successful physician, with a highly lucrative practice' (Mandelbrote, 2009, 146); and Banks's 'missions to transplant breadfruit from the Pacific to the West Indies, to gather samples of and information about cotton cultivation in India, to break the Chinese monopoly on tea production by transferring its cultivation to parts of India (Assam) and to place hemp manufacture in British possessions' do not deter the authors from judging him simply as a 'fascinating representative of the English Enlightenment, and a pioneer on a global scale of botany and zoology' (Chambers and Joppien, 2009, 225–42). These narratives are partial, and uninterested in the contexts from which such collections, knowledge and wealth were derived. Book history of this kind prefers the mechanics of forming grand collections, the idiosyncrasies of their classification and use, or collectors' personalities. Absorbing such collections into the national library further abstracts them from their complex contexts, bolstering the Library as the neutral 'storehouse' of 'the world's knowledge' (Box 11.1).

> **Box 11.1: Connections to slavery**
> Books collected through the use of wealth derived from profits of the British system of slavery are dispersed throughout the Library's collections. Outside of the major named collections there are other, smaller collections and individual items which have direct associations with wealth gained from such exploitation. Much provenance has been lost and must be carefully reconstructed, while other provenance research has yet to begin.

To leave the colonial histories of collectors and collections unsaid is not a passive act; rather, it is a powerful upholding of the status quo. It privileges outdated narratives that actively omit the often violent and exploitative historical facts of colonialism and imperialism. In connecting that diffuse imperial history to the experience of colleagues at the Library in the new bust captions, there is recognition of the active harm done by institutional silence. More than that, the Library has begun to connect its history to its present, its colonial entanglements to its coloniality as an institution, whether in relation to its staff or its users. As Errol Francis writes, 'I believe there is a connection between questions of what to do about colonial provenance, imperialist narratives of history and civilisation, the lack of diversity of the workforce and the lack of interest from BAME and working-class audiences in what museums are offering' (Francis, 2018). Through the link between the British Library's singular history, its role in shaping *national* heritage and 'the ongoing lived impacts of the colonial on knowledge production' (Crilly, 2019, 9), we might begin to tentatively talk about coloniality and decolonisation at the British Library.

Decolonisation Working Group

When the Decolonisation Working Group of the BAME Staff Network formed in 2018, it agonised, as it still does today, over the term 'decolonising' (as the broader staff network has over the 'BAME' moniker). There are several tensions around how the term is applied in the UK Galleries-Libraries-Archives-Museums (GLAM) sector.

- Removed from contemporary settler-colonial contexts (Americas, Oceania, Southern Africa, Palestine, Ireland), to what extent does our usage of the term harness its cachet to forward a generic racial justice agenda that decentres questions around repatriation of land and power, and the existential threats to Indigenous peoples? Tuck and Yang famously warn against the 'ambiguity between decolonisation and social justice work', which leads to the 'front-loading of critical consciousness' and the evasion of genuine decolonising action. The universal application of the term to all injustices might also be a 'settler move to innocence', which relieves the burden on the institution by paying lip-service to the injustice, while 'conceal[ing] the need to give up land or power or privilege' (Tuck and Yang, 2012, 10–21).
- Without institutional acknowledgement of the coloniality of its systems and practices, and without a subsequent commitment to structural and cultural transformation, decolonisation becomes a stand-in for 'equality and diversity'. To what extent are we limiting ourselves to rebalancing discussions around representation and diversification? To what extent do those rebalancing operations uphold the coloniality of an institution unbending to genuine fundamental transformation, maintaining 'marginalised narratives' as still marginal 'contributions' to a static and conventional universal narrative?
- Given this complexity and the potential hollowness of 'decolonising', institutions question how staff and users can relate it to their activities. Is there a place for more focused (and less political) language such as 'diversification', 'decentring knowledge', 'devaluing hierarchies', 'diminish[ing] some voices […] while magnifying others' (Appleton, 2019) when it comes to collections, and 'anti-racism' when it comes to the institution? Are there equivalent risks in moving away from more political and broad-picture language, towards specific, action-focused

initiatives? Can we use 'decolonising' as a useful umbrella term that allows us to move and speak about related approaches and activities between collections that are geographically, temporally and materially diverse, or does the very work require, indeed demand, nuance and specificity?
- Finally, is it even possible to decolonise collections that are fundamentally and literally constituted by colonialist, settler-colonialist and imperialist activities? For example, would the use of historic maps or treaty documents that evidence land claims by Indigenous groups be a radical upturning of institutionalised coloniality, or does it accept and follow the same logic (and law), reinforcing precedents that disenfranchise other groups in similar situations?

The Working Group is responsible to the BAME Staff Network and has always been led by members of that Network, rather than by the institution. Its initial aims were to provide a space for members to openly and safely discuss decolonisation and its implications for the Library, to provide learning opportunities on the subject for staff and to be open to challenging conversations. Embedded within the BAME Staff Network, those discussions have always been framed by the Network's core purposes of providing support, community and advocacy for BAME staff, whether in the form of Safe Space provision, Staff Development forums, events or education. In other words, theory and practice have always been connected through the underlying question: how is the colonial history of the Library linked to a systemic institutional coloniality, *and* how does that coloniality pervade the workplace as racial inequality and discrimination, and pervade our knowledge management systems as structural biases and problematic content? And how can we bring those connections to light to lead directly to the material uplift of BAME colleagues in the Library, and of existing and potential communities of BAME researchers and visitors? With that in mind, we might offer the following responses to the tensions around the term 'decolonising' outlined earlier.

Links to colonial and imperial history

It is worth repeating here that some of the British Library's major collections are inextricably linked to colonial and imperial history. There are direct links between some collections and profits derived from slavery and other forms of colonial violence and subjugation, or, in the words of the Library's own *Cultural Property Management Framework* 'parts of our collections [...] can be associated directly or indirectly with the British imperial expansion' (BL, 2018, 8). There are items that were taken from their contexts through British military expeditions (Derillo, 2019, 103). There are East India Company archives, artworks, weaponry even, some on display. And the historic libraries and archives that were integrated into today's national institution were established at a time when the *collection* of artefacts was part of a process of reclassification, representation and fragmentation of Indigenous knowledges and heritage to further a European epistemic tradition that created racial, ethnic and cultural hierarchies (see Smith, 2012, 20–60). That is the underside of cultural heritage approaches that explain away their collections as predominantly products of 'normal trade in objects either created to be traded or habitually traded' (BL, 2018, 7). The Library's claim to 'the world's knowledge', which might be said to 'assume a certain ownership of the entire world' (Smith, 2012, 58), is thus founded on the real historical and institutional experience of colonialism and imperialism.

That history leaves its structural mark on the Library in what we have referred to as coloniality, 'the logic, metaphysics, ontology, and matrix of power created by the massive processes of colonisation and decolonisation'; and 'the modern West, its hegemonic discourses, and its hegemonic institutions are themselves a product, just like the colonies, of coloniality' (Maldonado-Torres, 2016). The result is a privileging of the 'Western way of knowledge production' – which might include, for example, outdated and offensive catalogue records, or inaccessible and under-represented material related to marginalised communities – which 'has set up interpretive frames that make it difficult to think outside of these frames', and, worse, 'actively represses anything that actually is articulated, thought and envisioned from outside of these frames' (Mbembe, 2015). Such an approach also underpins fundamental Library principles, namely that publicly owned knowledge is 'for everyone' (BL, 2020b). This applies regardless of an item's original use, its continued specific meaning to a specific community of users, and the harm that may be caused by prioritising access over respecting community wishes. This is the fine line that must be navigated, with potentially even more caution by a library than a gallery, museum, or archive, given that access to information is *the* defining feature of libraries.

Professional inequalities

Real historical entanglements with colonialism and their subsequent systemic manifestation thus feed into professional inequalities and injustices, perpetuated by the normalisation of those structures. As Crilly puts it, 'coloniality is perhaps not always recognised but nevertheless informs and influences both the historical and ongoing development of collections and wider structures such as the whiteness of the library profession in the UK' (Crilly, 2019, 9). The umbilical link between the historic institution, its collections, its systems, structures and spaces makes the case for the pursuit of 'decolonising' at the British Library.

That pursuit, justified here by the link between past and present, has taken a decolonial approach in so far as British Library efforts 'do not isolate knowledge from action. They combine knowledge, practice, and creative expressions, among other areas in their efforts to change the world' (Maldonado-Torres, 2016). If decoloniality is about 'an *active* undoing, deconstructing, or delinking from coloniality' (Crilly, 2019, 9, emphasis added), the Working Group has developed into an active collective, collaborating widely both internally and externally, that has advocated for transformative action, all the more urgently as a consequence of the racial justice movements of 2020. It would be overstating the case to say that these efforts challenge the principles at the heart of Western knowledge systems, but it is certainly a starting point to asking questions about, and of, these principles from within.

A year of change

The global COVID-19 pandemic shed light on existing social inequalities in the UK, evident in large organisations like the British Library, where BAME staff either were disproportionately represented in roles that were front line (such as security and cleaning), often on a precarious basis via the use of fixed-term contracts and external contracting, or were without work to do due to site closure (such as basement retrieval). A combination of frustration with the uncontrollable externalities, remoteness or freedom from the structures of the workplace, time and space to reflect, among many other personal impacts of the pandemic, was the local context in which the murder of George Floyd and the resurgence of the Black Lives Matter movement entered.

As institutions across the cultural sector began to make commitments in the light of undeniable systemic racial inequalities of representation, pay and opportunity, the British Library too was driven by an ever-increasing group of BAME staff, allies and sympathetic colleagues into a process of self-reckoning. This genre of public statement saw the clearest, often platitudinous, acknowledgement of the link between institutional history and institutional present. The British Library's commitment followed this same two-pronged approach to 'anti-racism'. In July, the Library published a press release expressing its commitment to becoming an actively anti-racist organisation (BL, 2020a), and subsequently embedded that in its Strategy Refresh, stating: 'we are committed to an antiracism action plan that will guide our response to vital questions including representation within senior levels of our workforce, an open recognition of the colonial origins and legacy of some of our collections, and ensuring the inclusivity of our spaces, events, exhibitions and policies' (BL, 2020b, 12).

The steps that brought the Library to this point were hard won, and often bypassed conventional 'chain of command' means of communicating with senior management to do justice to the voice of a considerable body of staff. A letter addressing institutional racism and the custodianship of colonial collections was communicated directly to the Strategic Leadership Team (SLT). The letter asked that the Library make anti-racism a strategic priority and covered long-standing issues around representation, pay and grading, staff development and discrimination, as well as collections issues, including public acknowledgement of colonial connections, committing to conversations around decolonising, proper resource and expertise for under-represented collections and research and a rethink of public engagement and the ways in which we welcome and serve diverse audiences. Emblematic of the structural problem was the fact that the SLT, a group of over 30 senior managers, had no non-White members at the time. Similarly, across the collections area of the Library, there were only six self-identifying BAME curators among a total cohort of 120 curators, with no representation at all in Western Heritage Collections or Contemporary British Collections, which includes the entire Sound and Vision section (i.e. the UK's Sound Archive, which holds one of the largest world music collections globally).

Following the welcome integration of representatives of the staff networks (LGBTQ, Disability Support, Gender Equality and BAME) and unions into the SLT, the Library made its anti-racist commitment. That commitment, while not as far ranging as other statements in the sector, did inaugurate an Anti-Racism Project that has been given the independence and resource to translate that commitment into a plan of action. Involving over 70 volunteers, subgroups have been tasked to develop recommendations in areas covering values and behaviours, human resources, audiences, cataloguing and metadata, and collections and curation.

It is important to note that work towards decolonising has been ongoing in many corners of the Library for many years. If it were not for the long-standing commitment and work of colleagues around issues that have only now been given real credence, the projects detailed in the following section might not be so well ahead in some instances. And without the impetus of the Working Group, the opportunity for such a transformative future might have been missed. It is with one of the Working Group's projects that we begin the survey of decolonising activity at the British Library.

Activities

Public spaces

In 2019 the Working Group began to audit the objects on display at the Library's St Pancras site, with the premise of understanding how the Library was approaching Britain's Empire and its legacy and of focusing the Library leadership's attention on the necessity of a more critical approach to the items on display. No known effort had as yet been made to proactively detail imperial connections in the collections, with provenance information often deemed superfluous when it came to captioning. Further, the Library's branding as the centre of 'the world's knowledge' had been used for years without any attempt to contextualise the conditions under which that heritage had reached Britain. In 2019 the billboard on the north side of the Library advertised what the public could expect to find within the Library, listing, 'Shops – Cafes – The whole wealth of human knowledge, endeavour and experience to date – Events – Exhibitions'. Aside from the statement's hubris, it concealed the very processes that enabled it. To the extent that the Library contains the whole of human everything, this 'knowledge, endeavour and experience' was in part acquired through the workings of imperial power.

The public spaces, reading rooms, offices and meeting rooms are replete with paintings, busts and other artworks, most with minimal captions, many without any at all. Working with the University College London Legacies of British Slave Ownership Database and the *Oxford Dictionary of National Biography* (ODNB), among other sources, Working Group members detailed the object and personal histories behind those objects on display. This research revealed the extent to which the Library had unreflectively put figures related to Empire on (often literal) pedestals, and also the extent to which such imagery had been favoured over representations of more diverse figures and communities, not to mention the absence of figures related to anti-colonial and social justice movements.

This audit made recommendations to recontextualise and, in some cases, remove objects from view, ultimately leading to the formation of the group to reinterpret the entrance hall busts described and quoted at the beginning of this chapter. Many of the artworks that fell within the audit's remit were related to the East India Company (EIC), whose insignia, battle paintings and official portraits decorate the Asian and African Studies Reading Room in particular, a space the users and staff of which are predominantly from among the descendants of those on the receiving end of imperial violence. The audit report pointed, for example, to a painting of Lord Robert Clive (1725–74), first British Governor of the Bengal Presidency, as a particularly egregious example of imperial veneration, Clive bearing particular responsibility for the Bengal Famine of 1769–70. A related report which included a staff survey of EIC weaponry on display in one of the Library's offices revealed overwhelming staff malcontent at having to work every day underneath a brutal history of subjugation.

The internal distribution of the draft audit came after the Library had publicised its anti-racism commitment, further exposing the embeddedness of its coloniality, continuing to share knowledge and inspire conversations in the wider community of library staff and, significantly, sparking direct conversations with senior decision makers. Acknowledgement of the expertise gained from such research and of the lived experience of staff beyond the SLT has ultimately led to a more collaborative and democratised approach to anti-racist work. More than that, the work done to contextualise the public spaces has to be seen, to borrow from Achille Mbembe, as 'inseparable from the democratisation of access'; and by critically engaging with 'those colonial names, iconography, i.e. the economy of symbols, whose function, all along, has been to induce and normalise particular states of humiliation based on white supremacist presuppositions', we take a step closer to a renewed 'ownership of a space that is a public, common good' (Mbembe, 2015).

Custodianship
The limits of legal deposit
The British Library frequently states that, as a result of the combination of historical collecting with its legal deposit function, its 'documentation of the nature of life in Britain and of Britain in the world [is] unmatched by other United Kingdom cultural institutions in its inclusivity, in its breadth, and in its depth' (BL, 2018, 2). In practice, legal deposit cannot ensure that every local, ephemeral, community, do-it-yourself and online

publication is included in the collections. Even a form of collecting as apparently 'neutral' as archiving the UK's published output by crawling the UK web domain is far from neutral in practice. This is because many individuals without academic or institutional affiliation and many small groupings represent themselves online using larger, often US-based, platforms such as Facebook or WordPress because they are free of charge. These sites do not form part of the UK domain crawl, and so must be identified manually in order to be collected. The result is that official, mainstream institutions are over-represented in the archive. Similarly, print collecting is more straightforward where publishers use ISBNs or ISSNs, whereas considerable resources would be required to identify non-commercial or more marginal publications. Nor can the work of description, access and interpretation be consistent and rich in all areas. Beyond legal deposit, contemporary purchased collecting in the areas of serials, archives and manuscripts, European and Americas Collections, and Asian and African Collections strives to capture the same breadth and depth in global contexts, but is highly selective. It is this 'privilege to select' (Schmidt, 2020) that must be interrogated and unpacked if colonial hierarchies are to be undone in the way we produce knowledge at the British Library (Box 11.2).

> **Box 11.2: The influence of historic decisions**
> Historic decisions resonate in contemporary understanding of the Library's collections. For instance, many of the Library's early printed collections from Asia and Africa contribute to the reproduction of a very partial or even distorted understanding of the history of those countries. One example is the way that the collection of early Arabic publishing, driven as it was by Orientalist scholarship focused on Islamic learning, omits all but the faintest trace of early Arab feminist publishing. Library staff are encouraged to undertake research on the collections for exhibitions, digitisation projects or more general promotion, but if the collections are partial, the focus on collections works against a fuller understanding of the histories of the countries from which those collections are drawn.

Strategic priorities

The Library claims that it is nearly unrivalled in its comprehensive collections. Nonetheless, the 2020 Content Strategy conveys an understanding that much more can be done to focus on communities and experiences that are under-represented in the collections, or under-exposed due to being deprioritised for digitisation, cataloguing or exhibition projects, for example.

> [The Content Strategy] is also about ensuring that our collection reflects the full diversity of life and experience in the UK, and that our international collecting reflects the spectrum of views that make up the contemporary politics, society and culture of the countries from which we purchase material, including material that represents the voices of groups who are or have been marginalized in mainstream publishing.
>
> (BL, 2020c, 3)

One of the strategy's priority areas is Black Studies, which has already precipitated a project that engages widely across the Library. Approaches to content are enmeshed with questions around access, discovery and engagement, which are naturally highlighted in this strategy. Yet there are also questions around the naturalised injustices in the global research and publication systems, which often privilege familiarity, marketability and au-fait-ness with the strictures of an academic publication context dominated by European, US and predominantly Anglophone research. When it comes to the approval plan method of selection, which the Library does use for certain areas, where books are pre-selected by suppliers based on a collection profile, it is inevitable that what enters the purview of suppliers is influenced by 'what sells' and 'what sells is largely defined by social bias, which is thereby reproduced, and with it social injustice' (Schmidt, 2020, 319) (Box 11.3). This is not to say that curators at the British Library neglect this fact. Rather, it acknowledges that truly decolonial collection development for an international research library would necessitate the decentring of conventional and convenient sources in favour of those currently marginalised and neglected. As Schmidt has it, 'Researchers cannot voice demand for something that is invisible to them' (Schmidt, 2020, 316). The Library's international position means that it carries a responsibility to progress the rebalancing of that system.

> **Box 11.3: The bias inherent in Open Access**
> As research moves increasingly towards Open Access publishing models, inherent biases surface through the requisite pre-publication costs: 'researchers in privileged environments clearly are at an advantage once more. The constitution of open access as the new standard comes at a cost that often excludes "Global South" participation, since it requires advanced IT infrastructure and considerable staff resources' (Schmidt, 2020, 112).

Such progress is reliant on the resourcing and development of collections staff, and the integration of external community collaboration. To prioritise Black Studies, for example, requires expertise and lived experience to thread the discipline and the communities it engages into the Library's fabric. That would include: hiring curators responsible for the area directly; the development of a network of community curators; training for staff; long-term projects that centre these collections; or internal collaboration with staff networks. Black Studies serves as an important example for the future direction of the Library, as it refers not simply to content but to a methodology. As Kehinde Andrews underlines, 'Learning about Black people is not enough and we are developing methodologies for social change rather than simply analysis' (Andrews, 2018). The decolonial approach to custodianship must aim at reforming the systemic obstacles to representation, not just at representation itself, and that is always enmeshed in processes relating to broader and more fundamental social change.

One consequence of 'developing methodologies for social change' is a transformation in the positionality of the British Library. We have touched on the implications of ownership inherent in the strapline, 'the world's knowledge', but that sense of authority is also behind the Library's well-intentioned ambition of 'enabling access for everyone'. For one thing, a culturally sensitive approach to historic Indigenous material in the Library's collections would entail a parallel approach of *restricting* access to certain items, where culturally specific protocols allow access only to members of a community, as accounted for in rights management systems like Mukurtu (Box 11.4). Further, historic material that harbours potentially offensive and harmful metadata, imagery or content, ought not to be forgotten when championing the benefits of making *everything* accessible for *everyone*, and *forever*.

> **Box 11.4: Mukurtu**
> Mukurtu is an open source content management system designed in collaboration with Indigenous communities to ensure culturally appropriate use of Indigenous heritage online. Mukurtu offers the ability to provide differential access to community members and the general public as well as metadata that foregrounds Indigenous knowledge. It is developed and maintained at the Center for Digital Scholarship and Curation at Washington State University.
>
> 'Mukurtu is a grassroots project aiming to empower communities to manage, share, narrate, and exchange their digital heritage in culturally relevant and ethically-minded ways. We are committed to maintaining an open, community-driven approach to Mukurtu's continued development. Our first priority is to help build a platform that fosters relationships of respect and trust' (Mukurtu Mission Statement, https://mukurtu.org/about).

Models of distributed custodianship

More pertinent to contemporary collection development, the Library's responsibility as custodian of the UK's printed heritage might also retain a 'therapeutic model' of service, whereby users become 'beneficiaries' and the Library takes on the role of 'carer' (Lynch, 2017, 13), and where the authority of shaping and interpreting the nation's culture rests with the institution *on behalf of* communities. While the Library preserves niche, local, community content for the benefit of posterity, the connection often stops at collection, detaching that item from its context, losing sight of its relevance in the depths of the vast collections and offering little legacy impact for the publication community from which it came. To what extent should the Library continually take in content, and to what extent is that the best way of representing and preserving cultural heritage writ large? The question may be extreme, but it is worth posing. Of course, the Library must strive to collect under the broadest definition of cultural heritage, and the greater evil is surely still the omissions in our collections of various community and independent publications among other under-represented work – gaps which could ultimately perpetuate non-diverse narratives. That said, more could be done to relinquish authority on the part of the institution and to develop an approach that *also* facilitates archiving and discovery within communities, especially those communities who for many reasons have reservations about interfacing with government departments, public bodies and institutions like the British Library.

On an international level, the Library's Endangered Archives Programme (EAP; BL, n.d.) offers a successful model for resourcing and supporting community archival projects, while 'seek[ing] to ensure that the values of the people and communities from which the archives have come are respected and that they are consulted in any significant re-use of the digital material [held at the Library]' (BL, n.d.). Framing the EAP explicitly as a departure from the 'collecting activities of colonial explorers, soldiers and administrators', van Schaik writes, 'these collections are held in trust for the original owners and their descendants, and offer the potential for an approach to research based on a greater understanding of the custodians of the traditions, who have preserved and transmitted them through to the present day' (van Schaik, 2020). Similarly, the True Echoes project, which aims to reconnect 'indigenous communities with historic audio records of the sung and spoken cultures of Australia and Oceania', is founded on a premise to work 'in partnership with the communities whose cultures the recordings represent, enabling new understanding that is informed by local knowledge and cultural memory' (BL, 2021). These approaches might serve as a foundation on which to diminish the authority of the Library, developing instead a position elsewhere referred to as 'culturally humble neutrality' (Schmidt, 2020), 'radical empathy' (Caswell and Cifor, 2016) or 'radical trust' (Lynch and Alberti, 2010, 30). They entail, first, the genuine participation of communities and users in decisions about the preservation, access and interpretation of heritage; but also, importantly, they embrace an ethical imperative to consider the full complexity of our user base (academics, artists, community members, descendants of imperial subjects, etc.) and the 'need to build policies, procedures, and services with these users in mind, but even more so, [the] need to shift our affective orientations in service to these users' (Caswell and Cifor, 2016, 37).

Cataloguing and metadata

To focus on the affective impact for diverse users of the British Library collections there must also be a framework for ethical metadata. There are innumerable historic catalogue records that reflect outdated and oppressive attitudes, which reside in the range of British Library catalogues and in secondary platforms that link back to those catalogues, such as the BL Flickr page. For example, the India Office Records – 'archives of the administration in London of the East India Company and the pre-1947 government of India [...] complemented by deposits of private papers relating to the British experience in India' (BL, IOR, n.d.) – inevitably, as Chilcott glosses for historic archives generally, 'represent people of colour through a colonial lens, often describing individuals or communities using derogatory and racist language. This language is inherited by catalogue descriptions that remain in use today' (Chilcott, 2019, 359). Projects have already investigated interim means of correction and have to date looked at computational methods for identifying problematic terminology and its extent, using glossaries such as that included in the Tropenmuseum's publication, *Words Matter* (2018). An increasingly standard precautionary measure for archives and libraries online, and one which shows the bare minimum of empathy with users, is the inclusion of a cultural-sensitivity warning alerting users to potentially offensive descriptions. The Library does not yet direct users to a warning on entry into the Explore the British Library catalogue, but the

British Library Images Online commercial platform for digitised content does incorporate such a warning, which, at a minimum, ought to be expanded and made consistent across all the Library's catalogues.

The Library is also involved in international conversations addressing problematic aspects of subject headings, demographic terms and inflexible indexing schema (Box 11.5). Subject headings potentially harbour offensive language in themselves, but the rigidity of subject indexing systems also contributes to the obfuscation of content related to under-represented communities in the collections, above and beyond the vast number of records in the catalogues without any subject indexing at all. Users will continue to face difficulties in discovering records related to particular communities, unless more is done to privilege those records. One approach yet to be explored by the Library to its fullest extent is the potential for participatory methods of record enhancement. Embedding some flexibility within the catalogues themselves would provide an opportunity to combine both discoverability and community collaboration.

> **Box 11.5: BL participation in international standards development**
> The British Library participates in the development of metadata standards through membership of international bodies, including EURIG, representing the European RDA Region, European Dewey Decimal User Group (EDUG), FAST Policy and Outreach Committee (FPOC); Program for Cooperative Cataloging (PCC); International Standard Name Identifier (ISNI). Through its participation in these bodies the Library represents UK interests and perspectives and can influence choice of terminology, inclusion of appropriate subject headings, etc.

One area where discoverability has been improved is in 'the use of machine learning techniques […] in order to provide information about the language of content of the resources described' (Morris, 2019, 1). This language-identification project has successfully enhanced over three million legacy records related to pre-1970s printed material, which entered the catalogue without language codes and without any means for users to identify them by language. This innovative project encouraged human cataloguers and language specialists at the Library to quality-assure the machine-generated coding, most importantly for 'low resource' languages and for languages that are closely related and therefore more difficult to distinguish. The process might offer an insight into a future of record enhancement that combines computation with community collaboration (Box 11.6).

> **Box 11.6: Machine-generated language coding**
> There are challenges with machine approaches to language coding. For example, the program, and automatic language identification more broadly, has difficulty distinguishing between languages written in syllabary. Another complication is that available language codes are often inappropriate and do not reflect the complexities of language transmission, for instance where a community has been historically displaced and their language has evolved alongside others.

Such processes only begin to address racial hierarchies perpetuated by information management systems, however, when the focus is turned specifically on under-represented collections, rather than expecting any at-scale enhancement to naturally result in rebalancing the discoverability of materials of relevance to marginalised communities. This is yet another instance in which a rising tide cannot be expected to lift all boats. As Padilla notes, 'while the number of collections tuned for computation grows, it remains the case that the majority are the product of large Western institutions [...] corpora that overrepresent dominant communities and underrepresent marginalized communities' (Padilla, 2019, 15). The under-representation of certain communities in collections and their under-description and discoverability thus raises questions about the knowledge derived from computational methods. 'A critical historical perspective and resources are required to create corpora that remediate underrepresentation. Without these steps, libraries and researchers run the risk of reifying existing biases in a limited cultural record' (Padilla, 2019, 16). At worst, we run the risk of reproducing the offensive terminology itself, as 'scholars have begun to name and identify a growing tendency to reinscribe racist ideologies and codify damaging ideas about how we organize and create new knowledge as one drawback of mass digitization' (Purcell and Sutherland, 2021, 67). For instance, there are examples of tags algorithmically assigned to images in the Library's Flickr gallery, derived from their original book contexts, which include problematic language left unchecked and uncontextualised (www.flickr.com/photos/britishlibrary). As the Library experiments with computational methods for collections analysis, the duty of care to users must remain paramount, and processes of collaboration, quality assurance and community verification are crucial to an ethical approach to access.

Exhibitions

Increasing collaboration, internal and external, in the Library's exhibitions and interpretation work has proven important for the centring of diverse communities in the institution's most public output. Exhibitions on women's rights ('Unfinished Business'), gay rights ('Gay UK'), West African culture ('West Africa: Word, Symbol, Song'), the Windrush generation ('Windrush: Songs in a Strange Land'), and Khadija Saye's 'In This Space We Breathe' portrait series, among other smaller displays and online curated content, have showcased experiences and collections that have rarely figured before. More importantly, they have served as confident insertions into national discussions around issues of human rights, identity politics, citizenship, migration and racism. The Library has also worked to expand its permanent 'Treasures Gallery' to reflect both more contemporary material and more diverse experiences, incorporating items from the recently acquired Andrea Levy Archive (2018) – which marked the first occasion that the Library acquired the archive of a Black woman – and a letter by Ignatius Sancho, while initiating a longer-term plan to redesign that gallery with diversity and inclusion in mind.

Library leaders have taken steps to integrate the views of staff networks in the shaping of exhibitions, and opportunities are given to staff to provide comments in the nascent stages of exhibition development. It is undeniable that this is just the beginning of a long process of creating real diversity in the Library's exhibitions, and in the exhibitions programme as a whole. Community collaboration is often deemed supplementary to exhibitions, resulting in narrative and interpretive authority remaining with the institutional voice of the British Library. That voice is often articulated in limited captions that inevitably reduce the complexity of exhibited material. Again, there is a difference between consultation and collaboration, or between representation and inclusion. As exhibitions focused on under-represented experiences become less exceptional, the risk of co-option, exploitation (of lived experience, of community resource) or a kind of diversity-washing is heightened so long as meaningful participation, co-curation and co-responsibility with community collaborators remains underdeveloped. This comes with acknowledging that the collections in the British Library are not 'owned' by the British Library. Ways need to be found for the authority of interpreting national cultural heritage to be democratised, redistributed and complicated to reflect its real multiplicity, and thereby prevent the repetition of authoritative narratives and their intrinsic biases. Ultimately, 'if communities are not given the opportunity to record their own "history from below", what passes as the official collective past is neither one they find meaningful nor one they can relate to' (Hess, Jackson and Mutibwa, 2020, 159).

Conclusion

This chapter has aimed to outline the ways in which the British Library has engaged with what can tentatively be called decolonising. It has not been able to do justice to every project and every colleague that has fed into a necessarily continual process of institutional transformation. It has not explored the Library's multiple research projects, which contribute immensely to new understandings and approaches to material such as the North American Indigenous collections or the reception of BAME writing in Britain, to point to just two recent projects. Nor has it described nascent projects that are trying to introduce non-Western approaches in collection care and conservation, if not in the Library's fundamental understanding of 'cultural property'. These ideas scratch the surface and are testament to the readiness of colleagues for the kind of structural changes promised by the Anti-Racism Project. By framing that project as anti-racist, rather than 'decolonial', the Library has clearly acknowledged the existence of racial inequality in its structures today, as well as in its history and its collections. That is vital to decolonising the British Library, a process that must always endeavour to improve the real lives and experiences of marginalised staff, researchers and visitors.

However, it might also allow the Library to evade the more publicly contentious conversation around decolonising, which has been co-opted by anti-progressive political causes. It moves the institution a step away from acknowledging the connectedness of racist, colonialist attitudes to collections and the discrepancies in staffing roles and pay that this chapter has touched on. Tuck and Yang's warning about the 'ambiguity between decolonisation and social justice work' is real. Nonetheless, such a project requires the Library in its role as cultural institution to ask difficult questions of itself. It requires the Library to 'step away from current practice and challenge the fundamental cornerstone of an industry that has never been pre-colonial' (Minott, 2019, 2). It must interrogate itself confidently, transparently and collaboratively, opening itself up to challenge and, 'however laden with the problematic history and ideology of its institutional conception, [it] might position itself as a space for performance of critical citizenship in relation to wider hegemonic discourses articulated in politics and media' (Bryce and Carnegie, 2013, 1740). As *the* national library, the British Library has a responsibility to decolonise, to be actively anti-racist and to lead a sectoral transformation that will create the conditions for genuine diversity in the workplace and in senior roles, for genuine equality for that diverse staff and for genuine empathy towards the experiences of *all*.

Note

This chapter was co-written by a group of British Library staff members across various departments who have been part of the Decolonisation Working Group of the Library's Black and Minority Ethnic (BAME) Staff Network. It is based on our own experiences and research, as well as in-depth engagement with racialised staff, users and other Library stakeholders. In our work we have striven to find a balance between prioritising collective action and maintaining member anonymity while remaining mindful of the need that the work of each individual, and the emotional toll that takes, not be appropriated by others. This chapter represents one perspective of many within the Library, but hopefully one that does justice to the variety and complexity of conversations, projects and experiences.

References

Andrews, K. (2018) Preface. In Chantiluke, R., Kwoba, B., Nkopo, A. and Nylander, O. (eds), *Rhodes Must Fall, The Struggle to Decolonise the Racist Heart of Empire*, Zed Books.

Appleton, N. S. (2019) Do Not 'Decolonize' … If You Are Not Decolonizing: Progressive Language and Planning Beyond a Hollow Academic Rebranding, *Critical Ethnic Studies Journal Blog*, www.criticalethnicstudiesjournal.org/blog/2019/1/21/do-not-decolonize-if-you-are-not-decolonizing-alternate-language-to-navigate-desires-for-progressive-academia-6y5sg.

BL (British Library) (2015) Living Knowledge: The British Library 2015–2023, www.bl.uk/about-us/our-vision (accessed 16 March 2021).

BL (2018) Cultural Property Management Framework, www.bl.uk/about-us/freedom-of-information/5-our-policies-and-procedures (accessed 16 March 2021).

BL (2020a) British Library Commits to Becoming an Anti-racist Organisation, www.bl.uk/press-releases/2020/july/british-library-commits-to-becoming-an-anti-racist-organisation (accessed 16 March 2021).

BL (2020b) Living Knowledge for Everyone – The British Library's Role in Renewal, www.bl.uk/about-us/our-vision (accessed 16 March 2021).

BL (2020c) Enabling Access for Everyone – The British Library's Content Strategy 2020–2023, www.bl.uk/about-us/governance/policies/content-strategy (accessed 16 March 2021).

BL (2021) True Echoes, 9 February, www.bl.uk/projects/true-echoes (accessed 16 March 2021).

BL (n.d.) Endangered Archives Programme (EAP), https://eap.bl.uk/about (accessed 16 March 2021).

BL, IOR (India Office Records) (n.d.) www.bl.uk/collection-guides/india-office-records (accessed 16 March 2021).

Bryce D. and Carnegie, E. (2013) Exhibiting the 'Orient': Historicising Theory and Curatorial Practice in UK Museums and Galleries, *Environment and Planning A*, **45** (7), 1734–52.

Caswell, M. L. and Cifor, M. (2016) From Human Rights to Feminist Ethics: Radical Empathy in Archives, *Archivaria*, **81**, 23–43.

Chambers, N. and Joppien, R. (2009) The Scholarly Library and Collections of Knowledge of Sir Joseph Banks. In Mandelbrote, G. and Taylor, B. (eds), *Libraries within the Library: The Origins of the British Library's Printed Collections*, The British Library.

Chilcott, A. (2019) Towards Protocols for Describing Racially Offensive Language in UK Public Archives, *Archival Science*, **19**, 359–76.

Crilly, J. (2019) Decolonising the Library: A Theoretical Exploration, *Spark: UAL Creative Teaching and Learning Journal*, **4**, 6–15.

Derillo, E. (2019) Exhibiting the Maqdala Manuscripts: African Scribes: Manuscript Culture of Ethiopia, *African Research and Documentation*, **135**, 102–16.

Francis, E. (2018) It's Time all Museums Were Postcolonial, www.museumsassociation.org/museums-journal/opinion/2018/06/01072018-its-time-all-museums-were-postcolonial (accessed 3 March 2021).

Hess, A., Jackson, T. and Mutibwa, D. (2020) Strokes of Serendipity: Community Co-Curation and Engagement with Digital Heritage, *Convergence: The International Journal of Research into New Media Technologies*, **26**, 157–77.

Lynch, B. (2017) The Gate in the Wall: Beyond Happiness-Making in Museums. In Onciul, B., Stefano, M. L. and Hawke, S. (eds) *Engaging Heritage, Engaging Communities*, 11–29, Boydell Press.

Lynch, B. and Alberti, S. (2010) Legacies of Prejudice: Racism, Co-Production and Radical Trust in the Museum, *Museum Management and Curatorship*, **25**, 13–35.

Maldonado-Torres, N. (2016) Outline of Ten Theses on Coloniality and Decoloniality, http://fondation-frantzfanon.com/wp-content/uploads/2018/10/maldonado-torres_outline_of_ten_theses-10.23.16.pdf (accessed 7 January 2021).

Mandelbrote, G. (2009) Sloane and the Preservation of Printed Ephemera. In Mandelbrote, G. and Taylor, B. (eds), *Libraries Within the Library: The Origins of the British Library's Printed Collections*, The British Library.

Mbembe, A. (2015) Decolonizing Knowledge and the Question of the Archive, https://africaisacountry.atavist.com/decolonizing-knowledge-and-the-question-of-the-archive (accessed 6 January 2021).

Minott, R. (2019) The Past is Now. Confronting Museums' Complicity in Imperial Celebration, *Third Text*, **33**, 559–74.

Morris, V. (2019) Automated Language Identification of Bibliographic Resources, *Cataloguing and Classification Quarterly*, **58**, 1–27.

Padilla, T. (2019) Responsible Operations: Data Science, Machine Learning and AI in Libraries, OCLC Research Position Paper, www.oclc.org/content/dam/research/publications/2019/oclcresearch-responsible-operations-data-science-machine-learning-ai-a4.pdf.

Purcell, A. and Sutherland, T. (2021) A Weapon and a Tool: Decolonizing Description and Embracing Redescription as Liberatory Archival Praxis, *The International Journal of Information, Diversity, & Inclusion*, **5**, 60–78.

Schmidt, N. (2020) The Privilege to Select. Global Research System, European Academic Library Collections, and Decolonisation (dissertation), https://doi.org/10.5281/zenodo.4011295.

Smith, L. T. (2012) *Decolonising Methodologies: Research and Indigenous Peoples*, Zed Books.

Tropenmuseum (2018) *Words Matter: An Unfinished Guide to Word Choices in the Cultural Sector*, https://issuu.com/tropenmuseum/docs/wordsmatter_english (accessed 6 January 2021).

Tuck, E. and Yang, K. W. (2012) Decolonization is not a Metaphor, *Decolonization: Indigeneity, Education & Society*, **1**, 1–40.

van Schaik, S. (2020) The Endangered Archives Programme. Towards a Different Kind of Collection, *International Institute of Asian Studies Newsletter*, **85**, www.iias.asia/the-newsletter/article/endangered-archives-programme-towards-different-kind-collection (accessed 22 January 2021).

12
Cataloguing, Classification and Critical Librarianship at Cambridge University

Cambridge University Decolonising Through Critical Librarianship Group

Introduction

The Decolonise campaign at Cambridge University included an open letter from the FLY network, for women and non-binary people of colour, to the English Faculty, requesting that the Library 'move postcolonial books out of the basement and integrate them in the library cataloguing order' (FLY, 2017). Students were quick to recognise the importance of library systems in the preservation and organisation of knowledge, and they demanded a professional collaboration to address a transformation of the curriculum from within the library system. The student-led Cambridge Decolonise Network first began in 2015, and organised with the call for the University to 'Decolonise Disarm Divest' in 2018. Students organised protests and revised reading lists via Facebook groups and Google documents. The Network led to the creation of subject-focused working groups, such as Decolonise Sociology, Decolonise Law and Decolonise Anthropology. They collaborated with groups such as Black Cantabs Research Society, a 'counter-history project' designed to 'place Black students in the institution's past, present, and future', which in turn collaborated with the University Library on a 'Black Cantabs: History Makers' exhibition in 2018 (Cambridge University Library, 2018; Black Cantabs, n.d.). In its specific mention of library space and cataloguing, the FLY letter encouraged library staff to reflect on the flaws in the Library's cataloguing processes and to come up with a practical plan of how to learn differently.

Cambridge University Libraries

Cambridge is a collegiate university comprising 31 autonomous colleges, each with its own library, alongside more than 30 faculty and departmental libraries and numerous museums and special collections, all working with the legal deposit University Library. The federated nature of libraries in Cambridge creates obstacles as well as possibilities. Unlike universities with a single, centralised library, we are unable to instigate total and uniform updates. However, this multilayered library 'ecosystem' also meant that we could implement swifter changes at a local level. Several libraries were able to respond quickly: the English Library reclassified over 2,000 books under a new subject of Contemporary Global Literature in English; and the Modern Languages Library launched a programme of consultation on changes to the curriculum, reading lists and book recommendations with students and academics.

Many Cambridge libraries are not tied to larger institutional or international rules of classification but instead work according to in-house schemes. These schemes are often outdated but, equally, they are easy to update. For example, our reclassification of International Relations at Newnham College Library was informed by, but not tied to, Dewey categories. We could easily leave classmarks empty for future flexibility and introduce subsections, such as *Migration*, to make the scheme more hospitable to the growing literature of a rapidly developing discipline. In this project, the addition of a subdivision for *Empires* was a gesture of support for the Decolonise campaign as well as an acknowledgement of imperial practice as an ongoing phenomenon rather than a topic that should always be classified under *History*. Small and simple (if time-consuming) modifications such as this could bring about incremental change and contribute to the dispersed, collaborative and continuing nature of the campaign.

Decolonise the Curriculum: the Library response

We convened a workshop for librarians to find out more about the campaign to Decolonise the Curriculum and to address a topic that seemed daunting to many. In the initial workshops, attendees split into four groups: cataloguing and classification, information literacy, special collections and collection development. The cataloguing and classification group noted that subject headings were not (or need not be) limited to Library of Congress Subject Headings (LCSH). We discussed the politics of retaining a trace of outdated descriptions and the significance of multilingual records in challenging the Anglocentrism of 'controlled vocabulary'. In anticipation of future search functions, we considered the possibility of using alternative metrics to national borders for cataloguing, such as searching maps by geographic co-ordinates. Workshop participants proposed a glossary of decolonised terms and addressed the importance of reassessing hierarchies for a transformed browsing experience. In practical terms, we planned workflows for manageable changes, and discussed how to realistically update a collection in sections while maintaining a working circulating library.

The many different types of library in Cambridge also afford us access to a wealth of advice from colleagues. A college librarian who oversees a multidisciplinary library catering for undergraduates in every subject may not have regular contact with, for example, South Asian book vendors, but could consult a subject specialist at the University Library, or the relevant faculty librarian, for advice on specific international suppliers in order to improve their foreign-language holdings. For this reason, the development of a network was an important resource in itself.

In order to facilitate this exchange, we set up an online platform populated with case studies, resources and bibliographies (https://decolonisingthroughcriticallibrarianship.wordpress.com). We thought it most useful to present this website as a professional resource, aimed at colleagues rather than students or academics, and so address a gap in the Decolonise campaign around practical measures to incorporate its politics into library working methods. We also felt that a tailored professional resource would avoid the risks of making public claims that could divert attention away from the much-needed scrutiny of wider investigations going on within the University. We wanted to create a collaborative and continuing forum, and a place to share our efforts, rather than to claim any victories.

Following the workshop, we sent recommendations to the University's Cataloguing Advisory Group detailing our aims to update the terminology and organisation of different subject areas for those using in-house classification schemes; to collaborate on proposals to change subjects in international schemes, for those using Library of Congress Classification (LCC), Universal Decimal Classification (UDC), Dewey, Bliss and Library of Congress Subject Headings (LCSH); to explore ways in which we might adapt resource description to acknowledge interdisciplinarity and decolonise the categories and terminology of STEMM (science, technology, engineering, maths and medicine) subjects; to address language barriers and offer advice on cataloguing translations; and to consider the challenges of expressing diacritics and non-Roman alphabets in the library management system as a political problem as well as a technical hitch.

This chapter details case studies of practical progress made so far: reorienting from a geographic to thematic classification scheme to suit the collection at the African Studies Library; challenging bibliographic standards when cataloguing *cartoneras* at the University Library; and using collaborative and critical information literacy to decolonise classification at the Polar Library.

The case studies
Moving from UDC to LCC at the African Studies Library
The African Studies Library

The Centre of African Studies, Cambridge and its library were founded in 1965 by leading anthropologist Audrey Richards (first director of the East African Institute of Social Research, Makerere College, Uganda). The African Studies Library supports the research and teaching needs of the MPhil in African Studies programme, as well as those of the wider University, across all disciplines and at all levels of study and research (from undergraduate to senior academic). Our particular focus is on Africa south of the Sahara. The Library also supports the work of the Centre, and that of the Centre's constituent departments in the University, in promoting research from and on, and engagement with, Africa.

The main library collection holds 20,000 accessible items on the open shelf, including language grammars and dictionaries; audio-visual materials; and 304 (18 current) periodicals. In addition to the main collection, the Library holds a largely uncatalogued archive in closed stacks of approximately 18,000 items, consisting of posters, pamphlets and brochures produced by political parties and non-governmental organisations; official publications; newspapers; maps; photographs and film donated by families with relatives in the Colonial Service and ex-Colonial Service Officers; microform; and research paper collections donated by researchers mostly affiliated to Cambridge and the Centre. Much of the closed stacks material has strong ties to the colonial period, with a focus on development studies and anthropology – very much treating Africa and Africans as an object, or a problem to be solved. In recent decades, especially since the establishment of the interdisciplinary MPhil in African Studies programme in 2010, the focus of the open-shelf material has shifted from this elite archive perspective to contemporary collecting. Where possible, material published by African scholars and African presses is prioritised, with a focus on archaeology, art, gender studies, law, literature, philosophy, politics, sociology and the African diaspora.

Transition from UDC to LCC

The African Studies Library is in the process of transitioning from UDC to LCC. This change was prompted by a large, dated and underused development studies section (broadly speaking at *33- Economics*), which sat separately from the rest of a collection that was otherwise classed by region or country. Its separation into a dedicated space had justified retaining many more books than were used or necessary, including duplicating material held at other libraries. The process of reintegrating the (useful) books into the main body of the collection was a chance to tackle reclassification, which was in turn an opportunity to reappraise the collection and do some long-overdue weeding.

The LCC scheme is far from perfect. The ideal solution would have been to create a bespoke scheme with the freedom to adapt and expand. But time was a pressing factor, as the complications of UDC had contributed to a backlog of books that were not accessible on the open shelf. Students were struggling to locate material in UDC, where it was difficult to fathom the main subject amid the varying divisions of region and country. The challenges of using UDC for library staff were also reducing accessibility and discoverability, simply by extending the amount of time a book spent in the office before it reached the shelves.

There was also a vast range of interpretations of the endless potentials of UDC, and it was possible to identify the different classifying styles of previous librarians. For example, at the simplest level, in large classes such as *African literature (6):82*, many titles had been grouped with no subsections (poetry, drama, fiction, novels, speeches, etc.), until a new librarian had begun to drill down to more specific subject areas, but without applying these subjective specificities retrospectively. These varying styles caused confusion over the degree to which a book had been classified, leading to limited browsing benefit and discoverability: a novel by a Zimbabwean author could be found under general *African literature (6):82, Southern African fiction (68):82–3, Rhodesian literature (689):820* (820=old class for literature in UDC) or *Zimbabwean novels (689.1):82–31,* depending on the cataloguer.

The African Literature Book Club run by the Library benefits from the new organisation system, as readers can encounter books by authors from across the continent and diaspora, now subcategorised in classification *P* under *PN, PQ, PR, PS*, rather than focusing on one national literature. This means that users no longer need to explore more than 50 potential locations within the collection when looking to browse African literature. Previously, under UDC, our largest collections of literature from South African, Kenyan, and Nigerian authors would be bays apart at *(68:01):82*, *(676.2):82* and *(669):82*, respectively; they now sit comfortably on adjoining shelves. This has also meant that Francophone and Lusophone authors, and literature of authors from the African diaspora, are now within easy browsing reach, providing users a dedicated area to consult within the collection.

Classification by geography or theme

The move from UDC to LCC was a move from sorting geographically to sorting thematically. Arranging the collection by subject was a much more useful starting point for most research enquiries, and LCC lent itself to that system more easily. The inherited UDC system, which had prioritised regional or country facets, had become increasingly challenging as the collection developed with the discipline to include more international collaboration and comparative studies. The decolonising potential of sorting by theme or subject as opposed to nations became particularly apparent when articulating the taxonomies of material that crossed colonial borders, expressed Pan-Africanist thought, recorded local history or represented migratory or itinerant groups living between and across recognised national boundaries.

We began the process by classifying all newly received books in LCC; we then addressed the backlog, followed by donations, then core material on reading lists and any high-use titles. Library staff will continue to work through the remainder of the open-shelf collection systematically. Published material of an older, more fragile nature is stored separately within our closed stacks and will remain in UDC for the moment. This will be examined as part of a larger and more long-term project to identify, scope and catalogue our ephemera, grey literature and official publications. We recognise that the classification of these materials should be considered in terms of discoverability as part of the long-term project. However, as staff are currently required to retrieve these items from the closed stacks on behalf of students and researchers, they do not pose the same urgent cataloguing need or practical problems of user retrieval and effective browsing as open-shelf material.

In an elite university in the Global North, the African Studies Library faces extra challenges to cultivate research and collections by, with and from, and not only on, Africa and Africans. Cataloguing and classification processes can reinforce bias, and the over-representation of outdated development studies books was symptomatic of the historical disciplinary roots of the Centre and its collections. A thematic organisation of material can take the location of these studies for granted and allow the discipline a broad range of expression, as opposed to being defined primarily by its geographic area and national boundaries. What would be expressed in a silo if catalogued in a less specialist collection should in this space be located primarily by the subject. As articulated by the current director of our Centre in relation to the issues surrounding decolonisation and the African Studies Centre as a British institution, we must organise our library in a way that insists 'on the fact that African political thought is political thought, in addition to being African Studies; African economic history is economic history and African literature is literature in addition to being African Studies' (Branch, 2018, 85).

These inherent challenges of African studies as a discipline, and area studies more broadly, will continue to inform classification at the Library, which often must limit purchasing to the geographically classed confines of its collection development policy. This risks the under-representation of interdisciplinary subjects, or those with a broader global focus. For example, a course reading list 'Africa and Africans in the Atlantic World' highlighted the collection's limitations in terms of the history of the Caribbean and the Americas; a theme-based taxonomy allows for an easier articulation of shared histories and the incorporation of collections that are not primarily based in Africa.

Cataloguing cartoneras
Origins of cartonera publishing

Cartonera publishing has its roots in Argentina's economic crisis of the late 1990s and early 2000s. By December 2001, when the country's government defaulted on its public debt and froze citizens' bank accounts, tens of thousands of Argentinians were unemployed and homeless. Many resorted to waste picking to survive, with huge numbers of *cartoneros* collecting cardboard to sell to recycling plants. By 2003 books were not being sold, bookshops and publishers were shutting down and authors could not publish. A group of artists (Washington Cucurto, Javier Barilaro and Fernanda Laguna) started creating artistic books using discarded cardboard and photocopied paper, and funded a publishing co-operative called Eloísa Cartonera. In solidarity with the waste pickers, they bought cardboard directly from them at five times the market price and employed them to create the hand-painted covers (Eloísa Cartonera, 2020).

The result was a truly decolonial act: literature by peripheral authors with no access to mainstream publishers, as well as by established authors who donated their rights for free, all sold at cheap prices through alternative distribution paths. The model was incredibly successful. *Cartonera* publishers are present worldwide, not only in Latin America but also in Africa, China and Europe (University of Wisconsin–Madison, 2013). It is difficult to give a precise number, as new imprints are constantly emerging, and some have only limited lifespans, but the latest estimate puts the number of *cartonera* publishers at 250 (Bell and O'Hare, 2019, 3). Publishers are very heterogeneous, in the sense that they all adapt to their own local needs and social structures. Some focus on women's work, others give a voice to Indigenous communities, or LGBTQ+ groups, or refugees, or prisoners.

In 2017, Cambridge University Library became a partner in the two-year Arts and Humanities Research Council project 'Cartonera Publishing: Relations, Meaning and

Community in Movement', with the British Library, Senate House Library and Surrey and Durham Universities as partners (Cartonera Publishing, 2020). Cambridge University Library's main contribution to the project is a collection of 200 items bought in situ in Mexico, Brazil and Argentina by researchers from the universities involved in the project. One could argue that institutions in the Global North collecting and publicising books published in Latin America and Portuguese-speaking Africa is a way of broadening access to marginalised knowledge. However, Latin American publishing realities show us that, in fact, many voices are still lost to the demands of a global publishing market that is managed from Europe and the USA. Limitations on who can publish and what is published are more and more frequently dictated by these external forces. The phenomenon of *cartonera* books shows us that diverse models of independent publishing are leading the way in giving a platform to many of these missing voices.

Curatorial decisions about the collection

For an academic library, the collection presents many implications and dilemmas in terms of decolonisation: one of the main questions raised by a collection like this is the relative importance of conservation versus engagement. Cambridge University Library must balance its heritage preservation duty to conserve these publications with its responsibility to their creators' original intent and target audience, resisting the temptation to shut these books away in the 'ivory tower'. Consequently, workshops and active displays were organised, where the books could be handled as their creators intended and where visitors could engage with the process and create their own *cartonera* book.

Another important question is how much to collect. Collecting *libros cartoneros* may diversify our collections, but we must also bear in mind that these books have very short print-runs and too few libraries hold them in the places where they are produced. We have therefore decided that, after the end of this project, our library will no longer purchase *cartonera* items. The researchers involved in the project have also donated a *cartonera* collection to a local library in Mexico (El informador, 2019).

Decolonising bibliographic records

The Cartonera Collection also poses challenges to standard bibliographic records and demands a decolonised approach to cataloguing. How can we enhance accessibility? How far can we go? Can we be fair to all the agents involved in the creation of a book, regardless of their place in the 'canon'? Can we reflect the nature of a publication through its bibliographic record? How can the vocabularies we use influence accessibility and representation? Figures 12.1 and 12.2 on the following page are excerpts from a basic record for a *cartonera* book published in Paraguay, *Tatu ha jaguarete* by Miguelangel Meza. As is standard, the record displays information on the author, title and publication details.

100	1		$a Meza, Miguelángel, $d 1955- $e author.
245	1	0	$a Tatu ha jaguarete / $c Miguelángel Meza.
250			$a Primera Edision.
264		1	$a Luque : $b Mburukujarami Kartonéra, $c 2009.

Figure 12.1 *Basic cartonera record*

The record also contains information on the book's language, series, physical description and subject matter (Figure 12.2).

546			$a Guaraní text; parallel Spanish translation.
650		0	$a Small presses $z Paraguay $z Luque $v Specimens.
650		0	$a Cartonera books $z Paraguay $z Luque $v Specimens.
650		4	$a Editoriales cartoneras $z Paraguay $z Luque.
655		7	$a Cartón ondulado. $2 embne
655		7	$a Corrugated board bindings (Binding) $2 rbbin
710	2		$a MBurukujarami Kartonéra, $e issuing body.
830		0	$a Koleysione de Poésia, narratíva, dramatúrgia y koléyta de la oralida Sudáka-transfronterísa "Tupi'aveve" ; $v 68.

Figure 12.2 *Basic cartonera record, continuation*

In Figure 12.3, instead, we propose a record that goes beyond our standard cataloguing approach and aims to offer broadened access to the same book. The addition of richer bibliographical notes, taken from the book's preliminaries, not only allows for broader searches but also illustrates the intentions of the publishers and creators.

500			$a "Vilíngue du Pópuli ton nunga."
500			$a "Tápa écha kon karton xuntádo i/o komprádo en la vía púvlika de Lúke, Asunsion y por dónde séa, (Paraguái) a Gs. 1000 y pintáda a máno por Domadóra de Mainumby; Arami, 'Amor pasaxéro', S. T. F., Súni Veníte i demás pupilos en el Veráno del 2009 nel taller de MBurukujami Kartonéra, en Kurelándia a ful"—Page facing title page.
500			$a "Kómy de la páxina 22: José María Benítez"—Page facing title page.
500			$a "Tiráda: Inkalkulávle"—Page facing title page.
500			$a "Máde in Lukelándia, Paraguái. Agradesémo al autor su kooperasion, autorisándo la puvlikasion de éste lívro"—Page facing title page.

Figure 12.3 *Expanded cartonera record*

Interestingly, as Spanish speakers will notice, the added notes and series title reflect how standard Spanish orthographical rules have been subverted, reflecting spoken language in Paraguay and taking a clear stance in relation to the language imposed on the country by its colonisers. Cambridge University Library's standard cataloguing procedure is to produce English-language cataloguing records, using authorised LCSH, access points and controlled vocabulary. This is a system created by and for White English-language speakers in the Global North, so using it to deal with material created and consumed by non-English-speaking communities in the Global South reinforces White supremacist colonial structures and narratives.

Figure 12.4 is part of the record for another *cartonera* book, *O caçador de mariposas* by Wellington de Melo, published by Mariposa Cartonera in Recife (Brazil), where the addition of more representative notes helps to identify other relevant creative agents for whom we then assigned access points. We chose not to be limited by which agents were authorised or by the prohibitive workloads that authorising them would involve, and therefore we accepted a 'minimal encoding level' in the record's Leader field.

500		$a "Mariposa Cartonera integra a rede de cartoneras com Dulcinéia Catadora e Severina Catadora (Brasil), Eloísa Cartonera (Argentina), Sarita Cartonera (Perú), La Cartonera (México), Cephisa Cartonera (França) entre outras"—Title page verso.
500		$a "Em outubro de 2015, usando fontes Absara, do designer francês Xavier Dupré, nos espaçamentos 12/17.5, Patrícia Cruz Lima criou o projeto gráfico desta publicação, com capas em papelão confeccionadas inteiramente à mão pela Liga Cartonera, no Recife"—Colophon.
500		$a "Mariposa Cartonera é um selo editorial que confecciona livros com capas de papelão a partir de uma proposta editorial independente, fundado com a intenção de difundir a literatura de forma sustentável e alternativa. Todo papelão utilizado na confecção dos livros é coletado nas ruas, cortado e pintado artesanalmente pelo editor ou dentro do projeto das oficinas oferecidas em comunidades"—Page [42].
650	0	$a Cartonera books $z Brazil $z Recife $v Specimens.
650	0	$a Small presses $z Brazil $z Recife $v Specimens.
650	4	$a Editoras catadoras $z Brasil $z Recife.
655	7	$a Papelão. $2 larpcal
655	7	$a Corrugated board bindings (Binding) $2 rbbin
700	1	$a Cruz Lima, Patrícia, $e book designer.
710	2	$a Mariposa Cartonera, $e issuing body.

Figure 12.4 *Expanded cartonera record, continuation*

We chose to catalogue our *cartonera* collection by adding subject headings in the language chiefly spoken in the place of publication (Portuguese in the example above), referring to the most commonly used controlled vocabularies in each country (for Brazilian material we use the Brazilian LARPCAL [Lista de Assuntos Referente Ao Programa de Cadastramento Automatizado de Livros], but we found the most commonly used controlled vocabulary in Spanish was the 'Manual de indización de Encabezamientos de Materia Biblioteca Nacional de España'). We also chose to be geographically specific, recording $z information, where possible, to a local level. A further step towards presenting decolonised records would be the incorporation of free-text descriptive and interpretative notes which, together with the additions already mentioned, could allow for broader and more meaningful searches, legitimising a wider range of access points and keywords, in an attempt to decolonise the standard language of the catalogue.

Decolonising classification at the Polar Library
A unique classification scheme

The library of the Scott Polar Research Institute (SPRI) supports multidisciplinary research on the polar regions carried out by research staff and PhD, Master's and undergraduate students at the University of Cambridge, as well as the general public and visiting scholars from the global polar research community. Polar Library holdings cover diverse topics from glaciology to anthropology of the North and from climate science to polar geopolitics. The reference collection has been developed since the Institute's foundation in 1920 and includes over 50,000 monographs, 1,000 serial titles and 18,000 maps, as well as pamphlets, audio-visual material and theses. The collection comprises material in over 90 different languages, with extensive Russian-language holdings.

Like many other libraries across Cambridge, the Polar Library utilises a unique classification scheme to organise these resources. In 1945 it was decided to adapt UDC to better cater to material on the polar regions and the study of snow and ice, with major additions and revisions made to the Arctic and Antarctic geographic headings and subjects relating to glaciology. Unlike other libraries, SPRI also uses this unique controlled vocabulary for subject cataloguing. In the catalogue shared with other libraries across Cambridge, local Polar UDC subject headings sit alongside LCSH in Polar Library catalogue records, meaning the scheme is used for both cataloguing and classification purposes: doubly visible.

Alongside his work developing the Antarctic Treaty System, Brian Birley Roberts was instrumental in devising this unique scheme for organising polar libraries. Writing about the practical experience of cataloguing and classification at SPRI, he starts from the principle that 'collected material which cannot easily be found is of little use' (Roberts, 1960, 1). It is a familiar sentiment for cataloguers, and reverberates 60 years on, but the system that Roberts developed falls short today, especially when examined through a decolonial lens.

Coloniality of the classification system

SPRI was founded 100 years ago, at a time when geography as a discipline was being institutionalised under British imperialism; the Arctic and Antarctic in particular were seen as 'blank spaces' ripe for exploration, enhancing Western knowledge production and geopolitical formation. The tools of geography have often been used for colonial purposes, and this colonial presence endures at SPRI, not least in the library, whose space, collections and cataloguing systems reflect the Whiteness and imperial history of the Institute.

Polar UDC was seen as a collaborative, co-operative endeavour that was most productive when used by other participating libraries (Roberts, 1960, 5). But this aim for and assumption of universality – in perspective, language and priorities – at a polar library situated in the UK, whose involvement in the polar regions has almost always related to its imperial projects, demonstrates the inherent coloniality of the library classification system developed at SPRI.

Colonial attitudes are encoded in the classification scheme. For example, *Ethnography* is the only form of anthropology offered in Polar UDC. There are also numerous examples of subject categories that carry offensive connotations for Indigenous communities in the Arctic. Although ethnographic labels have been updated, with changes made going forwards, there are plenty of examples of offensive terminology, such as *Eskimo* and *Lapp*, that remain in the online catalogue and, more prominently, on the spines of the books themselves. With no better alternative available, *Traditional Ecological Knowledge* is crudely passed off as *Attitudes to nature*, and headings in the *Religion* and *Social Science* categories betray negative stereotypes and mischaracterisations of Indigenous culture, for instance, *392.123 – Infanticide* is a subdivision of *Social customs* rather than *Criminal law* and *398 – Native peoples, folk beliefs and tales* is the best option for describing Inuit cosmology. Headings such as *325.3 – Native policy*, used to describe governmental relationships with Indigenous populations, make it clear that the assumed perspective in the classification system is non-Indigenous.

Polar UDC has tried to keep pace with shifting geographical boundaries and place-name changes that often relate to Indigenous self-determination in the Arctic. However, the results in the library catalogue do not always mirror the real-world decolonial catalysts for these classification revisions. For example, in 1999 the political map of Canada was redrawn to create Nunavut; 'through political activism and long-term negotiations, a small, marginalised Indigenous group overcame many obstacles to peacefully establish a government that they controlled within the Canadian state, thereby gaining control of their land, their resources and their future' (Kikkert, 2020). Yet in Polar UDC, *(*440.2) – Nunavut* sits as a subheading of *(*440) – Northwest Territories*, now a distinct Canadian territory that included Nunavut when it was originally transferred to Canada from the British Empire in the 19th century. Hierarchical nuances betray lingering colonial attitudes. In another example of the deficiencies of Polar UDC, there is no geographical place name in the scheme that accurately describes Sápmi, the homeland region of the

Sámi people, which spans northern Finland, Sweden, Norway and part of Russia. Classification based on neat national borders in fact results in books on the same subject being scattered across the Library, and assigned classmarks according to the best guess of various librarians over several decades.

As Indigenous librarians Littletree and Metoyer point out, 'Words are powerful. The way we name and classify the world around us is indicative of our values and beliefs. The words we choose to identify elements in our world can illuminate, educate, and elucidate, or they can perpetuate stereotypes and misinformation' (Littletree and Metoyer, 2015, 654). It is important that the Polar Library does not preserve inaccurate and offensive terminology, or make northern Indigenous peoples feel 'othered' or unwelcome when they see the colonialist, outdated terminology that librarians chose to use. Controlled vocabularies may be a necessary feature of libraries, but, as Vowel points out, naming is tricky because it is so intimately tied up with the issue of identity: fluid and often self-defined (Vowel, 2016, 8). The intellectual task of updating the classification scheme and the manual labour of recataloguing thousands of records and relabelling items is huge, and all the more daunting because it is clear that decolonising work with the classification scheme can never be perfect.

Critical information literacy

Thus education, rather than mere correction, offered a compelling way of dealing with the flaws of Polar UDC. As Drabinski suggests, changing the language or structure of a classification scheme cannot deal with its fundamental limitations, its inherent universalising nature, but we can transform our users' relationship to the system through radical pedagogical work (Drabinski, 2008, 202–3). After discussion with teaching and research staff at SPRI, it became clear that there was enthusiasm for this educational approach to set about decolonising the classification scheme. Critical information literacy, with its focus on power dynamics and the political and social aspects of information, offered a particularly useful blueprint for the design of the workshop offered to undergraduate students who use the library for their Geographies of the Arctic course and, separately, to research staff and students at the SPRI Polar Humanities and Social Sciences seminar.

We put participants in the position of cataloguer and asked them how they would encapsulate a book of Sakha epic tales in a few keywords. As expected, everyone made different suggestions, and so the activity led us to discuss the practice of categorising knowledge, the contingency of language and the different biases and ways of thinking about the world that our categorisations reveal. Next in the workshop, we showed how different editions and translations of the same text in the library had been catalogued with different subject headings over time. We talked about the political context of using the autonym 'Sakha' over the Russian term 'Yakut' and the implications of 'folktale' over 'myth' or 'literature' in the subject headings.

The second half of the workshop was used to present the history of Polar UDC at SPRI and how it is used to organise the library, focusing in particular on its more problematic sections: an authentic problem with students and librarians as 'co-investigators' (Freire, 1996, 62). We asked the participants to critique sections of the classification scheme, with reflective prompts about what they found surprising, whose perspective takes precedence, the way the hierarchy works and the terminology itself. Students and researchers brought their prior knowledge but also their lived experiences to critique the classification scheme. Many were surprised to see the Library presented as a non-neutral force, with the workshop revealing the constructed nature of the ostensibly static and objective classification scheme and the people involved in creating and applying it.

In his experience of organising knowledge at the Polar Library, Roberts learned that 'some things need to be done and other things are impractical or unnecessary' (Roberts, 1960, 13). Overhauling the Polar Library classification scheme with a decolonial approach is logistically impractical; the time and labour involved in reclassifying is compounded by the need to first update the thesaurus itself and edit the subject headings in the catalogue. Yet this work is absolutely necessary to avoid the violence of reproducing colonial terminology. Workshopping a way forwards with students and researchers has not only promoted a deeper, critical understanding of the flawed information systems they work with and the implications this has for research, it has also helped the Library to make progress in thinking through its priorities for updating Polar UDC.

Crowe and Elzi envisage a '"meeting in the middle" for cataloguers, reference archivists and instruction librarians' to acknowledge the inherently problematic catalogue and use it as a valuable teaching tool, but also making sure not to shy away from the necessary work to address overt injustice in cataloguing practice (Crowe and Elzi, 2017, 271). Last updated in full in 1994, revision of the Polar UDC classification scheme is long overdue. The process will be labour intensive for a small team with no dedicated cataloguers. But for lasting, visible change, recataloguing work must take place. Our collaborative and critical pedagogical approach to decolonising the Library can help us to do so.

Conclusion

Each of these case studies demonstrates what can be done with limited time at a local level, and how the subject specialisms and linguistic expertise within a community of library workers can provide templates and workflows through which colleagues might learn by example. They cover collections that concentrate on various areas of the world with different politics and histories in relation to borders and colonialism, but common themes emerge.

Librarians at the African Studies Library and the University Library encountered different ways in which resource description can reinforce biases that impede discoverability: the former's reclassification project sought to improve upon a slow and inconsistent application of UDC that was hindering students finding books on shelves, and the latter's addition of extra bibliographic notes for *cartonera* records aimed to make the collection more discoverable to readers using a variety of search terms and local languages.

Each library also tackled the problems that arise when geography is used as the primary facet of classification: African Studies and SPRI both observe that hierarchies based on national borders scatter books on the same subject across a library and reinforce colonial boundaries. Where African Studies found that a more thematic order could accommodate shared histories across the continent, the University Library's Latin American and Iberian collections addressed the prevalence of nationality as the predominant locator with *more* geographical specificity, recording location to as local a level as possible in order to best articulate regional productions.

Language was another facet that appeared across multiple collections: although a linguistic order risks reviving former colonial categories, the African Studies librarian found that it was preferable to sorting books by nation, enhancing user access and allowing readers to browse and compare, for example, Lusophone and Francophone literatures from different countries. Prioritising the local over the national linguistically as well as geographically, the *cartonera* collections include subject headings in the language chiefly spoken in the place of publication, opting for regional accuracy over standard Spanish orthography.

Progressive changes often entailed overlooking certain cataloguing rules or settling for minimal levels of encoding, as the Latin American and Iberian department did in adding unauthorised agents to recognise *cartonera* creators, and as the Polar Library aims to do in challenging the assumed non-Indigenous perspective of Polar UDC subject headings. With support and perseverance, these incremental efforts might affect change at an institutional level, too. By demonstrating the potential for a more flexible and hospitable response to classification, professional networks formed around alterations to local schemes might highlight similar problems in international standards; in 2021 the Cambridge Cataloguing Advisory Group convened an open meeting to plan local treatment of outdated terminology in LCSH and agreed to update the Cambridge catalogue to display 'Undocumented immigrants' in place of 'Illegal aliens' and 'Noncitizens' instead of 'Aliens'.

These case studies demonstrate that cataloguing and classification, so often perceived as discrete, impartial and technical, in fact permeate every other aspect of library management, with particular implications for collection development and information literacy. The African Studies and Polar libraries both found traces of individual librarians' classification styles, suggesting that these practices are neither ahistorical nor neutral, even (or especially) when following mandated guidelines. The work to address inequalities in resource description is slow, boundless and subjective. In addition to the Decolonising through Critical Librarianship staff discussion groups, the Latin American and Iberian department's *cartonera* workshops with children honour the publishers' commitment to access and engagement, the SPRI student workshops invite the Library's readers to challenge the terms of classification themselves and a recent workshop with six graduate trainees and an intern from libraries across Cambridge marked an opportunity to discuss changes to library practices with new professionals (Decolonising through Critical Librarianship, 2021). Accessible and effective bibliography demands ongoing attention from as broad and critical an audience as possible and, through these case studies, a collaborative pedagogical method developed as the most promising way to maintain the critical engagement necessary for continued change.

A note about the Cambridge University Decolonising Through Critical Librarianship Group

The authors of this chapter, Jennifer Skinner (African Studies Library), Clara Panozzo Zénere and Christopher Greenberg (Latin American and Iberian Collections, Cambridge University Library), Frances Marsh (Polar Library, Scott Polar Research Institute) and Eve Lacey (Newnham College Library), work together as part of the Decolonising Through Critical Librarianship Group. More information on their case studies, resources and events for librarians in Cambridge and elsewhere can be found online: https://decolonisingthroughcriticallibrarianship.wordpress.com.

Inspiration for the *cartoneras* cataloguing project came from a workshop held at the LXIII SALALM (Seminar on the Acquisition of Latin American Library Materials) Conference in 2018 in Mexico City. The workshop was titled 'Edición cartonera como posible apuesta para descolonizar el mundo editorial y las bibliotecas', and was facilitated by Paloma Celis Carbajal and Laura Martin (University of Wisconsin), Wendy Pedersen (University of New Mexico), and Marc Delcan and Rosa Serna (Pensaré Cartonera).

References

Bell, L. and O'Hare, P. (2019) Latin American Politics Underground: Networks, Rhizomes and Resistance in Cartonera Publishing, *International Journal of Cultural Studies*, **23** (1), 20–41.

Black Cantabs (n.d.) Home, www.blackcantabs.org (accessed 15 March 2021).

Branch, A. (2018) Decolonizing the African Studies Centre, *The Cambridge Journal of Anthropology*, **36** (2), 73–91, DOI: https://doi.org/10.3167/cja.2018.360207.

Cambridge University Library (2018) Black Cantabs: History Makers, www.lib.cam.ac.uk/plan-your-visit/whats/black-cantabs-history-makers (accessed 15 March 2021).

Cartonera Publishing (2020) About the Project, http://cartonerapublishing.com/about-the-project (accessed 12 March 2021).

Crowe, K. and Elzi, E. (2017) Feminist Pedagogy and the Critical Catalog. In Accardi, M. T. (ed.), *The Feminist Reference Desk*, Library Juice Press.

Decolonise Sociology, Decolonise Sociology @ Cambridge, https://decolonisesociology.com (accessed 15 March 2021).

Decolonising Through Critical Librarianship (2021) Decolonising Through Critical Librarianship Workshop, https://decolonisingthroughcriticallibrarianship.wordpress.com/2021/03/15/decolonising-through-critical-librarianship-workshop (accessed 22 March 2021).

Drabinski, E. (2008) Teaching the Radical Catalog. In Roberto, K. R. (ed.), *Radical Cataloging: Essays at the Front*, 198–205, McFarland, www.emilydrabinski.com/wp-content/uploads/2012/06/drabinski_radcat.pdf (accessed 1 June 2019).

El informador (2019) Entregan acervo cartonero a SCJ [Secretaría de Cultura de Jalisco, Biblioteca Central], www.informador.mx/cultura/Entregan-acervo-cartonero-a-SCJ-20190731-0018.html (accessed 15 March 2021).

Eloísa Cartonera (2020) www.eloisacartonera.com.ar (accessed 15 March 2021).

Facebook, Cambridge Decolonise Network, www.facebook.com/DecoloniseCambridge (accessed 15 March 2021).

Facebook, Decolonising Anthropology, www.facebook.com/decoloniseanthropologycambridge (accessed 15 March 2021).

Facebook, Decolonise Law Cambridge, www.facebook.com/decolcamblaw (accessed 15 March 2021).

FLY (2017) Decolonising the English Faculty: An Open Letter, https://flygirlsofcambridge.com/2017/06/14/decolonising-the-english-faculty-an-open-letter (accessed 1 October 2019).

Freire, P. (1996) *Pedagogy of the Oppressed*, Penguin.

Kikkert, P. (2020) Nunavut. In *The Canadian Encyclopedia*, www.thecanadianencyclopedia.ca/en/article/nunavut (accessed 18 November 2020).

Littletree, S. and Metoyer, C. A. (2015) Knowledge Organization from an Indigenous Perspective: The Mashantucket Pequot Thesaurus of American Indian Terminology Project, *Cataloging & Classification Quarterly*, **53** (5–6), 640–57. DOI: doi.org/10.1080/01639374.2015.1010113.

Roberts, B. (1960) *The Organization of Polar Information*, Scott Polar Research Institute.

University of Wisconsin–Madison (2013) Cartonera Publishers Research Guide, https://researchguides.library.wisc.edu/cartoneras/cartonerasUW (accessed 16 March 2021).

Vowel, C. (2016) *Indigenous Writes: A Guide to First Nations, Métis, and Inuit Issues in Canada*, HighWater Press.

13
Re-membering Kenya: Building Library Infrastructures as Decolonial Practice

Syokau Mutonga and Angela Okune

Introduction

'What are you going to do with the lion's head?' I, Angela Okune (AO) asked Syokau Mutonga (SM), teasingly but genuinely curious. I was referring to a stuffed lion's head which seemed to have become somewhat of an infamous McMillan Library mascot among those who visited. The lion's head (Figure 13.1 on the next page) caught my eye during my first visit to the McMillan Library in February 2019; left atop a dusty table outside the second-floor Africana library, it looked as if someone had tossed it there years ago and had not bothered to move it since. The clear lack of regard for it – as if the librarians and library staff didn't know what to do with it – was perhaps what struck me as much as the very materiality of a decaying lion's head just laid out for anyone to touch. But a few weeks later, when I returned on a sleepy Saturday with my four-year-old son in tow, having enticed him to come with me by telling him he would get to see a real lion's head at the library, it wasn't there. It had been moved. Needless to say, my son was mad at me for making false promises. But the removal of the lion's head from public view also flagged for me its paradox. The lion's head was illustrative of a double bind that the staff at McMillan Library, not to mention others working on reviving and establishing libraries in diverse postcolonial and settler-colonial sites around the world, are grappling with – what to remember and what to forget in attempts to decolonise. What to do with the massive ivory tusks of some poor elephant who happened to be living at the wrong period of time, when Kenya was a colonial site of hunting expeditions for White foreigners, like Sir William Northrup McMillan (Box 13.1)? What to do with a decaying lion's head? These charismatic items are a strange delight for tourists to the library – Kenyans and non-Kenyans alike – although for regular library users they are quickly normalised as part of the Library's environment. Such artefacts give the Library 'character' and are material reminders of Kenya's colonial and imperial past and present. How to contextualise these materials and memories appropriately? Not to glorify or romanticise an adventurous past that centres the heinous deeds of White 'frontiersmen', but also not to erase them and their historical presence, since doing so risks ignoring the influence such colonial logics had and have on continued imperial formations.

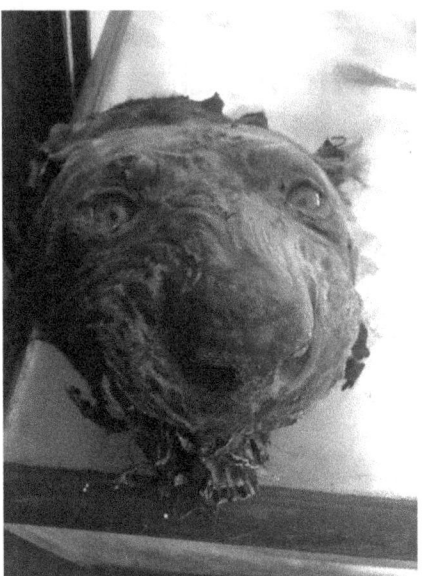

Figure 13.1: *The lion's head that can be found – sometimes – in McMillan Library's main branch, Nairobi, Kenya.*
Photo credit: Angela Okune

In this chapter, we reflect on these challenges and the work currently being undertaken by teams and individuals seeking to revitalise libraries in and for various Kenyan publics in Nairobi. We are in full-throated agreement with the need to decolonise libraries and other knowledge infrastructures (Box 13.2 opposite). However, without intending to misrepresent important and necessary decolonial work, we suggest that, in practice, decolonising might look similar to 'forget and move on', a force that we describe as having failed to address historic injustices and violence in the country. But if decolonising is in fact *not* the same as forgetting the British legacy, what is it? We suggest that looking to progressive librarianship (Durrani, 2014) might offer a counterpoint to 'forget and move on' and a way to think about what decolonising without forgetting might look like. We frame the work being done by Book Bunk, a not-for-profit trust undertaking restoration of the McMillan Libraries in Nairobi, as progressive librarianship and describe the ways in which the Book Bunk team are attempting to decolonise the libraries in ways that avoid getting caught in a culture of 'forget and move on'. The role of the academic library is not explicitly the focus of this chapter, but we believe that Book Bunk's experiences are applicable to other kinds of libraries, including Nairobi's university libraries.

Box 13.1: McMillan Library

The McMillan Memorial Library, one of the oldest libraries in Kenya, was established by Lady Lucie McMillan in memory of her late husband, US-born philanthropist Sir William Northrup McMillan. The Library opened its doors in 1931 to Europeans only until its management was handed over to the Nairobi City Council in 1962 on the eve of national independence. American millionaire William Northrup McMillan came to Kenya in 1904 on a shooting expedition and decided he would stay. He became a British citizen during the First World War and received a knighthood for his wartime services. He is well-known for having hosted former US President Theodore Roosevelt in 1909 at his lavish estate in Kenya. He died in 1925. To learn more about the history and context of McMillan Library, visit the digital exhibit 'McMillan Library' (Matathia and Okune, 2019, https://stsinfrastructures.org/content/mcmillan-library/essay).

> **Box 13.2: Knowledge infrastructures**
> The term 'knowledge infrastructures' refers to the people, artefacts, institutions and relations that generate, share and maintain specific knowledge about the human and natural worlds. In this chapter the term is pluralised to highlight, as Borgman (2020) notes, that knowledge infrastructures are not one system but are numerous, multilayered and adaptive systems, each with unique origins and goals, that are always interfacing and interacting. Included under the umbrella of the term are the infrastructures underlying academic and non-academic research, libraries, archives, data repositories and scholarly publishers – both the built material spaces of these institutions and the technical platforms and human and social networks that give them vibrancy and life.

Re-membering, decolonising, re-collecting
The African library

The African library did not originate in and with colonialism. In ancient Ghana's cosmopolitan city of Timbuktu, for example, the most profitable trade items were books. Under Mansa Musa's rule from the 13th to 17th centuries, Islamic learning centres, schools, universities and an incredible library were established in Mali. In the city of Chinguetti in Mauritania, libraries containing over 1,000 Quranic manuscripts survive to this day (Jurgens and Momoniat, 2020). Today, ancient manuscript collections, some dating back to the eighth century CE, are re-emerging across the continent. Nonetheless, the role of the library within African society is still up for grabs. 'You can tell who the library was supposed to serve simply by its placement in the city,' explained Trevas, a University of Nairobi anthropology student who was helping me (AO) to develop a crowdsourced map of libraries and archives in the city. 'McMillan was only for White settlers when it first opened and is in what today is considered "uptown" Central Business District, whereas Ismail Rahimtulla Walji Trust Library was meant for all people from day one and sits in "downtown".' Diverse libraries and archives are dotted all over Nairobi (Box 13.3, next page) – some in the heart of the Central Business District's hustle and bustle, some located within social justice centres in densely populated informal settlements and some far away from the residences of working-class Kenyans, located within foreign embassy compounds in leafy Gigiri. These libraries serve diverse users and agendas, funded by philanthropic donors, foreign and state governments, non-governmental organisations and individuals, Kenyan and non-Kenyan alike. There are also public libraries under the national government (Kenya National Library Service) and university libraries that primarily serve academics and students. A new cadre of Kenyan digital humanities specialists have also entered the Nairobi library and archives ecosystem and include the African Digital Heritage initiative (https://africandigitalheritage.com), focusing on the application of technology in the preservation, engagement and dissemination of African heritage; the Museum of British Colonialism (www.museumofbritishcolonialism.org) which has digitally recreated Mau Mau detention camps; WerJoKenya (www.werjokenya.com), an online journal that seeks to document, highlight, protect and celebrate Kenya's diverse musical history; and Paukwa (https://paukwa.or.ke), a counter-narrative online library of Kenya's histories.

> **Box 13.3: Nairobi's libraries and archives**
> Although this chapter is featured in a collective volume focused on libraries, there are also references to archiving, because many of the libraries in Kenya also house or have housed archival collections.
> A crowdsourced map produced in 2019 of libraries and archives in Nairobi can be found at https://researchke.ushahidi.io/views/map. Though not comprehensive, it is a start to aggregating information about the diverse libraries in Kenya. This map contributed towards another, more comprehensive map of Nairobi public libraries and archives published by Book Bunk in 2021 (available at their website www.bookbunk.org).

Trevas and I observed the varying levels of security at the different library locations. While some libraries like Alliance Français had security rivalling the international airport, others had no security, except perhaps their lack of marking. One could easily, for example, pass the Ukombozi Library hundreds of times without ever knowing its location. The books held by Ukombozi were once part of the Mwakenya movement's collection. Mwakenya, an underground Kenyan socialist movement especially active in the 1980s, was formed to fight for multiparty democracy, and these books, which became accessible to the public only in 2017, are today located on the third floor of a building largely constructed of cement and iron-sheet roofing across from the University of Nairobi. The well-worn stairs up to the library hint at decades of foot traffic.

Colonialism as dismemberment of Africa

For activist scholars, researchers and those working in the creative arts in Nairobi, the question of decolonising the library and broader centres of knowledge is not a metaphor (compare Tuck and Yang, 2012). It is a question of where to put the lion's head and elephant tusks, dismembered animal parts that are metonymic of the dismemberment of Kenyans. Kenyan philosopher Ngũgĩ wa Thiong'o (2009) describes Europe's contact with Africa as one characterised by dismemberment. During the first stage, he explains, the African personhood was divided into two halves: the continent and its diaspora. The second stage was the literal fragmentation of the African continent and its reconstitution into British, French, Portuguese, German, Belgian and Spanish Africa through the Berlin Conference of 1884. Finally, he mentions the additional dismemberment of the diasporic Africans who were separated not only from their continent and labour but also from their very sovereign being. When we write, then, of 're-membering', we are in conversation with Ngũgĩ and others' work on the dismembering of African personhood past and present and grappling with how to 're-member' the African body politic, who have been divided from their land, body and mind.

Decolonisation has become an important political and rallying cry across many contexts and parts of the world. We are decisively in agreement with the need to decolonise the library and other knowledge infrastructures. However, as digital data scholars Jane Anderson and Kimberly Christen (2019) have noted, there have been many blanket professional calls to decolonise archives and libraries without attention to the tools, techniques and technologies that perpetuate ongoing processes and attempts at dispossession of land, resources and knowledges. The symbolic renaming of streets and buildings is an important part of the practices of decolonising. Doing so renounces the colonial regime and its ideology and redefines a city's identity with symbols of nationalism and pan-Africanism. As Wanjiru and Matsubara (2017) have discussed, in the process, street names can act as sites for the restitution of justice, spatial memory and ethnic unity. However, without intending to misrepresent important and necessary decolonial work, we suggest that in these practices decolonising might also look similar to 'forget and move on', a force we describe as having failed to address historic injustices and violence in the country. Quoted in a 2014 news article in the local newspaper, Dedan Kīmathi Waceke, the grandson of leading freedom fighter Kīmathi wa Waciūri (who is known widely as Dedan Kīmathi), claimed that not enough was being done to honour the freedom fighters who helped to secure Kenyan independence from the British (Kimani, 2014). 'It's unfortunate that the people that are in this generation do not realise how painful a price it was to pay. They take it for granted,' he stated, causing a stir when he chained himself to a statue of his grandfather situated on Kimathi Street in Nairobi (renamed from the colonial-era 'Hardinge Street'). Michael Kīng'ori, another descendant of Mau Mau freedom fighters was quoted as saying: 'We are slowly killing our country's history. Naming of roads and erecting statues of honour is the only way we can remember the great freedom fighters of the country' (Kimani, 2014). Clearly though, renaming streets and erecting statues are not sufficient ends for 'decolonising'. In an article analysing the symbolism of the Dedan Kīmathi statue unveiled in Nairobi in 2007, Annie Coombes quotes an excerpt from periodical *The East African*: 'A better memorial would be an honest retelling of the story of his [Kīmathi's] struggle …' (Coombes, 2011, 210).

In the young Kīmathi's plea for remembering his grandfather, we hear a plea that goes beyond renaming another street but, rather, calls for greater structural changes towards realising the freedom fighters' vision of an emancipatory future for all Africans. In the following sections we share some of these dreams and critiques of the colonial and postcolonial governments as articulated by two generations of Kenyan activists, the Kenya Land and Freedom Army (colloquially known as Mau Mau) and the Mwakenya movement, to help move from 'decolonising' to thinking more practically about what it means to practise progressive librarianship. In this way we seek to expand the lens of practice and analysis, foregrounding voices from the past and present that should lead in discussions of what exactly 'decolonising' entails.

Here, then, decolonisation becomes not only about undoing the harms and legacies of colonialism but, importantly, about including a practice of (re)collecting radical imaginings of alternative futures (Kelley, 2003). By 'radical' we refer to addressing the root problem (rather than simply shifting rhetoric about the problem, for example).

Cultivating a capacity for such radical imagination is and will continue to be the task at hand for our generation and future generations who look to re-collect the vibrancy of Nairobi's public sphere in the 1960s and 1970s, when there was active and creative visioning of an Africa for and by Africans (Musila, 2019). A challenge to cultivating capacities for such radical reimagining comes from a mode of 'forget and move on' which has prevented important grappling with ongoing colonial habits and logics. In the next section we discuss what we have observed as a 'forget and move on' approach to national memory and trauma and join critiques by public figures like Patrick Gathara (2020b; 2020a) who argue that unfair, unequal and at times violent actions of state and non-state actors are glossed over through 'forget and move on' discourses.

Forget and move on: Kenya's institutionalised amnesia

Citing Milan Kundera, Firoze Manji has noted, 'When you want to liquidate a people's culture, the first step is to erase its memory. Destroy its books, its culture, its history, then have somebody write new books, manufacture a new culture, invent a new history. Before long the nation will begin to forget what it is and what it was. The world around it will forget even faster' (Manji, 2020). Manji (2020) argues that the last 30 years of neoliberal politics in Kenya have resulted in a profound dispossession of memory. Many Kenyans born or raised during or in the aftermath of Structural Adjustment Programmes (SAPs) have lost connection with their own history, partly due to the lack of investment in local institutions of knowledge and memory, as well as erasure of Kenyan resistance, silenced through state violence.

SAPs were a scheme of loans from the International Monetary Fund and World Bank in the 1980s and 1990s that were accompanied by policy conditions which included the liberalisation of trade and the privatisation of many government enterprises. Today, SAPs are recognised as having had widespread negative impacts on the well-being of citizens, especially those most marginalised in the country (Emeagwali, 2011). It is often assumed that SAPs primarily impacted on health access and social services; in fact, the deep impact of SAPs on the contemporary state of Kenyan schools, libraries, data infrastructure and overall scientific capacity cannot be overstated. In the period prior to the imposition of SAPs, academic libraries were part of a Kenyan university culture of student activism and decolonial strategising, a key site of student activism (Klopp and Orina, 2002). However, academic libraries in the region since the 2000s have had a limited role in contemporary decolonial movements. While the history and geopolitics of structural adjustment are distinct from the history invoked by decolonising the library, it is crucial to see the connections.

There is still little public discourse about the detrimental effects of the SAPs on/in Kenya. This is most likely because part of their legacy is that they limited funds for public services like libraries and public universities. Of course, this is not to discount the important work by Subbo (2007), Rono (2002), Oyugui, Kigozi and On'gwen (1997) and others on SAPs in Kenya, but to note that critiques of these programmes have largely been relegated to the academy and do not circulate in everyday conversation as we have learned, anecdotally, they do in other national contexts such as Zimbabwe. Any mention of the SAPs' lasting and ongoing effects on public services and systems is largely absent in both regular media reporting and educational curricula, including in history classes. This 'structurally adjusted' Kenya, whose public infrastructures have been defunded and local industries debilitated as a result of requisite financial policies imposed by the Bretton Woods institutions, offers a starting point for understanding how multinational private corporations today have such a captive audience for their 'free' services. We will expand on this at the end of this chapter.

First, we want to briefly discuss the Mwakenya movement, since the deliberate erasure of its legacy is important to understanding both the force of 'forget and move on' and also the foundations from which Durrani's concept of progressive librarianship (2014) developed and grew. We build on work by Joyce Nyairo, who writes: 'one of the glaring fault lines in the construction of the Kenyan nation is not the absence of memory, but rather the deliberate institutionalisation of amnesia' (Nyairo, 2015, 69). She refers to the 'deliberate erasure of ... any semblance of remembrance that celebrates a version of being or becoming in ways and forms that run contrary to the singular version that is inscribed by the state and the institutions that enable it' (Nyairo, 2015, 69). The work of Nyairo (2015), Gathara (2020b), Manji (2020) and others suggest that a dominant narrative in Kenya of 'forget and move on' glosses over unfair, unequal and at times violent actions of the state and non-state actors, and avoids tackling the underlying root of the issues (several key moments in recent Kenyan history include the post-election violence in 2007/8 and the terrorist attacks on the Westgate Mall in 2011, which have furthered a habit and national narrative of 'forget and move on', but which we do not have the space to expand on in this chapter). Such a lack of resolution at particular moments in Kenyan history leads to an increasingly disillusioned and cynical public who do not trust public narratives or institutions, and who are also missing a deep connection to their own liberation histories of resistance, where rich dreams of decolonial futures could provide the nutrition and support for their own to be established.

Kenya's Mwakenya movement

In the late 1980s the Moi government initiated a crackdown on an underground political movement known as 'Mwakenya' (*Muungano wa Wazalendo wa Kukomboa Kenya* or the Union of Patriots for the Liberation of Kenya) who were described by the government as a group of very dangerous individuals engaged in a guerrilla war. In fact, the Mwakenya movement was formed to fight for multiparty democracy, and its members, who included many Kenyan university faculty and students, advocated for the opening up of democratic spaces in Kenya. However, the movement was forced underground, due to state violence. Moi is quoted as saying: 'From today you should keep quiet. I don't want to hear anything again about Mwakenya.' 'Keep quiet,' Moi repeated. 'The government will deal with them one by one. We will collect them so don't mention Mwakenya again. Let's keep quiet and go on collecting them. I am happy that we have uncovered them and they are naming their fellow collaborators. This is very encouraging. If you were involved in this thing you should be worried' (Friedrich-Ebert-Stiftung and Citizens for Justice, 2003, 3–4).

Twenty years earlier, in the years following independence, the country was jubilant and ready for the start of a bright Pan-African future. The university was a key site for decolonial thinkers excited to reimagine society and rid it of colonial structures and logics. But by the late 1970s, these same intellectuals were labelled dangerous traitors by a government who saw them as potential high risks that could incite the public against the state. Ngũgĩ wa Thiong'o was one such leader. In 1977 his controversial play, *Ngaahika Ndeenda* (*I Will Marry When I Want*), written with Ngũgĩ wa Mirii, was performed at Kamirithu Educational and Cultural Centre. Because it was sharply critical of the inequalities and injustices in Kenyan society, unequivocally championed the cause of ordinary Kenyans and was committed to communicating with Kenyans in the local languages of their daily lives, in 1977 Ngũgĩ was arrested and imprisoned without charge at Kamiti Maximum Security Prison. Later, while Ngũgĩ was in Britain for the launch and promotion of his work, he learned about the Moi regime's plot to eliminate him on his return. This forced him into exile, first in Britain and then the USA, where he resides today (Thiong'o, 1981).

Ngũgĩ was one of many Kenyan intellectuals forced into exile during the 1980s. Using a 1982 coup as justification, the Moi regime arrested hundreds of faculty and students. The University of Nairobi and Kenyatta University were closed for one year, and on reopening in 1983 were divided into several faculty administrative units, part of divide and rule tactics. The Moi special police force invaded university libraries and removed all books by or on Vladimir Illyich Lenin, Karl Marx, Che Guevara, Malcom X, Franz Fanon, Ngũgĩ wa Thiong'o, Maina wa Kinyatti and Fidel Castro (Friedrich-Ebert-Stiftung and Citizens for Justice, 2003). Reading these books or others published by the Mwakenya movement led to quick detention. For instance, in the early 1980s security forces were deployed to look for copies of *Pambana*, the first underground anti-imperialist and anti-neocolonial newspaper since independence; anyone caught reading or distributing such material was arrested. Leading thinkers arrested at this time included Maina wa Kinyatti, Mukaru Ng'ang'a and Willy Mutunga (Gisesa, 2020). Despite Mwakenya's being branded as a terrorist organisation by the Moi government, Professor Isaiah Ngotho Kariuki, a former dean in the Faculty of Commerce at the University of Nairobi and Mwakenya leader is quoted in a 2013 news article debunking this claim: 'Our movement was not clandestine. It was a public movement where we gave open lectures and distributed literature to tell Kenyans what was wrong with the society and what we wanted changed. . . . It was a tool for democratic struggle, a progressive lobby group, and open forum that was only forced underground by unnecessary crackdown' (Oluoch, 2013).

Being forced to 'keep quiet' across generations fades many of these public memories and critical consciousnesses. By the early 1990s, for example, the term 'mwakenya' was used by some to refer not to the activists but, rather, to banned 'crib' booklets handmade by and circulated among high school students to peek at during midterm and final exams. In short, Moi's admonishment to 'keep quiet' worked to snuff out memories of the progressive politics and calls for democracy that the movement had stood for. Today, many Kenyan youth are unfamiliar with these names, this history of resistance and the Mwakenya movement. As Nyairo writes: 'nations are constructed by what they bury and forget, just as much as they are built on what they choose to remember' (Nyairo, 2015, 69). Thus, we see here the need for knowledge infrastructures that go beyond housing official histories, and which also offer safe spaces for archiving and sharing histories of resistance and subversive politics. The legacy of Mwakenya is little talked about today. Nonetheless, as the re-emergence of the library collection of the Mwakenya in 2017 and the growth of the Ukombozi Library reading clubs (Box 13.4) symbolise, the Mwakenya legacy is not gone. The movement remains active, albeit less public and less widely known than in its early days.

> **Box 13.4: Ukombozi Library**
> To learn more about Ukombozi Library, visit the digital exhibit PALIAct Ukombozi Library (Okune, 2019a, https://stsinfrastructures.org/content/paliact-ukombozi-library/essay).

Decolonising libraries as progressive librarianship

As alluded to in the previous section, in trying to understand what decolonised libraries in Kenya on their own terms might look like, there is a rich history of revolutionary and anti-colonial publishing in Kenya to turn to (Box 13.5). Crafting and practising decolonial ambitions for libraries and other knowledge infrastructures requires

> **Box 13.5: Publishing in pre-independence Kenya**
> In Durrani's rich history of Kenyan publishing prior to achieving independence in 1963, he details a history of publishing in Kenya that is diverse and reaches back to the end of the 1800s, noting that although colonial laws prevented Kenya's African population from owning printing presses or newspapers, that did not mean they lacked effective means of communication. Durrani spotlights the importance of oral communication systems and more fugitive methods in bypassing the embargo imposed by the colonial administration, such as writing 'Kiswahili cha ndani' ('Kiswahili of the inside') resistance messages on women's khanga cloth, worn as skirts or wraps, so that the message reached a wide audience right in their homes. Durrani also points to the newspaper *Nyota ya Kirinyaga* = Kirinyaga's Star (1949; 1951) to provide an example of the kinds of people who owned and ran the local radical press: 'among the editors were one carpenter, a shoemaker, driver, sign writer, one book binder and several clerks, traders and farmers' (Durrani, 2006, 191). However, this rich history of intellectual and activist social communication is at risk of being 'forgotten' (we use quote marks here to highlight the connection with the chapter's earlier discussion of 'forget and move on', in which we described how this kind of 'forgetting' has been intentional and institutionalised).

developing greater connection to and knowledge of these histories. Shiraz Durrani, a Kenyan-British library professional and political activist forced into exile to the UK in 1986, has published several important pieces that help us begin to better understand this past. In a monograph analysing publishing and imperialism in Kenya from 1884 to 1963, Durrani described a shift in tactics as Mau Mau freedom fighters came to realise that, despite winning what Durrani referred to as 'flag independence' from the British colonialists, Kenyans had not acquired real liberation, land or freedom (Durrani, 2006, 235). Durrani reprinted the opening of an analysis penned collectively by Mau Mau analysts that had been widely distributed in the form of a pamphlet at the Kenya African National Union Conference held in Nairobi, Kenya in December 1961, two years before the country was declared an independent nation. Recognising that the battle for independence had shifted from the military front to economic and political fronts, the Mau Mau writers articulated: 'The struggle for Kenya's future is being waged today on three distinct though interrelated levels: political, racial, and economic. It seems to us that we Africans are being allowed to "win" in the first two spheres as long as we don't contest the battle being waged on the third, all-important, economic level' (Durrani, 2006, 236).

The Mau Mau pamphlet noted that the neocolonial status of the country was that of continued economic control by the British government and the new imperialist power of the United States of America: 'Put into slogan form, this plan would be: LEAVE IN ORDER TO STAY' (Durrani, 2006, 236). 'There is clear evidence of a calculated plan on the part of the economic elite to partially dissolve racial barriers in order to use Africans as frontmen and spokesmen for its interests ... "Africanisation" is the term used for the process ...' (Durrani, 2006, 237). The pamphlet also critically assessed the concept of nationalism as a 'negative philosophy', no substitute for a 'positive ideology'.

We use this sharp critique by the Mau Mau to build our own argument that decolonisation is a double bind – it must feel the weight of history as it struggles to move on. As we point to in the next section, despite being distinct and usually opposing forces, 'forget and move on', in practice, may look similar to 'decolonising'. Thus, we seek to articulate a 'decolonising' that doesn't forget. For that, we find inspiration in the Mau Mau vision for a Kenyan future. In the same 1961 pamphlet, they wrote:

> 'Let us instead struggle against a "stability" which is in fact stagnation; let us struggle to liberate that vast reservoir of reactive ability which now lies dormant among our people; let us, in short, create a society which allows to each the right to eat, the right to the products of their labour, the right to clothe, house, and educate their children, the right in short to live in dignity among equals. It is a socialist society we should be struggling to build, a system which, unlike capitalism, concerns itself with the welfare of the masses rather than with the profits and privileges of a few.'
>
> (Durrani, 2006, 237)

The real task for those interested in decolonising knowledge infrastructures, then, is in fact not really a question of what to forget. Instead, it is about developing alternative ideas and practices to address people's needs. The Mau Mau analysts stated:

> 'Let us then refashion an ideology which will unify the vast majority of our people by articulating their needs and by advancing a program of socialist development which promises to eradicate poverty, disease and illiteracy, a program which will draw out the creative talents and energies of our people, giving them that personal dignity and pride which comes from socially constructive and productive activity. Let us, in short, provide our people with the ideological and organisational tools necessary for the achievement of genuine independence and development.'
>
> (Durrani, 2006, 237)

Durrani builds on these Mau Mau writings to develop the concept of 'progressive librarianship', which seeks to increase awareness among the people about their social, political and economic realities and the need for change from today's power relations. 'Progressive librarianship's great contribution to the development of theory and practice of librarianship is to re-establish the link between political and information struggles' (Durrani, 2014, 91).

Book Bunk: practising progressive librarianship

Figure 13.2: *The entrance to McMillan Library's main branch, Nairobi, Kenya.*
Photo credit: Angela Okune, taken March 2019

I (SM) have been engaged in work with Book Bunk Trust, a social impact trust founded in October 2017 by Wanjiru Koinange and Angela Wachuka. As part of our work, the team at Book Bunk have been tangibly working on how to materially and conceptually decolonise some of Nairobi's iconic public libraries, including the McMillan Library.

The McMillan Library

Opened in 1931, the library (see Figure 13.2 on p. 199) was built by Lady Lucie McMillan as a memorial to her husband, US-born Sir Northrup McMillan, who died in 1925. The oldest library in Nairobi and the second-oldest in Kenya, it is the only building in Kenya protected by an Act of Parliament. In its first three decades the Library was limited to use by Europeans only. The Library was taken over by the Nairobi City Council in the lead-up to Kenyan independence in 1962, at which point it was opened up to the general public. Four additional branches were opened in subsequent years but today only two of these branches are functional – Eastlands and Kaloleni. In March 2018, Book Bunk formalised a partnership with the Nairobi City County that grants the organisation a mandate to lead restoration efforts and resource mobilisation for the libraries. Book Bunk's responsibilities include sourcing and management of fiscal and other support; steering and management of architectural restoration; and management of these public library spaces, including design and delivery of programming. Towards realising a dream that public Kenyan libraries can be steered to act as sites of knowledge production, shared experiences, cultural leadership and information exchange, the Book Bunk team has been tasked with key decisions about several aspects of the libraries. Some of these include whether or not to use the Dewey Decimal library classification system; the kinds of books to have in the library; and whether or not to un/rename the Library.

What it means to decolonise the library

A core part of revitalising the libraries has revolved around what it means to decolonise the Library: 'When it was opened in 1931, this library was never intended for African users. So when it was handed over to the city, there was never an attempt to decolonise that quite purposefully. It is something that we are thinking quite deeply about, and it is a phenomenal amount of work,' the Book Bunk co-founders said in a documentary trailer (Okune, 2019b). For example, as we began cataloguing McMillan Library's many items in 2019, the Book Bunk team and I (SM) came across a rich photographic archive. It was stored in the Library's basement in a metal storage drawer, together with some glass-plate negatives in a vermin-infested metal crate. When we started combing through the archive, we came across photographs with captions that literally gave us shivers; for example, the photograph of the first institutional hanging, when Kenya was a British colony.

In 2020, after cataloguing all 137,705 items housed in the three libraries, Book Bunk created the first-ever digital catalogue of the libraries' collection and began digitising the archive. This included newspapers, gazettes and photographs that constitute Kenya's cultural heritage and have suffered from neglect and climate damage. The collection includes reports of key historical events during Kenya's struggle for independence, such as the Mau Mau revolution, political assassinations, social and cultural developments, human rights movements and exploitative land-acquisition laws. Through this ongoing digitisation process, the Book Bunk team has had to figure out how to frame and contextualise aspects of this colonial and postcolonial national history. Digitising the photographic collection has been a way of making space for what has largely been a silenced history of Kenyan identity and struggle during the colonial period. As Coombes (2011) has noted, although many institutional public history exhibits are met with scrutiny and critique, the debates they foster are nevertheless often constructive and important. Recognising that we may encounter fraught topics and material, we nonetheless employ an approach similar to Mimi Onuoha's work, 'On Missing Datasets' (Onuoha, 2018). Onuoha's mixed media installation of a metal filing cabinet with labelled files that do not contain any data is, in her words, a 'visible physical repository of those things that have been excluded in a society where so much is collected' (Onuoha, 2018). She explained: 'The word "missing" is inherently normative. It implies both a lack and an ought: something does not exist, but it should. That which should be somewhere is not in its expected place; an established system is disrupted by distinct absence' (Onuoha, 2018). By creating a digitised archive of colonial newspapers, gazettes and photographs, Book Bunk looks to call attention to the missing perspectives, voices and faces – to think about what 'ought' to be there. This is what de Sousa Santos has called practising the sociology of absences: 'whatever does not exist in our society is often actively produced as non-existent and we have to look into that reality' (de Sousa Santos, 2016, 21). If, as Onuoha writes, 'spots that we've left blank reveal our hidden social biases and indifferences', then Book Bunk seeks to make these materials available for public critique to inoculate against a public culture of 'forget and move on'. By analysing what has been left silent in colonial Kenyan histories and grappling with it through these physical and now digital materials, we seek to support a Kenyan public capacity for critical consciousness. This is a key role we see progressive libraries playing a part in. Part of figuring out ways to cultivate such critical consciousness is also a question of how to build a technical infrastructure for it; for example, ensuring metadata and critical commentary accompany each artefact so that it is experienced contextually. There are important ongoing lessons and work to be learned from those working on civic community archive development and its software development (cf. Fortun et al., 2021; Christen, 2011).

Shaping the collection

In libraries across the world, 'weeding' refers to a practice conducted periodically where books which are considered misleading, beyond physical repair, superseded (a newer edition is available), trivial (information can be found elsewhere) or otherwise unfit for a particular collection are removed from the library. After completing the digital catalogue in 2019, in 2020 Book Bunk embarked on weeding the Library's collection, which spanned 90 years. A question that continually resurfaces is what to do with all the books that write in a racist way about Kenyans and Africans. For example, in John Harris's *Dawn in Darkest Africa* (1912), British colonialism is exalted as a service to the 'primitive natives' of the African continent. The book's introduction praised Harris as 'having acquired a firm grasp of the main principles which should guide Europeans who are called upon to rule over a backward and primitive society' (Harris, 1912). Should such works be weeded from the collection entirely? How should a progressive library support critical awareness about scientific racism and racist imperialism, both past and present, while also promoting and opening space for Kenyan narratives and forms of self-expression that seek to move out of these over-determined frames? How do we move on and not forget? One of the ways Book Bunk is working around this is by updating the library's acquisitions and collections policy so that it does three primary things. First, the new collection housed in the McMillan Libraries is to be chosen by the public based on their own needs. We (SM) do this by asking library users who sign in daily to also write in their desired additions to our library collection. We prioritise new acquisitions based on user demographics in the different branches and have curated a wish list of books that are available through local bookstores. Kenyans around the city have begun to purchase these books for McMillan Library users from the available online list and we have now begun to receive monthly drop-offs of new books.

Using a similar approach, library events and programming are crowdsourced from the Kenyan public themselves. In 2019, Book Bunk solicited proposals for public events (examples can be seen at www.bookbunk.org/programmes/past-programmes) to be held at the Library. We (SM) received 66 applications and eventually selected 12. Each group was given both cash and in-kind support to run its proposed event at one of the library branches, helping to push forward a vision of the Library as a public space of art, memory, cultural heritage and knowledge production. Second, the predominant voices in the library collection are to be Kenyan and African authors writing about the people and the region (Box 13.6). We (SM) are currently working on an acquisitions and collection policy that details how we hope to promote bibliodiversity (Shearer et al., 2020) in the collection, including authors and genres that we intentionally prioritise. And third, Book Bunk will use the Dewey Decimal Classification (DDC) and other library cataloguing systems as inspiration for our own classification system that serves the needs of a modern Nairobi library more intuitively. Most libraries use the Dewey Decimal system, but the Glasgow Women's Library, who mentor the Book Bunk team, created their own classification system inspired by Indian feminists calling for the creation of alternative classification systems (Gandhi, 1995) that were less hierarchical and more inclusive of women's affairs.

> **Box 13.6: Languages in the McMillan Library collection**
> While there are over 40 spoken languages in Kenya, English and Kiswahili are the main languages of speech and writing. As such, most texts in the library will be written in English and Kiswahili, but the collection will also have books of other East African languages.

Drawing inspiration from this example, Book Bunk, too, is in the processes of developing its own classification scheme.

Progressive librarianship

McMillan Libraries are just one of a diverse ecology of libraries in Kenya and are certainly not the only ones that can be read as attempting to practise progressive librarianship. PALIAct Ukombozi Library, as another example, is explicitly founded by Shiraz Durrani, Kimani Waweru and others on the very principles of progressive librarianship. Durrani (2014) describes these efforts in detail in his book, *Progressive Librarianship*. By framing the decolonising work being done at McMillan Libraries as also working towards progressive librarianship, we seek to promote the idea that there is great heterogeneity in the libraries' attempting decolonisation. Instead of decolonisation as the goal in and of itself, greater collective attention to articulations of a public information system that meets the needs of the Kenyan working people is needed. As Durrani wrote: 'What was progressive a hundred years ago will not necessarily be progressive today; what is progressive in Kenya today may not necessarily be progressive in Britain today. The essence of progressiveness is that it is dynamic and changes with changing circumstances. Every revolution needs a relevant information system to ensure success' (Durrani, 2014, 50).

A diverse ecosystem of libraries, archives, digital repositories, and scholarly communities in conversation with each other and constantly reassessing information needs of Kenyan citizens is important because local collaborations, transnational alliances and an articulation of shared values and principles help to fortify against the commercial encroachment of digital knowledge commons which, as we detail in the next section, we have begun to observe in the Kenyan digital cultural heritage space.

Limiting decolonial possibilities: commercial dominance of the digital layer

In an October 2020 video message, Kenyan President Uhuru Kenyatta stated:

> We must look for our common vision in the dreams of our ancestors. We must seek out their wisdom and preserve their memory. We must bring them to life in a way that present generations can relate – through technology. You can begin that journey by visiting the National Museums of Kenya page on the Google Arts and Culture platform to learn the stories of our folk and cultural heroes, relive their experiences and draw the inspiration that you need from them in order to play your part in constructing and exemplifying our national ethos.
>
> (Itimu, 2020)

What does it mean when Kenyan youth are advised to turn to Google for the dreams of their ancestors? In this section we attend to the political economy of global knowledge infrastructure, pointing out the risks of increasing privatisation of digital knowledge commons by private corporations. Given the deep history of Kenyan resistance that we have briefly sketched, as well as the disinvestment in public memory and knowledge infrastructures enacted by the austerity programmes of structural adjustment, those who care about decolonised libraries must also care about protecting their public ownership. If we believe in the importance of progressive librarianship and scholarly knowledge for a vibrant civil society and public life, then we must pay attention not only to the physical structures and material content of libraries and archives, but also to the digital systems that structure how this knowledge is indexed, accessed, promoted and stored. The vertical integration of services provided by foreign corporate actors like Facebook and Google has far-reaching consequences for network sovereignty and (un)democratic control of digital infrastructures (Nothias, 2020). Toussaint Nothias (2020) has described how, despite often critiquing these foreign companies, civil society organisations find themselves increasingly reliant on the digital platforms run by the very same corporations, not to mention the explicit partnerships and philanthropic funding linked to tech industry fortunes. This makes resistance to such corporate projects particularly challenging, especially when the government, as evidenced in the section's opening quotation, is also in close collaboration with these corporations.

An approach of 'forget and move on' towards Kenyan national events has led to the normalisation of state incompetence and a distrust of its narratives and systems, fertile grounds for technology corporations to offer their 'free' services. Simultaneous with work by concerned Kenyans to reinvigorate libraries as open spaces for diverse publics, there have also been growing investments by technology corporations into these spaces, which we believe warrant critical attention from scholars, journalists and activists. A culture of 'forget and move on' has had debilitating effects not only on national memory but also on the actors seen as trustworthy and capable of managing and stewarding Kenya's past, present and future. Acknowledging this loss of trust in public systems and their agents is imperative for understanding the barriers to overcoming what Paulin Hountondji (1990) has labelled 'extroverted scientific activity', where scholarly work advances the theoretical needs and questions of the Western academy but does not serve the societies within which science is conducted. Individuals and library organisations alike, all of us, are increasingly caught within systems of platform capitalism (Srnicek, 2017) that establish dependencies that are hard to get out of and which reduce the possibilities of bibliodiversity (Shearer et al., 2020) and epistemic justice (Albornoz, Okune and Chan, 2020). Big tech, controlling the library, archive or data repository and mining its contents, would have us believe that they are best placed to reveal trends in data, from culture and thought to potential future pandemics. However, recent work by scholars of the archive reminds us to question the broad implications of technology corporations' investments in large-scale determination of knowledge. We add to these ongoing conversations by suggesting that without addressing the enduring imperial legacies that continue today in current established postcolonial knowledge infrastructures, there is no way to 'move on'. In an environment where funding is limited and government support is thin, libraries and archives are in an increasingly tight spot to come up with the funds to stay open and develop services such as digitisation of archives. When funding or in-kind support is offered, it is difficult to turn down corporate actors, many of whom seem very well intentioned. But we must reflect on the autonomy and decision-making power that is sacrificed when mega-corporations begin to get involved.

We take no issue with the President's sentiments that Kenyan youth can draw inspiration from the revolutionary leaders of the last 50 years; in fact, we are in full agreement. However, we do question why, instead of promoting and recognising, for example, the important efforts by Chao Tayiana at African Digital Heritage and the Museum of British Colonialism, Wairimu Nduba's work at WerJoKenya or Mwihaki Muraguri's work with Paukwa – to mention just a few – rather, the head of state called for citizens to turn to a multinational American company with a business model centred on data extraction. In light of this, supporting the organising of people and alternative socio-technical infrastructures that can enable digital humanities, archiving, artistic and scholarly experimentation for public interest appears as an important, growing role for Kenyan progressive libraries.

Conclusion

In the closing shots of a corporate marketing video, a thin, young Black woman looks straight into the camera, raises her fist and states resolutely: 'Forwards Ever, Backwards Never.' The video, from ThoughtWorks, a technology design company, is embedded in a company blog post titled 'Using Technology to Drive Change in Africa' (Rao et al., 2015) and talks about the company's relationship to the continent. 'Our vision for Pan Africa is that in five years' time, ThoughtWorks will have catalysed the development of accessible software-driven-technologies coded in Africa, for Africa, by diverse African teams,' the post states. However, five years down the line, the company no longer has any physical presence on the continent, having closed both of its Africa-based offices – one in Uganda and the other in South Africa. Its headquarters in Europe and North America remain open and active. The closure of ThoughtWorks' African offices is joined by more recent closures of technology start-up SafeBoda (Ayugi, 2020) and Google's Loon project (Wakabayashi, 2021), rendering void any illusion of a technologically driven linear progress narrative. Bestowing foreign technology companies – many of whom have quickly left once capital and profits dried up – with the country's 'roots', that is, historical artefacts and national memory, is an incredible risk. Even if external partners have the best intentions, their activities can be experienced as extractive if care is not taken to invest in strengthening local systems in the places where these materials were first created. All knowledge infrastructures reinforce authority, power and control (Acker, 2020; Dourish and Bell, 2007) and require upkeep, care and maintenance (Martin, Myers and Viseu, 2015; Murphy, 2014). Rather than putting Kenyan youth to work sweeping streets and digging trenches to 'keep busy' (Box 13.7), what if young people were instead mentored to contribute to, learn about and steward Kenya's knowledge infrastructure?

> Box 13.7: State programmes of youth employment
> State programmes designed to create employment for Kenyan youth have come in cycles, initiated with pomp and promise (and big budgets), only to end in scandal and missing funds and then to be resurrected again under a different name. For example, in March 2011, the government's Kazi Kwa Vijana initiative (with 4.3 billion Kenyan shillings allocated by the World Bank) was launched and aimed at creating 300,000 jobs countrywide. But barely six months later, claims of corruption and unaccounted for funds halted the programme (Aseka, 2011). Similarly, a 2018 scandal over 791 million Kenyan shillings (7.65 million USD) went missing as part of contracts associated with the Kenya National Youth Service (NYS) (BBC, 2018). The NYS continues to be plagued by corruption scandals (Mukii, 2021). Most recently, in 2020, *Kazi Mtaani* (which loosely translates to 'Neighbourhood Employment' in Swahili/Sheng) was launched and allocated 10 billion Kenyan shillings (91.2 million USD) to provide jobs to young people (Kinyanjui, 2020). Public criticism over the kinds of menial work being offered has surfaced in online spaces (see, for example, the satirical video https://twitter.com/i/status/1298924063570702336 circulated on Twitter).
> The latest youth employment scheme programme has been critiqued for offering menial work to Kenyan youth.

Kenyan philosopher Ngũgĩ wa Thiong'o wrote: 'Memory is the link between the past and the present, between space and time, and it is the base of our dreams' (Thiong'o, 2009, 28). If, as Ngũgĩ writes, '[m]emory and consciousness are inseparable' (Thiong'o, 2009, 29), given this chapter's exploration of Kenya's contested approach towards national memory and proclivity to outsource knowledge infrastructure, what are the implications for Kenyan consciousness? What kind of knowledge infrastructures, particularly libraries and archives, are needed if Kenyans are to (continue to) speak truth to power and rekindle and ignite consciousness not just in this generation but in generations to come? Here feminist historian of science and technology Michelle Murphy adds: 'the past as archive or as trauma is not what has already happened but instead a potential that can be variously actualized in the becoming of the future' (Murphy, 2014).

Going back to the paradox of the lion's head – what to remember and forget in attempts to decolonise – and layering this with contemporary and historical events that circle around questions of value and profiting from knowledge, it is clear that what to remember and what to forget is tied directly to the capabilities and ownership of the technical infrastructure. We cannot expect to retain a critical perspective of imperial formations if the very infrastructure itself is owned and bound up in that same hegemonic imperial power. The question of decolonising knowledge, then, is also one of decoupling from infrastructures owned by private Euro-American corporations. 'The need is for working people to own and control magazines and book publishing so as to reflect the world from their point of view,' Ukombozi Library founders Shiraz Durrani and Kimani

Waweru (Durrani, 2014; Durrani, Waweru and Kitchen, 2017) have suggested, reflecting on their experience and motivation for Ukombozi Library.

In this chapter we have shed light on what we characterise as an approach of 'forget and move on' towards national memory. Moving on instead of grappling with and bringing to account the injustices and wrongs carried out at particular moments in Kenyan history leads to an increasingly disillusioned and cynical public who do not trust public narratives or expect much from state institutions. Instead, citizens as well as the Kenyan state turn to external actors, outsourcing, for example, core knowledge infrastructures to foreign companies, including, most recently, national archival and library content to American technology multinational, Google. This has brought us to a contemporary moment where the President allocated 91 million USD to pay Kenyan youth to sweep the streets and dig trenches and advises them to turn to Google to learn about their ancestors.

If we are to truly stay with the discomfort of decolonising knowledge infrastructures, a first step is to develop and support community-owned systems, bringing together diverse people thinking and working on these issues. We do not need to know the answer in order to grasp that we must imagine and build something different together. We have no wish to simply replay the trauma and violence of imperialism over and over again, potentially overdetermining any kind of radical future imaginary. But by developing an understanding of colonialism's epistemic formations, we can better track its remnants and new formulations as they continue into the present and future. Instead of a culture of 'forget and move on', which does not in fact get us any closer to epistemic justice, we believe in the importance of infrastructuring and strengthening the connections that support those aspiring for decolonial knowledge through progressive librarianship to pay attention to existing oppressive systems and begin to imagine new modes of redress and freedom.

Acknowledgements

Thank you to Sylvia Nam, Sandy Wenger, Melissa Wrapp and Jen Zelnick for their invaluable comments and suggestions, which helped to push our early argument further. We would like to also thank Shiraz Durrani, Kim Fortun, Wanjiru Koinange, Regina Everitt and Jess Crilly for their review and suggestions. We would like to acknowledge the work being done by the teams at McMillan Libraries and Book Bunk Trust, especially Wanjiru Koinange and Angela Wachuka. We acknowledge Ukombozi Library and Vita Books for their dedication to the cause of progressive librarianship in Kenya, and Angela Okune would like to acknowledge the labour and work of Trevas Matathia, who supported her during her fieldwork in 2019.

References

Acker, A. (2020) Private Platforms, Metadata, and the Enclosure of Data Access: Urgent Issues for Knowledge Infrastructure Research, https://escholarship.org/uc/item/48c7b5p2.

Albornoz, D., Okune, A. and Chan, L. (2020) Can Open Scholarly Practices Redress Epistemic Injustice? In Eve, M. P. and Gray, J. (eds), *Reassembling Scholarly Communications: Histories, Infrastructures, and Global Politics of Open Access*, MIT Press, https://direct.mit.edu/books/book/4933/chapter/625156/Can-Open-Scholarly-Practices-Redress-Epistemic.

Anderson, J. and Christen, K. (2019) 'Decolonizing Attribution: Traditions of Exclusion', *Journal of Radical Librarianship*, **5**, (June), 113–52.

Aseka, C. (2011) 'Kenya: Kazi Kwa Vijana Good Project Dogged by Poor Planning and Usual Politics', *AllAfrica.Com*, 4 November, sec. News, https://allafrica.com/stories/201111040054.html (accessed 4 April 2021).

Ayugi (2020) SafeBoda to Close down Kenya Operations, *Tech In Africa* (blog), 16 November, www.techinafrica.com/safeboda-to-close-down-kenya-operations (accessed 4 April 2021).

BBC (2018) Head of Kenya Youth Agency Arrested in $78m Corruption Scandal, *BBC News*, 28 May, sec. Africa, www.bbc.com/news/world-africa-44280453 (accessed 4 April 2021).

Borgman, C. L. (2020) Knowledge Infrastructures in Past, Present, and Future Tense, https://escholarship.org/uc/item/5v73333z.

Christen, K. (2011) Opening Archives: Respectful Repatriation, *The American Archivist*, **74** (1), 185–210, https://doi.org/10.17723/aarc.74.1.4233nv6nv6428521.

Coombes, A. E. (2011) Monumental Histories: Commemorating Mau Mau with the Statue of Dedan Kimathi, *African Studies*, August, www.tandfonline.com/doi/abs/10.1080/00020184.2011.594628.

de Sousa Santos, B. (2016) *Epistemologies of the South: Justice against Epistemicide*, Routledge.

Dourish, P. and Bell, G. (2007) The Infrastructure of Experience and the Experience of Infrastructure: Meaning and Structure in Everyday Encounters with Space, *Environment and Planning B: Planning and Design*, **34** (3), 414–30, https://doi.org/10.1068/b32035t.

Durrani, S. (2006) *Never Be Silent: Publishing and Imperialism in Kenya, 1884–1963*, Vita Books.

Durrani, S. (2014) *Progressive Librarianship: Perspectives from Kenya and Britain, 1979–2010*, Vita Books.

Durrani, S., Waweru, K. and Kitchen, S. (2017) Vita Books, www.readafricanbooks.com/publisher-profiles/shiraz-durrani-and-kimani-waweru/ (accessed 4 April 2021).

Emeagwali, G. (2011) The Neo-Liberal Agenda and the IMF/World Bank Structural Adjustment Programs with Reference to Africa. In Kapoor, D. (ed.), *Critical Perspectives on Neoliberal Globalization, Development and Education in Africa and Asia*, SensePublishers, https://doi.org/10.1007/978–94–6091–561–1_1.

Fortun, K., Fortun, M., Okune, A., Schutz, T. and Su, S.-Y. (2021) Civic Community Archiving with the Platform for Experimental Collaborative Ethnography: Double Binds and Design Challenges. In *HCI International 2021 Proceedings*, http://centerforethnography.org/sites/default/files/artifacts/media/pdf/516458_1_en_3_chapter_onlinepdf_1.pdf.

Friedrich-Ebert-Stiftung and Citizens for Justice (eds) (2003) *We Lived to Tell the Nyayo House Story*, Friedrich Ebert Stiftung.

Gandhi, N. (1995) Let a Thousand Flowers Bloom: Creating Alternative Classification Systems, Akshara Centre, https://studylib.net/doc/7339644/let-a-thousand-flowers-bloom—creating (accessed 4 April 2021).

Gathara, P. (2020a) PATRICK GATHARA – Why Colonial-Era Edicts Will not Defeat the Coronavirus in Kenya, *The Elephant*, 23 March, www.theelephant.info/features/2020/03/23/why-colonial-era-edicts-will-not-defeat-the-coronavirus-in-kenya (accessed 4 April 2021).

Gathara, P. (2020b) On Westgate's 7th Anniversary, Kenya Is Repeating Its Mistakes, *Al Jazeera*, 21 September, www.aljazeera.com/opinions/2020/9/21/on-westgates-7th-anniversary-kenya-is-repeating-its-mistakes (accessed 4 April 2021).

Gisesa, N. (2020) Mwakenya Leaders Regroup to Tell Their Experiences, *Nation*, 18 March, https://nation.africa/kenya/news/mwakenya-leaders-regroup-to-tell-their-experiences-240084 (accessed 4 April 2021).

Harris, J. H. (1912) *Dawn in Darkest Africa*, Smith, Elder, http://archive.org/details/b29010639.

Hountondji, P. (1990) Scientific Dependence in Africa Today, *Research in African Literatures*, **21** (3), 5–15.

Itimu, K. (2020) Google and National Museum Partner to Showcase Kenya Superheroes Online, *Techweez* (blog), 19 October, https://techweez.com/2020/10/19/google-national-museum-kenya-launch-superheroes-online-exhibition (accessed 4 April 2021).

Jurgens, R. and Momoniat, Y. (2020) The Ancient Libraries of Africa, *GGA* (blog), 23 January, https://gga.org/the-ancient-libraries-of-africa (accessed 4 April 2021).

Kelley, R. D. G. (2003) *Freedom Dreams: The Black Radical Imagination*, Beacon Press.

Kimani, J. (2014) Mau Mau Descendants Want Roads Named after War Heroes, *Nation*, 29 July, https://nation.africa/kenya/counties/nakuru/mau-mau-descendants-want-roads-named-after-war-heroes-1009666 (accessed 4 April 2021).

Kinyanjui, M. (2020) More Youths to Be Hired in Kazi Mtaani Phase Two, *The Star*, 13 July, www.the-star.co.ke/news/2020-07-13-more-youths-to-be-hired-in-kazi-mtaani-phase-two (accessed 4 April 2021).

Klopp, J. M. and Orina, J. R. (2002) University Crisis, Student Activism, and the Contemporary Struggle for Democracy in Kenya, *African Studies Review*, **45** (1), 43–76, https://doi.org/10.1017/S0002020600031541.

Manji, F. (2020) FIROZE MANJI – The Failure of the Left in Contemporary Movements in Africa, *The Elephant*, 30 October, www.theelephant.info/op-eds/2020/10/30/the-failure-of-the-left-in-contemporary-movements-in-africa (accessed 4 April 2021).

Martin, A., Myers, N. and Viseu, A. (2015) The Politics of Care in Technoscience, *Social Studies of Science*, **45** (5), 625–41, https://doi.org/10.1177/0306312715602073.

Matathia, T. and Okune, A. (2019) McMillan Library. In Okune, A., Matathia, T. and Mutonga, S. *Scholarly Memory in Nairobi, Kenya: Care for Sites and Sources*. In Khandekar, A. and Fortun, K. (created by) *Innovating STS Digital Exhibit*, Society for Social Studies of Science (August), https://stsinfrastructures.org/content/mcmillan-library/essay.

Mukii, I. (2021) NYS Faces Fresh Multi-Million Scandal, *Kenyans.Co.Ke*, 16 February, www.kenyans.co.ke/news/62284-nys-spot-over-new-multi-million-scandal (accessed 4 April 2021).

Murphy, M. (2014) Abduction, Reproduction, and Postcolonial Infrastructures of Data, University of Toronto, 27 February, http://sfonline.barnard.edu/traversing-technologies/michelle-murphy-abduction-reproduction-and-postcolonial-infrastructures-of-data (accessed 4 April 2021).

Musila, G. A. (2019) Against Collaboration – or the Native who Wanders off, *Journal of African Cultural Studies*, **31** (3), 286–93, https://doi.org/10.1080/13696815.2019.1633283.

Nothias, T. (2020) Access Granted: Facebook's Free Basics in Africa, *Media, Culture & Society*, **42** (3), 329–48, https://doi.org/10.1177/0163443719890530.

Nyairo, J. (2015) *Kenya@50: Trends, Identities and the Politics of Belonging*. Contac Zones NRB.

Nyota ya Kirinyaga (Star of Kirinyaga) (1949; 1951). Gikuyu, Monthly.

Okune, A. (2019a) PALIAct Ukombozi Library. In In Okune, A., Matathia, T. and Mutonga, S. *Scholarly Memory in Nairobi, Kenya: Care for Sites and Sources*. In Khandekar, A. and Fortun, K. *Innovating STS Digital Exhibit*, Society for Social Studies of Science (August), https://stsinfrastructures.org/content/paliact-ukombozi-library/essay.

Okune, A. (2019b) Decolonizing the Library. STS Infrastructures, https://stsinfrastructures.org/node/4463.

Oluoch, F. (2013) Scores Arrested in Mwakenya Crackdown, *Nation*, 12 December, https://nation.africa/kenya/kenya-50/governance/scores-arrested-in-mwakenya-crackdown—925952 (accessed 4 April 2021).

Onuoha, M. (2018 [2016]) On Missing Datasets, https://github.com/MimiOnuoha/missing-datasets.

Oyugui, E., Kigozi, D. and On'gwen, O. (1997) Structural Adjustment and Public Social Spending, *Social Watch*, www.socialwatch.org/node/10596 (accessed 4 April 2021).

Rao, G., Byarugaba, F., Britten-Kelly, B. and Jonah, B. (2015) Using Technology to Drive Change in Africa, *ThoughtWorks* (blog), 8 May, www.thoughtworks.com/insights/blog/using-technology-drive-change-africa (accessed 4 April 2021).

Rono, J. K. (2002) The Impact of the Structural Adjustment Programmes on Kenyan Society, *Journal of Social Development in Africa*, **17** (1), 81–98.

Shearer, K., Chan, L., Kuchma, I. and Mounier, P. (2020) Fostering Bibliodiversity in Scholarly Communications: A Call for Action, *Zenodo*, https://doi.org/10.5281/zenodo.3752923 (accessed 4 April 2021).

Srnicek, N. (2017) *Platform Capitalism*, Polity Press.

Subbo, W. (2007) An Overview of Structural Adjustment Programmes in Kenya, http://erepository.uonbi.ac.ke/handle/11295/26326.

Thiong'o, N. (1981) *Detained: A Writer's Prison Diary*, Heinemann.

Thiong'o, N. (2009) *Re-Membering Africa*, East African Educational Publishers.

Tuck, E. and Yang, K. W. (2012) Decolonization is not a Metaphor, *Decolonization: Indigeneity, Education & Society*, **1** (1), 1–40.

Wakabayashi, D. (2021) Google-Linked Balloon Project to Provide Cell Service Will Close, *The New York Times*, 22 January, sec. Technology, www.nytimes.com/2021/01/21/technology/loon-google-balloons.html (accessed 4 April 2021).

Wanjiru, M. W. and Matsubara, K. (2017) Street Toponymy and the Decolonisation of the Urban Landscape in Post-Colonial Nairobi, *Journal of Cultural Geography*, **34** (1), 1–23, https://doi.org/10.1080/08873631.2016.1203518.

14
Challenging its Imperial Origins: Towards Decolonising SOAS Library

Ludi Price

Introduction

This chapter outlines the ongoing process of decolonising the library at SOAS, University of London (otherwise known as the School of Oriental and African Studies). It deals firstly with the history of SOAS and its library, highlighting its deep colonial roots, and secondly gives a narrative of decolonisation activities undertaken in the Library since late 2019.

Decolonisation, which has been discussed and defined in great detail in other chapters of this book, is often conflated with diversification (compare Makhubela, 2018; Blackwood, 2020). Let us first assume that this conflation is correct. SOAS Library, since its inception, is fortunate enough to hold a vast array of Indigenous material from around the globe (particularly Asia, Africa and the Middle East). One can therefore say that SOAS Library is extremely diverse, and that its material represents a wide range of languages, communities and cultures from across a vast swathe of the globe, particularly those of developing countries in the Global South (for want of a better term). Diversification is hardly necessary when it comes to SOAS's collections; many of our staff are non-White/Black, Asian and Minority Ethnic (BAME), and we already have a large network of overseas contacts from whom we purchase our acquisitions – valuable knowledge which has been built up over decades. In light of this, some may be puzzled to learn that decolonisation is on the Library's agenda at all. Some might consider SOAS Library fortunate – does this not all imply that half the legwork of decolonisation is already done?

Of course, we know that diversification and decolonisation are not synonymous; and that, while diversification may be part of the decolonisation process, simply having a diverse collection, filled with Indigenous voices, is only a fraction of that process. SOAS Library is not exempt from the need for decolonisation – far from it, in fact.

We possess many of the *tools* of decolonisation – but as far as our everyday ingrained practice at SOAS Library is concerned, it is not generally informed by a knowledge or a critical appreciation of decolonisation. While the goal of decolonisation is certainly to have it embedded within our everyday practice, such that it is no longer noticeable, the practices within SOAS Library that might be considered hallmarks of a decolonisation process are most certainly not so. They are the relics of age-old structures that are, in fact, deeply colonial, and the everyday business of librarianship means that one is barely cognisant of that fact. A process of decolonisation must surely mean an awareness, if not a constant reflection on how such systems come to be, and our awareness of SOAS's colonial past can inform our work with our diverse library collections, how we continue to build them and how we present them to the world.

It is worth noting that while SOAS Library does not formally frame its decolonising efforts within the rubric of critical librarianship, this chapter does approach decolonisation through that lens. Here, the definition used by Nicholson and Seale (2018, 2) is specifically used: '[critical librarianship] uses a reflexive lens to expose and challenge the ways that libraries and the profession "consciously and unconsciously support systems of oppression", thereby pursuing a socially just, theoretically informed praxis'. As part of an institution that is both colonial and yet possesses many of the tools of decolonisation by nature of its regional and ethnic specialisms, it is especially important to acknowledge and challenge the deeply embedded colonial underpinnings of SOAS Library. It is also important to reflect upon the tools at our disposal, and how we may best use them to combat the systems of oppression that exist without our space. To put this process into context, it is therefore important to briefly consider the history of SOAS itself.

SOAS: a brief history

It is not a secret that SOAS, like many institutions of its era, is one rooted in Britain's colonial endeavours. Its *raison d'être*, one might add, was explicitly to aid in those endeavours. As Brown, in the only book dedicated entirely to the history of the School, asserts: 'the School was established principally to train the colonial administrators who ran the British Empire in the languages of Asia and Africa. Founded in 1916 as the School of Oriental Studies, the institution was established with an explicitly imperial purpose' (Brown, 2016, 1). Africa would be added in 1938, after the Rockefeller Foundation promised a grant of £3,000 annually to go towards the research of that continent in 1931 (Lodge, 1968, 93). The School's inception came as a response to an awareness that Britain was lagging behind its continental counterparts in its study of the 'Oriental' languages, particularly Germany, which was a rival 'in commercial interests and Oriental expansion' (from the Reay Report, Appendix 1, 1909, cited in Lodge, 1968, 85). It was also in response to a recognition that Colonial Office officials would not be instructed in the language of the region they were to be posted in *before* they were shipped out, but by local teachers once they had arrived. The founding of a home-grown school would provide the necessary language education before officials reached their eventual destinations. But the Reay Committee, which released its report on the need for such an institution in 1909, considered a much longer list of potential beneficiaries of such a school:

officials being prepared for service in the East and in Africa ...; military naval officers being trained as interpreters; commercial men; those wishing to pursue Oriental scholarship ...; students from, in particular, India who wished to study the literature of their own language or to learn another Oriental language; medical practitioners, especially women, who intended to practise in India; missionaries; and officials, military and naval officers, and missionaries on leave.

(Brown, 2016, 14)

Here we can see the whole gamut of imperialist endeavour represented. However, it is worth noting, as Brown does, that this imperial training never reached the scale it was originally intended to. This is excepting the period of the Second World War, when finally efforts were made to fulfil this founding vision for the School. Nevertheless, it took a significant amount of time for the wartime government to actually utilise the School as a language-training ground for the war effort, and thus its teaching effort was not as organised or effective as the School itself had hoped, at least as far as we know from the Japanese-language classes offered at the time (Kornicki, 2018).

The School, then, did not quite fulfil the imperial dreams that engendered its creation. Nevertheless, it is a child of that imperial agenda, and of its time. Even as the decades passed, and SOAS's language instruction was outstripped by its instruction in the social sciences – law, politics, economics, anthropology and so on – its foundation as a site of imperial language training gave 'the School's historians ... political scientists, anthropologists, and economists, confidence that they possessed unmediated access to the beliefs and perceptions of the peoples and cultures that they were studying, enabling them to speak directly, both literally and figuratively, to and for Asia, Africa, and the Middle East' (Brown, 2016, 3–4). Despite Brown's claim that these scholars have become more self-reflective of this position in more recent years – and despite a general perception of SOAS as an institution that is radical and politically active – internally there is still a perception that SOAS is in some respects exempt from the need to decolonise, as a recent internal report by the Decolonising SOAS Working Group suggests: 'there was a feeling amongst some colleagues that some of the programmes offered at SOAS were inherently "decolonised" through their regional or methodological focus, for example courses on Art History of non-western Regions or non-mainstream economic approaches' (Decolonising SOAS Working Group, 2020, 6).

From this we can see the very real challenge SOAS faces as a colonial institution, as an institution that specialises in the languages and cultures of previously colonised regions and as an institution that enjoys a reputation as a home for socially and politically active students and staff. In 2016 the Decolonising SOAS Working Group was created in order to meet that challenge, and in direct response to the wider Decolonising the Curriculum movement. The aim of the group is nothing less than to decolonise SOAS, not merely through 'cosmetic' approaches but by being 'concretely focused on transforming praxis within our teaching and learning, our research, our collaborations, our institutional culture and our external partnerships' (Sabaratnam, 2018, 1), both collaboratively and collectively with the academic and student body.

SOAS Library

The library was considered an essential part of SOAS from the very outset, with the 1909 Reay Report suggesting that 'all the Oriental books now at University College and King's College would be concentrated' in this library (Reay Report, 1909, cited in Lodge, 1968, 85). The School, when it took up its first residence in the buildings of the London Institution (for the Advancement of Literature and the Diffusion of Useful Knowledge) in Finsbury Circus, inherited that institution's library. The collection was in bad shape, with minimal cataloguing having been done. Most of its content was not relevant to the mission of the School. Therefore, it was agreed that books from this collection would be exchanged for books on the 'Oriental' subjects from the University of London. The exchange took far longer than anticipated, due to the state of the London Institution library, whose collections had been boxed up, so the size and contents were poorly known due to the lack of cataloguing. Apart from this, the library relied heavily on donations, as it still does today.

Since 1961, and under the recommendation of the Hayter Report, SOAS Library has acted as a National Research Library and is provided with special funding under that status (Spina, 2010). Thus, it serves not only the SOAS community but also the public, and overseas patrons. Its current size is estimated at around 1.3 million volumes (SOAS Library, 2021); this does not include electronic items or material housed in its off-site stores. For an in-depth history of the Library through to the 1960s, Lodge (1968) provides an excellent overview.

Let us now turn, with a decolonial lens, to some individual aspects of SOAS Library.

Metadata, classification and cataloguing

As Crilly (2019a, 9) notes, '[c]lassification techniques form part of [...] epistemic control'. At SOAS, we use more than one classification system – modified Dewey, for the most part, with some in-house systems. The modified Dewey system adds regional/language codes as a prefix, thus allowing the classmark to be shortened, as the regional facets can be stripped out. Each region is given a code – for instance, CC for China, CCLA for Shanghai, CCX for Taiwan; KK for Hindi, KI for Gujarati; VK for Tanzania, VP for Francophone West Africa; and so on. The in-house classification systems are reserved for the Art and Archaeology collection and the Chinese-language collection. Suffice it to say that the classification systems SOAS employs have been criticised for being too complex and impermeable. Its classification by region can be problematic, especially when one considers territories whose borders are contested or controversial. For instance, some signage has been defaced within the Library in the past, with regard to Tibet's status as an autonomous region of China. As seen in the documentary *Change the Subject* (2019), it is the same case with subject headings (SOAS uses the Library of Congress Subject Headings). As librarians, we are often not aware of the trauma we can inflict on patrons through the classification systems we choose.

SOAS has considered reclassifying its collections by stripping away regional codes, but this does not mitigate the inherent Euro/Anglo/US-centrism of the Dewey system, and, in any case, the plan was shelved due to a lack of funds and manpower. However, the Library is now turning to decolonising its subject headings, which, due to the limited functionality of the library management system, have not been updated for several years.

Acquisitions

One strength of the Library is its sizeable network of overseas vendors and suppliers that has developed over the years. This has been vital in allowing us to build collections rich in Indigenous literatures. These relationships were built in part by previous generations of subject librarians reaching out to publishing houses or organisations overseas (Stevens, 1983), or going on book-buying tours (Colvin, 1976). While most libraries can no longer afford the luxury of book-buying tours, they are in many ways essential in the discovery phase for new sources of Indigenous material. As many developing regions are still not online, local publications, be they amateur or otherwise, are essentially invisible to the West, and it is these publications, and, I would argue, the voices they champion that are vitally important to the decolonisation process. For many books such as these, SOAS has relied on donations, both currently and historically, but these are by their nature ad hoc and inconsistent.

Nevertheless, SOAS benefits greatly from its overseas contacts, and we have begun work on putting a list together for other libraries to take advantage of.

Archives and Special Collections

There is great synergy between the Library and Special Collections: much of the material in the main library collection is old or rare enough to be considered part of Special Collections. Indeed, part of the background business of the Library is to transfer this material between the collections. One of the founding collections of the Library, donated by University College London in 1922, is the Morrison Collection of Chinese books. Robert Morrison (1784–1834) was the first Protestant missionary to China, and this rare and unique collection was part of an effort on his part to collect cheap and affordable books on every subject during the Qing period. These books rapidly deteriorated, are very scarce now and are of great historical interest (Wood, 2014, 29). Another collection of great historical value is the ex libris of Sir Reginald Johnston, a former SOAS professor and English teacher to the last emperor of China, Puyi 溥儀 (1906–67). To take these two collections as an example, neither consists of stolen or looted property, and the Library takes great pains not to ingest such material where its provenance is discernible. But what these collections do hold testament to is the colonial and imperial context of their background, which it is impossible to extricate from the objects themselves. These objects, these collections, provide the opportunity to assess, evaluate and critique our colonial past – if there is the will and the awareness to do so. Yet rarely have SOAS's collections been approached from this angle. Our large collection of missionary archives, while perhaps highlighting the colonial expansionist intentions of the British government, can also shed light on how missionary organisations 'led vigorous campaigns to protect the land rights and territorial claims of the people they served' (Rayner, 2014, 54). This is not to deny the condescending benevolence with which they may have done so, but to highlight that such resources give a wider and richer understanding of colonial (and decolonial) epistemologies.

Another problem is that of provenance. There are many parts of our Special Collections – particularly the early ones – that lack proper documentation of provenance. This leads us to a dilemma when trying to assess whether an item has been unlawfully obtained or not. When one considers the case for repatriation (or restitution) of such material, with such a lack of documentation, it often is not possible to know to whom it should be returned. Part of the problem may be solved by digital repatriation/restitution – but this too has its pros and cons. Baschiera (2020) has called for SOAS's Swahili documents to be returned, noting that those that are old enough to be considered 'artefacts' should be housed in museums in their originating countries. She praises digitisation efforts, yet notes the access difficulties often encountered in developing countries, suggesting that we 'explore how the digital collections can be better shared with the people and institutions of East Africa, especially Kenya and Tanzania' (Baschiera, 2020, 48). On the other hand, Davis (2019) has a much more cautious approach to repatriation/restitution, raising several points of concern, including the risk of splitting up collections, existing scholarship becoming unverifiable and copyright and licensing impediments. This is in addition to pointing out the internet access disparities which exist in many developing countries; open access is not the solution to all knowledge dissemination inequalities, as Istratii and Porter (2017) note. Instead, Davis suggests solutions such as adequate bursaries or scholarships to fund travel and accommodation for archival research – for more on this, her paper is well worth reading.

The library space

As Crilly (2019b, 88) and others have asserted: 'The academic library is currently a White space.' SOAS Library is lucky enough to have many BAME staff (54% at January 2021; it must be noted that several BAME staff were lost during the 2019 restructure). This is due in part to the need for regional and language expertise. While not all languages can be represented, it is validating and welcoming for many students to engage with staff in their native languages.

However, SOAS needs to consider other ways in which it can physically decolonise its both space and access to its materials. As mentioned earlier, how does the way we physically arrange and signpost our collections affect students? What parts of our collections do students feel are inadequate in representing their identities, cultures, backgrounds? Is the Library itself welcoming or intimidating – or even offensive – to students who come from BAME, low-income and/or working-class backgrounds? And let us not forget the virtual space either, especially during a pandemic that has forced learning and teaching to be conducted online. It is well known that some students from these backgrounds are less likely to have access to stable broadband internet connections. How does this affect their ability to access our e-resources?

These are questions that SOAS Library has not yet fully asked, let alone answered, and it is necessary for staff to listen to the voices of students in order to address the structural inequalities within the Library that they may not have thought of. This has been essential in other instances of library decolonisation, such as that outlined by Clarke (2020, 150).

The Library Decolonisation Group
The origins of the Group

The SOAS Library Decolonisation Operational Group began as an idea which was born during the inaugural meeting of the Chartered Institute of Library and Information Professionals' BAME network in September 2019. Attending this meeting brought to my attention how far behind SOAS Library was compared to other university libraries with regard to decolonisation. This seemed incongruous, considering the global nature of the Library's holdings, its colonial background and the work already achieved by its host institution via the Decolonising SOAS Working Group. If anything, SOAS Library should have been a leader in the effort to decolonise libraries, but there was not even a whisper of the word within the Library itself. This gave me the impetus to remedy this oversight and work to bring this group together.

The group was finally formed in the late autumn of 2019, holding its first meeting in December of that year. Despite a major restructure of the Library that unfortunately saw many of our BAME staff leave, one positive fallout was the creation by library management of several working/task-and-finish groups that allowed for a self-reflexive evaluation of the Library's structures and services that had not been undertaken for many years. At this point, I saw the opportunity to propose setting up a decolonisation group, which would finally put this important process formally on the Library's agenda. This proposal was approved, and the group was quickly promoted from task-and-finish group status to a more appropriate operational group status.

It should be noted that the work of the group – and indeed the group itself – is not ratified by all library senior managers, and therefore holds what I consider to be a 'semi-grassroots' status. The group was lucky enough to have some supporters who agreed to its formal inclusion within the working/task-and-finish group structure. Nevertheless, its membership is largely informal at present, though inclusive, and its agenda (as yet) is not considered by management as part of the core business of the Library. I am reminded of my early discussion with Elizabeth Charles, Assistant Director of Birkbeck Library, on how to set up a decolonisation group, and her advice to 'start from the bottom if you need to – don't wait for approval from the top'. This was excellent advice, and I would echo it to anyone else who is considering a similar initiative.

A challenging start

Having been approved, the group's work was almost immediately stymied by three significant events: (1) the UCU (University and College Union) strikes during February 2020; (2) the COVID-19 epidemic, which as of this writing still continues; and (3) another major restructure during the summer of 2020 which saw yet more colleagues either leave the Library or be transferred to other departments.

One of our first endeavours was to create a small, 'pilot' exhibition for LGBTQ+ History Month as a way of seeing how we might be able to put together a similar exhibition for Black History Month later in the year. This included a display of books, DVDs and a slideshow of streaming videos available within our collections. The physical materials were selected collaboratively by all regional and subject librarians, including books on sex, gender and LGBTQ+ topics in a wide array of different languages from across the regions collected at SOAS. These materials were free for patrons to pick up and browse on the spot, or to take out on loan. A link was also provided for patrons to give feedback on the display. Unfortunately, the exhibition took place during the UCU strikes, while there was minimal footfall in the Library; and while Reader Services staff did see the books being borrowed, there was nowhere near the level of engagement we had hoped for, and no meaningful data could be gleaned from the pilot.

Soon thereafter COVID-19 struck, and all staff had to work from home. Planned activities had to be put on hold while members got to grips with new ways of working, as well as the monumental task of delivering basic resources remotely. The situation highlighted another problem with decolonisation work in a digital era – that of the digital provision of Indigenous materials. The majority of the Library's collection is made up of texts that are rare or unique – some being the only copies available in Europe (or, indeed, the world) and a vast number of texts exist only in print form. The digital provision of texts outside the US/Anglo/Euro-centric world is not extensive or stable; therefore, there was a high demand for us to deliver print texts to patrons, largely satisfied by our Click & Collect service, which has run throughout the pandemic. However, there is still a struggle to provide access to patrons who cannot travel to campus to use the service. Scanning has been used to cover requests for materials that do not have a digital equivalent – which was challenging, as staff members could not read some Indigenous resources.

During the summer of 2020, SOAS was hit with another blow – a major restructure, the second in 18 months, that saw more staff losses and significant disruption. Again, the work of the group was interrupted, although we did have dislocated discussions during this period. One initiative that we discussed was decolonising our metadata, in particular tackling out-of-date and offensive subject headings. This is still a work in progress, largely because the functionality of our open source library management system (LMS; Kuali OLE) does not allow for global edits of subject headings (it does not house authority records), and any such work would involve exporting and manipulating the data in a third-party program. This point highlights an important consideration for systems librarians in the selection of LMS. We have found that technology itself can be either a powerful tool or a hindrance in the decolonisation process. Even open source software should not be accepted 'uncritically' (Barron and Preater, 2018, 106).

Another initiative discussed was a way in which SOAS could give its research back to the communities that were the subject of that research. This would involve, of course, the translation of that research into the languages of those communities, which was no easy barrier to surmount. The idea was to have this research hosted in *Decolonial Subversions*, a new, open access, online journal launched by SOAS academic Romina Istratii. The work of contacting scholars who would like to have their work (or a summary of it) translated (or to translate it themselves) and facilitating the project would be done by the Library's Scholarly Communications team. However, the restructure saw Scholarly Communications move out of the Library, and discussions on the project stalled due to the disruption of the restructure. An important development, however, was that the group became one of the Decolonising SOAS Working Group's newly formed 'clusters', responsible for all library-related decolonisation work. Thus, happily, the group was now formally a part of the wider SOAS decolonisation initiative.

Terms of reference

It was only in the winter of 2020, a full year after the decolonisation group had begun, that its work began again in earnest. For that entire year, members had been working on its Terms of Reference document, attempting to clarify what its aims were and what its remit was. After many drafts and rewrites, this was finally published in January 2021 (SOAS Library Decolonisation Operational Group, 2021). The aims of the group are as follows:

1   The decolonisation of our metadata, including reviewing and updating our subject headings, and looking to improve our classification systems where possible.
2   Continuing to reach out to publishers and suppliers from Asia, Africa and the Middle East, and supporting small publishers that encourage voices from the heart of these regions.
3   Working with departments and people throughout the SOAS community, to build reading lists that reflect Indigenous authors and engage with knowledge from across the globe, not merely the English-speaking West.
4   Facilitating the dissemination of our research to those who are the subjects of our research, particularly in Asia, Africa and the Middle East.
5   To champion digital repatriation or restitution through the SOAS Digital Collections, and to work towards other forms of restitution, where appropriate.
6   To assist in reviewing acquisition policies, especially in regards to donations, that will build a robust system for tracking the provenance of our collections; to refer new donations to the

Collections Committee where appropriate; and to review the provenance of sensitive items already within those collections.
7 To support our student body in the de-centring of Euro- and Anglo-centric epistemological structures by facilitating, as far as is possible, access to Indigenous resources from Asia, Africa, and the Middle East.
8 To work towards the decolonisation of our library space and collections, and access to that space and collections.
9 To work with our colleagues in other academic libraries to encourage/facilitate mutual sharing of best practice, knowledge of working with Asia, Africa and the Middle East, and to collaborate with them in the decolonisation process.
10 To involve the wider community in the decolonisation process, through engagement with, and access to, our collections.

It is important to add that these aims are not the means to the end of a linear process. Decolonisation is a dynamic process, and as the group navigates, and critically reflects upon, its practice, these goals may be subject to modification. None of us claims to be expert in what it means to decolonise; but we are dedicated to learning what it means through an ongoing journey, both within and without our home institution.

Conclusion

Despite existing for over a year now, the work of SOAS Library's Decolonisation Operational Group is still very much only just beginning. There are many challenges that face us. These challenges may not be easily met. We face technological challenges in updating, and in some cases modifying, subject headings. We have only just begun to engage with the Students Union about access to the library space. There is work, such as that on giving back the School's research to the communities we have studied, that was disrupted by the pandemic and other outside forces, and which needs to be continued. So far, our work has largely been 'driven by the individual activisms of those staff engaged in the initiative' (Clarke, 2020, 153), but we are slowly beginning to weave ourselves into the wider institution, primarily through the Decolonising SOAS Working Group. With our newly published Terms of Reference, we now have a solid foundation to build upon.

Acknowledgements

I would like to thank the members of SOAS Library's Decolonisation Operational Group, and all who have helped and supported our work over the past several months. Special thanks are extended to my co-chair, Farzana Whitfield, without whose encouragement and partnership this would never have got off the ground.

References

Barron, S. and Preater, A. (2018) Critical Systems Librarianship. In Nicholson, K. P. and Seale, M. (eds), *Politics of Theory and the Practice of Critical Librarianship*, Litwin Books.

Baschiera, A. (2020) Time to Address Repatriation of SOAS Swahili Manuscripts, *New African*, **603**, 48.

Blackwood, L. (2020) The Reality of Diversification Without Beginning the Process of Decolonisation, *Diversity Digest*, 28 May, https://blogs.kcl.ac.uk/diversity/2020/05/28/the-reality-of-diversification-without-beginning-the-process-of-decolonisation (accessed 13 January 2020).

Brown, I. (2016) *The School of Oriental and African Studies: Imperial Training and the Expansion of Learning*, Cambridge University Press.

Change the Subject (2019) [film] Directed by Baron, J. and Broadley, S.

Clarke, M. (2020) Liberate Our Library: Doing Decolonisation Work at Goldsmiths Library, *Art Libraries Journal*, **45**, 148–54.

Colvin, P. (1976) Report of a Book-buying Tour of the Middle East and North Africa, *International Library Review*, **8**, 271–81.

Crilly, J. (2019a) Decolonising the Library: A Theoretical Exploration, *Spark: UAL Creative Teaching and Learning Journal*, **4**, 6–15.

Crilly, J. (2019b) A Reflexive Lens: Critical Librarianship at UAL, *Art Libraries Journal*, **44**, 83–91.

Davis, J. (2019) Accessing UK Archival Holdings from South Africa, *African Research and Documentation*, **136**, 10–21.

Decolonising SOAS Working Group (2020) *Thoughts on Decolonising Teaching and Learning Practice at SOAS* [internal report], School of Oriental and African Studies.

Istratii, R. and Porter, H. (2017) Understanding the Possibilities and Limitations of Open Access Publishing for Decolonising Knowledge-making and Dissemination, *SOAS Journal of Postgraduate Research*, **11**, 185–94.

Kornicki, P. F. (2018) Frank Daniels' Report on the Wartime Japanese Courses at SOAS, *Bulletin of the School of Oriental and African Studies*, **81**, 301–24.

Lodge, A. (1968) The History of the Library of the School of Oriental and African Studies. In Saunders, W. L. (ed.), *University and Research Libraries*, Pergamon Press.

Makhubela, M. (2018) 'Decolonise, Don't Diversify': Discounting Diversity in the South African Academe as a Tool for Ideological Pacification, *Education as Change*, **22**, 1–21.

Nicholson, K. P. and Seale, M. (2018) *Politics of Theory and the Practice of Critical Librarianship*, Litwin Books.

Rayner, S. (2014) An Introduction to Archive Collections held at SOAS, *Legal Information Management*, **14**, 53–7.

Sabaratnam, M. (2018) A note from the Decolonising SOAS Working Group, *SOAS Journal of Postgraduate Research*, **11**, 1.

SOAS Library (2021) About SOAS Library, www.soas.ac.uk/library/about (accessed 12 January 2021).

SOAS Library Decolonisation Operational Group (2021) *Decolonisation Operational Group Terms of Reference*, www.soas.ac.uk/library/decolonisation-operational-group (accessed 12 January 2021).

Spina, B. (2010) SOAS Library: What Makes It Special, soas.ac.uk/library/about/what-makes-soas-library-special (accessed 12 January 2021).

Stevens, R. (1983) Acquisition of Serials from Asia and Africa at the School of Oriental and African Studies (SOAS) Library, *Library Acquisitions: Practice & Theory*, **7**, 59–70.

Wood, J. (2014) SOAS Library: Chinese Art and Archaeology Collection, *Art Libraries Journal*, **39**, 27–32.

15
Decolonising Library Collections: Contemporary Issues, Practical Steps and Examples from London School of Economics

Kevin Wilson

Introduction

This chapter examines the impact of decolonisation upon collection development, both in theory and in practice. It starts with a brief definition of collection development, how this has more recently evolved due to multiple influences and pressures and how it can be affected by bias. After, we reflect upon our analysis of London School of Economics and Political Science's (LSE) collections from a geographical perspective, assessing where our collections derive from. The relationship between collections and reading lists is then observed, particularly in terms of how library collections influence how reading lists are developed and how collections contribute to equity, diversity and inclusion issues. Finally, this chapter recommends some practical collection development steps that academic libraries can take, both individually and collectively, to make their collections more diverse, and also to support wider decolonisation initiatives within their parent institutions.

Collection development: an introduction

Library collections have historically been considered the heart of academic libraries, much as libraries have been said to be the heart of the university (Posner, 2019). Collection development is the work undertaken to build these collections and the decisions that are taken to determine how they evolve. Collection development includes many different activities, such as the selection and deselection of material, the acquisition of material and the evaluation of different access options (IFLA, 2020). Collection development is designed with the specific purpose to provide libraries with resources that meet the appropriate needs of their client populations (Gessesse, 2000) in a timely and economical manner (Evans, 1999).

The concept that collection development should 'advance scholarship and research' arguably refers back to Charles Coffin Jewett's tenure as the first full-time professional librarian in the USA, at Brown University in the mid-19th century (Desjarlais-Lueth,

1990). Over a century and a half later, this remains the consensus view (Jensen, 1977; Gonzalez-Kirby, 1991; Linden, Tudesco and Dollar, 2018; Scherlen and McAllister, 2019). Later, we will discuss the biases and inequities within curricula that have encouraged calls for greater change and levels of diversity. Therefore, we may question whether the role of collection development is solely to support teaching, learning and research and whether it should also be proactive in trying to influence it as well.

Collection development has been affected by technology and the promise of making processes more efficient, as well as by local pressures on time, staffing and finances. This has included centralising collection development and using approval plans rather than manual selection (Barstow, Macaulay and Tharp, 2016; Day and Novak, 2019) and using demand-driven acquisition to allow users to actively participate in selection (Blume, 2019; Day and Novak, 2019; England and Anderson, 2019). Where it was formerly the preserve of librarians (with some academic staff input), collection development has become more complex, with multiple stakeholders now involved. Librarians, however, retain a critical function in ensuring quality and maintaining the integrity of the collection (Levine-Clark, 2019).

The strategic direction for collection development is often defined by formal collection development policies. Having guidelines to follow and criteria to apply has many benefits for libraries (van Zijl, 1998). They demonstrate the direction of a library's collection building (Munro and Philps, 2008) and support and facilitate library decision making (Sanchez Vignau and Meneses, 2005). The absence of a collection development policy can lead to haphazard and inconsistent practice (Chaputula and Kanyundo, 2014). In contrast, it has been questioned whether collection development policies are 'the right weapon for this future battle' (Torrence, Powers and Sheffield, 2012), as they may not describe all the collection development strategies and criteria used (Papadakos et al., 2014) and changes in practice are not always reflected in policies (Hunt, 2017). Where policies diverge from practice, they can become the 'occupant of the last folder in the bottom drawer of a filing cabinet' (Snow, 1996), which indicates that successful collection development policies should be dynamic and adaptable, and change when the strategies and curricula of parent institutions change.

Bias in collection development

Libraries are increasingly reflecting on their collection development strategies and determining whether they are compatible with addressing equity, diversity and inclusion (EDI) concerns. This is part of a broader debate over EDI in libraries that also includes providing equal access to library resources and services for all, regardless of background or characteristics (ALA, 2019), and diversity in the workplace, including staff recruitment and career progression (Ishaq and Hussain, 2019; Schonfield and Sweeney, 2017).

A useful starting point for collection development librarians would be to consider some reflections on the nature of our libraries and our collections in terms of their significance and the values they possess and uphold. Libraries have never been neutral repositories of knowledge (Sadler and Bourg, 2015). They reflect the values and structures of their parent institution, and library collections have often developed according to those values. We often believe our collections have developed to be fair and balanced, but, in reality, every collection is biased in one way or another. The idea of the value-neutral decision is a myth (Quinn, 2012). These ideas may challenge some of our preconceptions about collections and collection development, but we should not shy away from confronting them.

Central to the debate about bias in collection development is concern about the decision-making process and whether it is possible for this to be truly objective and representative, despite the intentions of collection development librarians. The decisions made are inevitably biased (Morales, Knowles and Bourg, 2014), as they are based on the individual judgements and interests of librarians and libraries, although these would not necessarily be rectified by initiatives such as patron-driven decision making, as the systems that enable these have their own inherent biases, which are seldom understood.

Self-censorship can creep into collection development (Antell, Strothmann and Downey, 2013), often inadvertently, so it is vital for collection development librarians to pause and reflect upon each selection decision, especially if it affects a marginalised group that is under-represented in our collections. Multidisciplinary areas, such as LGBTQ, are usually underserved because they do not fit within a neat departmental structure and collection development budgets are usually allocated on a departmental basis (Graziano, 2016). Multidisciplinary areas also include race and gender, and these may be underserved or disadvantaged in library collections (Howard and Knowlton, 2018). Collaborative collection development strategies, where a small team of selectors develop these collections, have been recommended (Graziano, 2016). If there are more eyes on the selection process, there could be a reduction in unconscious bias in collection development.

When a narrow range of perspectives is represented in library collections, this often leads to a bias towards a narrow range of publishers, since more marginalised subject matter is often printed by smaller, niche publishers. This results in a degree of corporate control on library collections (Dilevko and Grewal, 1997), which are dominated by titles from the major international publishers, who represent an oligopoly (Larivière, Haustein and Mongeon, 2015) within the market. Within the UK, universities spent almost £1 billion on journal subscriptions between 2010 and 2019, with more than 90% of this spent with five companies (Elsevier, Wiley, Springer, Taylor & Francis and Sage) (Lawson, 2020). The 'big deals' signed with those publishers provide libraries with complete sets of their titles, eliminating the need to subscribe to individual titles. However, this means that library collections are often guided by the publishing decisions made by these companies, which are inevitably biased towards prestigious, highly cited journals from the highest-ranked universities, usually in the UK and USA. More diverse, regionally specific research authored by researchers from Global South universities will be edged out. Additionally, the financial implications of these deals often mean that libraries have limited funds to purchase titles from smaller publishers, reinforcing these disparities.

Political bias can also be found in library collections to varying degrees, with some views more represented than others (Hupp, 1991), often depending on one's geographical location and local political preferences. Many academic libraries take a line of supporting intellectual freedom and opposing censorship, therefore (in theory at least) they aim to be politically balanced.

There has been little discussion about the cognitive biases (Kahneman, Slovic and Tversky, 1982) that might influence collection development decision making. Some examples may include:

- dependency on collection development policies and strictly following their criteria to select resources (anchoring bias);
- using the strengths of a library's collection to further develop those collections rather than address weaknesses (status-quo bias);
- using data-driven or patron-driven acquisitions models of selection because we believe systems will redress biases, even when we do not fully understand the algorithms underpinning those systems (automation bias);
- becoming aware of a weakness in our collections, perhaps because it has been highlighted to us, which means we that notice it more and give it greater magnitude (selection bias).

Some of these cognitive biases overlap and contradict each other. However, as collection development librarians we should encourage ourselves to reflect upon how these biases will affect the selection we undertake. In our pursuit of developing what we perceive to be fair, neutral and balanced collections, our decision making may just reinforce pre-existing inequalities. Instead, we may need to become more proactive and interventionist, to ensure that marginalised and under-represented groups gain greater representation and prominence in our collections.

Evaluating collections

If collection development librarians wish to understand their collections more and to discover the outcomes of their collection development decisions, they should consider evaluating their collections. This allows libraries to identify the strengths and weaknesses of their collections, to consider whether collection development goals are being achieved and to determine the future direction of collection development (Agee, 2005). Evaluating collections allows libraries to discover whether their collections are fit for purpose and whether they meet user needs, provide value for money or support library and institutional strategies (Schmidt, 2016). They also allow libraries to demonstrate how they support the education and research missions of universities (Henry, Longstaff and Van Kampen, 2008; Hunt, 2017).

Collection evaluations can be labour intensive (Guise and Feinmark, 2003), time consuming and expensive, but worth the investment (Henry, Longstaff and Van Kampen, 2008). Libraries have adopted different approaches to evaluate their collections, often using quantitative tools such as WorldCat Collection Analysis (Henry, Longstaff and Van Kampen, 2008; Ciszek and Young, 2010), even though some believe the adequacy of library collections cannot be stated in purely numerical terms (Clapp and Jordan, 1989). Qualitative measures, such as the subject expertise of library staff (Agee, 2005; Ciszek and Young, 2010), or information on student numbers, academic departments and curriculum (Clapp and Jordan, 1989), can complement quantitative data. Successful and comprehensive collection evaluations should adopt a mixed-methods approach and include as much relevant information as can be obtained.

LSE collections

LSE Library collections are internationally recognised and a source of inspiration and pride for LSE (LSE Library, 2020a), and provide a resource of national and international importance for researchers working in the social sciences (LSE Library, 2020b). Camfield's (2016b) history of LSE Library's collections illustrates their development since the Library's foundation in 1896, identifying historical strengths in economics, political science, history, law and statistics, reflecting the earliest curricula at the school. Different collection strengths have emerged over the decades, including Russian social sciences collections from the 1920s onwards (Camfield, 2016a) and Latin American from the 1960s onwards (Camfield, 2016b). In an (unpublished) collection evaluation project carried out between 2015 and 2018, we identified our flagship collections (those with national significance in relation to their subject, quality and research value) as British economic and political history from the end of the 19th century onwards. Although we identified where collections are strong, we were less able to demonstrate where gaps and areas for future development existed.

Through using the analytics available via their library management systems (LMS), libraries can obtain rich insights into the composition of their collections by a range of criteria, such as age, classification, geography, etc. At LSE we obtained data obtained from our LMS (Ex-Libris's Alma) to look at the geographical division of our collections – specifically, which countries these titles were published in. Although this method would not tell us the backgrounds of their authors – this data would not be held in catalogue records (and therefore would need to be collected manually from, for example, staff profile pages) – we were able to rapidly find out whether our library collections reinforced publishing disparities.

We observed the division between titles published in the Global North and the Global South. However, we accept that this terminology is contentious, and definitions have often been debated and challenged (Caison and Vormann, 2014; Mahler, 2018; Horner, 2020). Such binary definitions are often unhelpful and hint at simplistic causes rather than more complex issues. Furthermore, there is no single division of Global North and Global South countries. The Brandt Report (Brandt, 1981), published during a particularly precarious period during the Cold War, provided an early distinction, with the 'North' represented by the Northern hemisphere and Australia and New Zealand, and the 'South' comprising most of Latin America, Africa and South Asia. These 'North' and 'South' boundaries have continued to evolve and the criteria previously used to determine the border between the 'rich' North and 'poor' South are no longer accurate and have thus become obsolete (Solarz, 2012), especially as there is clear evidence of shifting economic power in the 'South' (Lees, 2020), as seen in high GDP growth rates in some 'Global South' countries.

We used the Wikimedia classifications in our work to make some observations about the composition of our collections. However, this is not an endorsement of these definitions, nor a suggestion by us that these are the most 'correct' definitions. However, the Wikimedia classifications are relatively contemporary (developed between 2010 and 2015). According to this categorisation, the Global North comprises 65 countries (53 from Europe, 8 from the Asia and Pacific region and 4 from North America). The Global South comprises 182 (60 from the Asia and Pacific region, 50 from South and Latin America, 47 from Africa, 21 from the Arab States and 4 from Europe).

We assessed the three main print collections at LSE Library and ranked each collection by the number of titles published by country:

- Course Collection books (short-loan titles that are primarily used for teaching and are included on reading lists);
- Main Collection books (broader social sciences titles, often wider reading on reading lists);
- Main Collection journals (often print only, often ceased titles).

Course collection

We discovered that our Course Collection is comprehensively dominated by titles published in the Global North (98.44%). As shown in Table 15.1 opposite, 29,634 titles (93.7%) of Course Collection titles are published in just two countries; the United Kingdom (72.74%) and the United States (20.95%).

Other Global North countries are represented to a much lesser extent. The Netherlands is placed third because some major academic publishers are Dutch based. Other English-language countries, such as Canada and Australia, also feature in the top ten ranked countries, alongside other Western European countries such as Germany and France. Asian and Pacific countries feature even less frequently, with only Singapore and Japan appearing in the top 20 places of publication.

India is significantly the most common place of publication among other Global South countries for Course Collection titles, with 57.69% of all Global South published

Table 15.1 *Place of publication, Course Collection*

Country	No. of Course Collection items	% of Course Collection (n=31,628)
United Kingdom	23,007	72.74
United States	6,627	20.95
Netherlands	407	1.20
India	285	0.90
Germany	231	0.73
Canada	121	0.38
Australia	110	0.35
France	107	0.34
Switzerland	93	0.29
Singapore	61	0.19
Spain	54	0.17
South Africa	52	0.16
Belgium	52	0.16
China	42	0.13
Sweden	39	0.12
Ireland	39	0.12
Japan	33	0.10
Denmark	30	0.09
Philippines	26	0.08
Italy	22	0.07

titles (n=494) from India, which is the fourth-highest country for Course Collection titles (behind UK, USA and the Netherlands). The next Global South countries on the list are comparatively much, much smaller, with South Africa (10.53%) and China (8.5%) placed second and third. There are very small numbers of African and Asia and Pacific published titles, but many Global South countries are not represented at all in the Course Collection, with just 34 of the 182 Global South countries represented. Overall, there are 63 Course Collection titles published in the Global North for every title published in the Global South.

Main collection

Generally, the Global South is better represented in our Main Collection than in the Course Collection (Table 15.2, next page), which reflects its purpose as a wider research-related collection, as well as LSE Library's evolving collection development policies and practices since 1896. Of the Main Collection titles, 92.76% are published in the Global North, whereas only 7.24% are published in the Global South.

Table 15.2: *Place of publication, Main Collection*

Country	No. of Main Collection items	% of Main Collection (n=499,800)
United Kingdom	191,730	38.36
United States	68,398	13.69
Germany	51,495	10.30
France	34,164	6.84
Italy	18,217	3.64
Netherlands	11,216	2.24
Canada	10,956	2.19
India	8,801	1.76
Switzerland	8,512	1.70
Spain	7,984	1.60
Poland	4,804	0.96
Australia	4,752	0.95
Belgium	3,747	0.75
Sweden	3,594	0.72
Argentina	3,332	0.67
Mexico	3,327	0.67
Austria	3,313	0.66
South Africa	2,025	0.41
Ireland	1,788	0.36
Brazil	1,783	0.36

The Main Collection is much less dominated by the UK and USA, as compared to the Course Collection. Of the Main Collection titles, 52.04% are published solely in the UK and USA. Subsequent Global North countries in the list are Western European, non-English-speaking countries such as Germany (10.3%), France (6.84%) and Italy (3.64%). Other English-language countries are lower ranked (Canada is 7th [2.19%] and Australia is 12th [0.95%] on the list). LSE Library has a long collecting history of acquiring titles in the social sciences in Western European languages, which is reflected in their placings. India is also the largest Global South country of publication for Main Collection items. Although this comprises only 1.76% of the total Main Collection items, India provides 27.2% of the Global South items. However, the Main Collection has more even distribution across Global South countries than the Course Collection. A significantly greater number of Global South countries are represented in the Main Collection (148 of 182 countries) than in the Course Collection.

Africa is comparatively less well represented, with South Africa and Nigeria the best-represented countries. Asia (besides India) is represented even less often, with China and

Pakistan as the highest-ranked non-Indian Asian countries. The lower representation of African and Asian titles in our collections may reflect LSE's historical relationships with SOAS, University of London, where both libraries had informal reciprocal arrangements and have sought to maintain specialist social sciences collections from different areas of the world, and both libraries have attempted to avoid duplication and overlapping collections.

Three of the top 20 ranked countries are from the Latin and South American region, including Argentina (1.76%), Mexico (0.67%) and Brazil (0.36%). The presence of Latin and South American countries is no surprise. LSE Library historically had active collection development policies for this region and we have worked with specialist book suppliers for many decades to develop this collection. For context, we also looked at our collections on a regional level; the History of Asia (Library of Congress class DS), the History of Africa (DT) and the History of South/Latin America (F1201-F3799), and we discovered that the latter had greater representation from titles published in that region. While 86.33% of titles in the History of Asia and 82.28% of titles in the History of Africa were published in the Global North, this fell dramatically, to 69.17%, for the History of South/Latin America. This demonstrates some imbalance in our collections on a regional basis, therefore we need to make efforts to redress this by identifying new publishers and suppliers to increase our Asian and African collections. Overall, there are 13 Main Collection titles published in the Global North for every Main Collection title published in the Global South.

Main Collection journals

LSE Library's print journal collections comprise titles usually unavailable in online formats and are often historical, ceased titles. They are not usually used in teaching but are used in wider social sciences research. Main Collection journals are dominated by titles from the Global North, with 94% from this region, and just 6% from the Global South (Table 15.3, next page).

Around 38% of Global North periodicals were published in the UK and this dominance reflects that it has been easier to collect periodicals from the UK rather than elsewhere. While the USA is the second-highest country, with just over 8%, other Western Europe countries (France, Italy, Belgium, Germany and the Netherlands) and other English-language countries (Canada, Australia) feature highly among these collections. Their presence across all of our print collections reflects our dedication to specialising in these countries and regions, although it also identifies areas for future redress.

South Africa is the largest country for journals published in the Global South, comfortably ahead of India. Other African countries, often part of the Commonwealth, also feature prominently, including Zimbabwe, Egypt and Nigeria. South and Latin American countries are much less represented, with a small number of journals collected from countries such as Guatemala, Peru, Costa Rica and Paraguay, although these are

Table 15.3: Place of publication, Main Collection journals

Country	No. of Main Collection journal items	% of Main Collection journals (n=13,745)
United Kingdom	5,157	37.52
United States	1,120	8.15
France	972	7.07
Italy	456	3.32
Canada	266	1.94
Belgium	246	1.79
Germany	226	1.64
Australia	193	1.40
Netherlands	181	1.32
Poland	159	1.16
Spain	143	1.04
Austria	130	0.95
Sweden	121	0.88
Japan	107	0.78
Russian Federation	92	0.67
South Africa	88	0.64
Hungary	84	0.61
Switzerland	80	0.58
Finland	57	0.41
Israel	50	0.36

often banking reports and other financial accounts rather than more academic research-led journals. Overall, there are 17 print periodical titles published in the Global North for every title published in the Global South.

Library collections and reading lists

Reading lists reflect and represent the curriculum. They are an important influence upon students' learning and their understanding of subjects. Reading lists that comprise a narrow range of authors and perspectives will render students' learning both partial and incomplete.

There is often a slight contrast between academic staff and student perspectives of the purpose of reading lists. Academic staff believe they provide guidance and a sense of direction (Beard and Dale, 2008; Stokes and Martin, 2008; Brewerton, 2014; Cameron and Siddall, 2017), but they are concerned about student reliance on reading lists and that they should use them purely as 'starting points' before they embark on more independent reading (Siddall, 2016). Students agree on the sense of direction (Thompson, Mahon and Thomas, 2004), but often find the lists overwhelming (Siddall and Rose, 2014) and then employ a means–end approach to managing the amount of reading they can achieve (Stokes and Martin, 2008). Students may rely on reading lists more than academic staff imagine, and choose to prioritise reading the titles on these ahead of those they would find themselves from independent research. This means that students are greatly influenced by, and dependent upon, the titles that academic staff select, and any lack of diversity among those titles will be reflected in how students learn about their subject.

What is perhaps missing from the reading lists debate is a discussion of their authority and power. They may be benignly designed as tools to support learning, to guide students through the vast terrain of academic literature and direct them towards the most relevant sources, but this cannot be a 'neutral' process. Much as we considered that cognitive bias may lead to collection-development decisions that reinforce pre-existing inequalities that negatively impact on the marginalised and under-represented, the same could easily apply to reading lists. More understanding of the rationale behind the inclusion and exclusion of titles is required.

Academic staff may not believe there is anything intrinsically problematic with how they develop reading lists, but there is growing evidence of bias within reading lists, both at discipline level and more widely across the academic spectrum. This is particularly acute in the politics and international relations discipline, where marginalisation occurs on reading lists according to both gender (Phull, Ciflikli and Meibauer, 2018) and race (Choat, 2020), but also in African Studies, where a comparison of the reading lists of both African and non-African universities revealed startling differences regarding the frequency with which African scholars were included (Africa at LSE, 2019). Whereas 15% of items on reading lists from African universities were from African scholars, it was fewer than 2% in UK universities. This means that UK researchers, for example, are missing out on potentially significant regional research that may offer different perspectives to Western researchers. Another study that looked at both science and social science reading lists discovered empirical basis for concerns that university curricula are dominated by White, male and Eurocentric authors (Schucan Bird and Pitman, 2020).

Higher education is also becoming increasingly globalised. There is dynamic movement of people across the world for educational purposes, often from the Global South to Global North universities. Student populations in the Global North are more diverse than they have ever been. Just over one million or 5.5% of students in universities in the USA are classed as international students (Institute of International Education, 2020), whereas in the UK this is just under half a million, or 20.38% of students (HESA, 2019). This level of internationalisation has encouraged students and academic staff to ask questions about the curricula at their universities, particularly whether they are representative of their student populations, whether they reinforce inequalities and whether they disadvantage or alienate some students. If reading lists effectively represent the curricula, then the inequalities evident in the reading list may be evident in other aspects of the course. This will lead to a concern that students' understandings will only ever be partial or reductive, because they are missing insights and experiences through not including a diverse range of viewpoints and experiences in the curricula.

Reading lists and collection development have a symbiotic relationship. They depend on each other. We understand that collection development is designed to support teaching and research, but equally, many academic staff design their curricula and develop their reading lists based on the resources available in their library's collections. Therefore, if the diversity of reading lists is questioned, then the same could apply to library collections because they may not provide academic staff with a sufficiently diverse range of collections. Libraries should reflect upon their own approaches and processes and consider how they can change these, so that they can best support greater diversity for reading lists. Libraries should be proactive and stay ahead of the curve, rather than being reactive. By doing this, we give ourselves opportunities to collaborate with academic staff and to influence the shaping of curricula. We can use our knowledge and expertise to advise academic staff on appropriate resources and suggest that those selected should encompass a broader range of perspectives. This may take some perseverance, since librarians are not typically active in reading list design. However, this can start small, with a few good examples to develop momentum, before being scaled up, particularly if universities begin more institution-wide curricula reviews.

Practical next steps

Based on both the work we have undertaken at LSE and the work undertaken by libraries across different countries and continents, there are a range of collections-related activities that most academic libraries should be able to engage with if they are keen on decolonising their collections. Some will be quick and simple, while some may be more complex. Individual libraries should work within the scope that suits them, based on the time and resources they have.

Active commitments to equality and diversity

It may not be enough for librarians to commit to a 'neutral' approach to collection development. As we have discovered, sufficient subjective bias (whether intentional or not) influences selection to ensure that this neutrality is never truly achieved. Is 'neutrality', however we define it, an appropriate outcome? Does it just reinforce existing inequalities? Therefore, we may need to exceed this and be more assertive in addressing inequalities in our collections. Libraries do not necessarily need to devise their own commitments, but they could adopt or adapt existing commitments, such as those of the American Library Association or the Chartered Institute of Library and Information Professionals (CILIP). Librarians should also consult EDI colleagues in their institutions and discuss suitable approaches and, where possible, align with institutional strategies. In a more practical sense, collection development librarians should consider whether they should commit to actively and aggressively collecting resources by and about under-represented groups to ensure their collections reflect a commitment to diversity (Morales, Knowles and Bourg, 2014). This may involve using existing reading lists designed to support and promote under-represented groups and simply purchasing the titles not currently available in their libraries.

If you need to have a collections policy, make sure it is fit for purpose!

As we have discovered, collections policies provide strategic guidance and direction for collection development activity and allow libraries to communicate this to different stakeholders, but they can often be inflexible, unresponsive to changing teaching and research needs and perpetuate biases within collections. Where libraries wish to continue using collections policies, it is essential that they consider how they can be most effective. Most importantly, collections policies should be living and dynamic documents that can adapt to the rapid change that libraries and universities are experiencing, and reviewing them should not be an administrative task that librarians undertake periodically.

At LSE, we undertook a project to review our collections policy, which comprised a small project team of staff in different library roles, not just those in collection development. We worked with our EDI team and used an equality impact assessment framework (for assessing policies, processes and services) to review the current collections policy. We then identified the various areas in which the policy did not actively promote equality or could be perceived as discriminating against various groups. Having an established framework in place allowed us to conduct this activity objectively. When writing a new policy, we decided not to lean too much on the previous policy. It is tempting for librarians to reuse as much of an old policy as possible and just remove and replace sections as necessary. However, we wanted to start with much more of a clean slate. Our new policy starts with an introduction to our collections, identifying their strengths, and then places specific importance on supporting EDI and decolonisation of the curriculum. The policy also covers every aspect of the collections lifecycle, from how we select material to how we manage it. We explain all processes involved with each aspect and outline how our decisions are made, so that our diverse stakeholders are fully informed, and also that they are reassured that the Library is making decisions based on sound judgement.

Work with academic staff to diversify reading lists

Different institutions will take different approaches to how they decolonise or diversify their curricula. We should first note that there is a distinction between these terms and they are not interchangeable. Diversification may often include an adjustment in content of the curriculum, rather than a change in pedagogy or institutional cultures, practices or processes (Lemos, 2018). Diversification often leads to softer reforms than decolonisation requires (Makhubela, 2018). Some may take top-down approaches, with a mandate or direction for most or all departments to review their curricula, such as University College London's Inclusive Curriculum Healthcheck (UCL, 2018), whereas others will encourage a more bottom-up approach, where individual academic staff or departments will engage in this activity. At LSE, this has occurred at department level, on an optional basis, rather than being part of a university-wide strategy. Several departments have reviewed their reading lists, particularly looking at the authors represented on the lists and how broad this representation is. Our academic support librarians have worked with departments in identifying areas for improvement where they have noted a lack of diversity of authors. Whichever approach an institution takes, librarians should consider how they can support this activity.

If your library manages an online reading list platform on behalf of your institution, you should think about how you can leverage this data to provide academic staff or departments with information about their reading lists. With Talis Aspire, for example, an all-items report can provide the raw bibliographic information about all titles on reading lists, but this can be easily filtered by a specific course or department. Academic staff or departments evaluating their reading lists may be interested in finding out the gender and ethnicity of authors, where they are based, where their research is published, etc. Reading list data is unlikely to provide these answers. At LSE, we were able to use the metadata management system ID (MMSID) of reading list items, which are unique identifiers. These were then entered through our LMS (as Talis Aspire data does not provide the geographical data about titles) to discover where items on reading lists were published. However, the gender and ethnicity of individual authors can be discovered only by finding staff profiles from their institutional websites. Therefore, from a data perspective, it is important to remember that what we can provide as librarians may be of limited use, but it can act as a starting point for further qualitative analysis.

The value of librarians may be more in terms of making connections. Through our liaison work, for example, we will be aware of pockets of decolonisation activity in departments, which may be undertaken in isolation, with academic staff unaware that colleagues in other departments may be performing similar work on which they would value each other's support or feedback. We are also likely to have good relationships with colleagues in teaching and learning centres, who may be leading or advising on decolonisation. Connecting these dots across institutions may be more valuable than the data we may be able to provide from our systems.

Seek out and actively acquire from new publishers and suppliers

In the UK, various library purchasing consortia frameworks will determine supplier preference for books and e-books. The benefits for libraries include price discounts, agreed processing standards for print books and agreed accessibility and licence standards for e-books. These frameworks are based on various criteria. Currently, there are no specific diversity-related criteria that suppliers are assessed by (price and service support are among the highest-ranked criteria). However, this is likely to be an area of change, as librarians have raised these issues regularly and non-English-language suppliers are likely to be brought into next versions of these frameworks. This means, for now at least, that libraries may be limited in certain aspects of collection development, as the titles that users can access depend on what the supplier provides. Libraries will have much freer rein on supplier choice for collections beyond the scope of these frameworks, for example, non-English-language titles. However, due to potential complications in purchasing these titles (financial, metadata, etc.), incorporating them into these existing frameworks may be preferable for libraries.

At LSE we have used approval plans and patron-/demand-driven acquisitions, but the titles available from these are dominated by a small number of large publishers. Smaller publishers providing titles on more niche topic areas may be absent or less visible. Major academic publishers in Africa, Latin America and Asia publishing important research in English or local languages may be present in some supplier platforms, but not all. Maintaining the status quo may mean that libraries continue to neglect Global South scholarship (Schmidt, 2020) and our collections continue to reflect the biases that exist in knowledge production more widely, where research published in the Global North remains dominant and research published in the Global South is marginalised (Collyer, 2018). Libraries wishing to obtain more diverse titles may need to reflect on their acquisitions and cataloguing practices and consider how they can absorb new suppliers that may pose additional challenges related to cost (as titles from small, specialist publishers could be more expensive), invoicing, delivery or catalogue records. Although we have spent recent years trying to simplify and automate processes as much as possible, we may need to accept that some more manual work may need to start taking place. It is advisable for libraries to start small; perhaps purchase a small number of titles from a specific supplier first, and assess how the acquisition and cataloguing experience was, before scaling up.

More collaborative collection development

Perhaps the most effective means of reducing bias in collection development is to introduce a plurality and diversity of voices and experience in the selection process. This may, to some extent, contradict the efforts librarians have made to streamline collection development work; for example, technology and other time-saving methods are used often because of reduced time and staffing. Librarians have already encouraged users to participate in collection development through patron- and demand-driven acquisitions, although libraries may not assess the difference that makes in reality. For example, is it just a small number of users who participate? Do they come from similar academic disciplines? Do they study at the same academic levels? What are the backgrounds of these users? We cannot treat our users as a homogeneous entity and assume that by handing control over some aspects of collection development to them this will automatically reduce bias. In fact, it might just replace one form of bias with another. Likewise, the algorithms underpinning patron-driven acquisitions may not be neutral themselves, and may recommend certain titles over others (based on a user's keywords during searching), therefore undermining any sense of 'choice'.

Collections policies should also be written collaboratively. At LSE we have consulted groups working on decolonisation to ascertain their feedback on how our policies would support more EDI activity. By seeking these collaboration and engagement opportunities, we provide our different stakeholders with a sense of 'shared ownership' of library collections and reinforce that they are able to highly influence how they develop.

Improve discoverability and redress classification bias

Understanding how our library systems work is vital to learning whether any biases are present and reflected back to users. We use discovery layers so users can find our resources, while we also allow users to select books for purchase or rental on e-book platforms. What we may be less certain about is how or why users get the results they receive when they search for terms. There has been much recent research on gender and racial bias in search engines and online activity (Cohn, 2019; Kay, Matuszek and Munson, 2015; Noble, 2018; Williams, Brooks and Shmargad, 2018). Timnit Gebru, a Google researcher, was sacked in December 2020 for co-authoring a paper on the ethics of artificial intelligence and whether it reinforces gender bias and offensive language (Simonite, 2020). Bias against women, the LGBTQ community, Islam, race and mental illness have been highlighted in the algorithms used in library discovery systems (Reidsma, 2016). In their broader analysis of the power relations between librarians and software vendors, Barron and Preater (2018) highlight how discovery layers promote content owned by their parent company rather than content provided by their competitors. Librarians should raise these issues with the vendors providing these services and ask for greater clarity on how results are indexed and ranked. In information literacy teaching, librarians often recommend that students have greater confidence in results found through library discovery systems rather than search engines. While in broad terms this still applies – the vast majority of content libraries provide is intended for academic audiences and undergoes rigorous criteria such as peer review prior to publication – we still need to encourage students to reflect on the results provided by library systems, to understand that 'relevance' is a loaded term (and therefore to not just accept the first set of results for any search) and to think just as critically as before.

Librarians and their users are becoming increasingly aware of the bias in how collections are classified. The most recent and controversial example of this is the debate over the term 'illegal aliens', which was first cancelled by the Library of Congress (Library of Congress, 2016), then overturned by the House of Representatives (Congress, 2017). The documentary 'Changing the Subject' (Dartmouth College, 2019) outlines the campaign that Dartmouth College staff and students led to advance and promote 'the rights and dignity of undocumented peoples'. This is one of many subject headings that remain in classification schemes that remain offensive to many groups and reflect historical biases. Even where these have been identified, progress is often slow or there is resistance to change. The early work around updating Library of Congress Subject Headings was by Sanford Berman in the 1970s, and only two-thirds of his recommendations were made either partially or in full (Knowlton, 2005).

Libraries are increasingly taking matters into their own hands. Frustrated by the lack of change, they are looking at what they can do locally to make their catalogue records more modern and representative. Libraries face the challenge of the international use of these standards affecting what they can do, as local, manual changes might not be sustainable in the longer term, particularly if deviations from existing subject headings are overridden by LMS. Many libraries are choosing to work together for collaborative solutions at international level, through initiatives such as Cataloguing Lab (The Cataloging Lab, n.d.) and OCLC Metadata Managers groups (LSE contributes to both).

At LSE, we are documenting specific areas of concern so colleagues can identify patterns and areas that may require attention. We may consider 'cultural sensitivity' messages on our library catalogue regarding the use of terminology, or we may look at options to maintain metadata in our LMS but hide it from display on our discovery layer, though this needs to be weighed against discoverability issues this loss of data may cause.

Ringfencing collections for retention

Academic libraries often make collection management and retentions decisions according to quantitative measures, such as how often items are borrowed or when they were last borrowed. Since academic libraries define their mission as supporting teaching and research, it is perhaps natural that they would prioritise the material that is in regular use or being used for a specific purpose. In addition, academic libraries will be making difficult decisions based on space concerns, since many would have lost shelf space over the previous decades to accommodate more study space or other facilities.

The risk is that this turns retention purely into a numbers game or popularity contest, where the materials that academic libraries retain are those that are already held in many other libraries and are usually easy to obtain. Materials that are consulted less frequently may be of interest to a smaller number of potential researchers but are no less valuable, and these will often be rare, possibly held only in that specific library. It is likely that material from a non-Anglocentric background will fall within this category. Therefore, academic libraries should consider a more nuanced approach to how retention decisions are made and not just rely on borrowing statistics alone. We do not necessarily need to develop a more complex set of criteria that makes decision making difficult or just results in inertia, but during this process we should ask ourselves what the impact would be of not retaining certain materials. Would we be depriving researchers of potentially vital material? Are we just encouraging homogeneity and reinforcing the national and regional biases in our collections? This may mean that certain collections are just separated from the decision-making process and are retained, come what may. Although theoretically we should suggest that every title should earn its place in the collection, a balance needs to be maintained in our collections to ensure that they are as representative as possible.

Review and assess your collections

As we have seen, many academic libraries have already undertaken collection assessments and have found value in doing this, such as identifying collection strengths and determining whether their collection development approaches are succeeding. While it is absolutely correct for libraries to discover which aspects of their collections are strong, it is equally important for libraries to also discover where the weaknesses and gaps in their collections are and address them accordingly. At LSE, we learned that our strengths were in 19th- and 20th-century British economic, political and social history, which is appropriate, as our library also has a role as the British Library of Political and Economic Science. At the same time, we identified that our African, Asian and, to a lesser extent, Latin American collections are comparatively weaker. Now that we know this, we can consider which approaches we can take to redress this, while still maintaining our collection strengths – with the intention of developing the most balanced and extensive social sciences collections possible.

Academic libraries need to consider what approach will work best, based on the resources available. Libraries should leverage the data that can be obtained from their LMS to develop knowledge about their collections. This may include assessing by classmark, language, place of publication or any other relevant bibliographic information, although it is likely that any assessment would include several criteria to obtain deeper insight. As LMS are likely to export this data as spreadsheet file types to be used in Excel or elsewhere, it is also important for librarians to be confident and skilled in managing, manipulating and visualising data. Based on what libraries discover, they can then consider their approach for how to take this forward. Although in some cases subjective decision making may be necessary, this can be complemented with a data-driven approach.

Collaborate with other libraries

As much as academic libraries should develop relationships and bring expertise together within their own institutions, they should equally do so within their sector. Many UK libraries may be interested in decolonisation and are searching for inspiration for how to start. Many of us are undertaking or have undertaken projects and have shared our findings internally, but not externally. We have a responsibility to share our knowledge and experience with our peers and assist each other where we can. Fortunately, this has been an area in which many libraries have been doing excellent work, so there are many opportunities to share our findings. In the UK there have been a number of conferences that have allowed libraries to discuss their projects (De Montfort University, 2020; Goldsmiths, University of London, 2020).

A decolonisation JISCMail list (2019) has allowed libraries to connect with each other and discuss issues. Some libraries have developed a Google Sheet (Decolonisation Best Practice and Case Studies in HE Libraries, 2019) of decolonisation best practice and case studies, where libraries can outline the area of practice they have worked on and to summarise their projects and provide a link to where more information can be found. The intention was that libraries working on similar ideas could find inspiration and have a named contact to reach out to, if necessary. Libraries should look more widely than the UK and think about how they can collaborate with global peers where circumstances may differ from those in the UK.

Conclusion

Collection development librarians should seize with both hands rapidly emerging opportunities to support wider institutional strategies of decolonisation and diversifying library collections. They require librarians to reflect and take stock of their current approaches and consider whether they are truly supporting EDI in their work. Part of this also requires reflecting on our own assumptions and beliefs about balance and fairness and accepting that these shape the collection development decisions we make, which can lead to inadvertent bias affecting how we build collections. This can be a personal and difficult challenge for librarians, but a challenge we should tackle head on.

In this chapter we have identified some practical steps that collection development librarians should consider. By taking a data-driven approach and analysing our collections, we will learn more about whether our approaches have been successful, and identify areas for improvement in collection development. By fostering strong and effective relationships with academic staff and other stakeholders we can introduce a plurality of voices and experiences into the collection development process and also influence curriculum design and reading lists to make this equally representative. Through working with publishers and vendors, we can lobby for greater access to more diverse resources, as well as understand how the systems we use to provide access to content influence how our users make use of that content. Underpinning all this activity should be a guiding principle that we commit to supporting EDI more broadly, and this should become an integral part of all the collection development activity we undertake in future.

The tragic deaths of Breonna Taylor in Kentucky and George Floyd in Minnesota, among others, and the resurgence of the Black Lives Matter movement in 2020 have yet again shown the need to reflect on systemic injustice and to consider the changes we can make to our personal and professional lives. This has led to a growing commitment among librarians to review their services, policies and practices. Although the shock of the COVID-19 pandemic has led many institutions to refocus on core teaching and learning, this has not dissuaded those working in universities from continuing to plan and implement larger strategic projects, such as reviewing and changing curricula. Librarians, too, continue to focus on initiatives such as collection reviews, forming partnerships across their institutions and reviewing suppliers and other acquisitions processes. Supporting decolonisation activities and delivering change remains an important priority for many librarians, even in difficult circumstances.

References

Africa at LSE (2019) How Diverse Is Your Reading List? (Probably Not Very …), *Africa at LSE* (blog), 12 March, https://blogs.lse.ac.uk/africaatlse/2019/03/12/how-diverse-is-your-reading-list-probably-not-very.

Agee, J. (2005) Collection Evaluation: A Foundation for Collection Development, *Collection Building*, **24** (3), 92–5, https://doi.org/10.1108/01604950510608267.

ALA (2019) Access to Library Resources and Services, www.ala.org/advocacy/intfreedom/access.

Antell, K., Strothmann, M. and Downey, J. (2013) Self-Censorship in Selection of LGBT-Themed Materials, *Reference & User Services Quarterly*, **53** (2), 104–7, https://doi.org/10.5860/rusq.53n2.104.

Barron, S. and Preater, A. (2018) Critical Systems Librarianship. In Nicholson, K. P. and Seale, M. (eds), *The Politics of Theory and the Practice of Critical Librarianship*, Library Juice Press.

Barstow, S., Macaulay, D. and Tharp, S. (2016) How to Build a High-Quality Library Collection in a Multi-Format Environment: Centralized Selection at University of Wyoming Libraries, *Journal of Library Administration*, **56** (7), 790–809, https://doi.org/10.1080/01930826.2015.1116336.

Beard, J. and Dale, P. (2008) Redesigning Services for the Net-Gen and Beyond: A Holistic Review of Pedagogy, Resource, and Learning Space, *New Review of Academic Librarianship*, **14** (1–2), 99–114, https://doi.org/10.1080/13614530802518941.

Blume, R. (2019) Balance in Demand Driven Acquisitions: The Importance of Mindfulness and Moderation When Utilizing Just in Time Collection Development, *Collection Management*, **44** (2–4), 105–16, https://doi.org/10.1080/01462679.2019.1593908.

Brandt, W. (1981) North-South: A Programme for Survival, Commonwealth Information: News Release 81, Commonwealth Secretariat.

Brewerton, G. (2014) Implications of Student and Lecturer Qualitative Views on Reading Lists: A Case Study at Loughborough University, UK, *New Review of Academic Librarianship*, **20** (1), 78–90, https://doi.org/10.1080/13614533.2013.864688.

Caison, G. and Vormann, B. (2014) The Logics and Logistics of Urban Progress: Contradictions and Conceptual Challenges of the Global North-South Divide, *The Global South*, **8** (2), 65–83, https://doi.org/10.2979/globalsouth.8.2.65.

Cameron, C. and Siddall, G. (2017) Opening Lines of Communication: Book Ordering and Reading Lists, the Academics View, *New Review of Academic Librarianship*, **23** (1), 42–59, https://doi.org/10.1080/13614533.2016.1224769.

Camfield, G. (2016a) The Beginnings of the Russian Collection at LSE, *LSE History* (blog), 22 June, https://blogs.lse.ac.uk/lsehistory/2016/06/22/the-russian-collection-at-lse-library.

Camfield, G. (2016b) LSE Library: A History of the Collections, www.lse.ac.uk/library/about/history/home.aspx.

Chaputula, A. H. and Kanyundo, A. J. (2014) Collection Development Policy: How Its Absence Has Affected Collection Development Practices at Mzuzu University Library, *Journal of Librarianship and Information Science*, **46** (4), 317–25, https://doi.org/10.1177/0961000614531005.

Choat, S. (2020) Decolonising the Political Theory Curriculum, *Politics*, October, https://doi.org/10.1177/0263395720957543.

Ciszek, M. P. and Young, C. L. (2010) Diversity Collection Assessment in Large Academic Libraries, *Collection Building*, October, https://doi.org/10.1108/01604951011088899.

Clapp, V. W. and Jordan, R. T. (1989) Quantitative Criteria for Adequacy of Academic Library Collections, *College & Research Libraries*, **26** (5), 371–80.

Cohn, J. (2019) *The Burden of Choice: Recommendations, Subversion, and Algorithmic Culture*, Rutgers University Press.

Collyer, F. M. (2018) Global Patterns in the Publishing of Academic Knowledge: Global North, Global South, *Current Sociology*, **66** (1), 56–73, https://doi.org/10.1177/0011392116680020.

Congress (2017) H. Rept. 114–594 – Legislative Branch Appropriations Bill, 2017, Legislation. 2015/2016. 2017, www.congress.gov/congressional-report/114th-congress/house-report/594/1.

Dartmouth College (2019) Change the Subject – a Documentary about Labels, Libraries, and Activism, https://sites.dartmouth.edu/changethesubject.

Day, A. and Novak, J. (2019) The Subject Specialist Is Dead. Long Live the Subject Specialist! *Collection Management*, **44** (2–4), 117–30, https://doi.org/10.1080/01462679.2019.1573708.

De Montfort University (2020) Decolonising the Academic Library, Digital Conference Mercian Collaboration Event 16 June 2020, https://decolonisingdmu.our.dmu.ac.uk/library-work-stream/decolonising-the-academic-library-digital-conference-mercian-collaboration-event-16-6-20.

Decolonisation Best Practice and Case Studies in HE Libraries (2019) https://docs.google.com/spreadsheets/d/1NyBVaHlJKTrLM9S1tCfSv8rlDwpqpx5A0mkgAKiSY2g/edit#gid=0.

Desjarlais-Lueth, C. (1990) Brown University and Academic Library History, *Libraries & Culture*, **25** (2), 218–42.

Dilevko, J. and Grewal, K. (1997) A New Approach to Collection Bias in Academic Libraries: The Extent of Corporate Control in Journal Holdings, *Library & Information Science Research*, **19** (4), 359–85, https://doi.org/10.1016/S0740-8188(97)90026-8.

England, M. M. and Anderson, R. (2019) Demand-Driven Acquisition of Print Books: Applying 21st-Century Procurement Strategies to a 5th-Century Format, *Collection Management*, **44** (2–4), 95–104, https://doi.org/10.1080/01462679.2018.1564715.

Evans, E. G. (1999) *Developing Library and Information Center Collections*, 4th rev. edn, Libraries Unlimited Inc.

Gessesse, K. (2000) Collection Development and Management in the Twenty-first Century with Special Reference to Academic Libraries: An Overview, *Library Management*, **21** (7), 365–72, https://doi.org/10.1108/01435120010372551.

Goldsmiths, University of London (2020) Decolonising the Curriculum – the Library's Role, Decolonising the Curriculum – the Library's Role, https://decolonisethelibrary.wordpress.com.

Gonzalez-Kirby, D. (1991) Case Studies in Collection Development: Setting An Agenda for Future Research, *Collection Building*, **11** (2), 2–9, https://doi.org/10.1108/eb023298.

Graziano, V. (2016) LGBTQ Collection Assessment: Library Ownership of Resources Cited by Master's Students, *College & Research Libraries*, **77** (1), https://doi.org/10.5860/crl.77.1.114.

Guise, J. and Feinmark, D. (2003) ARL's Collection Analysis Project: Continuing Feasibility for a Medium-sized Academic Library, *Library Management*, **24** (6–7), 332–6, https://doi.org/10.1108/01435120310486057.

Henry, E., Longstaff, R. and Van Kampen, D. (2008) Collection Analysis Outcomes in an Academic Library, *Collection Building*, **27** (3), 113–17, https://doi.org/10.1108/01604950810886022.

HESA (2019) Where Do HE Students Come From? www.hesa.ac.uk/data-and-analysis/students/where-from.

Horner, R. (2020) Towards a New Paradigm of Global Development? Beyond the Limits of International Development, Towards a New Paradigm of Global Development? Beyond the Limits of International Development, *Progress in Human Geography*, **44** (3), 415–36, https://doi.org/10.1177/0309132519836158.

Howard, S. A. and Knowlton, S. A. (2018) Browsing through Bias: The Library of Congress Classification and Subject Headings for African American Studies and LGBTQIA Studies, *Library Trends*, **67** (1), 74–88, https://doi.org/10.1353/lib.2018.0026.

Hunt, S. (2017) Collection Development in UK University Libraries, *Collection Building*, **36** (1), 29–34, https://doi.org/10.1108/CB-09-2016-0026.

Hupp, S. L. (1991) The Left and the Right, *Collection Management*, **14** (1–2), 139–54, https://doi.org/10.1300/J105v14n01_09.

IFLA (2020) About the Acquisition and Collection Development Section, www.ifla.org/about-the-acquisition-collection-development-section.

Institute of International Education (2020) IIE Open Doors, https://opendoorsdata.org.

Ishaq, M. and Hussain, A. M. (2019) BAME Staff Experiences of Academic and Research Libraries, SCONUL, www.sconul.ac.uk/sites/default/files/documents/BAME%20staff%20experiences%20of%20academic%20and%20research%20libraries_0.pdf.

Jensen, K. O. (1977) Structure and Organization for Collection Development: A Centralized Model, *Library Acquisitions: Practice & Theory*, **1** (3), 173–9, https://doi.org/10.1016/0364-6408(77)90028-X.

JISCMail (2019) LIS-DECOLONISE, 2019, www.jiscmail.ac.uk/cgi-bin/webadmin?A0=LIS-DECOLONISE.

Kahneman, D., Slovic, P. and Tversky, A. (1982) *Judgment under Uncertainty: Heuristics and Biases*, Cambridge University Press, https://doi.org/10.1017/CBO9780511809477.

Kay, M., Matuszek, C. and Munson, S. A. (2015) Unequal Representation and Gender Stereotypes in Image Search Results for Occupations. In *Proceedings of the 33rd Annual ACM Conference on Human Factors in Computing Systems*, CHI '15, Association for Computing Machinery, https://doi.org/10.1145/2702123.2702520.

Knowlton, S. A. (2005) Three Decades Since Prejudices and Antipathies: A Study of Changes in the Library of Congress Subject Headings, *Cataloging & Classification Quarterly*, **40** (2), 123–45, https://doi.org/10.1300/J104v40n02_08.

Larivière, V., Haustein, S. and Mongeon, P. (2015) The Oligopoly of Academic Publishers in the Digital Era, *PLOS ONE*, **10**, (6), e0127502, https://doi.org/10.1371/journal.pone.0127502.

Lawson, S. (2020) Journal Subscription Expenditure in the UK 2010–2019, *Zenodo*, https://doi.org/10.5281/zenodo.3657776.

Lees, N. (2020) The Brandt Line after Forty Years: The More North–South Relations Change, the More They Stay the Same? *Review of International Studies*, **47**, 1–22, https://doi.org/10.1017/S026021052000039X.

Lemos, S. (2018) Decolonise Not Diversify, *The Social History Society* (blog), 30 September, https://socialhistory.org.uk/shs_exchange/decolonise-not-diversify.

Levine-Clark, M. (2019) Imagining the Future Academic Library Collection, *Collection Management*, **44** (2–4), 87–94, https://doi.org/10.1080/01462679.2019.1610680.

Library of Congress (2016) Library of Congress to Cancel the Subject Heading 'Illegal Aliens', www.loc.gov/catdir/cpso/illegal-aliens-decision.pdf.

Linden, J., Tudesco, S. and Dollar, D. (2018) Collections as a Service: A Research Library's Perspective, *College & Research Libraries*, **79** (1), https://doi.org/10.5860/crl.79.1.86.

LSE Library (2020a) Collection Highlights, London School of Economics and Political Science, www.lse.ac.uk/library/collection-highlights/home.aspx.

LSE Library (2020b) Library Collections Policy, London School of Economics and Political Science, www.lse.ac.uk/library/about/library-collections-policy.aspx.

Mahler, A. G. (2018) *From the Tricontinental to the Global South: Race, Radicalism, and Transnational Solidarity*, Duke University Press.

Makhubela, M. (2018) 'Decolonise, Don't Diversify': Discounting Diversity in the South African Academe as a Tool for Ideological Pacification, *Education as Change*, **22** (1), https://doi.org/10.25159/1947-9417/2965.

Morales, M., Knowles, E. C. and Bourg, C. (2014) Diversity, Social Justice, and the Future of Libraries, *Portal: Libraries and the Academy*, **14** (3), 439–51, https://doi.org/10.1353/pla.2014.0017.

Munro, B. and Philps, P. (2008) A Collection of Importance: The Role of Selection in Academic Libraries, *Australian Academic & Research Libraries*, **39** (3), 149–70, https://doi.org/10.1080/00048623.2008.10721347.

Noble, S. U. (2018) *Algorithms of Oppression: How Search Engines Reinforce Racism*, New York University Press.

Papadakos, J., Trang, A., Wiljer, D., Mis, C. C., Cyr, A., Friedman, A. J., Mazzocut, M., Snow, M., Raivich, V. and Catton, P. (2014) What Criteria Do Consumer Health Librarians Use to Develop Library Collections? A Phenomenological Study, *Journal of the Medical Library Association*, **102** (2), 78–84, https://doi.org/10.3163/1536-5050.102.2.003.

Phull, K., Ciflikli, G. and Meibauer, G. (2018) Gender and Bias in the International Relations Curriculum: Insights from Reading Lists, *European Journal of International Relations*, August, https://doi.org/10.1177/1354066118791690.

Posner, B. (2019) Insights From Library Information and Resource Sharing for the Future of Academic Library Collections, *Collection Management*, **44** (2–4), 146–53, https://doi.org/10.1080/01462679.2019.1593277.

Quinn, B. (2012) Collection Development and the Psychology of Bias, *The Library Quarterly: Information, Community, Policy*, **82** (3), 277–304, https://doi.org/10.1086/665933.

Reidsma, M. (2016) Algorithmic Bias in Library Discovery Systems, https://doi.org/10.5281/ZENODO.47723.

Sadler, B. and Bourg, C. (2015) Feminism and the Future of Library Discovery, *The Code4Lib Journal*, 28 (April), https://journal.code4lib.org/articles/10425.

Sanchez Vignau, B. S. and Meneses, G. (2005) Collection Development Policies in University Libraries: A Space for Reflection, *Collection Building*, **24** (1), 35–43, https://doi.org/10.1108/01604950510576119.

Scherlen, A. and McAllister, A. D. (2019) Voices Versus Visions: A Commentary on Academic Library Collections and New Directions, *Collection Management*, **44** (2–4), 389–95, https://doi.org/10.1080/01462679.2018.1547999.

Schmidt, J. (2016) Developing a Library Collection Today: Revisiting 'Collection Evaluation, the Conspectus and Chimeras in Library Cooperation', *Australian Academic & Research Libraries*, **47** (4), 190–5, https://doi.org/10.1080/00048623.2016.1250598.

Schmidt, N. (2020) *The Privilege to Select. Global Research System, European Academic Library Collections, and Decolonisation*, Lund University, Faculties of Humanities and Theology, Lund Studies in Arts and Cultural Sciences, https://doi.org/10.5281/zenodo.4011296.

Schonfield, R. C. and Sweeney, L. (2017) Inclusion, Diversity, and Equity: Members of the Association of Research Libraries, *Ithaka S+R* (blog), https://sr.ithaka.org/publications/inclusion-diversity-and-equity-arl.

Schucan Bird, K. and Pitman, L. (2020) How Diverse Is Your Reading List? Exploring Issues of Representation and Decolonisation in the UK, *Higher Education*, **79** (5), 903–20, https://doi.org/10.1007/s10734-019-00446-9.

Siddall, G. (2016) University Academics' Perceptions of Reading List Labels, *New Library World*, **117** (7–8), 440–8.

Siddall, G. and Rose, H. (2014) Reading Lists – Time for a Reality Check? An Investigation into the Use of Reading Lists as a Pedagogical Tool to Support the Development of Information Skills amongst Foundation Degree Students, *Library and Information Research*, **38** (118), 52–73.

Simonite, T. (2020) A Prominent AI Ethics Researcher Says Google Fired Her, www.wired.com/story/prominent-ai-ethics-researcher-says-google-fired-her.

Snow, R. (1996) Wasted Words: The Written Collection Development Policy and the Academic Library, *The Journal of Academic Librarianship*, **22** (3), 191–4.

Solarz, M. W. (2012) North–South, Commemorating the First Brandt Report: Searching for the Contemporary Spatial Picture of the Global Rift, *Third World Quarterly*, **33** (3), 559–69, https://doi.org/10.1080/01436597.2012.657493.

Stokes, P. and Martin, L. (2008) Reading Lists: A Study of Tutor and Student Perceptions, Expectations and Realities, *Studies in Higher Education*, **33** (2), 113–25, https://doi.org/10.1080/03075070801915874.

The Cataloging Lab (n.d.) Cataloging Lab – Experiment with Controlled Vocabularies, https://cataloginglab.org.

Thompson, L., Mahon, C. and Thomas, L. (2004) *Reading Lists – How Do You Eat Yours?* University of Wolverhampton, https://wlv.openrepository.com/wlv/handle/2436/3693.

Torrence, M., Powers, A. and Sheffield, M. (2012) Something's Gotta Give: Is There a Future for the Collection Development Policy? In *Something's Gotta Give*, Against the Grain Press, LLC, https://doi.org/10.5703/1288284314888.

UCL (2018) The UCL Inclusive Curriculum Healthcheck, *Teaching & Learning*, 4 December, www.ucl.ac.uk/teaching-learning/education-strategy/1-personalising-student-support/bame-awarding-gap-project/ucl-inclusive.

van Zijl, C. (1998) The Why, What, and How of Collection Development Policies, *South African Journal of Libraries and Information Science*, **66** (3), 99–106.

Williams, B. A., Brooks, C. F. and Shmargad, Y. (2018) How Algorithms Discriminate Based on Data They Lack: Challenges, Solutions, and Policy Implications, *Journal of Information Policy*, **8**, 78–115, https://doi.org/10.5325/jinfopoli.8.2018.0078.

Afterword: Challenging the Narrative of the Storyteller

Regina Everitt

Decolonisation is not about deleting or re-writing history, it's about telling stories from different perspectives or that have never been told. It is also about challenging the narrative of the storyteller. In Chimamanda Ngozi Adichie's TED talk about the 'Danger of a Single Story' (Adichie, 2009) she speaks about her experience at an American university where her room-mate was confused when she learned that English was the official language of Nigeria and that Adichie's favorite music was that of Mariah Carey. The room-mate had a single story about Africa and its people – that of poverty, famine and war. It was unfathomable that Adichie, a middle-class Nigerian, would have so much in common with an average American student. In fact, Adichie grew up in a household with live-in domestic help. And just as her American room-mate knew a single story about Africans, so did Adichie have a single story about the boy who worked for her family. Adichie could see only his poverty until she visited his village and learned more about his life and family. If we hear only the single story, we do a disservice to the protagonist by flattening them to one dimension. And we rob ourselves of the richness and complexity of the full picture often blindly leading us to incorrect conclusions. As stewards of information, it is the role of librarians to encourage users to look beyond, even question, the veracity of that single story. Moreover, librarians should encourage users to write new stories.

A standard storytelling technique is to have a hero and a villain. In old western films, the hero normally wore a white hat and the villain the black hat. Familiar imagery? The simplicity of the story makes it easy for the audience to follow. The audience cheers on the guy in the white hat because the narrative is shaped to reinforce that he is the hero. The audience sees the story from that single perspective and, in the absence of any other evidence, believes it. And that is the danger of library collections if they tell stories from a single perspective. Even if the stories tell the students that they are not clever enough, not pretty enough, or paint them as villains – there is the danger that students will believe it. This negative self-image impacts students' outcomes and lives. For example, a 2019 UK Advance HE report shows a degree-awarding gap of 23.4% between White and Black students (80.9% of White students receiving 1st/2:1 or A/B grade compared to 57.5% of Black students) (Advance HE, 2019a). This is exacerbated by the dearth of role models for Black, Asian, and minoritised ethnic (BAME) students in UK higher education institutions. According to another 2019 Advance HE report, 23.9% of UK higher education students and only 9.8% of staff identify as BAME (Advance HE, 2019b). And as discussed in this book, the 2015 CILIP/ARA survey found that 97% of the respondents identified as white. Although it cannot be claimed that these factors cause some BAME students to have poor outcomes, they are contributing factors.

Another technique for storytelling is multiperspectivity, telling a story from multiple perspectives, as defined in Wikipedia. A single event is witnessed or experienced by more than one person. How each person tells the story will be through the prism of their experiences, attitudes and beliefs. In his book *Talking with Strangers*, Malcolm Gladwell (2019) deconstructs the story of the arrest and eventual mysterious death of Sandra Bland based on his interpretations of their perspectives. In July 2015, Sandra Bland, an African American woman, was pulled over by a Texas law enforcement officer for failing to use her turn signal (Fieldstadt, 2019). The exchange between Bland and former State Trooper Brian Encina became heated resulting in the arrest of Bland. She was later found hanging in the Texas jail cell. Gladwell hypothesises that Bland's and Encina's responses to their encounter were influenced by their experiences and perspectives. So, Bland's activism against police brutality and social injustice would have influenced her response to being pulled over and her exchange with Encina. Encina's expectation of how one responds to someone wearing a police badge, in a position of 'authority', would have been challenged – by a Black woman, no less. Each would have feared for their life. For four years, the only video perspective that was available was from Encina's dashcam. In 2019, footage from Bland's mobile phone was released and her perspective finally aired. By then Bland had lost her life.

So, the storyteller determines the perspective. During the writing of this book, the world was living with a coronavirus (COVID-19) pandemic that led to millions of deaths worldwide, unprecedented economic damage as businesses had been forced to close and people told to stay at home to mitigate the spread of the virus, catastrophic job losses, disruption to education, and damage to the mental health and well-being of many. The virus disproportionately impacted members of BAME communities, who were more likely to die from the disease. According to a June 2020 Public Health England report, BAME people have a 10% – 50% higher risk of death when compared to White British people (Public Health England, 2020). Contributing factors, according to the report, include dwelling in urban areas and/or extended-family households (called 'crowded households' in the report) as well as presence of illnesses such as diabetes and hypertension. A dangerous underlying narrative here is that BAME people brought this on themselves due to living conditions and lifestyle. However, one must consider the systems and structures that lead to poverty and poor healthcare. In addition, BAME people tended to work in healthcare, cleaning, and front-line roles such as transportation, hospitality, and retail where they were in continuous contact with the public.

So how will the story of COVID-19 be told to future generations and from whose perspective? During the first lockdown in late March 2020, there were TV appeals from celebrities encouraging people to stay at home to stop the spread of the virus. The most ill-conceived appeals came from those sitting around their swimming pools telling people to enjoy the time at home with loved ones. Meanwhile, many people lived in cramped flats (apartments) with children that they had to home-school and with restricted or no access to technology. Still others endured domestic violence and other abuse or suffered with addiction without access to support. As the success of the vaccine rollout in wealthy nations like the UK, USA and Europe is celebrated and politicians pat themselves on the back, the stories of those marginalised people who suffered loss of loved ones, jobs, businesses, security and lives must be documented and remembered as well as those of the privileged.

More storytellers are needed. Librarians need to inspire curiosity in their students, members of local communities through citizen science, and themselves to dig into the past and tell untold stories. Dr Miranda Kaufmann, Senior Research Fellow at the Institute of Commonwealth Studies, part of the School of Advanced Studies at University of London, took part in a virtual question and answer session at University of East London (UEL) about her research for her book *Black Tudors: The Untold Story*. She talked through the 'forensic' process of looking through photos, reading letters and manuscripts, following leads from related research and building stories from disparate sources. Fascinating but meticulous work! The UEL library team is working collaboratively with academic colleagues to embed research-informed teaching in the curriculum supporting students in the use of primary sources from the institution's archives in their studies. Perhaps this work will inspire some students to become researchers.

With more storytellers come more stories from different perspectives evidencing different experiences. As libraries are not neutral spaces, librarians will need to document their curatorial decisions and signpost users to collections that offer different perspectives. Librarians have the responsibility to guide users beyond the single story and help them to experience a multidimensional world.

References

Adichie, C. N. (2009) The Danger of a Single Story, TED talk, 16 October, www.youtube.com/watch?v=D9Ihs241zeg (accessed 8 May 2021).

Advance HE (2019a) *Equality in Higher Education: Students Statistical Report*, www.advance-he.ac.uk/guidance/equality-diversity-and-inclusion/using-data-and-evidence/statistics-reports (accessed 8 August 2020) [available only to Advance HE members].

Advance HE (2019b) *Equality in Higher Education: Staff Statistical Report*, www.advance-he.ac.uk/guidance/equality-diversity-and-inclusion/using-data-and-evidence/statistics-reports (accessed 8 August 2020) [available only to Advance HE members].

CILIP and ARA (2015) *A Study of the UK Information Workforce*, https://archive.cilip.org.uk/research/workforce-mapping (accessed 24 January 2019).

Fieldstadt, E. (2019) Newly-aired Sandra Bland Cellphone Video Shows Traffic Stop from Her Vantage Point, *NBCNews*, 7 May, www.nbcnews.com/news/us-news/newly-aired-sandra-bland-cellphone-video-shows-traffic-stop-her-n1002756 (accessed 8 May 2021).

Gladwell, M. (2019) *Talking with Strangers*, Little, Brown and Company.

Kaufmann, M. (2017) *Black Tudors: The Untold Story*, Oneworld.

Public Health England (2020) *Disparities in the Risk and Outcomes of COVID19*, https://assets.publishing.service.gov.uk/government/uploads/system/uploads/attachment_data/file/891116/disparities_review.pdf (accessed 11 June 2020).

Index

360-degree appraisals 14

Aberdeen University Museums and Special Collections xxv
Aboriginal activists group 10
academic literacies, academic research 26–8
academic practices, decolonising *see* decolonising academic practices
acquisitions
    London School of Economics (LSE) 238–9
    SOAS 217
ACRL *see* Association for College and Research Libraries
African library, Kenya 191–2
African Studies Library
    Cambridge University Libraries 175–8, 185–7
    classification schemes 175–8, 185–7
agency and identity, decolonising academic practices 30–1
Ahmet, Akile 21
Akomolafe, B. 142
ALA (American Library Association) 136
allies' role 7
American Federation of Labor and Congress of Industrial Organizations Department for Professional Employees (DPE) 135–6
American Library Association (ALA) 136
'antagonistic forces' in HE, racism 63–4
appraisals, 360-degree 14
Archives and Records Association (UK and Ireland) (ARA), staff survey 135–6, 252
Association for College and Research Libraries (ACRL), critical information literacy (CIL) 76–8

Balshaw, Maria 18
BAME staff *see* Black Asian and Minority Ethnic staff
Banks, Sir Joseph xxiv, 153, 154, 156
Barnett, Ron 142
Benin Bronzes xxv
bias
    see also classification bias
    collection development, LSE 226–8
    Open Access bias, BL 164
BL *see* British Library
Black Asian and Minority Ethnic (BAME) staff 39–53
    BAME Staff Network, British Library (BL) 154, 157, 158, 170
    community engagement 51
    critical race theory (CRT) 49
    diversity advancement 47–8
    equality advancement 47–8
    ethnic diversity 46–7
    ethnic monitoring 52
    ethnicity impact 42–3
    'glass ceiling' 41
    leadership 51
    lower pay 40
    occupational segregation 40–1
    occupational structure 46
    outreach work 51
    promotion opportunities 46
    racial discrimination 40
    racism 40, 43–5, 50
    research design and approach 42
    research findings 42–8
    research participants 42
    resilience 53
    self-identity 42–3
    training and development opportunities 45
    undervalued 40
    vertical segregation 41

work experience in UK organisations 39–41
workplace diversity lack 41
The Black Curriculum (2019) 127–8
Black Lives Matter (BLM) xxiv, 5
Black Studies, British Library (BL) 163–4
BLM (Black Lives Matter) xxiv, 5
Book Bunk Trust, Kenya 190, 199–203
British Library (BL) xxiv, 153–70
  BAME Staff Network 154, 157, 158, 170
  Banks, Sir Joseph xxiv, 153, 154, 156
  Black Studies 163–4
  cataloguing and metadata 166–8
  colonial past 155–7
  COVID-19 pandemic 160–1
  custodianship 162–6
  Decolonisation Working Group 153–70
  distributed custodianship 165–6
  exhibitions 168–9
  expansion and scope 155–7
  historic decisions influence 163
  international standards development 167
  legal deposit limits 162–3
  links to colonial and imperial history 158–9
  machine learning 167–8
  Open Access bias 164
  professional inequalities 159–60
  public spaces 161–2
  slavery connections 154, 156, 158, 161–2
  Sloane, Sir Hans xxiv, 154, 156
  strategic priorities 163–5
  unique institution 155
  University College London Legacies of British Slave Ownership Database 161–2
British school system 57–68

Cambridge University Libraries 173–87
  African Studies Library 175–8, 185–7
  cartonera cataloguing 178–82
  case studies 175–85
  classification schemes 174, 175
  Decolonising Through Critical Librarianship Group 187
  organization 173–4
  Polar Library 182–7
Canadian academic libraries *see* Indigenising Canadian academic libraries
cartonera cataloguing
  Cambridge University Libraries 178–82
  classification schemes 178–82
challenging the narrative of the storyteller: storytelling perspectives 251–3
Chartered Institute of Library and Information Professionals (CILIP), staff survey 135–6, 252
Churchill, Winston xxv
CIL *see* critical information literacy
CILIP (Chartered Institute of Library and Information Professionals), staff survey 135–6, 252
Civil Rights Act (1964) 74
classification bias
  Dartmouth College xxiv, 240–1
  Library of Congress xxiv, 75, 116, 174–5, 240–1
  London School of Economics (LSE) 240–1
classification schemes
  African Studies Library 175–8, 185–7
  Brian Deer Classification System 116–17
  Cambridge University Libraries 174, 175
  cartonera cataloguing 178–82
  McMillan Library 202–3
CLR (Creative Library Research) workshops 143–5

INDEX 257

collaboration
  internal and external, Goldsmiths University of London 134–5
  London School of Economics (LSE) 242–3
collaboration and integration, decolonising academic practices 32–3
collection development, London School of Economics (LSE) 225–8
collections policy, London School of Economics (LSE) 237
colonial imprint
  academic libraries 98–101
  White LIS profession 98–101
colonial legacy, library and information science (LIS) education 92–6
colonialism as dismemberment of Africa, Kenya 192–4
colonialism impact, library and information science (LIS) education 97–101
coloniality xxiii–xxiv
Colour of Power Index, UK organisations 67
colour-blind racism 64
Colston, Edward xxv
Commission on Race and Ethnic Disparities (CRED) report 67–8
commitments to equality and diversity, London School of Economics (LSE) 236–7
community engagement, BAME staff 51
constructionism vs positivism, research methodologies 25
coronavirus *see* COVID–19 pandemic
COVID-19 pandemic
  British Library (BL) 160–1
  critical information literacy (CIL) 80–1
  SOAS 220
Creative Library Research (CLR) workshops 143–5
CRED (Commission on Race and Ethnic Disparities) report 67–8
critical information literacy (CIL) 73–84
  Association for College and Research Libraries (ACRL) 76–8
  COVID-19 pandemic 80–1
  critical race theory (CRT) 82–3
  Georgia International Conference on Information Literacy 82
  LOEX (Library Orientation Exchange) 82
  Open Educational Resources (OERs) 83–4
  Polar Library 184–5
  QAnon 79
  Reclaiming Native Truth (RNT) project 82
  Trumpism 78–81
critical librarianship xxiv
  Decolonising Through Critical Librarianship Group, Cambridge University Libraries 187
  SOAS 214
critical pedagogy 77, 140
critical race theory (CRT) xxiv, 61–2, 67, 75–6, 127
  see also racism
  BAME staff 49
  critical information literacy (CIL) 82–3
  origins 61
critical reading and writing skills
  decolonising academic practices 32–3
  Goldsmiths University of London 32–3
CRT *see* critical race theory
cultural racism 64
curricula
  The Black Curriculum (2019) 127–8
  colonialism impact 97–8
  decolonisation framework/steps 101–2
  Decolonising the Curriculum xxi, 6, 62, 174–5
  library and information science (LIS) education 92, 97–8
  research-informed teaching 253
  Whiteness impact 97–8, 99

Dartmouth College, classification bias xxiv, 240–1
De Sousa Santos, Boaventura 26, 129, 201
decanonisation 141
decolonisation
   critical pedagogy 140–1
   defining 25–6
   explorations 140
   nomenclature and meaning xxi–xxiii, 3
   objective 13
   tensions in use xxi–xxiii, 157–8
decolonisation framework/steps
   curricula 101–2
   library and information science (LIS) education 101–2
decolonisation movement, future 10–11
decolonisation project, University of East London (UEL) 66
Decolonise Education campaign 9–10
decolonising academic practices 29–33
   collaboration and integration 32–3
   'community of practice' 29–30
   critical reading and writing skills 32–3
   Global North thinking 33
   Global South thinking 26, 35
   identity and agency 30–1
   inclusive citation 33
   reflexive pedagogy 31–2
Decolonising LSE Collective 3
Decolonising SOAS Working Group 215–16, 219, 221
   see also SOAS, University of London
Decolonising the Curriculum 62
   Cambridge University Libraries 153–70, 174–5
   Keele University xxi, 6, 8, 67
Decolonising Through Critical Librarianship Group, Cambridge University Libraries 187

degree-awarding gap, library and information science (LIS) education 94–6
designing-in intelligence 21–2
   imagery, on-campus 21
   workplace design 22
discoverability, London School of Economics (LSE) 240–1
disinformation vs misinformation 74
diversification of the workforce and activism 135–6
diversity advancement, BAME staff 47–8
'double–edged sword', decolonisation as a 6–7
DPE *see* American Federation of Labor and Congress of Industrial Organizations Department for Professional Employees

education purpose 4
emotional intelligence 13–14
equality advancement, BAME staff 47–8
ethnic diversity, BAME staff 46–7
ethnic monitoring, BAME staff 52
ethnicity impact, BAME staff 42–3
evaluating collections, London School of Economics (LSE) 228–9
exhibitions, British Library (BL) 168–9

Fair Housing Act (1968) 74
future, decolonisation movement 10–11

Galleries-Libraries-Archives-Museums (GLAM) sector 157
GARA (Goldsmiths Anti-Racist Action) 131–2
Georgia International Conference on Information Literacy, critical information literacy (CIL) 82
GLAM (Galleries-Libraries-Archives-Museums) sector 157
'glass ceiling', BAME staff 41
Global North thinking 62
   decolonising academic practices 33

Global South scholarship, London School of Economics (LSE) 239
Global South thinking 62
   decolonising academic practices 35
Goldsmiths University of London
   academic literacies 27
   collaboration, internal and external 134–5
   critical reading and writing skills 32–3
   Goldsmiths Anti–Racist Action (GARA) 131–2
   Goldsmiths Learning, Teaching, and Assessment Strategy (LTAS) 132
   Liberate Our Library 127, 130–2
   Liberatemydegree collection 132–3
   Open Access for Resistance Researching 133–4
   student activism 130–2
   student engagement 5–7
Grosfoguel, Ramon 26, 129–30

Hack Your Library workshop 148–50
Hall, Tracie D. 128
Hayden, Carla, Library of Congress 136
Historically Black Colleges and Universities (HBCUs) 75

identity and agency, decolonising academic practices 30–1
'illegal aliens' 75
imagery, on–campus 21
increasing BAME student populations, library and information science (LIS) education 93
Indigenising Canadian academic libraries 105–22
   Aboriginal Reconciliation Council (ARC) 115, 116
   Aboriginal vs Indigenous 109
   Brian Deer Classification System 116–17
   Chong, Rachel 107–8, 119–22
   confederation of Canada 109–10
   Decolonising the Library Interest Group (DIG) 116
   Deer Classification System 116–17
   Edwards, Ashley 107, 119–22
   experiences within educational institutions 119
   Indigenisation 121–2
   'indigenous', defining 105–6
   Indigenous Curriculum Resource Centre (ICRC) 107, 116–17
   Indigenous Information Literacy 117–18
   Indigenous representation 120–1
   Indigenous Student Centre (ISC) 115
   Kwantlen Polytechnic University (KPU) 117–18
   library education 120
   referring to Indigenous Peoples 108–9
   reflections 119–22
   Simon Fraser University (SFU) Library 107, 116
   Stó:lō Research and Resource Management Centre (SRRMC) 107
   terminology 105–6, 110–11
   Truth and Reconciliation Commission (TRC) 110, 111–12, 114–15
'inequality regime' 49
information literacy *see* critical information literacy
Institute of International Visual Arts (INIVA) library 144–5
institutional racism 62–4
   racial identity 65–6
   White allyship 65–7
institutional resistance to change 75
integration and collaboration, decolonising academic practices 32–3
international standards development, British Library (BL) 167

Jim Crow laws 74

Kaufmann, Dr Miranda 253

Keele University, Decolonising the
   Curriculum xxi, 6, 8, 67
Kenya
   African library 191–2
   Book Bunk Trust 190, 199–203
   colonialism as dismemberment of
      Africa 192–4
   commercial dominance of the digital
      layer 203–5
   decolonising libraries as progressive
      librarianship 197–203
   institutionalised amnesia 194–5
   knowledge infrastructures 190–3, 197,
      199, 203–4, 205–7
   Mau Mau 191, 193, 198–9
   McMillan Libraries 189–90, 191, 199,
      200–3
   Mwakenya movement 195–7
   Nairobi's libraries 192
   Ngũgĩ wa Thiong'o 192, 196, 206
   publishing in pre-independence
      Kenya 197–8
   Structural Adjustment Programmes
      (SAPs) 194–5
   Ukombozi Library 192, 197, 203,
      206–7
   youth employment 205–6
Kenyatta, President Uhuru 203
Kew Gardens xxiv
King, Martin Luther, Jr., education
   purpose 4
knowledge democracy 129–30
knowledge infrastructures, Kenya 190–3,
   197, 199, 203–4, 205–7

LCSH *see* Library of Congress Subject
   Headings
leadership, BAME staff 51
Liberate Our Library, Goldsmiths
   University of London 127, 130–2
Liberatemydegree collection, Goldsmiths
   University of London 132–3
library and information science (LIS)
   education 91–102

colonial imprint 98–101
colonial legacy 92–6
colonialism impact 97–101
curricula 92, 97–8
decolonisation framework/steps 101–2
degree-awarding gap 94–6
increasing BAME student populations
   93
predominant Whiteness of the LIS
   profession 100–1
racism 94–6
reading list audit 97–8
student and staff perceptions 97–8
White privilege 94–6
'Whiteness' of campuses 92–6
Library of Congress
   classification bias xxiv, 75, 116, 174–5,
      240–1
   Hayden, Carla 136
Library of Congress Subject Headings
   (LCSH) 174–5, 216–17
Library Orientation Exchange (LOEX),
   critical information literacy (CIL)
   82
LIS *see* library and information science
   education
literacies, academic *see* academic
   literacies
LOEX (Library Orientation Exchange),
   critical information literacy (CIL)
   82
London College of Communication
   (LCC), Wikipedia workshops 147
London School of Economics (LSE)
   225–44
   acquisitions 238–9
   bias in classification 240–1
   bias in collection development 226–8
   classification bias 240–1
   collaboration 242–3
   collaborative collection development
      239–40
   collection development 225–8, 239–40
   collections policy 237

INDEX 261

commitments to equality and diversity 236–7
Course Collection 230–1
discoverability 240–1
evaluating collections 228–9
Global South scholarship 239
Library collections 229–36
Main Collection 231–4
Main Collection journals 233–4
reading lists 234–6, 237–8
review and assess your collections 242
ringfencing collections for retention 241–2
lower pay, BAME staff 40
LSE *see* London School of Economics
LTAS (Goldsmiths Learning, Teaching, and Assessment Strategy) 132

M25 Library Consortium conference 66–7
machine learning
British Library (BL) 167–8
machine-generated language coding 167
Mau Mau, Kenya 191, 193, 198–9
McMillan Libraries
Kenya xxiv, 189–90, 191, 199, 200–3
languages in the McMillan Library collection 202
minimisation of racism 64
misinformation vs disinformation 74
Mukurtu 165
multiculturalism, racism 63–4
Mwakenya movement, Kenya 195–7

Nairobi's libraries 192
(Smithsonian) National Portrait Gallery 15
National Trust xxiv
National Union of Students (NUS) xxvi, 4
see also student...
collective action 8–9
Decolonise Education campaign 9–10

Goldsmiths University of London 5–7
'natural' intelligence 58–9
naturalisation, racism 64
Ngũgĩ wa Thiong'o 192, 196, 206
NUS *see* National Union of Students

occupational segregation, BAME staff 40–1
occupational structure, BAME staff 46
OERs (Open Educational Resources), critical information literacy (CIL) 83–4
Open Access
e-library 9
Mukurtu 165
platforms 141
Wikipedia workshops 145–7
Open Access bias 164
Open Access for Resistance Researching, Goldsmiths University of London 133–4
Open Educational Resources (OERs), critical information literacy (CIL) 83–4
outreach work, BAME staff 51
Oxford University xxvi, 21

Peace Corps 18–19
Pitt Rivers Museum xxv
Polar Library
Cambridge University Libraries 182–7
coloniality of the classification system 183–4
critical information literacy (CIL) 184–5
decolonising classification 182–5
unique classification scheme 182
positivism vs constructionism, research methodologies 25
progressive librarianship 197–203
promotion opportunities, BAME staff 46

QAnon, critical information literacy (CIL) 79

Race at Work Charter 50
Race Equality Charter 50
racial discrimination, BAME staff 40
racial identity, institutional racism 65–6
racism
   see also critical race theory
   'antagonistic forces' in HE 63–4
   BAME staff 40, 43–5, 50
   colour-blind racism 64
   cultural racism 64
   institutional racism 62–7
   library and information science (LIS) education 94–6
   manifestation 43–5
   minimisation of racism 64
   multiculturalism 63–4
   naturalisation 64
   Race at Work Charter 50
   Race Equality Charter 50
   'weight of whiteness' 63–4
   White allyship 65–7
   workplace 43–5, 50
reading lists
   diversifying 237–8
   London School of Economics (LSE) 234–6, 237–8
   reading list audit, library and information science (LIS) education 97–8
Reclaiming Native Truth (RNT) project 82
reflexive pedagogy, decolonising academic practices 31–2
research methodologies 25–35
   academic literacies 26–8
   constructionism vs positivism 25
   Western canon 25–6
research-informed teaching 253
resistance research and writing 28–9
review and assess your collections 242
Rhodes Must Fall campaign xxvi, 8–9, 21, 130–1
ringfencing collections for retention 241–2

RNT (Reclaiming Native Truth) project 82

SAPs (Structural Adjustment Programmes), Kenya 194–5
School of Oriental and African Studies *see* SOAS, University of London
school system, British 57–68
Scott Polar Research Institute (SPRI), Polar Library, decolonising classification 182–5
self-identity, BAME staff 42–3
slavery connections 131–2
   British Library (BL) 154, 156, 158, 161–2
   University College London Legacies of British Slave Ownership Database 161–2
Sloane, Sir Hans xxiv, 154, 156
Smith, Linda Tuhiwai 130
Smithsonian National Portrait Gallery 15
SOAS, University of London 16, 19–20, 213–22
   acquisitions 217
   archives and Special Collections 217–18
   COVID-19 pandemic 220
   critical librarianship 214
   Decolonising SOAS Working Group 215–16, 219, 221
   history 214–16
   library space 218–19
   metadata, classification and cataloguing 216–17
   missionary archives xxiv, 218
   provenance 218
   restructuring 220–1
   SOAS Library 216–19
   SOAS Library Decolonisation Operational Group 219–22
social intelligence 13–14
SPRI *see* Scott Polar Research Institute
storytelling perspectives: challenging the narrative of the storyteller 251–3

Structural Adjustment Programmes (SAPs), Kenya 194–5
structural oppression 73–84
  libraries 75–6
student activism 8–9
  see also National Union of Students
  diversification of the workforce and activism 135–6
  Goldsmiths University of London 130–2
student and staff perceptions, library and information science (LIS) education 97–8
student engagement 5–7
students' union *see* National Union of Students
Syed, Matthew 18

teaching and learning practices and spaces 7–8
Temple University 17–18
training and development opportunities, BAME staff 45
Trumpism 78–81

UAL *see* University of the Arts London
UCL *see* University College London
UCT *see* University of Cape Town
UEL *see* University of East London
Ukombozi Library, Kenya 192, 197, 203, 206–7
undervalued BAME staff 40
University College London (UCL)
  University College London Legacies of British Slave Ownership Database 161–2
'Why Is My Curriculum White?' campaign 4, 9
University of Cape Town (UCT) xxi, 130–1
University of East London (UEL) 13, 21
  decolonisation project 66
University of the Arts London (UAL) 19, 142–4, 146–7, 148
  Wikipedia workshops 147

vertical segregation, BAME staff 41

'weight of whiteness', racism 63–4
Western canon, research methodologies 25–6
White allyship, racism 65–7
White privilege
  defining 95
  library and information science (LIS) education 94–6
Whiteness impact on curricula 97–8, 99
'Whiteness' of campuses, library and information science (LIS) education 92–6
Whiteness Studies 75–6
'Why Is My Curriculum White?' campaign 4, 9
Wikipedia workshops 145–7
work experience in UK organisations, BAME staff 39–41
workplace design 22
workplace diversity lack, BAME staff 41
workplace racism 43–5, 50